For my good friend, Jack

Bob M. Michael

ONE MAN'S OBSESSION

Robert McMichael

Prentice-Hall Canada Inc., Scarborough, Ontario

Canadian Cataloguing in Publication Data

McMichael, Robert, 1921-
One man's obsession

Includes index.
ISBN 0-13-566-944-8

1. McMichael Canadian Collection. 2. McMichael, Robert, 1921- . 3. Painting, Canadian – Ontario – Kleinburg. 4. Painting, Modern – 20th century – Canada. 5. Group of seven. I. Title.

N910.K57M36 1986 759.11'074'0113547 C86-094445-X

Prentice-Hall Inc., Englewood Cliffs, New Jersey
Prentice-Hall International, Inc., London
Prentice-Hall of Australia, Pty., Sydney
Prentice-Hall of India Pvt., Ltd., New Delhi
Prentice-Hall of Japan, Inc., Tokyo
Prentice-Hall of Southeast Asia (Pte.) Ltd., Singapore
Editora Prentice-Hall do Brasil Ltda., Rio de Janeiro
Prentice-Hall Hispanoamericana, S.A., Mexico
Whitehall Books Limited, Wellington, New Zealand

Production Editors: Sharyn Rosart, Lois Weir Ferguson
Design: Rene Demers
Manufacturing Buyer: Don Blair
Composition: Fleet Typographers
Jacket Painting: A.J. Casson
ISBN: 0-13-566-944-8

Printed and bound in Canada by John Deyell Company

1 2 3 4 5 JD 90 89 88 87 86

TABLE OF CONTENTS

In memory of my mother and father
Evelyn and Norman.

ACKNOWLEDGEMENTS

My editor, Joyce Forster, became at once my severest critic and a one-woman cheering section. She unsplit countless infinitives and more importantly, she prevented my narrative from wandering into mazes of unnecessary detail from which many readers may have emerged asleep.

Editors Sharyn Rosart and Iris Skeoch and production manager Rand Paterson at Prentice-Hall Canada made innumerable suggestions with a very sensitive red pencil and reorganized sequences so thoughtfully that the story became more easily readable.

My typist, Mary Ciggaar, at times must have become bleary-eyed while deciphering seemingly endless scrawls before the screen of a word processor. She and her electronic magic lantern worked miracles.

Gibson Henry, nephew of Tom Thomson, provided helpful records related to the artist and his family members.

Beth Southcott, author of *The Sound of the Drum*, read the section dealing with Woodland Indian art and made several helpful suggestions.

Bud Watson's photograph of Signe and me, invariably unphotogenic subjects, demonstrated a certain genius behind his camera.

Chuck Matthews' slides of many artists and friends present a photographic "Who's Who" of the McMichael Collection through the years.

Pierre Berton, our longtime friend and neighbour, not only encouraged me to write but also showed me how to catch the essence of our adventures in art. For his patience and discernment I am most grateful.

To wrap it up, I called on my dearest friend, artist A. J. Casson to paint an oil panel which is the jacket-cover for this book.

INTRODUCTION

This is the story of a singular adventure in art. It is also a story of love and dedication and sacrifice.

The now famous McMichael Canadian Collection began quite accidentally, out of the deep affection of its founders for their country and its painting. It grew inevitably into a unique institution which has become a place of joy and understanding for literally millions of Canadian and foreign visitors. Through its exhibits, visitors have also come to know the physical face of Canada which the Group of Seven and their contemporaries portrayed so dramatically from one coast to the other.

Few art galleries in the world possess the splendidly bucolic setting of the McMichael Canadian Collection. Even fewer come to mind as rivaling the natural beauty of its spirit and ambiance, chosen by Bob and Signe for their original home. Like everything else about the Collection, it bears the stamp of their creative personalities. Subsequent changes to the galleries have failed to diminish its unique character.

Too often, the creative figures who timelessly reflect and shape the true character of the nation are ignored in public places. It is nice to know that the McMichael Canadian Collection exists as a unique testimony to the total dedication of a couple who have given their lives to the spiritual and cultural enrichment of their fellow citizens.

Too few personal statements have emanated from the world of Canadian art. This story of Bob and Signe McMichael adds a warm and affecting testament to that small legacy.

Paul Duval
Monaco, July 1986

1

There was very little in my early life that would lead anyone who knew me then to expect that Canadian art would become my obsession.

Norman McMichael, my father, was born in St. Thomas, Ontario. Though his roots were in Ayrshire, Scotland, our branch of the family emigrated to the American colonies in the 1700s. Dad once showed me the chapter in a treasured old book which described Captain Edward McMichael's service in the American Revolutionary War. He had lost an eye in the Battle of Trenton and was with Cornwallis at the Yorktown surrender on October 19th, 1781 while his wife Elizabeth, a member of a prominent Philadelphia family, tended the wounded.

In 1787 Edward McMichael, with his young family and the few possessions they could carry, headed for the northern British colonies. They crossed the Niagara River in August and joined the Niagara Settlement, where they remained until 1794. That year they moved further west to the tiny Lake Erie settlement of Long Point where Edward built a log cabin, the first McMichael homestead in Canada.

After his boyhood and school years in St. Thomas, Dad got his first job in the bank in nearby London where he met my mother, Evelyn May Kennedy, whose grandparents had emigrated to Canada from Ireland. In 1919, after Dad's service in the Canadian Army in World War I, they were married and moved to Toronto. Two years later, on July 27th, I was born in our house on Runnymede Road in the city's west end. Just over a year later we moved six blocks further west to the city's very limits, Armadale Avenue, amidst the woods of Jane Street, where my brother Don was born.

After school hours at Runnymede Road Public School, Don and I and our friends became explorers of the nearly untouched valley of the Humber River, whose only building was the rustic Old Mill Tea Garden beside the fascinating ruins of an old stone grist mill. During the summer months we paddled in the river, catching minnows and watching the swarms of little yellow birds which we called "wild canaries" bobbing through forests of willows on the banks. In the springtime we took pussy willows home to our mothers and in the autumn we collected apples from an ancient deserted orchard, and with them, in spite of repeated warnings, a good many tummy aches. Nor were those our only mishaps. More than once we came home drenched to our armpits after we had decided to prove that the ice on the frozen river was plenty thick enough for skating.

At about fourteen, when we reached "maturity" and were allowed to stay out after dark, the valley became the site of glorious corn or weiner roasts and singsongs. Our parents insisted that the valley could be a dangerous place, although it wasn't until we had suffered through a few burnt fingers and several dark nights when we lost our way home that we began, for the first time, to realize that our parents knew more than we had been prepared to give them credit for.

Growing up wasn't all fun. During my early teen years, in the midst of the Great Depression, the furniture company that Dad had joined when he left the bank was closed. There were no job openings for the secretary-treasurers of failed furniture companies and few opportunities for any kind of gainful employment, and unemployment insurance had not yet been invented.

Don and I shared a room to leave one available for a boarder who paid seven dollars a week, meals included. During the winter months we earned quarters shovelling snow from walks in nearby Baby Point, where the "rich" people lived, and in the summer months we earned a dollar a day as delivery boys for a local drug store. We learned early the truth of the old maxims, "Waste not, want not", and "A penny saved is a penny earned", and they have never entirely disappeared from my thinking even in this age of free spending and planned obsolescence. In those days, when impossible debts and foreclosed mortgages were the rule rather than the exception, I promised myself I would never become needlessly overextended.

At Humberside Collegiate as sub-goalie on the school's hockey team (I spent more time on the bench than the ice) I learned the value of teamwork but I was always a little wary of counting too much on others for support in the scrambles. "Do it yourself or it won't get done" was a principle which worked equally well for me when I worked on the school yearbook, *Hermes*. I wrote stories for it and later, when I became its advertising manager, I found it more difficult to get my fellow students to sell ads to local merchants than to simply go out and sell them myself. One year I sold almost all the advertising in the book. For that I was given the gold *Hermes* pin, presented by the principal in the school auditorium.

That auditorium was a special place, not merely as the site of my minor triumph, but because one long wall was a huge mural of several panels which illustrated various aspects of Canadian history and life. I learned that the name of the artist who had painted it over a five-year period was Arthur Lismer.

It was the largest mural ever painted by one of the Group of Seven and had been completed by Lismer between 1927 and 1932. One panel was painted each year and paid for by that year's graduating class, through a fund known as the Literary Society of Humberside Collegiate. Lismer had been engaged to carry out the design and painting by the head of the school's art department, Salem B. Hatch, and principal John S. Wren, both of whom were still at Humberside when I entered its classrooms some ten years later.

The central panel, completed in 1927-28, is allegorical and shows several life-sized figures for which students of the school acted as models. A mother represents Devotion and Care while a stream flowing beside her suggests the River of Life, with turbulent passages and quiet pools encircling a young pine tree, symbol of the sturdy quality of the nation's youth. A little girl with a dove is Innocence and the figure of a maiden attended by a fawn, a picture of woodland grace, is Beauty. Beside a path stands a pilgrim who represents Courage and the Aspirations of Youth. He gazes upwards toward mountains and the figure of Truth, the highest of all. The other panels show the early explorers and the development of the nation up to the generation for whom it was painted — young nurses, scientists and aviators looking to the skies.

The great mural left a strong impression on me and, I'm sure, on almost everyone who saw it during the formative teen-age years.

In the 1970s most of Arthur Lismer's papers were given to the McMichael Collection archives and among them were pencil sketches, photographs and letters related to his work on the Humberside mural in the late 1920s. It was an enormous achievement and it seemed to me it had been purchased for a mere pittance, especially when now, half a century later, one of his canvases of the 1920s, far smaller than the Humberside panels, might fetch as much as $100,000. His best-known works of that time, such as *Rock, Pine and Sunlight, Isles of Spruce* or *September Gale* could not be bought at any price today.

Poring over the old records I couldn't help reflecting how unfair it was that the artist had not lived long enough to enjoy the recognition and praise his work now receives. Yet his bold, brilliant brush strokes of fifty years earlier had not undergone the slightest change, nor had his letters and records.

I read a letter from principal John S. Wren, written to the artist after three of the Humberside Collegiate panels had been completed:

Arthur Lismer, Esq., *18th November, 1931.*
69 Bedford Park Avenue,
Toronto.

Dear Mr. Lismer,

I was very pleased to receive your letter. I have sent the account to the Board of Education, and they no doubt will pay you. I note that you are out $25.00 for frames, $16.00 for sewing and $140.00 for canvas. The Board have already paid you $44.00, and no doubt will pay the $100.00. This leaves a balance of $37.00 which you are out, and which we feel you should be paid. I am therefore enclosing a cheque for $649.00, made up as follows:

For Panels	*$550.00*
Bills	*62.00*
	37.00
	649.00

I must say that we are very pleased with the way you have been dealing with us. We think that we would like you to complete the other two panels. If you would give us a sketch of what you think would be suitable, and also the price, we would then have a staff meeting and you would likely be given the job.

Please let me know if you do not get the cheque from the Board of Education.

Yours very truly,
John S. Wren

When Humberside Collegiate underwent major alterations and additions, the Lismer murals were insensitively removed to a less prominent area of the school. Now, years later, a committee is actively raising funds for the restoration of the impressive panels to their original place of honour in the school's new auditorium, as bids at Canada's auction houses go ever upwards for paintings by Arthur Lismer.

Lismer's original paintings have, of course, not undergone any change. It is we, and our perception of what is important — what has lasting meaning and real value — that have changed.

During my high school years I took my first small step into journalism, which I hoped would be my career, by writing a weekly column which reported news, social events, sports and gossip from the three high schools in the city's west end in a neighbourhood paper, *West Toronto Weekly*. Student reporters I had recruited in the other two schools, Western Technical and Commercial School and Runnymede Collegiate, fed me stories and the column, "Collegiate Chatter", proved so popular it inspired another idea at the end of my final year at Humberside.

Lloyd Hodgkinson and Ben Holdsworth, my two representatives at Runnymede Collegiate, and Carl Thuro of Central Technical School and I came up with the idea of a weekly high school newspaper filled with youth news, sports, fashion, gossip and, of course, advertising, specifically directed to the teen-aged market, which could be distributed in the forty or more high schools in the greater Toronto area. We knew that many high schools in the United States had their own newspapers, but as far as we could see, Canadian secondary schools lacked any medium of communication. We thought we saw an opportunity to meet a real need and at the same time build a unique publishing business by offering advertisers direct access to an untapped market. We had enthusiasm, energy and, we believed, the know-how, but alas, our pooled financial resources wouldn't have equalled a hundred dollars.

During the summer of 1940, we began casting around for someone who might be willing to foot the bill for one issue of a newspaper that would be published at the time of school's opening. The previous year, a store called the Book Exchange had passed out its advertising pamphlets on opening day. The store was in the west end, on Bloor Street near Christie, and so we called on owner Carl Cole. To our delight he liked our idea and agreed to supply a small office space, with a phone, in his warehouse, and to pay the costs of the first issue of an eight-page newspaper crammed with Book Exchange advertisements which would be called *The Student*. Cole's involvement in newspaper publishing ended with the first issue of "the world's largest student newspaper" but the vision that led him to give us his support stood him in good stead. Carl Cole went on to establish one of the world's largest book store chains, Cole's Book Stores.

That first issue, crude as it later appeared, got us off and running. I found a rundown office at 73 Adelaide Street West which could be rented without lease for fifteen dollars a month. At least the location was good. Years later it became the site of the entrance to First Canadian Place. We also found a small newspaper plant a block away, The Northern Miner Press, which agreed to print for us with no guarantee except our four smiling young faces.

Thus *Canadian High News* was born, its first edition reaching out to schools from Weston to Scarborough on October 23, 1940.

After the first issue, which registered a loss of about five hundred dollars, two of the partners, Holdsworth and Thuro, dropped out to continue their education. Lloyd Hodgkinson and I became publishers, editors, writers, space salesmen and distributors (in a rented truck) of the world's largest and most underfinanced student newspaper.

Nevertheless, our phone soon began to ring with responses to our appeals for volunteer reporters in high schools as far north as Willowdale and for three issues, between October and the Christmas holidays, I sold enough advertising to almost meet the printer's bill. Unfortunately, we still had to think about the rent, the phone, typewriter rentals and a pile of other bills. The year's end found us almost $2000 in debt with a request from our printer, Mr. Pierce, for a little meeting. How, he asked us, did we expect to meet our expenses now and in the next six months?

The infant newspaper was attracting wide attention but it was considered to be just an experiment. Educational authorities and advertisers remained skeptical — in fact, the first two issues in January 1941 were so short of advertising that we began to hear rumours that we were controlled by "hidden backers", or maybe even "Communists"!

Until that point our editorial material had been mostly devoted to school activities, sports, fashions and big bands like Glen Miller and Tommy Dorsey. We needed a cause. It had to be one which would be of interest to students and yet appear worthwhile to the principals and members of boards of education who were searching our columns for devious motives. Without at least tacit acceptance from educational authorities, distribution at schools and the recruiting of volunteer reporters and helpers among students might become impossible. Nor could we look forward to the full-page advertisements from stores like Eaton's or Simpson's which we so desperately needed unless we could shake our fly-by-night image.

With the coming of spring and the threat of wartime food shortages, high school students were encouraged to take summer jobs in agriculture, where labour shortages were becoming critical. Making money while contributing to the war effort seemed to me to offer a golden opportunity to high school kids. Perhaps if we put our weight behind this programme we could make a real difference to its success and, at the same time, acquire for our fledgling publishing venture the respectability we so badly needed.

We had a natural medium for reaching nearly forty thousand potential student farm labourers. Unfortunately our natural medium was in serious financial difficulty. It seemed unlikely that we would survive long enough to carry out our good intentions. Then one day, while I was struggling with our financial problems, I heard a radio appeal from Ontario's premier, Mitchell F. Hepburn, for student help for Ontario farmers. It triggered an idea!

I asked our part-time *High News* artist, Jack Walton, to make a drawing of Mr. Hepburn with farm fields, cattle and barns in the background and sat down at my typewriter to draft an appeal from the Premier to our readers. Then nervously, but brazenly, I picked up the phone and asked for the premier of Ontario. When an assistant enquired why I wished to talk to the premier, I told him, with a bravado I did not feel, that I was the editor of the world's largest youth newspaper and that we were planning a front page appeal, complete with a picture of the premier, urging young people to help on the farms. The message, I insisted, needed his approval and a copy of his signature for printing. The assistant hesitated, so I forged ahead with what I hoped sounded like confident assurance, "I'm sure the premier will be pleased with the drawing we have made of him for the front page but he may wish to edit the message...I could finish my meeting with him in less than five minutes."

To my astonishment I was told to come to the premier's office at Queen's Park on the following Thursday morning at ten o'clock.

On the appointed day, having borrowed my dad's leather briefcase and walked ten blocks, I found myself climbing the steps to the impressive front portico of the Ontario Legislative Buildings. Once inside, I was directed to the premier's second-floor suite. Taking a deep breath I tried to look like the sort of newspaperman who interviewed important people every day of the week. My nonchalance diminished considerably when I was ushered into Ontario's highest office which also, at that moment, seemed its largest and most impressive. The man whose face was so familiar through news photographs shook my hand, asked me to be seated, gave me an encouraging smile and said nothing.

"Mr. Premier," I said nervously, breaking the silence, "I hope you like this picture we've drawn of you for our newspaper, *Canadian High News*, and the message we plan to run with it."

The premier began to read the message, and to my relief, broke into a broad grin.

"Perhaps I would have said it a little differently," he said at last, "but the idea's right. May I suggest a few changes?"

Naturally, I got busy with my pencil. When the message was finished I plunged again. "This week's message will reach over forty thousand young people," I told the premier as I handed him a copy of *High News*, "and we'd like to go on bringing them the message in every issue. We know we're both popular and influential with high school students but we're just getting started and right now it looks as though we won't have enough money to keep publishing."

The premier looked thoughtful. "I'm sure your paper would be an excellent way to recruit students for the farm programme but we can hardly subsidize a newspaper — yours or any other. Still, we might buy a full-page advertisement to tell your readers how important the farm programme is to the war effort. How much would that cost?"

I was flabbergasted. We had never had a full-page advertiser. "Two hundred and fifty dollars," I blurted.

"That seems quite modest," said Mr. Hepburn, pushing a button and speaking to someone outside. In minutes I was headed for the Department of Agriculture and a signed contract for space at two hundred and fifty dollars per page.

Back at our Adelaide Street cubbyhole our celebration was loud and long. We knew that with one stroke we had solved both our financial and our image problems. Soon we were publishing weekly instead of every two weeks and could boast of contracts for a full-page advertisement each week from Toronto's two largest department stores. Our pages increased from eight to twelve and, on occasion, to sixteen, and we hired a small full-time staff, some of whom were earning the princely wage of twenty dollars a week! Mr. Pierce, our printer, began to look a lot happier.

With the coming of summer and school's closing I found a job as a reporter next door at the *Toronto Daily Star*, which kept me busy until the fall when *High News* began publishing again. It was great experience working under editors like Jimmy Nichol and critical old pros like picture editor Charlie Stead. (To meet *High News*'s needs, I had started to learn news photography, so that I could double as photographer and reporter, when necessary.)

By the following autumn, *High News* had become the accepted news medium for Toronto's young people, gaining steadily in advertising lineage. Through its network of student reporters it was often able to report changes and developments in the educational system ahead of the other papers, so that it was becoming required reading for the other papers and radio stations. Bright young writers saw it as an excellent training school and years later I got a lot of satisfaction from knowing that national figures like Knowlton Nash of the CBC, Robert Fulford of *Saturday Night*, Arnold Edinborough of *Financial Post* and others like Frank Rasky and Senator Keith Davey had been part of our staff. James Nelson, one of our first news editors, later became press secretary to Prime Minister John Diefenbaker.

During the second summer I was hired as a sort of junior consultant on marketing to the youth market by Jack Brockie, a public relations and merchandising executive at Eaton's. Marketing people were just beginning to see teenagers as a special market. I knew that market, and no promoter could have had a more receptive audience.

That first summer we developed plans for Eaton's Junior Fashion Council, a group of popular girls (and later, boys, in the Junior Executive Council) who met with company advertising and merchandising people every Saturday morning to discuss current trends, fads and activities. The company could use this information to direct its advertising to the lucrative teen market. The whole idea was really just an extension of the thinking that had led to our successful *High News* editorial board.

In late summer I began developing another idea for Eaton's to consider which, I hoped, would bring together the best musical talent to be found in city schools. I knew that Eaton's owned a small concert hall in their Margaret Eaton staff building at the corner of Yonge and McGill Streets, which was rarely used. I persuaded the company to lend it for the auditions and rehearsals of a teen radio programme featuring a twenty-five piece teen orchestra, a teen chorus and soloists and a teenaged announcer, all under the direction of Howard Cable, a talented arranger and conductor just out of Parkdale Collegiate. Each programme was also to include a short skit which focused on some phase of the war effort.

Finally, after weeks of after-school rehearsals, the forty-member troupe was ready to present a one-hour programme to the president and some of Eaton's senior executives, with high hopes that the company would sponsor a weekly programme on a network of Ontario radio stations. A rude shock awaited us. The company's conservative management did not approve of radio advertising and our hopes for a radio programme were dashed. However, the executives were impressed by what they had seen and heard and offered to sponsor an evening concert at their prestigious Eaton Auditorium.

Even one concert, I was quick to recognize, offered a perfect opportunity for a full-dress audition for executives of other companies. Surely someone would want to sponsor us in a weekly network radio show. Howard continued to rehearse and improve the sound of the impressive young orchestra and chorus. I became, willy-nilly, a twenty-year-old impresario seeking out and offering reserved seats to executives of companies which I thought might be potential sponsors. I had complete faith in the quality and potential appeal of our program, but I also recognized that we would have to have some sort of special angle if we were going to capture a sponsor. We had to find a company that needed us as much as we needed it.

In those days, advertising alcoholic beverages in any form was illegal. Surely this was an industry that would be responsive to any proposal which fell within the law. O'Keefe's Brewery, I knew, also owned a ginger ale company whose products were sold under the same name. Suddenly I could hear commercials for our radio show in my mind. We would promote the flavour, the zest, the tang of "O'Keefe's". "Enjoy an O'Keefe's...enjoy the sparkling flavour of Ontario's favourite beverage, O'Keefe's." The name could be played to the limit. On occasion we could even add the words "ginger ale".

Excitedly I pressed my one good Tip Top Tailors suit and arranged an appointment with Mr. James Smith-Ross who had been appointed to run O'Keefe's by its chairman, E. P. Taylor.

When *The O'Keefe Show* hit the airwaves it was accompanied by large supporting advertisements in major Ontario daily newspapers. They featured photos of the youthful orchestra and glee club with the big name stars who were brought in for guest appearances in short dramatic skits related to Canada's war effort. The half-hour programme ran on a large radio network in Ontario for twenty-six weeks and received extremely favourable reviews and publicity.

Small wonder. In that youth orchestra were violinist Victor Feldbrill, who became conductor of the Winnipeg Symphony Orchestra, and Jack Grube, who became a leading member of the renowned Hart House String Quartette. Trumpeter Ellis McClintock went on to head a perennially popular dance band, and trombonist Teddy Rodderman became leader of a well-known musical group. Trumpeter Fred Davis, who stood in as band leader, became the well-known moderator of television's *Front Page Challenge* and our teenaged announcer, Lloyd Bochner, has had a lengthy and successful career in Hollywood. Denny Vaughan became an international singing star and formed his own band, and another of our young singers, Royce Frith, became a Canadian senator.

Back at *High News*, my partner Lloyd Hodgkinson had decided to accept the position that led to his many successful years at Maclean-Hunter, where he eventually became Group Vice-President of the Magazine Division, so I invited Bill Torgis, our advertising manager, to become my co-publisher. When I joined the Royal Canadian Navy a few months later I sold my interest in the paper to Torgis, who was exempt from service because of a childhood bout of rheumatic fever.

As a result of my experience at *High News* and the *Toronto Star* I was assigned to the Navy's photographic section and posted to the large convoy base at St. John's, Newfoundland, then a British Crown colony. In nearly two years at St. John's I took thousands of official photographs ranging from highly technical and secret equipment to the funerals of sailors whose ships had been torpedoed in the Battle of the Atlantic. At the time of Germany's final defeat I photographed the first German submarine to surrender to the Allies, some fifty miles off the Canadian Navy's base at Bay Bulls, Newfoundland.

Those were high points, but much of my work involved the boring routine assignments that are the lot of the armed services in every war. To relieve the monotony I spent many off-duty hours photographing the weddings of my fellow members of the services. They preferred the candid photographs that I took to the traditional posed portraits favoured by the local studio. They also liked my prices — seventy-five cents a print. The low price was possible because, although I bought my film, flashbulbs and other supplies from a local Kodak store, I was allowed to use our Navy darkroom and enlarger in the evenings when they were not being used for service work.

At war's end I returned to Toronto and just went on doing what I had been doing. I opened a photographic studio in Toronto which was to be devoted exclusively to weddings. I continued to defy convention by making candid records of each wedding. These were then bound in an attractive white leatherette album which I titled "Wedding Casuals".

As long as I can remember, it seems to me, I have understood instinctively the need for the little merchandising extra which can often make the difference between mere survival and success. Another idea that attracted attention to my studio was the attire of my photographers — they wore Oxford grey director's suits. These were in real contrast to the baggy pants and loafers which many other photographers wore to weddings. The distinction was soon noted, and as a result we found ourselves photographing many of the city's most important weddings and social events.

When I first met her, Signe Sorenson was employed as a continuity writer at radio station CKEY. Impressed with the care and attention she gave to writing and scheduling the brief, inexpensive bridal commercials I purchased, I found that I was also personally attracted to her. In spite of the small salary I could offer I was able to lure her to work at my photographic studio.

As studio receptionist, Signe worked with hundreds of brides-to-be, whose weddings ranged from small private occasions to grand cathedral ceremonies with receptions in huge glittering ballrooms. They had often asked for, and received, her help and advice. But no wedding Signe had ever helped to plan received as much thought and attention as the nuptial ceremony that was scheduled for February 1949: our own.

Late in 1948, after a fruitless search for an apartment, still in very short supply in booming postwar Toronto, we had decided to convert and redecorate two rooms at our photographic studio on Avenue Road. One became a small bedroom, the other an even smaller kitchen. The studio's reception area, we decided, would become our after-hours living room. Armed with hammer and nails, paint scrapers and brushes, we set out to create our first home together in the already overtaxed space of a growing business. It served — just. So a year later, now an old married couple approaching our first anniversary, we undertook our first real construction work, adding a small apartment and large portrait studio to the rear of the old Victorian house which I had purchased with the aid of a sizeable mortgage three years earlier. By comparison, this new living space of nearly eight hundred square feet was luxurious, but it soon became apparent that our expanding business would need even more space, and it had nowhere else to grow. We were beginning to realize that living twenty-four-hour days with little separation between our business and personal lives was a mistake. Somehow, we were never off-duty.

December 1950 brought the usual round of festive parties, many of which we were too busy to attend, but an invitation from our friends Jack and Helen Lynette who lived in a delightful colonial style home north of the tiny village of Kleinburg, was one we always found hard to refuse. Jack and Helen owned the city's leading flower shop which bore her maiden name, Helen Simpson. One of the joys of their Christmas parties was their special way with flowers, pine boughs and pioneer implements which made their home a beautiful place, especially in the holiday season. They even had an old sled filled with colourfully wrapped presents.

That year, carried away by the surroundings, I told Jack that Signe and I hoped some day to find a few acres of wooded land like theirs, not too far from the city, where we could build a home. He gave me a smile which suggested that it was not the first time a guest had enthusiastically announced an intention to move to the country. I wondered myself if I hadn't perhaps been to the frosted punch bowl once too often, until I remembered a promise which Signe and I had made to ourselves long ago — one day we would have a home in the country with lots of trees and hills and maybe even a brook.

We spent that Christmas in Edmonton with Signe's sister Astrid, her husband Rogers and our three captivating nieces, all of whom I was meeting for the first time. I was impressed equally by my new-found family and my first glimpse of western Canada. Penny and her two younger sisters, Timmy and Deanna, seemed determined that I should not miss any western sight which could be packed into five days. My pleas for mercy simply reinforced their resolve to make this Yuletide a memorable one — presumably before I dropped dead of exhaustion.

Early in January 1951, a few days after our return from the west, I received a telephone call from Jack Lynette informing me of a "For Sale" sign on property just south of Kleinburg that we might wish to investigate. I hadn't expected he would remember my comment of a few weeks earlier, let alone follow it up so soon. We had no immediate intentions nor, indeed, the wherewithal to purchase more real estate, but I made a note of his directions and thanked him for his interest.

January is a slow season in the wedding photography business and by the following Saturday my curiosity had been piqued enough for me to drive to Kleinburg while Signe minded the store.

I had no difficulty locating the sign which Jack had mentioned, since it stood next to the stone foundation and charred ruins of a burnt-out barn. Inquiries, it said, could be made across the road at an old red brick farmhouse, liberally decorated with Victorian gingerbread.

A silver-haired man with piercing light blue eyes answered my knock on the weather-beaten door. Cecil Mitchell's overalls and faded plaid shirt seemed to submerge his small frame, obscuring the wiriness and strength that came from working the land for over fifty years.

In the linoleum-floored parlour I met his two sisters, Irene and Annie. Irene would have been the perfect model for Grant Wood's *American Gothic*. She wore her black hair in a tight bun and a lightly patterned apron over a dark cotton housedress. Her dark beady eyes peered through steel-rimmed spectacles and did not miss much, I was sure, particularly when she was sizing up a visiting stranger. Annie, a huge hulk of a woman, overflowed a sturdy old oak chair of vast dimensions, constructed (I supposed) to bear her weight and that of a huge black and white cat draped in slumber across her lap. Her dim eyes, unkempt straggly hair and toothless grin were somewhat misleading, because her eyes and mind could quite suddenly sharpen when money matters were discussed.

The previous fall, at Hallowe'en, young boys had been seen running from the Mitchell farm. When the nearest volunteer fire brigade arrived, it was helpless against the massive fire which consumed the hay-laden building and wiped out a dozen head of cattle. Worn out by years of hard work, the Mitchells had no heart for the task of rebuilding and had decided to sell at least ten acres, if not all of the farm, but to retain the house.

We sat around the old, black, wood stove for a few minutes in expectant silence and I was pleased that I had worn blue jeans and a heavy sweater, appropriate for the occasion. Finally I broke what seemed like an interminable pause by saying off-handedly that I might possibly be interested in the land they were planning to sell. Eyes lit up all around as Cecil began to extol the merits of his road frontage immediately adjacent to the village and its potential as a profitable subdivision development in a postwar market still crying for new homes. Irene chimed in with the statement that anyone buying it was bound to make a fortune. I searched for a way to tell them that I was not interested in wall-to-wall housing; that I would be much more attracted to some wooded acreage far from the road where I could build a single house. When I told them I really wanted to look at land far from the road and useless for agriculture, they assumed immediately that I couldn't afford "the good part" and looked with sadness and compassion on one who would be banished to a backwoods life of lonely toil.

Pondering my unhappy future for a few moments, Cecil hesitatingly suggested, "There's some hilly, scrub land at the back near the river. We used it for pasture."

Quickly shifting gears, Irene added, "Really pretty back there in the spring when wildflowers and apple blossoms come out. I used to walk back to pick daisies and the like."

Big Annie remained silent, her eyes darting between her brother and sister and my face, which I hoped didn't reveal the strong interest I was beginning to feel with Cecil's mention of hills and a river.

"Would you like to go back and see it?" Cecil asked finally.

I would. The old farmer pulled on rubber boots and slipped easily into a well-worn parka. Again I was grateful for my warm clothing and all-weather boots.

We trekked along a rutted wagon track bordering ploughed fields, the land treeless and slightly undulating, for about half a mile, which seemed longer on this damp, cool January day. In the distance were tall pines and bushy cedars standing out from leafless hardwoods. Promising, I thought. When we arrived at the top of a steep descent to a broadly sweeping river valley, I caught my breath.

"Is this all yours?" I gasped.

"Yep."

"How far does it go? What part would you be interested in selling?" I asked, stirred by the view and the woods and also mindful of how easily we had walked to this hidden forest overlooking a river which snaked through overlapping hills. But practical considerations were far from my mind as I looked around me. My pulse quickened and I knew I was falling in love at first sight; an affair that would last a lifetime.

That evening, as I tried to describe the forests and hills above the yawning valley with its twisting river, and my meeting with Cecil and his sisters, Signe smiled and, I could see, was making allowances for gross exaggeration. The next day I drove her to Kleinburg to explore my Eden in the Mitchell's back forty.

Fresh snow had fallen overnight and we felt like children stepping into a magic kingdom. The air was crisp and still and snow decorated every tree limb with glittering prisms sending out multi-coloured glints in the morning sunlight. The silence was punctuated only by the chirps and riffs of winter birds. There was no sign that man had walked this land. At the valley's rim under the outstretched arm of an enormous pine it was hard to believe we were less than twenty miles from the centre of the city. I think we knew in that moment that the unspoiled earth on which we stood in silence would change our lives.

Eventually the spell was broken and we romped down to the valley and a river which gurgled where it penetrated its sheathing of ice. In the deep woods we came upon more ancient pines so large we tried in vain to encircle them with our arms. Beneath our feet were green-needled seedlings and masses of leafless deciduous youngsters coming to life in the forest. Did we sense companions unseen, the painters who would one day walk with us through those very woods? I like to think they were there.

Sunday afternoon is visiting time in the country. Now we were anxious to pay another visit to the Mitchells in the hope of discussing seriously a purchase of some of this rough, untended scrub land at the back of their farm.

We knew Cecil wanted to continue to farm the toplands but we convinced ourselves that the back forty was useless even for grazing since he no longer had cattle. We would willingly take this sub-marginal tract off his hands. We would require only a registered right of way along the south border of the rich, fertile, treeless lands which stretched out from his farmhouse.

When it comes to business, never underestimate an old Ontario farm family, particularly one of Scottish extraction!

Cecil and his sisters received us cordially, but after the customary mention of weather and road conditions, when talk turned to land and money, they looked at us like bankers approached by strangers wanting an unsecured loan. They knew all about rising land prices and how "lots of folks were now giving up city living," in favour of the suburbs and even the country. They were also aware of local zoning by-laws under which they could not sell fewer than ten acres. If we didn't have enough money for that they would be only too happy to take back a mortgage at going rates of interest, but they were in no hurry to sell. We abandoned the driver's seat and took up a more humble position.

As discussions continued, Cecil let us know they had in mind a thousand dollars an acre but if the land we were interested in was mostly hillsides and valley they were prepared to consider a lesser price of seven hundred dollars per acre, provided we would pay the cost of surveying and the grading, ditching and gravelling of a right of way. The precise way in which the terms were stated made it clear that he had done his homework and that there was little room for bargaining. On one point we took a firm position which he found reasonable and was prepared to accept: we would delineate precisely the area we wanted, provided it was not an island in his acreage which would make the balance difficult to use or sell. In effect, a corner of our property must coincide with existing boundaries.

The following weekend, we walked the hills and valleys while above us a small, two-seated aircraft hovered. A friend and weekend flier, Cam Warne, was the pilot and aboard was Hugh Thomson from my studio making aerial photographs.

Back at our cozy studio-apartment, we thought about the serene woods and hills of Kleinburg and the money necessary to make them ours. We hoped to avoid a mortgage, reasoning that we would need one when we were ready to build and a second mortgage might be impossible to obtain on such a remote rural site. Our bank manager, Don Fluker, seemed amused as I extolled the wonders of our newly discovered haven up-country, and surprised me by asking only a few questions before coming through with a loan of seven thousand dollars.

Two weeks later I was climbing hills and walking fence lines deep in the woods with an elderly but very robust surveyor named Leitch who, I learned, had participated in the original surveys of Canada's Northwest Territories. He staked out ten acres bounded on the west by an Ontario Hydro easement from which topland spread about two hundred yards to the valley's rim and down the wooded hills to the centre of the broad valley through which flowed the east branch of the Humber River. A right of way shared with the Mitchells, half a mile long and twenty-five feet wide, was the lifeline between our hidden paradise and the world. When the necessary title searches, closing and registrations were completed we became owners of Part of Lot 23, Concession 7 of the Township of Vaughan; the exact, if not very romantic, address of our piece of wilderness.

With the coming of spring, like the birds, we turned our energies to nesting. Ours was a small prefabricated cabin, which arrived in seven pieces with a box containing nuts and bolts and instructions for its assembly. We lugged a dozen cement blocks, nearly the undoing of our car springs, for footings, and with the help of a local handyman, erected our first country home.

In one corner of the twelve by sixteen foot cabin an old cupboard with open shelves served as kitchen and library as well as a communications and music centre; it was equipped with a small battery radio. Beside the bed (our only seating) was a small folding table which became eating place, desk and workbench. Kerosene lamps, art prints and a rag rug gave the hut a coziness we would enjoy through many days and nights over the next three years, before it became the equipment shed and construction office for a much larger building project.

Spring was also planting time. As if we hadn't enough trees around us, we ordered five hundred cedar seedlings at one cent each from the provincial Department of Lands and Forests, which was encouraging reforestation. By early April I was making daily checks at the old Kleinburg railway station, which had been built years earlier on the rail line three miles west of our village and around which another village, Nashville, had sprung up.

All that we had read about planting young trees stressed getting them into the ground promptly since their tender roots could dry quickly, causing them to die in childhood. With only our little VW bug to transport them, I counted on several trips to the station to move five hundred trees — a really staggering project. When the stationmaster called to say our shipment had arrived, we left work at closing time laden down with shovels, balls of twine, water buckets and an assortment of cardboard boxes, fully equipped to undertake our first major conservation project — planting a forest.

At the station we were handed a corrugated package about the size of a breadbox. Perhaps they had sent a sample ahead of the main shipment? They had not. To my astonishment the carton contained five hundred flat little cedars, only inches tall and packed sardine-tight, their bare roots kept moist by a layer of moss. My five hundred potholes vanished in an instant. Instead we found it was desirable, and infinitely easier, to slit the earth with a square spade, pry back an inch and insert the roots, following up with heel pressure to close the slit which allowed the tiny tree to begin growing. Over the years most of those little cedars have been transplanted to other areas of the grounds but a number have grown to over twenty feet in height where we first planted them, and they now tower over Tom Thomson's shack, which we later reconstructed nearby.

In those early years our little cabin stood with its back to stately pines and hemlocks on the site now occupied by the log home provided for our maintenance superintendent, just across from the present gallery's main entrance. It had no electricity or plumbing. Drinking water came with us from the city in large jugs, and a barrel caught rainwater from the roof for washing. But the lack of amenities did nothing to dampen our spirits when we were cutting dead wood in our small forest or scything waist-high weeds to make an open space for softball, catch and horseshoe pitching with our friends. (Today, that open space is part of the gallery's front lawn.) On warm days, a dip in the river seemed more luxurious than any Jacuzzi, and a swing suspended by ropes from a sturdy pine limb provided Signe with the best hair dryer she ever owned.

In the long summer evenings we walked our land trying to decide the best location for the house which was beginning to take shape in our minds. Evenings in the cabin we dreamed of a house that would nestle into the natural setting as though it had just grown there. We weighed the advantages of reclaimed brick and natural wood, but when we asked ourselves what a house, perhaps built by pioneers, would look like, we knew at once what our choice would be. Our home in the woods would be built of massive, hand-hewn logs and would have a large stone fireplace.

Not surprisingly, our reading ran to books dealing with nature, history and art. One evening I was dipping into a book my father had saved from his school days when I came across a quotation from a little-known speech of Joseph Howe, the Nova Scotian Father of Confederation:

> *In every village in our infant country we have the quiet graves of those who subdued the wilderness, who beautified the land with their toil and left not only the fruits of their labours but the thoughts and feelings that cheered them in their solitude, to cheer and stimulate us amidst the inferior trials and multiplied enjoyments of a more advanced state of society.*

Thirty years later those lines move me as much as they did the first evening I read them — they express so perfectly our feelings for our country, the pioneers who hewed the first homes from our forests, and the first artists who painted those forests through Canadian eyes. When we did, finally, see our dream become reality, we had Claude Taft carve those stirring words into a very wide pine board from an old log house whose timbers became part of the woodland home which would do so much "to cheer and stimulate us amidst the inferior trials and multiplied enjoyments of a more advanced state of society."

Over the years, a few pseudo-sophisticates masquerading as architectural purists, have insisted that our reuse of massive hand-hewn logs for the construction of Tapawingo was, at best, sentimental, at worst, idiosyncratic and impractical. If, by that, they mean that we were determined to go our own way, free of the clichés of modern architecture and textbook planning, they're certainly right. We created our sturdy building of pioneer logs in its unspoiled natural setting to reflect an earlier and simpler way of life, far removed from the tensions created by the inhumanity of concrete and steel. A cultural fortress, impressive, but intimidating, would have been totally foreign to our natures. Instead, we envisioned a welcoming door, sheltering roofs and large windows which would encourage nature to embrace the celebration of natural beauty within our walls.

We also wanted our home to be practical and durable. From our research we knew that in Europe there were many log buildings which had withstood the ravages of centuries without serious deterioration. We believed our building would be equally durable so long as we made sure that practicality, strength and lasting quality were never sacrificed or compromised in favour of the merely picturesque.

When Vaughan Township Fire Chief James Davidson approved our first building plans he praised us for building with massive logs because they are extremely fire retardant. He told us of his experiences as a fire warden during the London Blitz. After nights of white-hot incendiary bombing, fire fighters found that steel and concrete buildings had collapsed, their metal frames bent and buckled from the intense heat. In contrast, buildings with massive wooden beams were found to be surface-charred but still standing. We were astonished when, years later, Davidson joined the small chorus of bureaucrats who questioned the gallery's fire safety.

Hewn logs eight inches thick and twelve to twenty inches wide are not listed in building codes nor are they to be found in lumber yards. In two years of searching, we came to know most of the back roads and farm lanes of the neighbouring townships. West Gwillimbury, Garafaxa, Amarinth and Chinguacousy became as familiar as our own Vaughan and we marked promising sites on large-scale maps of each region during our long and often frustrating searches for abandoned or nearly abandoned log houses and barns.

Our first find was the remains of a building whose roof had long since disappeared but whose four walls of broad hemlock timbers seemed sound when I tapped them with a hammer, a test I had been told to apply by our builder, Buck Bayliss. It was something like tire-kicking in a used car lot — really a bit of bravado — since, when it came to buying old buildings, I had no experience and even less expertise.

The skeleton of the old shed stood awkwardly in the centre of a barnyard and as I worked my way around its walls its owner, a Mr. Surr, said, "It's in the way of things, and I'd like to get rid of it."

Trying to appear knowledgeable, I muttered offhandedly, "Twenty-five dollars."

"Now let me get this straight," said Surr, "Do you pay me twenty-five dollars, or do I pay you twenty-five dollars to take it away?"

I resisted temptation and paid up. Unfortunately, not all of our purchases were so easy.

It did not really surprise us to find that many unused farm buildings suddenly became useful, almost indispensable, and very valuable, the moment we showed an interest in buying them. One owner thought the bargain should include a new barn for him. He finally settled for two hundred dollars for the unused log section of his barn and our undertaking to close in the remaining frame section with a new wall.

The northern parts of Albion and Mono Townships near the Hockley Valley proved to be our most productive hunting grounds. After making seven separate purchases we set aside a day to tour our acquisitions with an indulgent and slightly amused Buck Bayliss. We had been forced to buy several buildings to get enough long logs, eighteen feet or more, for our plans. Often we had to buy several derelicts to get two or three of the long logs we needed from each.

Following his tour of inspection and more professional log tapping, Bayliss assured us I had been an astute pupil, and most of our old logs were sound. A few "dozey" ones would have to be discarded when the time came to dismantle the old buildings and gather up their timbers.

After countless walks along our hilltops and several changes of mind we had finally decided on the site for our dream house. Our difficulties had come because there was a bewildering number of possible sites, all accessible, all with magnificent views. However, save for the transplanting of some small trees, no work had been done on the site when, on a morning in the early spring of 1954, Leo Venchiarutti, our architect, and I arrived with transit, tape measure and string to peg the precise borders of the excavation for our concrete-and-stone foundation.

Bayliss and his crew were still building bungalows in King City; the McMichaels, on the other hand, were already mentally hanging pictures. The best promise we could get from Buck was "before the summer's out". That could mean the loss of several of our best building months so, with Buck's blessing, we arranged to have a highly regarded Kleinburg builder, Len Patterson, contract with local excavators, the Bell brothers, and a crew of stonemasons to build the eighteen-inch-thick masonry walls which would enclose the lower level of our log lodge.

From the beginning of May, Signe and I slept in our little cabin nearly every night that we were not working in the city, so we could check with Len and make sure he and his men had all the materials and equipment they needed and that the electricians and plumbers were available when required. A month earlier, Joe Beedham, our electrician from Woodbridge, had installed wires and poles along our right-of-way, from which vital electricity was now flowing to the cabin and, from it, to power saws and drills.

The house was to be L-shaped with the main stem cutting through the broad hilltop. This would permit the lower level doors and windows to face the south valley on one end and provide a view into another heavily wooded valley on the north side. At right angles to the north end, the excavation formed a basement, above which would be our two bedrooms and a bath. A hallway from our front door faced into a very large living room with a cathedral ceiling. It would be forty-two feet long with a glass wall on the south framing a panoramic view of our broad river valley. Under it was another large room of almost the same size and a smaller room which became our first library.

In keeping with the natural patina and texture of our old logs we had decided on split cedar shakes to shingle the roof. Although they were widely used on the west coast where they originate, in the 1950s they were almost unknown east of the Rocky Mountains. Thus began another search for an unusual building material. Large companies like Vancouver-based MacMillan Bloedel knew of them but had never sold them, at least in the east. Fortunately, we learned of a mill in Alford, British Columbia that produced shakes from the stumps of logged-over stands of red cedar.

A month later a huge tractor trailer loaded with shakes, which had been packed around hundreds of cases of canned salmon, pulled up to Shaw's hardware in Kleinburg to ask for directions to our site. Sitting in his rocking chair outside the store front, old Earl Shaw cast keen eyes over every detail of our shipment as he gave the driver the directions he needed. For months Kleinburg believed we were building a seafood restaurant.

Finally the time came for Buck Bayliss and his crew to begin dismantling the forsaken cottages and sheds we had bought, to give them a new lease on life in Kleinburg. Buck hired trucker Doug Welsley and his huge tractor-drawn float. It must have been an incongruous sight as we manoevered up and down the dusty roads with my little VW bug in the lead.

It always astonished me that the crew knew exactly how to position the huge flatbed float against the wall of each log building. After removing blacksmith-made iron spikes and wooden dowels from drilled holes, they would then secure the top log with a rope around the next lower timber, still firmly in place, using it as an immovable windlass to lower each heavy beam to the truck bed.

As the truck's stack became large with the weight of several houses I began to worry that we would never get back to Kleinburg. Buck and Doug just smiled indulgently and insisted that we move on to still another log building until the pile held in place by girdling chains was taller than the buildings we were dismembering. As more and more timbers were levered with loggers' cant hooks onto the now mountainous load, I noticed that the float's eight huge tires were noticeably flattening.

It had been a long, hard working day but the crew seemed cheerful when, toward sunset, my little red bug led the mobile log mountain back to our hilltop in Kleinburg. Their cheer surprised me when I thought guiltily of the back-breaking job of unloading which still lay before them. But when Doug's float truck pulled to a stop at our building site I saw with astonishment that he was now alone. Bayliss and his men had gone home. It took all my self control to keep from shouting a warning as I watched him climb expertly up the towering stack on his truck which, to my horror, had stopped with one side on the road, the other in a ditch, and was listing badly. After examining the chains, he slid down to the ground and began using a crowbar on a chain-locking device which he referred to as "bear claws". In the next instant there was a clank from the taut chains and a groan from the mountain as, in slow motion, the timbers tumbled to the ground with a noise like thunder. With my blood pressure back to normal I said, rather severely, "Weren't you afraid some logs would break under that awful shock?"

"If they had, you wouldn't want them," said Doug, with impeccable logic.

The following morning, Buck and his three men, using cant hooks, ropes and round logs for rollers, waded into the immense pile and began sorting the timbers by length and thickness into neat piles. By day's end large logs were placed around the perimeter of our stone foundation. The walls of our haven had finally begun to rise! At one corner, a second course of logs, separated by two-by-four-inch spacers from the first, was begun. Since each log added up to thirty square feet of wall, the building was taking form with amazing speed. A twelve-foot gap would be filled later by a massive split-granite fireplace, the anchor and heart of our new-old home.

To support the living room floor and maintain the equally large room beneath it without supporting partitions or columns, our plan called for five enormously strong beams in the ceiling of the lower room. Heavy joists would run between them. Each of the beams was to be twenty-five feet in length with dimensions of twelve by sixteen inches. They had to be fashioned from that strongest of woods, west-coast Douglas fir.

At about this time construction had just been completed on the first leg of Toronto's first subway under Yonge Street. During the building period of two or three years, streetcar and motor traffic had been carried on decking made up of thousands of Douglas fir timbers. After completion of the rapid transit line these were replaced by steel, concrete and paving to restore the street to normal. It seemed to me that the Toronto Transit Commission must have an enormous surplus of giant timbers from that temporary structure. To my surprise, it took only a telephone enquiry to direct me to a vast storage field where I was able to buy the five beams I needed for ten dollars each. They had already proven their stength, but they were also perfectly seasoned against shrinkage and cracking after three years of exposure to weather. When they arrived at Kleinburg, Buck's versatile crew, wielding broadaxes and adzes, soon gave them the same hand-hewn surfaces as the old pioneer logs. It pleased us to think we would have a little portion of Toronto history built right into our home.

Our autumn woods were ablaze by the time the heavy two-inch roof decking was spiked and splined into place and by Thanksgiving weekend the roof was sheathed with coarse-textured hand-split shakes.

"The weather can't beat us now," Buck said with satisfaction, "we're in the dry."

To this benediction, Signe and I added thankful "amens".

In pioneer days, the spaces between logs were chinked inside and out with clay or coarse cement applied over randomly placed hand-wrought nails which acted as cleats or lathe, holding and reinforcing the chinking material. Between the inner and outer layers, moss was often stuffed to provide additional insulation against the weather. Modern building materials allowed us to achieve the desired result more efficiently. Metal lathe, cut in long strips about eight inches wide, was bent using a two-by-four plank as a moulding form to hammer it into a broad U-shape. The sides were then nailed between the logs to provide a two-inch deep recess of lathe to receive and hold the cement which, as in early days, was considerably reinforced by adding horse hair to the wet mixture. The cavity between interior and outer chinking was filled with Fiberglas insulation.

Toward mid-October we had reason to be doubly pleased that our walls and roof were firmly in place and the exterior chinking was complete. Weather reports were warning of a tropical storm which might bring gale-force winds and heavy rains as far north as southern Ontario. By Thursday, October 14th, it was evident that Tapawingo, still without window panes and doors, was in for a siege of heavy weather. Since both ends of the building were wide open, this could have a disastrous imploding effect, so all hands were set to the task of closing in vast window areas with every available piece of plywood.

Then Hurricane Hazel struck!

For two days and nights the torrential rains never ceased. It seemed as if the heavens had stored an ocean and were emptying all of it over York County. Although it was obvious that a lot of rain was falling, Signe and I had no idea the situation was becoming critical so, as usual, on Friday October 14th, after work, we set out for Kleinburg. When we reached the northern section of Avenue Road, the water on the streets was up to the car doors and our little red bug was all but floating. Our windshield wipers slapped ineffectually against the cascades of blinding water. Anxious as we were about Tapawingo in its partially finished state, we had no alternative but to head back to our midtown apartment.

The hurricane's formidable winds held vast accumulations of moisture as it moved northward over the United States and across Lake Ontario. Meeting a cooler front, the moisture condensed and fell, causing watersheds to become saturated and rivers to flood as they had never done before. That night, eighty-three people in the area were drowned and hundreds were left homeless. Property damage totalled millions of dollars. On four of the approaches to Kleinburg, bridges had been washed away and on the one which still held, emergency measures were in force and only residents of the immediate area were allowed through. On Sunday we were allowed to cross the one bridge in Woodbridge, to the south, which had withstood Hazel's ravages, and by a circuitous route finally reached our lane near Kleinburg. We were filled with dread as we headed for our construction site.

When we finally slogged to the hilltop we could only stare in disbelief — the river below was no longer a gentle stream but a roaring tumult of water which covered the broad floor of the entire valley and carried with it not only chicken coops and outhouses, but also sections of whole houses and barns. Slowly, through a field of mud, we made our way to our partially completed log home. Buck's preventative measures had served us well. Tapawingo had weathered its first major storm.

Through the next two months Bayliss and his crew, reinforced by plumbers, electricians, tinsmiths and glaziers, worked to bring Tapawingo to completion. They seemed to understand how anxious Signe and I were to spend Christmas in the log house which had been in our dreams for so long.

A week before the holidays, although there was still a lot of finishing to do, we could wait no longer. We moved into the one nearly finished bedroom and the workmen helped us hoist a fifteen-foot Christmas spruce into place under the towering peak of our living room. Dad was with us for the holiday and we spent a joyous Saturday evening dressing it with decorations saved from our childhood Christmases. At the last moment on Christmas eve the electrician wired up our record player and amplifier.

As the strains of "The First Noel" poured out we sat before our crackling fireplace on that holy night and gazed out at the country sky filled with stars. Tears of joy filled our eyes.

At first, living in our cozy hilltop home, we felt as though we were in a dream world come to life. The honks of car horns, constant background music on Avenue Road, were replaced by the distant honking of great Vs of Canada geese high in the sky, which never failed to bring us running to the nearest door or window. The cooing of city pigeons gave way to the chirps and joyous trills of woodland birds, which at times seemed to be pouring out their songs just for us. Mischievous little white-breasted pine squirrels peered at us with curiosity from our windowsills.

The ever-changing light on the hills and valleys, and deepening shadows in our woods drew us to the quiet contemplation that we could not have imagined in the bustle of Avenue Road and Bloor Street. The snow was so pristine that we hated our footsteps to mar it, yet the patterns of small animal tracks never seemed like intrusions.

Through the early months of 1955, Bayliss and his carpenters, now joined by our local handyman, Lyman Marwood, continued to finish countless details, inside and out. While they trimmed windows and doors and installed cupboards, shelves and baseboards, Signe and I applied elbow grease, steel wool and sandpaper during our evenings and weekends, part of the loving care which transforms a house into a home.

Along the length of the highest timbers in our living room walls we mounted flat iron tools and implements from pioneer days, which we had rescued from local barns and auction sales. Their shapes, many of which resemble abstract sculpture, provided a harmonious counterpoint to the hewn, textured surface of the old logs. A wooden shoulder yoke which had borne the weight of countless water and syrup pails as a functional artifact was suddenly reborn as a sculpture in the manner of Henry Moore. An Eskimo ulu and the silhouettes of other centuries-old designs would, we thought, have given pleasure to Picasso. Most of these humble blacksmith's creations had been retrieved from junk piles; few cost more than five dollars.

At one sale the auctioneer held up the frame of a small, armless rocking chair. Obviously old, its upholstered seat and back were missing except for some black cloth shreds still clinging to its loose-jointed skeleton. As it was held up for all to see, the seat frame fell loose from the back uprights — a pathetic jumble of wood which met with derisive hoots from the assembled farmers. While the embarrased auctioneer dangled the misshapen object, vainly seeking a bid from his laughing audience, I stared at the wooden components which appeared to have been hand fashioned rather than machine turned.

"Fifty cents," a daring hunch.

"Sold!"

To the laughter of the crowd, he dropped the bundle of junk into my outstretched arms as I sheepishly made my way forward. Walking down the lane, trying to support the twisted frame to prevent further separation of its wooden members, my hands felt the lovingly carved and rubbed wood and I was certain it could be rescued and restored to its former beauty.

Fragments of black cloth clinging to the open frame convinced me that the chair had probably been upholstered with petit-point patterned cloth. After visits to several yard goods outlets I found the material I was seeking. With my old chair and new cloth my next stop was at a shop advertising expert antique furniture repairs. The proprietor assured me that he could reglue and upholster the little rocker without too much expense and confirmed my belief that it had been handmade with care and skill and that its elements were, in fact, made of three different woods. The rockers and rungs were of ash, the seat frame of pine and the gracefully curved back of butternut. Our relationship was cemented when he referred to my junk as "a little gem". A few weeks later when I picked up the little rocker, again complete, it was exactly that — a little gem carved and created by some rustic pioneer who had, perhaps, no idea that he was an artist.

Living in an unspoiled woodland setting, we became more acutely aware not only of the seasons but of nature's infinite variety. From the silent valley mists of early morning to moments when raucous winds swept through the tall pines, from violent gale-driven torrents of rain to soft, caressing sunlight, nature's moods filled us with awe. We rejoiced at springtime's bursting new growth and mourned the death of old forest giants.

Looking at the beauty that surrounded us at Kleinburg many people have wondered why we could not be content. Why, in fact, did we find it so imperative to reproduce that beauty through our collection? Every day we could see and experience valleys and hills, forests, a flowing river, a patch of wild flowers...

Of course we loved our natural surroundings. Most people do. But what we saw in the paintings was not a reflection or a photographic reproduction. We saw inspired designs extracted from nature in the mass; interpretations, not merely of trees and hills, but of the artists' intense feelings about those trees and hills, their desire to express in paint a stronger and deeper impression than the natural objects could give. We saw, above all, the joy they must have felt in capturing the simplified but concentrated essence of their insights.

Whatever part our earlier experiences and education played in focusing our attention on Tom Thomson and his fellow painters, the sweeping views and intimate glimpses of nature surrounding Tapawingo greatly enhanced our appreciation of their art. We recognized that nature and the art derived from it are separate but related forms of beauty. We needed both.

After a day's work in the bustling city and a fairly long drive through traffic-clogged arteries we felt for our home in the woods something of the same fervour nomads must feel when they find a desert oasis. Nestled among the giant pines and cedars, it appeared small and lonely until we filled it with the joy of our homecomings.

The word "nationalism" often conjures up an excessive and narrow patriotism, an isolationist philosophy or a creed of rugged independence. Although we seldom use the word in conversation, Signe and I have always accepted its simplest meaning: wholesome pride in our country, its vastness and grandeur, its history, its accomplishments, its people.

Yet although we love this large piece of geography called Canada and all it represents, like most Canadians we seldom display our patriotism, which is another word we use sparingly.

We are more likely to talk about our country when we are not in it. On occasional jaunts to the United States or overseas, we find ourselves talking more about Canada than we do at home. We deplore the lack of knowledge and understanding of Canada we find beyond its borders. We try mightily to correct false impressions and where bland conceptions of our nation exist we strive to compensate by doing a little bragging. But not at home.

Here, to speak of "our great nation from sea to sea" and its proud symbols seems like flag-waving, naive, ever so slightly embarrassing. Perhaps this is the result of our not having, until a few years ago, our own flag to wave. Most adult Canadians still remember when they had no legal right to assert a Canadian nationality; when there was no such thing as Canadian citizenship. Our youngest adults and many of our children will recall the day we finally patriated our constitution. How many times have we felt compelled to explain to our American cousins that we have our own governments, that we are not governed from across the Atlantic? Perhaps their ignorance is pardonable since the first coins and dollar bills they use at entry points bear the image of Elizabeth II.

Through the ages, man has recognized the need to create and salute symbols which represent the things he reveres, such as his land and his society which, unlike their symbols, cannot be seen at a glance.

Given Canada's aboriginal and colonial histories, our mixed parentage and a population thinly stretched across our enormous land, it is hardly surprising that we have been tardy in adopting national symbols which could be universally accepted.

With time, a stronger appreciation of national symbols will come — a time when, regardless of race, religion, or language, we learn to take more pride in calling ourselves Canadians and drop our French, English, Ukranian or Chinese prefixes. Paradoxically, that feeling of togetherness will most likely come when our population has doubled or tripled, as it almost certainly will. When our native land is shared by vast numbers from diverse backgrounds, Canada will become our great common denominator, an even deeper source of pride.

Most visual symbols are derived from nature or art. In both, Signe and I have discovered the symbols that have the most meaning for us. Nature had always been there and has blessed us twice. Without nature, the art we admire most, that of our aboriginal peoples and of our nationalist painters, could not have been created. When we searched out a site in the unspoiled countryside, built a shelter of natural materials and filled it with art drawn from nature we felt we had somehow created a symbolic microcosm of our nation.

In our early days at Tapawingo, Viljo Revell, the brilliant Finnish architect of Toronto's new city hall, visited us with his dinner host, our Kleinburg neighbour, Pierre Berton.

Seated in a pine rocking chair, Revell peered at the dense woods and sweeping valleys which could be seen through the steeply peaked windows in our massive walls. He made a penetrating observation which we treasure still. He said that after many visits to this country in connection with the new city hall project, at Tapawingo he was experiencing, for the first time, the architecture, the spirit, and the feeling, which he had always imagined he would find in Canada.

Revell's reaction to Tapawingo was echoed in different words by many visitors throughout the years. Countless people have told us they bring guests, particularly those from other countries, because they believe the setting, the gallery and the Collection represent the very essence of what it means to be Canadian. A Toronto newspaper columnist, with some hyperbole, wrote "When I visit there, I'm so proud to be Canadian, that I feel as if I'm about to sprout maple leaves."

Reactions like these were very heartening for us, especially during the early years. They reinforced our own conviction that even though we don't talk much about it, the feelings of most of us for our country run very deep.

Through the earlier years and occasional visits to art galleries we had seen some works by Tom Thomson and his friends. Often they were displayed among other well-accepted but more conventional works, most of which were very detailed and literal. By comparison, the older landscapes, notwithstanding their wild subjects, appeared tame. Of course, at that time (the years after the Second World War) most Canadians, except for a comparatively few astute collectors, still felt more comfortable with the traditionally highly detailed renderings of the Canadian landscape.

Although the Group's paintings had been available for years, many fine works by each of its members could easily be found and purchased. Yet, partly because of his early death and consequently small production, Thomson's works, even then, were rare and difficult to acquire. (Thomson, of course, was never actually a Group member, having died in 1917, three years before the Group of Seven was founded.)

Looking back, I think that at first our interest in Thomson was sparked by the awakening pride of country we shared with most Canadians in the post-war era. Perhaps it went hand-in-hand with our love of the wilderness, which Thomson and his artist pals had painted. Our hearts' content was bound up with the forested hills around Kleinburg and the hewn-log home we were building there. This probably deepened our admiration for the bold paintings which so faithfully embodied the spirit of the ruggedly beautiful Canadian wilderness. With each viewing our appreciation increased.

Eventually we were drawn closer, not to Thomson's subjects, but to the paintings themselves. We were intrigued by their bold, heavy-laden strokes of almost pure colour. The sureness, the spontaneity with which each work had been created, filled us with wonder. It was not long before our admiration and enthusiasm changed to a passionate desire to see more and more of Thomson's paintings. From there it was a natural step for us to want to possess one. That desire became a tingling, sensuous urge as impossible to explain as it was to resist.

As a general rule, it is unwise to mix business with pleasure. Nevertheless, there were times, when by pure chance, delicious opportunities to view the paintings that I coveted arose through my business activities. I was not about to pass them up.

By 1954 most of my working hours were centred on our new advertising business so there was little time for our photographic studio except for weekly staff meetings. At one of these, photographer Hugh Thomson, knowing of my interest in painter Tom Thomson (no relation) casually mentioned that while photographing a wedding the previous week, he had been shown a Tom Thomson painting in the home of the bride's parents. Since I had never seen a Thomson outside of the few displayed in public galleries my ears perked up and I decided at once that I should deliver this particular set of wedding picture proofs personally.

A few days later, calling at a home in Forest Hill, I was welcomed by a mother and father as anxious to see the wedding pictures as I was to see their Tom Thomson. I learned that the family, whose name was Brodie, were distant relatives of Thomson's and did indeed have a Thomson oil panel and a smaller watercolour which they had bought in the late thirties. Their only regret was that they had not bought more.

I was immediately struck by the rich colour, the sureness and the sheer power of the two small pictures. The visual force of the painting on a small birch shingle was so great I could only stare in wonder. It was the beginning of a lifelong love affair and for thirty years has been enough to send me scurrying in search of any example of the great artist's work. With each discovery I still marvel at the spontaneous, unerring strokes and powerful splashes of colour in his paintings, the all-too-limited legacy of a solitary genius.

My excitement must have been obvious and the Brodies recognized that I was more than a casual admirer. Perhaps because of that they told me that the artist's sister, Margaret Thomson Tweedale, lived in west Toronto and had a "house full" of her brother's paintings. It was all I needed to set me on the trail.

"But don't ask to buy one," warned the Brodies. "The pictures are not for sale at any price. She would be embarrassed, perhaps even offended, to be asked."

I was surprised to learn that Tom Thomson's youngest sister Margaret and her husband, Bill, lived on Glenlake Avenue, just two blocks away from the house where I grew up. After a phone call in which I told Margaret of my intense interest in her brother's work, I was warmly, if a little cautiously, welcomed into a modest brick house, typical of the first homes built around 1920 in west Toronto.

Margaret was a petite, silver-haired woman whom I guessed to be in her seventies. At the mention of her brother's name, her blue eyes twinkled with pride. Although she was slightly hard of hearing, she needed little encouragement to reminisce about the brother for whom she had an admiration almost amounting to veneration.

The walls of the living and dining rooms were covered with Thomson paintings, often three deep. Not all by Tom, she quickly pointed out. Her other brothers, George, Henry and Frazer had all taken up painting after Tom's death, as had she, so the display included paintings by five members of the Thomson family. A dozen of the works stood out boldly from among the others. They had been chosen from Tom's estate shortly after his death in 1917 and each of the panels was clearly a jewel from his last great years. I attempted to focus for a minute at a time on each of the little paintings, trying to absorb the unmistakable technique and colour of each composition before moving in awe to the next.

It was hard to pick a favourite.

At first I was drawn to an Algonquin lake ringed by dense conifers backed by hills of hardwoods exploding in autumn crimson and gold. A stunning glimpse of the north Thomson had known and loved. A different perspective of a northern lake seen through a screen of golden tamaracks, captured their ragged, asymetrical foliage against chill water with unequalled sureness and freedom. Then, nearby and totally dissimilar, was the most striking still life I had ever seen — a pattern of wildflowers against an unlikely ground of cobalt blue. The delicate subject nevertheless showed a toughness of design that was further heightened by the dazzling use of pure colour. The little panel had all the power of a true masterwork.

Seeing these stunning works for the first time in this unpretentious setting had an enormous impact on me. Some day, some way, I vowed, there would have to be a place where all Canadians could see what I was seeing. Not an ordinary art gallery where a few paintings would be brought from the vault for periodic display at a curator's whim, but a unique, accessible sanctuary for the art of Tom Thomson and the other artists who had been the first to be inspired by our country to produce a truly Canadian art.

I realized that in the past few days I had actually seen fourteen original Tom Thomson paintings, privately owned and hidden from public view. There must be many more, closely held, screened from the eyes of all but a fortunate few. Like the Brodies and Tweedales, their owners would undoubtedly be loath to part with their treasures. But with time, I thought, they might be persuaded that their pictures should have a permanent home where they would be protected forever, and on view at all times for the enjoyment of present and future generations of Canadians.

Whatever it cost in time, energy and patience I knew that a home had to be provided and, fantastic as it seemed, I felt that somehow Signe and I would have a hand in providing it.

(We would return again and again to the Tweedale's — who became close friends — but nearly twenty years would pass before the twelve small masterpieces came to the home they had inspired.)

Although the magical Thomsons continued to fascinate us every time we saw them, we understood without really being told, Margaret's resolve not to part with them. At times, especially after 1965, when we opened our collection to the public, the temptation to pressure her was nearly overwhelming, particularly as she and Bill were frequent visitors to Kleinburg and we often enjoyed afternoon tea at their new home in nearby Etobicoke. Several times we drove to Owen Sound with them to visit Margaret's oldest brother, George, then in his nineties and still spry enough to pay us an occasional return visit. Her youngest brother Frazer and his wife Ina also became our friends through their many visits to our home and collection.

One thing we did grasp quickly. Our first encounters with privately held Thomsons proved to us just how scarce his paintings were and that few of those who owned them were willing even to consider selling. We left our names with several dealers and made it known to almost everyone even remotely connected with art and collecting that we were most anxious to buy a Thomson, but it often seemed that we might more easily find a Rembrandt or a Renoir for sale.

During the next few years, it became a happy habit for me to spend a good part of many lunch hours in art dealers' shops near my Avenue Road office. The nearest was Laing Galleries, where I came to know founder Archie Laing, and his son Blair. Through the years, Laing had handled more paintings by Thomson and members of the Group than any other dealer. My long chats with him while I viewed his paintings were an education in appreciation and collecting. When there were no other visitors, he would reminisce about his experiences with artists and their estates and collectors. With evangelic zeal he described the joys of owning fine paintings. At the same time, he lamented the difficulties of educating some of his clients to the aesthetic as well as the investment qualities of a unique work of art. He cited case after case of former clients suffering everlasting regret at not having purchased on his recommendation only to realize too late that such opportunities usually come only once. This happened most often, he said, with those who could easily afford major works. Returning for a second cautious look, they often became bitter when they found *their* picture had been sold.

More than once I had mentioned to Laing our abiding interest in Tom Thomson, only to have him reply rather condescendingly that there was very little hope that I would ever get even a small work by the scarcest of all Canadian painters. Not only were Thomsons almost impossible to obtain but also, he told me, even if he was able to acquire one, it would be difficult for him to offer it to me. Many of his best regular customers were also anxious to buy a Thomson, any Thomson. I was a newcomer to art collecting and to the Laing Gallery, even though I had been making frequent visits over several months. It did not help, he confided, that his son and partner, Blair, considered Thomson and Morrice our two greatest painters. Blair all too often consigned works which came in to storage for his own personal collection, a practice that Archie was endeavouring to discourage.

A few days later, during one of my noon visits, Archie again got onto the subject of Tom Thomson panels. By now he correctly sensed that I might be looking elsewhere in my search for one of the rare oil sketches. That could be dangerous. My anxiety could make me a gullible victim of unscrupulous people who were offering very doubtful works for sale. The very thought of a trusting and willing beginner buying something less than genuine brought an expression of pain to his face. With fatherly concern, he emphasized the need for extreme caution. I should not even consider purchasing anything claimed to be a Thomson except from a very reputable dealer. Even then, I should purchase only if the work had a clear history of past owners and would stand up to close examination by experts.

One day on his return from lunch, Blair joined in the discussion and a few minutes later invited me to the Laing apartment on the third floor of the gallery building. Proudly he pointed to a Thomson panel, a still life of wildflowers that was less dramatic, but similar in technique to the one which had so impressed me in Margaret Tweedale's collection. Before I could get my hopes up Blair promptly informed me that it was not for sale. Still, even these disappointing encounters were useful. With each new exposure to Thomson's work I was becoming more expert at recognizing his technique.

We continued to search and spread the word that we hoped to find a Tom Thomson for sale. One day, a friend who worked at the *Toronto Star* on King Street West mentioned that he was quite sure he had seen a small Tom Thomson for sale in Haynes Art Gallery just across the street. Dubious that a Thomson would be so openly available, but eager to follow up any leads, I visited Haynes Gallery the next day.

Sure enough, there was an eight-and-a-half by ten-and-a-half inch oil panel. On the attractive new frame was a brass plaque — Tom Thomson, 1877-1917. A foreground stretch of water ringed by wooded hills in the middle distance under a boldly painted sweep of sky was painted with fairly heavy impasto and the freedom so typical of Thomson. Momentarily stunned, I could not take my eyes away from the little picture until a portly man in a well-cut dark blue suit approached. Immediately sensing my interest, he told me that they had just had the picture cleaned and reframed and that they felt very fortunate to have a rare work by the great painter. He introduced himself as Leslie Lewis.

As I stood transfixed before the little painting, he removed it from the wall and showed me a circular imprint on the back side of the panel. He explained that this was the Thomson estate stamp, designed by one of the artist's friends to certify, after his death in 1917, each of Thomson's panels. Most, and undoubtedly this one, were painted in Algonquin Park.

Almost dizzy with excitement, I tried to remain cool and dispassionate, mindful of Archie Laing's advice. Still, this was a fairly large, well established gallery filled with dozens of other fine paintings. And this little one, from all I had seen, looked right, especially with the circular identification stamp which I had seen on the backs of some of Thomson's other panels. Still, Laing's stern warnings about doubtful pictures echoed in my mind.

"Can you tell me where the picture came from, its former owners?" I asked.

"We don't like to disclose that information because our sources usually have other pictures and they don't want to be bothered by collectors. But since you seem very serious about purchasing, I don't mind telling you. It was owned by Mr. Ernie Poole of Edmonton, who has a fine collection of paintings by Thomson and the Group of Seven. Mr. Poole is head of Poole Construction Company, one of Alberta's largest. That is confidential and I trust you won't bother him since he is not intending to part with any other pictures."

His answer sounded very forthright and the little picture was looking better by the moment. Right size, right subject matter, identification stamp and, yes, painting quality. Who else but Thomson . . . ?

Hesitantly, I asked the price. So few Thomsons had changed hands in recent years that I had very little idea of what to expect. When he said "six hundred dollars," I was not surprised. I knew that Jacksons at the time were selling for one hundred dollars and up and the larger Harris panels for over two hundred. Considering the rarity of a Thomson, the price sounded right.

The following day, I could hardly bear the wait until lunch time and the moment I would show our first Thomson panel to Archie Laing. I felt sure, since I believed I had followed his advice, that he would compliment me on my good sense and good fortune.

When I showed him the framed panel, he studied it intently for what seemed a very long minute. Then, like electronic scanners, his eyes studied the forms of trees and clouds and water. Picking up a magnifying glass he began zeroing in on strokes of paint. Silently he moved the painting away to arm's length and back to within a few inches of his horn-rimmed glasses. With a poker face which didn't give a hint of his thoughts he continued to examine every millimetre of the panel, back and front. I began to feel like a patient waiting for a pathologist's report. But he wasn't finished his examination yet.

To my amazement he reached for a wall switch and turned off the overhead lights. With the precision of a brain surgeon he hovered over the little painting, now lying face up on a table, with a formidable looking machine known as a black light, because of its invisible rays. Motioning me to come closer, he slowly moved the ultra-violet beam across the painted surface. Under magnification the thickly applied paint appeared like mountains in purple moonlight. Under this magic light, oil pigment which is sometimes added years after the original was painted, usually for purposes of restoration, stands out like the proverbial sore thumb.

During this close inspection, Archie picked up minute traces of cotton swab material clinging to the higher ridges of paint. A good sign. The painting had been cleaned, probably by a professional conservationist.

As he was finishing the thorough inspection, Blair appeared in the doorway, curious about what was going on. Together they walked into an adjoining room, Archie carrying our panel as tenderly as a newborn, which I prayed it wasn't.

When Blair and Archie returned wearing the solemn expressions of jurymen, I anticipated the bad news. In their carefully considered opinion, the painting was not from the hand of Tom Thomson, but since I was not paying for their opinion, under no circumstances should I quote them. Certain as they felt about their verdict, they were unwilling to get into a controversy with another dealer which might lead to legal action.

On the positive side, they had determined that it had not been painted recently and therefore, except for the circular imprint on its reverse side, was not an obvious forgery. It was the right size and had been skilfully painted. Archie said it might be by J.E.H. MacDonald but Blair simply refused to speculate. It was a good little painting, but it was not by Tom Thomson.

Years earlier, the Laings had handled the sale of a major portion of the Thomson estate and probably had sold more works by the painter and his friends in the Group of Seven than any other art dealer — a long history which had included the sale of such major works as MacDonald's *Tangled Garden.*

Against their expertise, my knowledge was rudimentary. I was forced to accept the fact that I had bought my first phony or, to put it more charitably, misattributed painting. Fortunately, it would also be my last.

With some reluctance, Haynes Gallery returned my money and I was off to a fresh start, sadder, but much wiser. In my increasingly reduced spare time, still mainly during lunch hours, I continued to haunt art dealers' showrooms in the midtown area, now considerably more conscious of the reputation and expertise of each. Among the few well-established dealers, besides the Laings, who seemed regularly to have paintings by members of the Group of Seven, was another gallery on Yonge Street. A short walk from my Avenue Road studio-office across Yorkville Avenue led almost directly to Roberts Gallery, located at that time just north of Bloor Street. I began alternating visits between it and Laing's.

Although still determined to turn up my first Tom Thomson, I was also greatly attracted to a number of oil panels by the founding member of the Group of Seven, Lawren Harris, which Roberts had received from the artist. One in particular, painted in Algoma in the autumn of 1920, impressed me by its strong treatment of a typical northern subject: a foreground screen of shaggy balsam firs looking across water to a far shore, boldly painted in chopping strokes, the crimson and gold of the northern autumn hardwoods intermixed with deep green conifers. Because of its subject, composition, and the free application of rich pigment, it created an impression not unlike that of a Tom Thomson. This was not surprising since only three years after his death his influence on his friend and admirer had undoubtedly remained strong.

If we couldn't have a Thomson at this time — and it appeared we couldn't — this brilliant Harris panel would certainly be, at the very least, the next best thing. Browsing at Roberts, I found myself returning over and over again to the ten-and-a-half by thirteen-and-three-quarters-inch picture which Harris had painted on Algoma's Montreal River.

The debts accumulating from continuing construction at Tapawingo were much on my mind but I felt certain that if I did not act now we would lose the most appealing picture I had seen offered for sale. The price was two hundred and fifty dollars, a sizeable amount in our circumstances. Fortunately, Jack Wildridge and his father, the gallery owners, were willing to accept a down payment of fifty dollars with four monthly payments of fifty dollars to follow. Lawren Harris' *Montreal River*, still in the white and gold frame designed by the artist, thus became the first painting in what would one day be the largest permanently displayed collection of works by the Group of Seven. To this day the little picture, painted in the year of the Group's founding, remains for us and the millions who have viewed it, a special favourite.

As much as we enjoyed *Montreal River*, our desire to have a Thomson grew even more intense with the passing months. Signe and I sought out other members of the artist's family and other friends as well as his fellow painters and some of the city's best-known elderly collectors. I also continued my visits to Laing Galleries, where Archie and Blair continued to caution me not to be impetuous.

During one discussion, I vented my frustration. "I'm sure your advice is very sound and well meant. But the day ... the hour may come when I'm offered the genuine article. If and when that happens, I sure don't want to reject it because I'm overcautious. And I'm trying hard to make it happen."

"I know you are, Robert," said Blair patiently, "and we'd like to help you. But I've spent over twenty years studying Thomson's pictures ... not just for a few minutes ... but living with them. I've known the people who knew Thomson personally and who had his pictures. You can hardly expect to duplicate our long experience in a short time. For the present, you must depend on the ability and integrity of the few dealers who have actually handled Thomsons."

Blair went on to recommend that I try to see every known Thomson I could in public galleries, to study them and absorb his technique, composition and colour. That would take a lot of time and looking and still be only a start. Almost equal in importance to visual recognition, he continued, is the picture's history, its provenance. I must find out where the present owner got the picture. Not some vague reference, like "a little old lady in Rosedale", but a real name which could, if necessary, be traced and, if possible, who had it before that, right back to the artist himself. Evaluating such information properly, he stressed, can be very tricky and there is no substitute for experience and knowledge. Certain names, places and times ring the right bells ... others are meaningless and must be seen as casting doubt on a picture. However, names and places which had no meaning for me might strike the right note with the Laings. That's where experience comes in, he concluded.

I had my work cut out for me. During my business travels, mainly in Ontario and Quebec, I usually managed to steal a few hours to visit art galleries, dealers and individuals who might lead me to our first Thomson. But in spite of my persistence it still eluded me. Then, early in September 1956, a telephone call came from the most likely, or perhaps, in view of my experience, unlikely source.

"Robert, are you coming in today?" Archie Laing asked.

"I could. Anything special on your mind?"

"Yes. Just be sure to see me."

Archie had never called me before. His brief message sounded urgent. I left for an early lunch hour with a mixture of curiosity and excitement.

The elder Laing welcomed me with a beaming smile and invited me into the private viewing room at the rear of the gallery, something he had never done before. We had always sat on a bench in the main gallery, where he could mind the store and oversee the comings and goings of browsers or come smartly to attention at the sight of an established customer. With an old trader's eye he could infallibly spot a potential buyer — or seller. Those who come to sell are often as important to the dealer as those who come to buy.

In the smaller room, its walls lined with shelves of art books, Archie Laing sat beside me on a large comfortable sofa facing a velvet-draped display easel. On it was a small, framed oil panel of pine trees and rocks against a cloud-swept sky. On the large easel, strikingly lit by a strong adjustable light, the little picture had all the drama of a solo performer in the spotlight on a great theatre stage.

Giving me time to absorb a first impression, Laing spoke in an almost conspiratorial voice, "It's a Tom Thomson!"

Here at last, was the object of what had seemed an endless search. As if to leave me alone with a loved one, Archie remained silent as I stared at the painting, the fulfilment of what I had begun to think was an unattainable goal.

I had seen many genuine Thomsons in public galleries and private homes, but none had been for sale. When we had been offered paintings they had proved to be of doubtful authenticity.

This was the first unquestionably genuine Tom Thomson I had ever had the opportunity to purchase.

Thomson's finest paintings were all completed in the brief period between 1914 and his death in Algonquin Park's Canoe Lake three years later. The panel I was viewing had been painted during a brief stay with Dr. McCallum at his Georgian Bay summer home in July 1914, although most of the other works from the great period that was only beginning would come from his beloved Algonquin Park.

Painted very early in Thomson's greatest period, the pine tree sketch displayed much of the freedom and sureness, the spontaneity, which marked his final, triumphant years. It did not have as much appeal for me as some of those I had seen at his sister's home or such stunning sketches as *Bateaux*, which I had seen in the Art Gallery of Toronto. Those pieces were, of course, the *crème de la crème*. I could hardly expect our first conquest to fall in that category. It was good, I knew, but not great.

But it was a Tom Thomson, in his classic size, technique and period. My desire to possess these eighty square inches of genius was overpowering.

Archie had not spoken a word during my examination and a frightening thought crossed my mind. Was the painting being shown to me as a favour? Would it then be kept by Blair or offered to one of Laing's long-standing and more affluent clients? I was almost afraid to look at Archie, who seemed suddenly to have taken on the appearance of a judge about to pass sentence.

Hiding my anxiety, I assumed what I hoped was an offhand manner. "It's a nice sketch. How much?"

Silence. Deeply furrowed brow. Then, "Robert, it's a thousand dollars." But quickly, "We didn't expect this one to come in and we had to pay a lot of money. It may seem high to you but how can you put a price on it? They are so rare, we may never get another."

At that time, it was probably the highest price ever asked for a Canadian painting of this size. But we could have it — if we were willing to pay.

"I'll be perfectly honest, Robert," Archie said. "Blair would like to hold it for himself, but I've told him we must turn these things over, no matter how much we like them, for the sake of our business. We are, after all, dealers."

That did it. Blair wanted to keep it and certainly many of their wealthier clients would jump at it. But it was a big move for us. Signe and I, as children of the Great Depression, had always avoided spending money we did not actually have. Other than modest mortgages on our Avenue Road and Kleinburg properties we had a rigid no-personal-debt policy. Still, I knew this would have to be the exception.

"We'll take it," I said bravely. "But I'd like Signe to see it. She and I will figure out how to pay for it."

"Robert," he said, "I'm willing to help you. Give me a cheque for one hundred dollars with today's date, and nine post-dated cheques for the next nine months — and you may take the picture home with you."

That really did it. I asked Laing to put the picture out of sight, promising to return in less than an hour with Signe ... and our cheque book. In much less time than that we were both writing cheques and placing them in a little pile on Archie Laing's desk. Yet before we had even signed the final cheque, he was holding up for inspection another framed painting exactly the size of the Thomson.

"You should have this one too," he told us. "It's a painting of Tom Thomson's camp in Algonquin Park, painted by his friend Arthur Lismer in 1914. We acquired it recently, directly from Lismer."

Signe and I looked at the picture and then at each other. The two pictures belonged together. It was fate that we should get not only our first Thomson, but also a unique and historic painting of his tent in the woods by another artist of the Group. We had to have both.

"How much?" I asked, resigned to another reckless plunge.

"Normally," said Archie, always the most astute of dealers, "A picture of such historic importance would sell for much more but, since you're buying two, you can have this lovely Lismer for just two hundred."

After having committed ourselves to a thousand dollars for the Thomson, two hundred struck us as modest. We nodded in unison. Never one to leave a good closing dangling, Archie shook both our hands and handed our treasures to his preparator for careful wrapping.

As we waited, we noticed several stacks of framed pictures leaning against a wall at the rear of the gallery. Another visitor was looking through one containing Lismer and Harris paintings and we began to look too. Bending down for closer examination we were soon in conversation with a man who shared our passion for the Group of Seven. As we chatted I noticed that Archie had returned to the desk with our parcel and appeared desperately anxious that we break off our conversation. Finally he came over and asked us quietly to return to the private room with him.

"I hope you didn't mention the Thomson to him," he said unhappily, then heaved a sigh of relief when we shook our heads.

"That man is an avid collector," he explained. "He would be terribly upset if he knew we had not offered the Thomson to him. In fact there are a number of people in the tight little collectors' world who would also be upset and word gets around like wildfire. It was partially because we believed you are outside those cliques that we offered the picture to you first. I hope you will be discreet about it."

"Of course," I said, "but just who *is* that man we were talking to?"

"That is James Coyne, Governor of the Bank of Canada," said Archie, reaching into his pocket for a dollar bill. "That man has his signature printed on every blessed dollar in this country." He pointed to the signature at the bottom right-hand corner of the bill in his hand.

Quietly, but smugly, we left the gallery with a brown paper parcel securely tucked under my arm.

2

The 1950s brought dramatic changes in both our professional and our personal lives. We gave up the development of film for the development of new ideas. In this watershed decade, we abandoned our home/office in the heart of Toronto. A log cabin on a hilltop in the woods of Kleinburg became our home; my working office moved to Rockefeller Center on Fifth Avenue in the heart of New York.

During the fifties, as our photographic business became more successful, I found I was giving more and more of my energies to a new advertising concept which had evolved from a unique promotional idea that I had devised to increase sales at the studio. Our business was primarily wedding photography and its success came from a then-new idea — the production of a wedding "storybook" of pictures taken at the home, the church and the reception, rather than the formal studio portraits and poses which had long been the custom.

One of our successful promotions was an informative forty-page booklet dealing with wedding etiquette. To cover its production costs, I sold one-page advertisements to a well-known florist, a caterer and a formal clothing rental service. The booklet was mailed to brides-to-be, who responded to radio commercials that we bought on station CKEY. Even though the promotion was moderately successful, I kept trying to think of some way to make it more exciting, more effective.

One day I noticed an advertisement from the Richard Hudnut Company which offered a free trial-size bottle of Egg Creme Shampoo to anyone who mailed in the coupon in the ad. I thought this was an excellent way to increase customers, but I was puzzled because, quite aside from the cost of the product, it seemed to me that the costs involved in advertising, handling the coupons, mail packaging, labelling and postage must be considerable. Our promotion, the etiquette booklet, was successful only because it was underwritten by advertisers who wanted to reach a specific and very select market. Surely there was a lesson to be learned? Why couldn't an attractive and exciting package of non-competing products be put together ... and what better market than brides-to-be?

I knew very little about the toilet goods industry but the more I thought about my idea, the more logical it seemed. I asked Signe to mail in the Richard Hudnut coupon and about two weeks later the mailman brought her a trial bottle of shampoo. We were quite surprised that it was not a tiny sample but a generous bottle, sufficient for several hair washes. I examined and noted the corrugated outer packaging, the typewritten address label and the postage stamp. Without counting the cost of the magazine advertisement, my conservative guesstimate of cost for this method of sample distribution added up to between nine and twelve cents per unit over and above the cost of the product itself.

That set me to thinking of the negative aspects of any mail-in programme. It seemed to me to be both wasteful and inefficient. No great flight of imagination was required to picture thousands of children collecting the samples for fun and other thousands of people who could not normally afford to buy the product sending in coupons.

It was only a step to a new idea. I saw our wedding booklet surrounded by useful and glamourous nationally known products such as perfume, toothpaste and soap. Why, we could even include a silver spoon! A package like that would give us a blockbuster promotion and at the same time assure quality, wasteless distribution to a prime market group at much lower cost than mail-in coupons. And having a third party, in this case our studio, present the products would imply an endorsement that would be much more effective than a direct sample distribution.

Convinced that we were breaking new ground in sales promotion, I was soon spending most of my time working out the possibilities of my idea. First, I decided, I needed a model. In drug and variety stores I bought the smallest retail sizes of several toiletries and proprietary drug products which I felt might be candidates for inclusion in our "Bridal Shower." A dozen or so of these products were attractively set out in a mock-up box with a silver-plated spoon and our etiquette book on top.

My earlier years as salesman-publisher of *Canadian High News* stood me in good stead. I knew there was no substitute for legwork so, full of evangelical enthusiasm, I set out to call on sales and advertising managers in the toiletries field to tell them in person of this brilliant new promotion. Lower cost, a controlled market, no waste or duplication, direct access to potential purchasers with third-party endorsement; how could I miss?

It seemed only right that the first to hear of Bridal Shower should be George Plewman, sales manager of Richard Hudnut. A bottle of Egg Creme Shampoo almost glowed in the central position of my carefully arranged mock-up.

Plewman studied the package and generously agreed that the idea might have merit ... until I proudly stated that the gift would reach at least twenty or thirty brides each week.

He winced. "That's not enough to make even a little jiggle on our sales charts ... even if it achieved one hundred percent conversion among recipients ... which it won't. The idea is attractive, but the numbers are wrong for us."

Quickly regrouping, I said, "Mr. Plewman, if I had suggested distribution of say, one hundred per week, could your company afford to give away fifty-two hundred bottles of shampoo a year?" It sounded like a large amount to me.

"Not really," he replied. "We'd be much more interested in fifty-two thousand."

In those few seconds, my marketing education advanced by miles. For us, winning another bridal customer meant another one hundred dollars or so in sales for our studio; more for our co-advertisers in catering, flowers or formal rentals. National advertisers in the toiletries field may make only a few cents profit per customer but their volume is measured in millions.

I saw my miscalculation immediately. As George Plewman had said, my numbers were wrong. My enthusiasm was far from dampened; however, I began to imagine the almost limitless possibilities for a revised concept: multiple sampling of non-competitive products to much bigger markets than brides. After all, brides were less than one percent of the toiletries market. I went home a little sadder, but certainly wiser, to think things over.

With exquisite tact, Signe sensed that my first call had not been an outstanding success and asked no questions until after a nearly silent dinner. Finally she could stand the suspense no longer. Her voice filled with sympathy, she asked, "Was the amount of shampoo you wanted too much for them?"

I told her about my meeting with Plewman.

"Fifty thousand? I don't think there are that many weddings in the whole country."

"There aren't," I agreed. "But the message is clear. They are not interested in advertising or distributing samples to the numbers we're talking about."

"Surely they don't send that many bottles out through magazine coupons like the one I sent in?"

I explained what George Plewman had told me. "Those sample requests give them a figure which they multiply by some magic number or percentage. It supposedly tells them how many people read their advertisement and from that they get some measure of the effectiveness of the publication. All very complicated, but the gist is that getting the sample to a potential buyer is only a secondary purpose."

During the next few days I considered this new information. One thing was certain. I still believed we were onto a new advertising-public relations medium and that my idea was sound. The brides' package would be fine for testing or market research, but to achieve the distribution we needed, I had to think of a much broader application. The solution seemed to lie in attracting a third party who would also benefit, and who had access to a lot more people a lot more often than once in a lifetime.

All of this was on my mind one Saturday evening, when we visited our friends Don and Marne Insley. Don was programme director of radio station CKEY, the station we used to advertise our etiquette book, and I hoped to get his ideas about how we might achieve the necessary distribution for Bridal Shower. Leaving nothing to chance, I took along my mock-up, knowing that Don had years of experience in radio promotion. I was sure he would give me his honest opinion and possibly some good suggestions.

His reaction was everything I could have hoped for. "It's a natural ... great idea ... why didn't I think of it first?"

As always, Don was ready to back his judgement with action: a proposal that radio station CKEY become a co-sponsor of Bridal Shower. The station would provide three commercials every day, mentioning our studio and the names of the products, on a rotating basis. CKEY would be promoted as co-sponsor.

I was absolutely delighted. To begin with we would be tripling our commercials at no cost to us. Manufacturers, I knew, would jump at the chance for free product mention. Our numbers problem would be solved and the money we had been spending for radio time could now be used to pay our postage bills. We would have achieved that dream of all advertising people — a self-liquidating or zero-cost promotion.

Don phoned a few days later to say that the plan had been approved by CKEY's owner, Jack Kent Cooke, and we were on our way. Within weeks we had lined up a dozen top manufacturers and were producing thousands of Bridal Shower packages.

Brides responded just as enthusiastically as we had expected to the much more enticing offer and more frequent radio announcements. Many of them even sent thank-you notes for the regular-size products they received. (Manufacturers had no need to restrict themselves to sample sizes since the controls we provided made it impossible for merchandise to fall into unscrupulous hands and be resold.) We had created a new sales medium that was low in cost (compared with older sampling methods), waste-free, direct to a specific and controlled market and had real appeal.

It was also easy for us to conduct market research to determine brand preferences, since we had a complete list of names and addresses as well as the dates on which the packages had been sent. The research was carried out among a cross-section of brides who had received Bridal Shower. The results were then tallied and compared to results among a similar group of women who had not received packages. The number of apparent conversions in brand preferences was extremely impressive.

Although our volume had grown well beyond our earlier estimates, it was still far too small to warrant the formation of a company with the purpose of developing the new medium. For that we needed to find a broader application for the packages and more third-party companies who would purchase and distribute them.

Eventually I found what seemed to be the ideal solution. My research turned up a company in the United States which was producing packs somewhat smaller than ours. These were customized for hotels who bought the handy packs to give to their guests at check-in time as a gesture of service and goodwill. There seemed no good reason why the idea wouldn't also work in Canada, so I formed a company and with a new mock-up package made my first sale to Bigwin Inn on Ontario's Lake of Bays.

Fortunately, Signe and our photographers, Ted Dinsmore and Hugh Thompson, were well able to manage our photographic business. I was off and running with a brand new medium, determined to make a mark in the world of advertising and sales.

We were already sharing our living space with the studio. I had no wish to add another business to the household, and besides, I was anxious that my two businesses should not be confused, so I rented office space in a two-storey building at the corner of nearby Bloor and Bay Streets. Sales representatives Bud McClean, Tommy Hunter and Gordon Crocker (who doubled as package designer) and secretary Margaret Betty became the staff of my brave new enterprise, Travel Pak Limited.

After the first year we found we had supplied Travel Paks by the tens of thousands to hotels and resorts from Harrison Hot Springs in British Columbia to Keltic Lodge on Nova Scotia's famous Cabot Trail. It was time, I felt, for market research to provide us with even more ammunition for our sales pitch.

Reply cards were inserted randomly in Travel Paks with the hope that they would enable us to measure consumer response. By early autumn we had hundreds. They showed clearly that resort and hotel guests enjoyed receiving the handy kits and approved of the assortment of well-known and useful products they contained. We were even told of cases where the products had helped overcome minor emergencies. That part of our research was very pleasing.

What shook us to the very foundation of our programme was the undeniable fact that the finest hotels and resorts in Canada were occupied — as much as eighty percent — by Americans! Great for the tourist industry, but unfortunately Canadian toilet goods manufacturers, even subsidiaries of American firms with the same brands, would never get Brownie points for the follow-up sales which would, of course, occur south of the border.

We knew that by revealing this hitherto unsuspected situation to our clients, and we certainly felt obligated to, we were sounding the death-knell of hotel paks in this country. To stay in business we would have to find an entirely different form of distribution. It was as simple, and as difficult, as that.

This setback had one positive aspect. It forced us to realize that we were still focussing on a narrow market. It took no particular insight to see that hotel guests, particularly on weekdays, were usually males or that household purchases, particularly in those days, were usually made by females. Our new distribution system would have to be broader if we were to do a better job for our manufacturers. Somewhere out there, I was convinced, was the right distributor, the right industry which would find our Travel Paks the ideal medium for their messages.

The harder we stared into our crystal ball, the murkier it became. Travel Pak's potential as a premium was obvious, but we were not in the premium business, and furthermore, we were convinced our ultimate success lay in developing a new advertising medium. Our circulation must not be conditional on or based on making a sale. Our Paks must be true gifts, no strings attached.

After days of thrashing around I was finally able to look beyond my anxiety and, as usually happens, the picture began to clear.

"What is it that almost everyone has in common?" I asked myself. Answer: almost everyone works for someone. In most cases that someone is a company; most people are employees. What's more, enlightened companies see their employees as major assets. With mounting excitement I developed this thought. Wouldn't Travel Paks be a nice way for companies to say thank you to this valuable asset at vacation time. That was it ... Vacation Paks!

My second question was easier to answer. "What is it that almost everyone, whether typist or chairman of the board, has in common?" Answer: regardless of our status, we all use toothpaste and, when headaches come, an analgesic or, when mosquitos strike, an insect repellent.

My third question was downright simple. "Since virtually all companies have both male and female staff members, what products should we put in a Vacation Pak?" Answer: all products should be asexual; no perfumes and no shave creams. A handy package useful to all would have, perhaps, suntan lotion, Band Aids, toothpaste, a headache remedy, antiseptic ointment — a sort of utility first-aid kit which would get people and families through minor emergencies.

Now my thoughts raced ahead. Each run of Vacation Paks would be customized with the name of the company which was giving the gift to its employees. I could already imagine how pleased our manufacturers would be to receive the tacit endorsement of other companies for their products. Names like DuPont, Air Canada, Toronto-Dominion Bank and General Motors, blue chips all, flashed through my mind.

I could hardly wait to discuss the new idea with our staff who, having faced the loss of our hotel business, were beginning to think more about new employment than about new ideas.

It seemed to me that at one stroke I had solved the problem of reaching a cross-section of Canadian consumers. All we had to do was switch our sales pitch from hotel managers to industrial relations executives, which I felt shouldn't be too difficult. From Gord Crocker's drafting table new designs for Vacation Paks directed to employees would soon emerge. Already I saw themes like "Enjoy a Happy Vacation ... Have Fun".

We decided each Vacation Pak should contain twelve travel-size items with a retail value of more than three dollars. Since product manufacturers paid us three cents for the inclusion of each item distributed, it was possible to provide the customized Paks to employers for only forty-five cents each.

Our first mock-up Paks were designed with colourful cartoons of vacation activities like swimming, boating and camping. Each Pak was about the size of a one-pound box of candy and fit easily in a car's glove compartment or an over-the-shoulder travel bag. They were attractive, valuable and desirable, and so low in cost, I was sure it would be difficult for any employer not to jump at this easy way to build employee goodwill.

Confidently I made appointments with several directors and vice-presidents of personnel in companies which employed between five hundred and a thousand employees. (I felt these would be our average customers, and they were not so big that an approach on the executive level was difficult.) After two or three calls and no sales, I was baffled. The Paks should have been a roaring success. Seeking advice, I sat down with my friend and business associate, Pete Esling, public relations director of Goodyear Tire and Rubber Company of Canada, to discuss my lukewarm responses. All company executives had agreed that the Pak was very attractive, appealing and remarkably low priced and each had conceded that employees, or anyone for that matter, would be happy to be given such a package, I told him, yet there were no sales.

We reviewed my presentation, essentially the same as the one which had met with such success among hotel owners. We looked hard at the package design and contents. We could not see any way to improve either. Perhaps, we reasoned, the companies would like a more customized design or a number of different designs from which to choose.

Gordon Crocker went back to the drawing board and produced a variety of pleasing designs with slogans such as "Enjoy your Vacation", "Have a Happy Holiday", and "Enjoy a Safe Vacation". I went to the library and began reading books on employee relations, hoping to increase my understanding of the field, still convinced we had a place in it.

More determined than ever I set out on more calls, this time to companies who were known to have, and foster, especially good relations with their employees. Again there were compliments; again no sales. In desperation I even offered the Paks to a couple of companies as a free promotion. When these offers were politely declined I decided I had nothing more to lose.

On my next round of calls I determined that I would listen very carefully for possible reasons for our rejection or even go a step further and ask outright for the real reasons we were being turned down rather than the polite "It doesn't fit our thinking" that I had been hearing thus far.

The break came during a meeting with a vice-president of industrial relations, whose judgement I respected. I noticed that he had become thoughtful about one of our package designs. I held my breath. When I could stand the suspense no longer I asked tentatively, "Does that design appeal to you?"

"It's alright," he replied, "but it's the wording ... 'Enjoy a Safe Vacation' ... That says something we are constantly trying to communicate in our factories. Safety is big with us. We have posters throughout our plants which stress safety and we're rather proud of our accident-free record. In fact, we have a large sign showing the number of accident-free days. Both we and our employees are very proud of this because it's good for both of us. It would be consistent, and it might be good for us, to continue to communicate the safety theme into vacation time. In fact, we have given out safety and first-aid pamphlets with vacation pay cheques in the past. But a more tangible package such as this would be more exciting — and not that much more expensive. Perhaps we could include a brochure or letter in the package which would make it more personal. We would think of the package as an employee-management communication."

Bingo! We had been tantalizingly close but, until now, we had not recognized the subtle but all-important difference between a "gift" and a "communication". Management is not interested in giving gifts to employees nor do employees expect gifts in the normal course of their working relationship. But management has many things to communicate to employees and well-conceived communications are well received. Marshall McLuhan's famous aphorism was never more appropriate. Each Pak, attractive and useful though it was, would not be a mere gift but a medium of communication. An "envelope" for a personal letter from the company's chief executive to each employee, urging safety during the hazardous vacation season, it would say, in effect, "You are an important member of our team. Practise safety and moderation because we want you back, safe and sound."

We had found the formula! From then on we sold the sizzle, not the steak, and our sales climbed. Corporations in every field found the unique programme helped them to tell their employees that their welfare was extremely important to the company they worked for.

In the vacation seasons that followed we produced Vacation Paks for Air Canada, Dupont, Toronto-Dominion Bank, General Electric and even municipal governments such as Toronto's Borough of York, as well as hundreds of smaller companies in all parts of Canada. Response from employees was so favourable that many company presidents received hundreds of letters of thanks. Tom McCormick, president of Dominion Stores, told me, "Some years ago we introduced an employee pension plan which cost us millions. We sent a booklet explaining it to employees and received hardly a peep of response. The Vacation Pak programme cost us peanuts and we received an overwhelming response."

With Vacation Pak now successfully established, I began to think of ways in which our new medium could be used for other messages. I knew from my long association with them that pharmaceutical and toiletry manufacturers were very anxious to reach new mothers. Families expecting a new arrival in any given year represent less than three percent of the population, so mass media such as television and newspapers are very costly and inefficient ways to reach the primary market for diaper rash ointment or baby powder. To reach this market without waste we created a Pak for new mothers with more than fifteen products of particular use to mothers and babies.

Of course, creating the Pak was the easiest part. Finding the right third-party distributors who would buy the Paks for distribution as a means of increasing their own businesses again required considerable research and thinking. Hospitals or physicians were obvious first choices, particularly since their implied endorsement of the products would be of great value, but they had no need or desire to promote their services. We ruled them out. We then considered diaper and laundry services, among several others, and finally decided on the one we all agreed was the very best choice: the leading drug store or pharmacy in each community. The pharmacists had both a reason and a need to communicate to the new mother: "Our professionally trained staff are anxious and willing to provide the best products for your baby, and professional service and advice in co-operation with your physician." Each pharmacy could choose its own wording, using one of a series of suggested letters, to be inserted in each Pak, which would have an attractive mother-and-child design and the individual pharmacy's name and address. We had learned our communications lesson well.

The idea was so well received in Ontario that it was not long before we had additional sales representatives in the Maritimes and on the West Coast. In a surprisingly short time we had Mother Pak pharmacies in most communities from Victoria to St. John's.

As part of our contract with pharmacies, we required them to supply us with lists of the mothers who had received the Pak. This not only verified distribution but also provided a controlled group of names which could be used for market research. Within weeks of first distribution we were delighted to learn that mothers were sending glowing thank-you letters to our pharmacies.

As we moved from success to success there was only one cloud on the horizon. I realized that it would not be long before some entrepreneur south of the border learned of our success. There was nothing to prevent an outsider from exploiting the programmes in a vastly larger and more lucrative market, the United States.

Our success had brought some financial rewards. In addition to paying the finishing costs of Tapawingo and adding a number of small paintings to our cherished collection, we had managed to put aside a few thousand dollars in Canada Savings Bonds for the proverbial rainy day. Signe, with the help of our two excellent photographers, Ted Dinsmore and Hugh Thomson, plus a small staff, was operating our photographic business successfully and the advertising package business in Canada had reached a stage where it could continue to prosper and grow with minimal help from me. It was time to decide whether to attempt to reap the rewards of the huge American market or let it go by default to someone else.

Through my membership in the Toilet Goods Manufacturers Association and the Proprietary Association I had some knowledge of the American market, but I trembled to think of the money and the physical and mental effort that would be necessary to launch and maintain a successful company on a national scale in the United States. But ... caution aside, one thing seemed sure — it was now or never!

On a cool Sunday evening in October 1959, carrying a small suitcase and my attaché case stuffed with sample Paks, letters of praise from mothers and pharmacies and a big blank note pad, I boarded a noisy Trans-Canada North Star for New York. Five days later, after exploratory talks with lawyers, immigration officials and a few potential clients, I returned to Kleinburg for a long, long talk with Signe.

I had become convinced that Americans would receive us just as enthusiastically as had Canadians. We could achieve a successful launch and at least four or five times the volume and profitability of our Canadian operation. Unfortunately, the costs of this success would be considerable. For a start, I would be away from home and Signe would be alone with Sam, our Labrador, at least five days a week — not just for the next few months — for years. Furthermore, our modest financial resources would be stretched to their very limits. It was an all-or-nothing situation. We would be betting everything that an all-out commitment of our resources would prove the worth of our ideas in the largest and most competitive marketplace on earth.

We braced ourselves ... and jumped.

Over the next few weeks I was X-rayed, blood tested, photographed, fingerprinted and cross-examined, and I finally received from the United States Consulate a "green card," which proclaimed me to be a legal resident alien of the United States of America. Between appointments with doctors, photographers and even police, I made calls on several of our drug and toiletry manufacturers to learn as much as I could about their American parents and any product or marketing differences I should consider.

Finally, on a Sunday in November 1959, I was scheduled to depart for New York on an early evening flight. I was like all emigrants, I suppose, stricken with homesickness and suddenly aware that Signe and I would be apart and that I would be seeing little of Tapawingo. As I walked around our woods with Signe and Sam I found myself taking mental pictures to store up happy memories against the many lonely evenings that I knew lay ahead. We tried to keep up our spirits by planning the weekends we would have together, but even Sam seemed to know: this was a time of parting.

Through the next six years our lives revolved around airline schedules. Whether I was living in New York or staying in any of the hundreds of other places where business took me, Friday evenings almost always found me returning, like a homing pigeon, to Toronto International Airport and Kleinburg. Before long, the imagined glamour of almost constant travel began to wear thin. Flight cancellations, usually caused by poor weather conditions at one end or the other, became a real problem. All too often a lonely hotel room provided an uncomfortable substitute for Tapawingo's rough-hewn charm.

I'm certain that at such disheartening times it was only the dream of building our collection in the wooded hills of Kleinburg and my recognition of the business success required to accomplish it which provided my determination to push ahead in the highly competitive, if often rewarding, jungle of commercial advertising.

The first member of the Group of Seven I met was Arthur Lismer. It was late autumn 1955. For several years Signe and I had been devouring all of the Group's exhibition catalogues and the few books that had been written about the Group or any of its members. The ink was hardly dry on John McLeish's study of Arthur Lismer, *September Gale*, but our copy was already well-thumbed and we had nearly committed it to memory, as if cramming for an important exam. It was the first book on a Group artist since Robert Hunter's *J.E.H. MacDonald*, which appeared in 1940 and Paul Duval's *A. J. Casson* (1951). While it revealed something of Lismer's personality it dwelt more heavily on the man as an academic who was deeply involved in children's art education. This scholarly profile had hardly prepared me for a sensitive intellectual who could dismiss his talent and accomplishments with tongue-in-cheek offhandedness.

Lismer's best-known works were *Isles of Spruce*, in the collection of the University of Toronto's Hart House and *September Gale*, at the National Gallery in Ottawa. Even one viewing of these monumental paintings had been enough for me to put him on a very high pedestal among Canadian "greats". We had already purchased the small oil panel, painted in 1914, of his friend Tom Thomson's camp. Unlike his later bold style with its brilliant colours and writhing forms, the little painting was interesting as an example of his sombre, English-influenced work, painted during his first years in Canada. It was as well an historic record of the early friendship of the two artists.

My advertising business required frequent trips to Montreal. On one of them, shortly after checking into the Mount Royal Hotel, I telephoned the Children's Art Centre of Montreal's Museum of Fine Arts, determined not to let any business commitments interfere with a meeting I had looked forward to for so long. Over the years I felt my business experience had made me something of a super salesman on the phone. This was different.

Dr. Arthur Lismer, R.C.A., was a revered elder statesman of the arts, one of the fabled Group of Seven, already a giant and legend in his own time. I was not used to talking with giants and legends. I got through without delay.

"Dr. Lismer? My name is Robert McMichael. I'm visiting Montreal and I'd like very much to meet you. My wife and I are very interested in Canadian art, especially the Group of Seven."

"What? You mean the Group of Old Fogies?"

I relaxed a little — the legend had a sense of humour. "We greatly admire your paintings and we have just read your biography."

"Don't believe everything you read," said the irrepressible Lismer and then, to my relief, suggested that I drop around to the old house that housed the Children's Art Centre the next morning at ten.

In his tiny cluttered office, Lismer appeared larger than life. Unwrapping his long legs from behind a small desk and grasping my hand, he suggested we take a walk through part of the adjoining Museum of Fine Arts. Though not exactly what I had in mind, I agreed that it would be very enjoyable. A stroll through the galleries was his very civilized way of shifting the focus from himself and his art to a wider world and, in the process, getting to know me and something of my interests. Perhaps he also wanted to escape from this small, disordered room in which, I learned later, he had stored nearly all the paintings he still owned.

"This is the only Tom Thomson painting which the Museum has," he said, pausing before *In the Northland* and studying it closely as if for the first time. Then, as an afterthought, "It's rather a nice one."

I told him we had recently bought a Tom Thomson oil panel and also one he had painted at Thomson's camp in Algonquin Park back in 1914 and was pleased when he said, "Hmmm ... you must have got it from Blair Laing. I let him have a few things not long ago. Nice to know you have that one."

Fortunately, and perhaps purposely, he was leading me through gallery rooms featuring early twentieth century Canadian painters who were now becoming so familiar to me I could identify most without squinting at name plates. Prudently I confined my opinions to nodding approvals of his running commentary. With my limited knowledge, I was well aware that saying more might have resulted in an embarrassing gaffe. In any case I was content to savour the experience as he shared his thoughts about the people, events and paintings which had so profoundly affected the course of Canadian art.

During our impromptu tour I had become more relaxed and sufficiently confident to ask if I might see some of his paintings with a view to purchasing one or more. On our return to his office he began digging through cupboards and shelves. The closets were crammed with drawings and watercolours on paper as well as oil panels and canvases in a variety of sizes, ranging from note pads to full-scale paintings, boards and canvases, many in rolls. They were stacked in frightening disorder, piled helter-skelter with sketch pads, pencils, erasers, pieces of string and even a rusty teaspoon. Small wonder that as he began selecting pictures for me to view he seemed quite surprised, as though many of them had been long forgotten.

One of the larger panels was a forest subject painted in British Columbia where the Lismers had vacationed in recent summers. Its central focus was a huge long-dead tree bleached by time and nature to a silver grey, a ghost tree. With a twinkle in his eye he reached for a copy of his biography, *September Gale*, and said, "I believe you've read this great volume. This painting is reproduced in here."

I told him I remembered it well.

"Rather a remarkable picture," he grinned. "Most people seem to think it looks just as good upside down." He handed me the open book. *Ghost Tree* was indeed printed upside down and I had walked into his little trap — he knew I had not spotted the error. It was small comfort when he told me that of a dozen people he knew who had seen it, none had spotted the mistake.

As he began spreading out panels on the floor I realized that several were from his earlier 1920s period with the Group and I hoped he would not exclude these from those he was willing to sell. His later work was strong, but the earlier and usually smaller panels had the freedom, the spirit and the power so characteristic of the band of young painters who would change Canadian art and the way Canadians saw their country forever.

To my relief, the panels he indicated he wanted to keep, "Nothing special — just a sentimental attachment" were primarily from his South African period or of other subjects with personal meaning for him. Nearly all of those painted thirty or forty years earlier remained spread out before me like pages from a book on art history. Georgian Bay, the Rockies, Algoma, Quebec and Nova Scotia; oil panels, watercolours and drawings — I could hardly believe my good fortune. It seemed miraculous that he still had them until I remembered reading his wry comment of years earlier when sales were lean, "I have the world's largest private collection of Lismers."

Signe and I had long since found that expanding our little collection gave us far more satisfaction than new clothes or expensive entertainment, but our fine collection of unpaid bills for the building of Tapawingo always had to be remembered. The riches spread before me I felt were priceless, but I had to ask about price.

I think he must have sensed my dilemma. "Perhaps it would make things easier," he said, "if I simply marked the back of each with a price. The prices will be about what I think those fancy showrooms on Sherbrooke Street or Bloor Street would ask. You may cut these prices by half ... that's how much they mark them up." He set to work. Each painting seemed to receive only a moment's consideration before he marked a price on its back with a stubby piece of crayon.

Waiting tensely, I tried to appear casually confident while frantically deciding at what price each would be a bargain and what price would prove to be more than we could afford. The flaw in this system was, of course, that his judgment of quality was much superior to mine. Perhaps I should jump at those on which he placed the higher prices? Yet I knew artists often found it difficult to be objective about their own work. I had seen them pass over gems of spontaneity with a shrug while treasuring a lesser work with special personal, emotional or sentimental significance. This sort of thinking was getting me nowhere. I would go with my own eyes, a bit of book learning and a lot of gut feeling.

First in line was a strong Georgian Bay impression of leaning, twisted pines against a sky of wind-blown clouds dating from the 1920s or early 1930s. About twelve by sixteen inches, it had a concentrated power surpassing many larger canvases I had seen by other painters. On a scrap of wood his brush had captured not only the misshapen gale-tossed pines but their strength and will to survive.

I had to possess these pictures!

Feigning nonchalance, I turned over a panel. The small crayon marking stood out on the dark grey board like neon light ... 200. Surely this didn't mean that the cost to me would be a modest one hundred dollars! Lismer assured me that the one hundred dollar figure was correct!

Incredulous, I responded, "Sold!"

Studying the other panels he had laid out, I felt the same thrill of discovery and delight. There were more than a dozen. More than half had been painted in recent years, mostly on the West Coast. From these I selected one small, richly painted canvas which I moved to the centre of four smaller earlier panels, hoping that my obvious preference for his early work would not offend.

Finally, he picked up the panels one by one, looking at each wistfully and examining their backs for the pencilled notations made so long ago when he and his friends were the young rebels of Canadian art. I was terrified he would change his mind and decide not to sell after all, especially when he said, "These are filled with memories for me." And then to my relief, "But I can't keep them forever."

With a shrug, he began adding figures on the back of a discarded envelope. I wrote a cheque and my treasures were loosely wrapped in some used brown paper.

That evening, my hotel room became a small private gallery. I moved the unframed paintings around, viewing them from different distances, almost unable to believe that in one brief hour our little collection in Kleinburg had doubled in size. I could hardly wait to show Signe.

A few months later, on another business trip to Montreal, I had a second meeting with Arthur Lismer. When I called, he seemed pleased to hear from me again and suggested that I come to the Children's Art Centre about four o'clock when the day's classes would be over. Arriving a few minutes early, I found the lanky old painter in the Centre's main hallway, helping a six-year-old into her snowsuit. Oh, for a camera!

Since my first meeting with Lismer, Signe and I had met and shared an evening at Tapawingo with Alfred and Margaret Casson, so we talked about the Cassons and our enjoyment of my previous purchases before I got up the courage to ask if I could see more of his work.

"My, my...you're a beggar for punishment," he said, but led the way once more to his office.

From long closed cupboards he began pulling out panels and works on paper. A roll of paper, secured by an elastic band, was about to be pushed back in the cupboard when some sixth sense — I thought it might be a poster for one of his or the Group's exhibitions — led me to say, "That looks interesting. May we look at it?"

With some hesitation, almost as if he was trying to remember the subject, Lismer removed the elastic band and, to my amazement, revealed a magnificent watercolour of twisted pines on a small island.

I had always thought of watercolour as a delicate medium, best suited to soft pastels. This was different. As boldly painted as his landscapes in oil, the deep green boughs and the vivid blues in the water and sky gave it the brooding power which the rocks and gnarled pines demanded. Tormented trees and limbs, living and dead, clinging to the harsh rock-bound islets of Georgian Bay, were the subject of many of Lismer's best-known works, particularly those of the 1930s.

"It's called *Pine Wrack*," he told me. "I worked up a similar canvas which became my Academy picture. It was submitted to the Royal Canadian Academy when I became a member."

Obviously such a historic work would not be for sale. But, once again, the irrepressible old man surprised me and once again he wrote a crayoned figure as casually as though he was writing an item on a shopping list.

It was our first watercolour and, at about thirty inches, the largest painting in our blossoming little collection. I also bought a lovely oil panel of a rocky shore with a dazzling clump of scarlet maple saplings at its centre. Then, at the rear of an open shelf, I noticed a smaller panel of a mother and child, unusual subjects for Lismer. The young mother on a park bench with a bent shadowy figure in the background was solidly painted with heavy dark accent lines and shadows, and although the painting was unmistakably a Lismer, I was strongly reminded of Roualt or perhaps the German Expressionist, Kirchner.

"A little thing I did on a lunch hour one day, in the park in Dominion Square. Do you like it?"

"Yes, but it seems so unlike your other work."

"Perhaps you should have an unusual Lismer to place among all the usuals that you have... a gift of the artist," he said with a wry grin as he handed it to me.

In the late 1950s a small salesroom known as The Park Gallery opened in a slightly renovated old house at the corner of Avenue Road and Cumberland Street, just across from our photographic studio. A few days after it opened (for what proved to be a short life) I dropped in during one of my usual lunchtime gallery cruises, curious to know what they were offering.

To my surprise the first picture which caught my eye was a

Lismer which had been illustrated in black and white in his biography, *September Gale*. It was a medium-size canvas but the white card under it carried no title, only the price of three hundred and fifty dollars. I was aware, however, that its name was *Canadian Jungle* and that McLeish, Lismer's biographer, and the artist himself, had thought enough of it to use it as an example of Lismer's best work in the 1940s.

At first sight it seemed to be nothing more than a disordered mass of tangled tree roots and twisted vegetation which filled almost the entire picture. After a moment's concentration, however, a slab of rock, nearly covered with the exposed, writhing roots of a pine tree whose base was only partially visible, became clearer. There was a tiny glimpse of open water at the top right-hand corner.

The more I looked at the snake-like roots and the masses of discordant colour in the teeming undergrowth the more I began to feel the disarray and turmoil that Lismer had striven to portray.

What at first sight appeared to be a jumble of intermixed and overlapping forms only vaguely defined was taking on an entirely new meaning. The tremendous vitality I felt in the painting implied the essential life force — a celebration of that promiscuous generation in nature that guarantees not only growth but change and adaptation.

It was clear that the artist's pleasure had lain in the opportunity to paint a brilliant creation of pure light and colour, to wrestle from clashing hues and contrasting tones an image that, although often raw in its parts, is finally a resolved, complete composition.

So absorbed had I become in the unusual canvas that it was only when I touched it that I realized it had been mounted with some type of adhesive on a board. In some areas it had begun to pull away, forming quite large, loose pockets of air, while in other, larger areas it seemed so firmly affixed to the board that the adhesive had saturated the canvas, holding it in an iron grip. I prayed the grip could be broken by an expert conservator without damage to the painting.

I drew this sorry condition to the attention of the gallery's manager who hastened to his own defence by assuring me that the painting's unfortunate condition was the reason for its extremely low price. When it was removed from the wall I could see that the rather thin canvas material had been glued to a piece of thin, rough plywood which was showing unmistakable signs of warping. The manager indicated very clearly that in buying the picture I must agree to accept it as is, that this would be indicated on the invoice, and further to that, it would not be returnable.

Mentally I cursed the uncaring and certainly unprofessional vandal who had perpetrated this crime against art, but I also realized that if it had not suffered this ham-handed remounting, the picture undoubtedly would not have been for sale. Until now we had never acquired a painting which was in such poor condition. Some had been very dirty and others in need of cradling or repair to minor paint damage, but this one, I felt, would be a nightmare for the most expert restorer.

I turned it face up again and knew I was lost. I couldn't allow this vibrant, pulsating work to get away. Unwarrantedly confident that a top-rank conservator could work miracles, I wrote a cheque and tenderly carried my violated beauty across the street to my studio-office.

During a month-long restoration, skilled picture doctor Ed Zakowski separated the canvas from the plywood, thoroughly cleaned away the dirt and glue and relined the painting on fine-quality canvas on a sturdy stretcher. Finally, *Canadian Jungle* came home. All traces of its former mistreatment were gone and now its rich colour and texture glowed, giving even greater emphasis to the lusty, contorted agonies of life and growth in its tangled, yet compelling, composition.

During my next visit with Arthur Lismer I was anxious to tell him about our rescue of *Canadian Jungle*, hoping he might shed some light on the inexpert mounting and the resulting condition in which it had first come to us. When I spoke of rough plywood and glue, I felt, more than saw, a nearly imperceptible flash of embarrassment. Then, sheepishly, more to himself than to me, the old artist passed off an awkward moment with, "I wonder what fool would do that?"

The painting has never again suffered mistreatment but it has certainly suffered misunderstanding. Over the years we heard startled visitors call it everything from "a can of worms" to a "snake pit," yet *Canadian Jungle* was destined to become a star! Nearly thirty years after we first saw it, Lismer's daring and powerful composition of roots and vegetation was assigned the leading role in the first major exhibition of the artist's later work.

This comprehensive retrospective of works from the last forty years of Lismer's life came about after years of work by the Art Gallery of Ontario's brilliant curator of Canadian historical art, Dennis Reid, and opened at the AGO in October 1985. To my delight and vindication the cover of the exhibition's impressive catalogue was a full-colour reproduction of the picture and the title of this important show was — "Canadian Jungle"!

Colour plate number one, a full page, second in importance only to the cover, was given over to *Pine Wrack*, the large watercolour I had purchased from Lismer. Of it, Dennis Reid wrote:

> *This very large watercolour version of* Pine Wrack *is far from being a copy of the original oil. All the elements are repeated — the basic arrangements of the branches, the rocky mound upon which the tree stands, the bright sapling to the right — but they relate one to another in new ways, the image of the tree itself is larger, and because the format is more horizontal in shape than the oil, the tree pushes out of the top edge and presses more closely to the bottom, drawing the whole image forward. As well, the configuration of the rocky outcropping is entirely different. All of this tells us that the watercolour was painted without access to the earlier oil. That probably explains why it is a work of such uncommon vigor, one that stands entirely on its own merits as an image of visual experience.*

In their seventies, Arthur and Esther Lismer enjoyed their summer vacations at Long Beach, Vancouver Island. Lismer found the cathedral-like forests of giant firs and cedars, and the king-sized skunk cabbages and tangled vegetation on the forest's dappled floor as irresistible as the derelict wharves and jumbles of anchors and floats he had painted on the other side of the country in Nova Scotia. I was fascinated by Emily Carr's monumental tributes to the same landscape — her native British Columbia — but Lismer's Atlantic and Pacific Coast work always had less appeal for me than his earlier paintings of Georgian Bay and the Pre-Cambrian Shield, where I felt his inspiration was deepest.

If asked, I might have said my visits with this Canadian old master were purely acquisitive. I would have been wrong. Talking with him, gaining a first-hand insight into the years of joy and sorrow and the triumphs and trials of Canada's first truly national art movement helped to form and feed my resolve that Group paintings should find a home together in an unmistakably Canadian setting.

Another project had grown from our research and study of the Group. We soon became aware that there were very few good photographs of Thomson or other members of the historic band who were no longer living. One early, rather flat portrait and some small snapshots were the only photographic record of MacDonald. A small oil portrait made from a 35 mm slide by his cousin Fred Haines and some not very clear snapshots were all we could find for Franklin Carmichael. We made copies of the few existing prints of Thomson which we borrowed from his sister Margaret, as well as of the painted portrait of Carmichael, but it was a very meagre record.

We could do little about Group members long gone, but I was determined to see that the situation did not worsen. A few weeks after my second visit to Lismer, he came to Toronto to speak at the Art Gallery and took time to come to my studio. As a result we have him clearly, and I believe characteristically, recorded on film.

Throughout the sitting he held his pipe, a natural prop which made him feel more comfortable, and kept a note pad and pencil in his lap. From time to time he scribbled on the pad — notes for his lecture, I supposed. But at the end of the session, he tore off a page and handed me one of his famous cartoons showing me and one of my employees adjusting large lights on either side of the large portrait camera mounted on an even larger Saltzman camera dolly. The dark-suited sitter appears small in the foreground dwarfed by the banks of lamps, snaking cables and camera stand. A question mark appears above his head as if to ask, "All this attention for me?" This spontaneous caricature still hangs in my den, a reminder of a great artist and his puckish sense of humour.

In the following two years we were able to persuade A. Y. Jackson, Lawren Harris, A. J. Casson and Frederick Varley to sit for their portraits and I was pleased to hear that they and their families were delighted with the pictures, the latest, perhaps the best and, in more than one case, the only recent photographic portrait they had.

Years later, these framed and mounted portraits hung in the retrospective galleries, one of which was devoted to each of the artists at Kleinburg. Most visitors thought they were by the great Ottawa photographer, Karsh. I was pleased by this tribute but even more pleased when Yousuf Karsh and his wife visited the McMichael Collection in 1967. He told me jokingly that if he hadn't known better he would have thought they were from his own studio. He then gave me a copy of his book, *Karsh Portfolio*, inscribed, "To Signe and Robert McMichael, whose untiring efforts have helped preserve the arts in Canada".

Throughout the 1950s and 1960s I continued to call on Arthur Lismer in Montreal. Our relationship grew into a warm friendship as I gained a much deeper understanding of this remarkable man, his thoughts, his art and his part in a mission which would make his name immortal.

I remember my last meeting with him in 1968. I had telephoned from Kleinburg suggesting a meeting in Montreal at four o'clock in the afternoon. He suggested three o'clock or even earlier, if possible. Somewhat surprised, I managed to catch an earlier flight and was ushered into his office just before three.

He had correctly assumed that I was interested in seeing and possibly purchasing more paintings although his inventory was now greatly diminished. He was far from his usual relaxed self. In fact he seemed abrupt and, unusual for him, nervous. After a quick handshake he showed me three oil panels. Two I knew I wanted. The third, I could live without.

Over ten years had passed since our first meeting. In that period there had been many happy get-togethers as more Lismer paintings and drawings had moved from Montreal to Kleinburg. We had talked together about galleries, art education, dealers and his fellow artists, and I had learned much about him, his philosophies and his art. I laughed at his frequent puns and delighted in his amusing anecdotes. We had always felt very much at ease with each other. Yet on this blustery November day he seemed to have little time for talk. There was no chat about dates and locations. Instead, he placed the three panels briskly on a table, indicating that he agreed with my quick appraisal.

"These two are your kind of thing," he said, adding, "this third one didn't quite come off."

By now our transactions had become a ritual. Turning the panels over, I noted his prices — a little higher, but still very modest — and wrote a cheque.

Suddenly, as though he sensed my bewilderment at his abrupt manner, he gave me one of his kindly smiles and explained, "A very aggressive collector will be coming in, probably within the next few minutes. He doesn't look at pictures very carefully, but he's determined to buy. I'll let him have that one, if he wants it." With that he handed me my two chosen sketches in used wrapping paper tied with bits of knotted string.

As I walked down the steep Ontario Street (now rue de la Musée) hill toward Sherbrooke Street I saw another figure leaning into the snow squalls as he climbed toward the Art Centre entrance. It was a well-known collector from Ottawa.

The following year, Arthur Lismer, the first of six Group artists I had come to know as friends, died at the age of eighty-four. At that time I met his daughter, Marjorie Lismer Bridges of Ashton,

Maryland, for the first time. Her friendship has helped to happily extend our fond association with the Lismer family and she has continually added more of her father's paintings, drawings, cartoons and archival material to the McMichael Collection, so that we now have an extraordinarily rich collection of art and writing from the hand of the artist who once joked that he owned "the largest private collection of Lismers".

Lismer was the first to be buried in the little cemetery we had established on a hilltop surrounded by pines and maples on the grounds of the Collection. Group members A. Y. Jackson, A. J. Casson and Frederick Varley, artists Yvonne Housser, Isobel McLaughlin, Carl Schaefer and other old friends stood at the graveside as Barker Fairley's resonant voice delivered a fitting eulogy to the nearby woods and river as well as to the television cameras of the national networks.

Lismer would have smiled at the scene, so reminiscent of one of his cartoons in which he had depicted seven grave sites by a lone wilderness tree with the caption "Here lies the Group of Seven". "Dynamic Symmetry" was a popular artistic philosophy in the 1920s and Lismer had been unable to resist one of his outrageous puns. The cartoon is entitled "A Dynamic Cemetery".

From February 1949, when we married, until November 1954, when we moved into a partially finished Tapawingo, Signe and I had shared the old red brick Victorian house at 38 Avenue Road with my photographic studio. Early in 1955 our living quarters in the building's rear became the offices of my newer company, Travel Pak Limited, and we became daily commuters between Kleinburg and Avenue Road.

Our growing interest in Tom Thomson and his fellow painters had begun to take root, but it was only after a pilgrimage to Montreal for my first meeting with Arthur Lismer that I learned that another original Group member was living so close to 38 Avenue Road that the backyards of our workplace on Avenue Road and his home on Lowther Avenue adjoined.

Frederick Horsman Varley, then in his mid-seventies, had moved into 13 Lowther Avenue with Donald McKay and his wife Kathleen. He was to stay at the McKay home for the rest of his life. In 1912, a year after the arrival of his fellow Yorkshire artist, Arthur Lismer, Varley had emigrated to Canada from Sheffield, England. Like Lismer, Varley found employment in Toronto at the art studios of Grip Limited, where he joined Thomson,

MacDonald, Johnston and Carmichael. These men, with the addition of his friend Lismer along with Harris and Jackson, were to become Canada's most famous art movement.

When Kathy McKay first introduced us in a room which had been set aside for his painting, Fred Varley shook my hand abstractedly while he continued to scowl at a canvas on his easel which obviously did not please him. It was a mountain scene painted in moonlight, and after some uncomplimentary muttering to the painting itself, he told me with some frustration that he had scraped the paint from the sky twice. Now, after a third repainting, he was still not pleased with the result. Kathy assured him that she liked the painting but his mood remained sombre.

It was late afternoon and he had obviously been totally immersed in the painting for hours. A quick glance at his watch seemed to surprise and unsettle him; he apparently had no idea of the time. Then, with a sudden change of mood. he turned to me. "My good man, do you have a car?" he asked, his manner almost courtly. "I seem to have left it very late, but I need to make a short visit to the liquor store on Davenport Road. Could you possibly oblige me? This confounded picture may look better after I have a wee nip."

The short drive to Davenport Road was a forerunner of many such urgent appeals which usually surfaced just before closing time.

Unlike most members of the Group of Seven, Varley did not subscribe wholeheartedly to the creed which held that the Canadian scene should be painted in a Canadian fashion. Although his best-known painting, *Stormy Weather, Georgian Bay*, with its pine trees bent by the wind above the waves of the great bay, is in the classic Group spirit, he was not, as Arthur Lismer was to comment much later, really attracted to the wild, untamed country which so fascinated the other members of the Group. In fact, he was too much of an individualist to be bound to anything except his own desires — to paint well those things that fired his creative imagination.

During the nearly fifteen years between our first meeting and his funeral and burial at the Collection's memorial grounds in the autumn of 1969, we enjoyed uncounted visits with Fred Varley at Tapawingo and at the McKay home in Unionville to which he moved with Kathy shortly after her husband's death in the late 1950s. She had become protector, confidant, business manager and companion as well as chauffeur to the artist whose temperament, veering between tranquility and turbulence, was so well reflected in his work.

I recall one glorious autumn Sunday afternoon when Varley and Kathy, with several other friends, were our luncheon guests at Tapawingo. Fred and I were strolling along a path on the nearby hogsback ridge where tall maples and beeches formed a tunnel-like canopy of scarlet, gold and bronze. As we kicked through a pillow of leaves, Fred reached to pick up a newly fallen, crimson-streaked leaf. Holding it in the open palm of his hand he stared at its veined, translucent form in a tiny patch of sunlight. Then, in a voice that combined awe with humility, he said quietly, "No human artist can achieve that."

At other times, when his painting or his life seemed fraught with insurmountable difficulties, his moods could be tempestuous or despondent. Most often, when he was in the company of others, his gallant and courtly manner and soft voice charmed all around him, particularly if the group included attractive women. The glint in his eye by no means diminished with age.

In both the magnificent drawing of a little girl given to us by Dr. Viola Pratt and scores of sensual figure studies and striking portraits, Varley's women far outrank (in the eyes of collectors, at least) his competent, though often arresting, pictures of men. His agent, Jack Wildridge of Roberts Gallery, could always sell almost any female subject by Varley, often at twice the price of equally well-painted men. Many of his portraits, like those of Vincent Massey, Sir George Parkin and "Dr. T.", as well as the glowing immortalization of his son John, are treasured in major public collections. But his many drawings and paintings of his favourite model Vera and his almost mystical *Dharana* plus a host of masterly drawings made it inevitable that for many, Fred Varley will always be associated primarily with depictions of the female face and form.

Senior Bank of Nova Scotia executive Robert Dale, a modest collector of Group works, was particularly interested in Varley's work. Early in the 1960s he commissioned the artist to paint his portrait while agreeing to come periodically to Unionville for sittings. On his first and subsequent visits he thoughtfully brought Fred a present of a bottle of good Scotch whisky. Varley so obviously appreciated this gesture that it became an accepted custom. However, while some work on the painting was accomplished with each sitting, Dale began to sense that Varley seemed to be so preoccupied with achieving perfection that he seemed to be progressing more and more slowly with the picture. Only gradually did he begin to suspect that Varley might be intending their happy arrangement to continue indefinitely — which it did. Years later, after Varley's death, the still incomplete portrait was finished by conservator Ed Zakowski.

Throughout most of his life Fred Varley experienced recurring financial crises so severe that he often lacked money not only for painting materials but even for food and shelter. During these crises, even though he had no source of income but his work, Varley was willing to exist at a barely subsistence level unless he had something to say. Whatever his minor defects of personality and temperament, he had integrity. He never permitted himself the indulgence of repetition or compromise. He was a painter's painter.

Over the years we were able to gather for the Collection a very fine selection of Varley's works, ranging from his 1920 paintings in Georgian Bay through his period on the West Coast to the watercolours he painted on his travels in the Arctic and the Maritimes.

The works which most distinguished him from the others in the Group, his portraits, have been more difficult for the Collection to acquire. Since they are portraits, very perceptive ones, they are usually treasured by the families of his subjects as much out of affection as for their value. Many, of course, were commissioned for public reasons and continue to hang in appropriate public places. Except for a finished drawing of Dr. Arnold Mason which was the preparatory sketch for a canvas, our eight portrait drawings and oils, most of unknown subjects, were painted because of Varley's interest in the faces, rather than for private or public commissions.

One of the most outstanding among them is an oil on canvas of an enigmatic subject entitled *Girl in Red*, which was brought to us by a former Torontonian, then living in California, who wished to sell a picture that her late husband had purchased in the 1920s. She knew very little about it. We brought the painting to the attention of Mrs. E. L. Rous, widow of the founder of the commercial art house which played such a significant role in the lives of Varley and many of the other artists who banded together in the Group. Mrs. Rous purchased the portrait and donated it to the Collection in memory of her husband, but neither she nor we knew the name of the subject. It was an intriguing question.

When *Girl in Red* had been cleaned, reframed and photographed, we circulated excellent prints to the Toronto newspapers with a news release which asked, "Who is this woman?" The story was quickly picked up by television and newspapers across Canada and even though the model would be at least forty years older, we hoped someone who recognized her would respond. More than one person who had known Varley in the early years had made vague allusions to a girl who had worked in the glove department of Eaton's and who was known to have modelled at times for the artist, but no one came up with a name. She remained *Girl in Red*.

Still, it was a great human interest story and, following its wide circulation in print, thousands of visitors poured into the gallery, many asking at the front entrance, "Where's the *Girl in Red*?" *Where* we know, but will we ever know *who*?

Another strong oil portrait, *Negro Head* (1940) was a bequest of the late Charles S. Band from a collection of Varley's work which he had lovingly assembled over nearly forty years. The strong, extremely sensitive drawings, *Indian Girl* (1927) and *Eskimo Woman* (1938) demonstrate Varley's masterful draftsmanship and the diversity of the subjects that caught his interest.

I recall talking with Fred during one of his last visits to our collection. We were looking at a small, powerfully painted Tom Thomson panel and I remarked, with what may have seemed to be naïve enthusiasm, on the texture, the sheer thickness of paint on the small sketch.

Fred Varley's response was quiet but firm. "It's not the thickness of the paint that counts, Bob. It's the spirit and skill with which it is applied!"

To make my first call to A. J. Casson I cranked the handle of our wooden, wall-mounted telephone three turns and gave our local operator his number in Toronto. It's hard to believe now, but the Kleinburg system was that primitive in 1955.

After introducing myself, I told him as best I could of our enthusiastic but still fledgling interest in Canadian art and invited him and his wife Margaret to dinner, hoping they would find their way without difficulty to our home on the eighth concession of Vaughan Township. Looking back I am astonished that with so little to go on he accepted my invitation at once.

Thus began a friendship neither of us could have foreseen; one which would grow warmer and deeper through the years, never wavering, and enduring for the rest of our lives.

That was thirty years ago. Islington Avenue had not been named, Highway 400 did not exist, and Major MacKenzie was not a busy east-west artery, but our local member of the Ontario Legislature. Kleinburg was a remote hamlet. Fortunately, because many early sketching jaunts in a Whippet or Model T Ford had taken him through the byways of up-country Ontario, Casson knew, and had painted, our small hamlet years earlier. He had little difficulty locating the narrow half-mile laneway that led to Tapawingo.

Old buildings on the back roads of Ontario had always been favourite subjects for Casson's paintings. Our buildings of old logs and stone suited him as comfortably as his well-worn tweed jacket and slacks fitted his trim figure. He seemed impressed with the care and skill which had gone into constructing our new home of pioneer broad-axed timbers and we were delighted when he noticed the weathered silver patina we had carefully conserved on the massive logs. He and Signe, both enthusiastic gardeners, became immediate friends when he noted the old-fashioned rockery plants at our front door.

Although we were well aware that our little assembly of Thomson, Harris, Lismer and Jackson panels was far from being a significant collection, Casson sensed our pride and pleasure and responded as he might have to an array of major works. As he praised each as a little gem, we dared to hope that on this first visit he was beginning to share our dream.

At dinner Casson reminisced about early Group days, recapturing the spirit and the joys and sorrows of those momentous years. We felt we had been born too late when he talked about now-famous paintings the artists had been unable to sell, even at give-away prices. It seemed impossible that collectors and galleries could have been so blind. Casson explained:

"In the twenties and thirties and even up to the forties, most people who could afford good pictures bought second-rate European work or Canadian work in the nineteenth century European manner ... misty pastorals of windmills, stone bridges and thatched cottages. That kind of painting was considered to have prestige. A few collectors like Dr. Mason, Stanley McLean and Vincent Massey bought good Canadian art, some from Group members.

"I'm not exaggerating when I say that, at times, Jim MacDonald, Alex Jackson and Fred Varley came close to starving. Without commercial employment like I had, or teaching, it was almost impossible to get by, let alone support a family."

Did he have regrets or a feeling of bitterness about those lean years of hard work with so little reward?

"Not for myself. I had a steady job and I could get in my painting on Sundays and during holidays. But men like Jim MacDonald had so much to offer ... worked so long and hard. He didn't receive much acclaim during his life ... or money. Between commercial art and teaching he managed to work in his own serious painting but his health was never robust, and in the end he worked himself to death."

As the evening progressed, we became more and more fascinated. Casson had taken our folk heroes and idols and turned them into real people. The past came into perspective and as he reminisced we learned about his own life and association with the Group.

Around 1920, after two short-lived jobs with small engraving firms, Alfred Joseph Casson had joined the well-known commercial art firm of Rous and Mann. Here he met and became apprenticed to artist Franklin Carmichael, a member of the newly formed Group of Seven. A friendship developed that led to many weekend and holiday sketching trips. Five years later, Carmichael left Rous and Mann to join Sampson Matthews Limited, and two years after that Casson joined him there as assistant art director. Their very close relationship continued until Carmichael's sudden death in 1945.

After the Group's formation and first exhibition in 1920, Carmichael introduced his younger friend and protégé to other members of the Group over lunch at the Arts and Letters Club in Toronto. Casson soon became a regular visitor at the Group's table. Over the next few years his friendship with the painters grew closer and in 1925 he and Frank Carmichael were invited to join A. Y. Jackson and Lawren Harris on a sketching trip to Lake Superior.

The following year, on their way home after a party at Lawren Harris's house on Queen's Park Crescent, Casson recalled that Carmichael said, almost casually, "How would you like to be one of the Group?" When Casson replied that he would be honoured, Carmichael, who had already talked with Harris and some of the others, stated simply, "Well, you are one." Frank Johnston had resigned from the Group a few years earlier and Casson's acceptance filled the vacancy, so the Group once again had a full seven members. The appointment came just in time for Casson to exhibit for the first time with the Group in their fifth exhibition in 1926.

Casson has always acknowledged a debt to his "boss", Carmichael. His senior by eight years, Carmichael had studied at Toronto's Central Technical School, the Ontario College of Art and Antwerp's Académie Royale des Beaux Arts. To this day, Casson says with pride, "Anything I came to know about the organization of paint on canvas originated with him." So strong was Carmichael's influence on his painting that Casson found it necessary, in later years, to greatly reduce the amount of time the two painted together so as to establish a style of his own.

About 1945, Casson moved temporarily into a slightly abstract, cubist style of sharp, geometrically controlled lines, not unlike the effect produced by the prisms of an optical kaleidoscope. A decade later he had returned to more literal treatments, heightened by dramatic contrasts and an enriched colour palette.

When we first knew him Casson had worked in commercial art for nearly forty years and was still employed as art director at Sampson Matthews Limited. Through all those years, landscape painting had been a weekend and holiday avocation. Then aged fifty-seven, he began giving serious thought to quitting commercial art at sixty to devote his remaining years to full-time landscape painting. Early retirement from a long commercial career was considered a very novel idea at the time.

As his sixtieth year approached, Cass and I had many serious talks about his desire to make the break. My concern was not entirely disinterested. Although I was twenty-three years his junior I had also been giving serious consideration to leaving commercial work so I could pursue my dream for Canadian art on a full-time basis.

Casson's decision was made difficult by a discouragingly sluggish art market and his natural concern for his family's security. He had enjoyed steady employment through the Great Depression of the 1930s but had known many self-employed artists who had all but starved on the dole. Like most Canadians of his age, Casson had been indelibly marked by those terrible years.

Even though it was now the mid-1950s, company pensions were not universal and were often meagre. The Canada Pension Plan and universal medical plans did not yet exist. Inflation was beginning to cast its dark shadow. Yet the prices paid for paintings, particularly Canadian paintings, seemed to remain nearly static.

For example, the going price for a Casson oil panel, ten by twelve inches, was seventy-five dollars; for a medium-to-large-size canvas, Casson usually received something between two hundred and five hundred dollars. He had no regular dealer representing him, nor were purchasers beating a path to his door.

Nevertheless, in 1958 A. J. Casson courageously withdrew to work full time in the bedroom-size studio of his north Toronto home, for the first time fully committed to his art.

Through almost forty years of part-time painting, he had never been represented by any one agent or dealer. Several well-known commercial galleries had from time to time displayed his paintings, usually on consignment, meaning that he was paid his portion of the sale price only if, and when, a painting was sold. This arrangement often led to misunderstandings, requests for discounted prices and, in more than one case, underpayment for pictures which had been sold at higher prices than predicted by dealers. Prompt payment after a sale was a rarity.

Now that painting was a full-time career, it was essential that Casson become associated with a dependable dealer. Eliminating those with whom he had experienced difficulties, his choice was narrowed down to the few he held in high regard. Among these, Roberts Gallery on Yonge Street in Toronto's midtown stood out. Gallery manager Jack Wildridge seemed to be Casson's kind of person, but he sought advice from a number of friends, including Signe and me, before making his decision. As it happened, we had purchased our first Group painting, a Lawren Harris panel, from Wildridge. We had been pleased when he allowed us to pay for the picture over a period of several months. We also felt that he and his father operated their gallery in an efficient, businesslike manner, without the high pressure tactics we had experienced on occasion with other dealers. Without hesitation, we endorsed his choice.

It was a wise one. For almost thirty years, artist and dealer have enjoyed a warm relationship which has also been profitable for both.

All of this was, of course, in the future when, a few weeks after our first evening together at Kleinburg, the Cassons returned our hospitality. Our most vivid memory of their home is of a richly coloured mural framed by the open archway of their dining room. Installed as a permanent wall, the huge canvas — a mass of flaming hardwoods — dominated the room. From behind two of its stylized trees, two deer, almost incidental to the large composition, peered timidly. It was an extraordinary display both of Casson's mastery of design and of his deep appreciation of the natural wilderness.

Margaret's food was delicious, but Signe and I were soon feasting on different fare — four medium-size canvases from Casson's various painting periods which were just a prelude to dozens of smaller oil panels.

Dinner over, Casson led us to his upstairs painting studio.

For all his relaxed personal manner, Alfred Casson is very orderly in his working habits and in his approach to art. In his studio several neat piles of small paintings on panels were laid out on an uncluttered workbench beside his large easel. These were ready for us to carry down to the living room where the light was better.

Ten or twelve at a time were spread out on the carpet. Since most were of the panel size that Casson preferred, he could easily slip any painting of special interest into an empty frame he kept handy. It is amazing how much a frame changes and enhances a raw panel, especially for people who had (as we had in those days) little experience with unframed work.

We could hardly believe our good fortune. Row on row of landscapes appeared before us; a dazzling selection ranging from Casson's earliest to his most recent periods and from sombre winter moods to dazzling celebrations of autumn colour. In the presence of such riches we were alternately exhilarated and confused — even somewhat intimidated — as silent old farms and quiet streams were followed by the massive rocks and crystal lakes of the Pre-Cambrian Shield, and leaping waterfalls gave way to brooding forests. Casson's first loves seemed to be tiny old villages, often deserted, and remote miners' and woodsmen's shacks on little-travelled back roads. In some we found a cheery feeling of snug, if spartan, living; others suggested only abandonment, decay and death. Yet whatever the subject, Casson remembered every detail of his pictures and kept us entranced with a running commentary of dates, times and circumstances that we found phenomenal. Glancing quickly at a panel he would say something like, "On this trip in the fall of 1931 Frank Carmichael and I ran into poor sketching weather. The skies were just blah. Now the canvas of this sketch I sold to J. S. McLean. I think it still hangs out at Canada Packers. This one is the sketch, quite early, 1920, for one of my early canvases in the National Gallery."

Then turning to Margaret: "Do you remember that trip to Haliburton? We had a hard time finding a housekeeping cabin for rent ... but just off the highway we spotted just what we wanted ... right in the midst of old farms with dilapidated houses. Real beauts ... the kind of thing I wanted to paint." And Margaret, whose memory was equally vivid, would add domestic details.

Of one panel he said frankly, "That one is not up to scratch. The light wasn't very good but I made it just for the record. I like strong contrasting light ... and lots of clouds. Bright sun and cloudless skies are what most people hope for on a trip. Not me. I like the texture you get from cross-lighting, when the sun is darting behind clouds and creating interesting effects both in the sky and on the ground."

We felt a little like the proverbial kids in a candy store, but I realized that we should get down to selecting our own picture or pictures. Casson had given us some insight into his preferences but I felt we should also exercise our own judgement. In the end we narrowed the choice by focussing on several that Casson liked and from these selecting the ones which most appealed to us. Absorbed as we were with the Group, it was hardly surprising that most of our choices were from work produced in the 1920s.

Price was also a consideration. Holding up one favourite early sketch, I asked Casson how much he would expect for it — hoping it would not be more than one hundred or one hundred and fifty dollars. To my astonishment he said, almost apologetically, "Would seventy-five dollars be all right?" It certainly was!

With our budget now magically expanded, we had no difficulty choosing five favourites from among the dozen or more which Casson had rated among his better works. Though the price seemed modest, even in those days Signe and I hated the thought of debt, so we limited ourselves to those we could pay for right away. However, we had scarcely made our hard and final decision when Signe pointed to a sixth panel pleading, "We didn't get that one and I love it." The budget developed even more elasticity and Casson smiled as I picked up the sixth and added it to our treasure pile.

We had purposely chosen our six paintings to represent different subjects and treatments and felt that with this major addition to our little collection we had achieved a mini-retrospective of Casson's work through two earlier decades.

It was late evening when we returned to Tapawingo but we could not resist the urge to set up the panels in the glow of a table lamp. Then and now, I consider three of these lovely little works to be the choicest of our choice. *Rock and Sky*, painted in 1921, we feel is very much in the manner of Tom Thomson. Heavily painted, a single dead and limbless tree stands like a sentinel in the middle foreground of a rocky precipice, against a glowing sky in which cumulus clouds are gathering. *Norval*, painted in 1929, is a richly coloured portrait of a small Ontario village. An empty buggy stands beside a winding gravel main street flanked by rural houses and shops. The effect is of a toy country village with billowing three dimensional clouds floating lazily in its summer sky, while *Flaming Autumn* is a flatly rendered clump of richly coloured hardwoods against a distant range of cobalt blue hills, an enduring testament to Casson's abilities as a designer and colourist.

Framing was our next task. Alex Campbell, a framer who had

made the original frames for many Group works, had a shop on Brunswick Avenue a few blocks west of our studio on Avenue Road. The morning after our dinner with the Cassons, old Mr. Campbell and I selected clean-cut mouldings from which frames finished in grey and off-white would be made. Knowing how eager we were, he completed them in just a few days. In my little workshop at Tapawingo my tack hammer and a handful of small finishing nails completed the job. I cannot count the times this enjoyable exercise has been repeated over the years but I still experience a tingle of excitement the first time we hang a newly framed acquisition and there is a special thrill if it happens to be one that has just received a much-needed expert cleaning and a fresh coat of varnish.

In 1956, Thoreau MacDonald still lived in the white clapboard Victorian farmhouse on eight acres of land where his father, J.E.H. MacDonald, had painted a famous and controversial canvas, the *Tangled Garden*, some forty years earlier.

From his early childhood, after the turn of the century, he lived here with his parents and after their deaths continued to maintain the house and its lands. A sensitive artist, he was content to spend his solitary days meticulously drawing and painting from nature and the pioneer farms and buildings surrounding the village of Thornhill. His sanctuary was thickly wooded with tamarack, pine, spruce, maple, basswood and elm, interspersed with wild apple trees and all manner of planted and wild country flowers. Thoreau, who had never married, tended his woods and open fields and the creatures of nature which inhabited them with a love and power of observation which would have done credit to his namesake, Henry David Thoreau.

As the years passed, he became known as a very private person, with few very close friends. Fortunately for us, Alfred Casson had been one of these for many years and was able to telephone the MacDonald home and introduce me before my arrival there one Saturday morning in the summer of 1956.

The house was set back a considerable distance from old Highway 7, and as I walked the footworn path and crossed a small plank bridge spanning a brook, I realized that nature had been allowed to do most of Thoreau's landscaping. The trees and flowers seemed to grow in natural profusion, rather than by design. Actually, most of them had been planted by Thoreau himself, decades earlier, with a feel for natural order upon which a landscape architect would have been hard-pressed to improve.

The vine-covered front door obviously had not been used for

years, so I went around to the back shed where I was greeted by a denim-clad man wearing a peaked cap. His weathered skin testified to a life spent outdoors.

Introductions over, he invited me into the house and I was able to tell him how much we admired his father's work and a little about Tapawingo. He wanted to know all about our miniature wilderness, particularly the profusion of hawks, owls and foxes which Signe and I watched with such fascination from our hilltop.

He told me rather sadly that he was seeing less and less wildlife as development and highways came closer. "I guess that's what they call progress," he said wryly, "but I'd rather have more birds and fewer buildings."

I agreed with him and said, with unwarranted confidence, that we felt reasonably safe since Kleinburg was still quite isolated from the mainstream of traffic and population growth. "After all," I went on, "we're so far back from the road that we can't see any sign of civilization."

Eventually the talk turned to his father. "Alfred Casson mentioned that you would like to see some of my father's paintings." Delighted to get to the purpose of my visit, I told him that although I had seen a few of the better-known works, I was surprised that the big galleries did not hang them more often.

"Yes," he said unhappily, "the galleries have lots of his work, but I guess it's stored away in vaults and they just forget about it."

This was my cue. I had wanted from the start to tell him of our dream ... our *intention*, to create a public gallery which would be almost entirely devoted to the Group. This would not be a community gallery, we hoped, but a national institution devoted entirely to a truly Canadian art. I knew I must sound like an impractical dreamer but I wanted him to see that our dream was as real to us as though it were already an accomplished fact. We were absolutely confident that it was only a matter of time.

Finally, I finished. "Signe and I are only beginning, of course," I told him, "but we already have several works by Thomson, Harris, Jackson and Lismer."

Thoreau's response was to turn slowly in his chair and open the door of a small pine cabinet. On the shelves inside were carefully piled four different groups of oil-on-panel sketches which appeared to have been sorted and classified. He lifted out one of the stacks, containing perhaps fifteen unframed panels, and began handing them to me one by one, referring to some writing on the reverse side. J.E.H. MacDonald usually noted the place and sometimes the year of his paintings, occasionally adding other information such as "stormy weather" or "hillside at dusk". I soon learned to identify his neatly written script. I also noted other markings, in pencil and in larger lettering, which had been added by Thoreau. The most common and prominent of these were the letters "NFS" — not for sale. I learned that, just as J.E.H. had made a die stamp for Tom Thomson's panels, so had Thoreau made one with the initials "J.M. 1932" for his father's pictures. While I was devouring the striking little paintings with my eyes, Thoreau supplied a running commentary on the location and date of each, often with an interesting anecdote about the painting which seemed as fresh in his mind as when his father had painted it. I found these masterly little works were attracting me almost as strongly as had the Tom Thomsons.

Perhaps it was because MacDonald and Thomson had been very close friends from the time in 1907 when Thomson had joined the staff of Grip Limited, where MacDonald was a senior staff member. A trained artist and master designer, MacDonald had helped and encouraged Thomson and was one of the major influences in his development. Conversely, the dazzling works which Thomson produced in his last years were to have a profound influence on MacDonald's work.

By 1916, members of the Group were widely dispersed, mainly because of World War I. MacDonald alone was in regular contact with Thomson. After Thomson's death, it was MacDonald who organized and helped in the building of a cairn in his memory at Canoe Lake in the autumn of 1917. He designed the bronze plaque and composed the poignant epitaph:

To the memory of Tom Thomson

Artist Woodsman
and Guide

Who was drowned in Canoe Lake
July 8, 1917
He lived humbly but passionately
with the wild. It made him brother
to all untamed things of nature.
It drew him apart and revealed
itself wonderfully to him.
It sent him out from the woods
only to show these revelations
through his art and it took
him to itself at last.

While he was helping Bill Beatty to erect the cairn at Canoe Lake, MacDonald had painted a little eight-by-ten-inch panel of Canoe Lake and the forested hills which surround it. This beautiful little painting, now in the McMichael Canadian Collection, is so much in the manner of Tom Thomson that one wonders if MacDonald was not purposely emulating Thomson's technique as a final tribute to his friend.

As Thoreau and I continued to look at the sketches, I hesitantly asked whether he would consider selling one or more to me. He said he was not anxious to part with them, but there were some he might be willing to sell. Others, particularly those marked "NFS", he would keep. Finally, we agreed on two Algoma panels and one Georgian Bay panel which, to my delight, he permitted me to take back to Kleinburg.

That evening Signe and I spent in what had become our favourite pastime — revelling in our new acquisitions. We marvelled at J.E.H. MacDonald's astonishing capacity to capture the very spirit of the land. The colours and the spontaneity in these little panels had a lyrical quality. By the elimination of extraneous detail, he reduced to its essence an enormously complex wilderness. Whether his subject was an intimate view of a little brook tumbling over a rocky Algoma hillside or a vast panorama of northern canyons, MacDonald could extract the substance of a subject and, while reducing it to an eight-by-ten-inch panel, actually magnify its power by intensifying its most outstanding features. His brush, loaded with pure colour, had a direct and unerring sense of design.

That first meeting with Thoreau was the start of a tradition. Each weekend we got together, usually at his home, but often at Tapawingo. His vivid recollections, not only of his father, but of Tom Thomson and the other painters in the Group, gave me an understanding of them which no books or other records could ever provide.

Thoreau was only in his teens when he first met Tom Thomson, in the shack behind the Studio Building in Toronto's Rosedale ravine. Recalling one day when Thomson asked him to stay for lunch, his eyes became misty. While Tom in his usual blue denims and open-necked shirt prepared a pot of mulligan stew on the wood stove, Thoreau browsed through piles of sketches and drawings. Already a budding naturalist, Thoreau lingered over three drawings of deer. Noticing his absorbed interest in the little pencil sketches, Thomson asked if he would like to have them. Thoreau said he felt his face light up and he promptly asked to have the three little drawings signed.

Young Thoreau quite naturally assumed that the quick pencil sketches had been made in Algonquin until Tom casually mentioned that since he lived in Toronto during the winter months, his viewing of wild animals was confined to nearby Riverdale Park. The drawings had been made at the Toronto zoo!

Authenticated Thomson drawings from this peak period of Thomson's life are rare. A series, no matter how slight, with such detailed first-hand documentation of time and circumstances was virtually non-existent. The merest scribble from the reclusive Thomson's hand when he was scaling heights which are still unmatched by any Canadian painter is important to those who strive to understand the shadowy figure whose works were to dominate Canadian art.

Hardly daring to hope, I asked him if he still had the deer drawings.

He blushed and hung his head slightly. "No. In a weak moment I sold them to Doc Kenny."

"Doc Kenny?"

"He's sort of a private picture dealer who used to come around to see me occasionally."

"A dealer? Do you think he would still have them?"

"Oh, I don't know. A lot of people seem to be interested in Tom Thomson."

"Is his real name Doctor Kenny? Do you think I could reach him?"

"No, Doc is just a nickname and I think he lives in the east end."

That evening we searched through the Toronto telephone book and came up with a number. Without mentioning the Tom Thomson drawings, I arranged a meeting with "Doc" Kenny. It was an incredibly successful meeting! It turned out he still had the drawings and I was able to buy them as well as considerable archival material — letters by Thomson and various members of the Group, cartoons of the Group by Lismer, and other original pieces which added to our growing knowledge.

Saturday visits with Thoreau usually included his gentle friend, Julia Berakova, who shared the MacDonald house at Thornhill. The get-togethers became such a natural regular habit that I telephoned only on the rare occasions that I was unable to drop in for a relaxed chat at the spartan, but inviting, old farmhouse.

As art mistress at Upper Canada College, Julia was known to generations of boys at the famous prep school as "Miss B". In the late 1920s she and her sister Alexandra had emigrated to Canada from the turmoil of post-revolutionary Russia. A trained painter, she gravitated toward the young rebels of Canadian painting soon after her arrival in Toronto, becoming a friend and admirer of J.E.H. MacDonald, who was then principal of the Ontario College of Art. In those times few Canadian artists could eke out even a modest living from painting. Like many of the rebels in Severn Street, she turned to teaching while making her home at the Studio Building. After J.E.H. MacDonald's death in 1932 she moved into his Thornhill home with Thoreau and his widowed mother.

Thoreau and Julia became frequent guests at Tapawingo. Although they were strict vegetarians who did not believe that animals should be sacrificed for human consumption, Signe's imagination never failed to produce delicious meatless menus, usually with acceptable fish as a main dish. As our relationship warmed Thoreau became more deeply interested in and involved with our progress. He was not only willing but anxious that we should acquire more works by his father. In addition to offering us some of his choice sketches (even those marked "NFS") at very modest prices, he often searched his memory for the names of people who had acquired some of the elder MacDonald's prime pieces, years earlier.

Although Franklin Carmichael was a member of the original Group of Seven, only a small amount of his work was in public galleries at the time we began serious collecting and little had been written about either the artist or his art.

Born in Orillia in 1890, Carmichael was the youngest of the original members, but a mere five-year lag behind Harris and Lismer would hardly account for the disparity in gallery holdings and public recognition. In *A Canadian Art Movement*, the first major book about the Group, Fred Housser lists ten works by Harris and eight by Lismer in public collections at that time, but only three by Carmichael. By comparison with his friends Thomson, Jackson, Varley, MacDonald, Harris and Lismer, all of whom had been given major retrospective exhibitions by the National Gallery and the Toronto Art Gallery, we found that he was almost unknown. After seeing some of his masterly watercolours, canvases and panels, Signe and I became curious about the apparent neglect of this outstanding artist.

We found that during his entire painting career, Frank Carmichael had been closely associated with commercial art. Like others of the group he went to work for the Toronto firm of Rous and Mann, in 1916. In 1925 he moved to Sampson Matthews as art director. Finally, in 1932, he became head of graphic and commercial art at the Ontario College of Art. Alfred Casson was his assistant at both Rous and Mann and Sampson Matthews and they remained close friends until Carmichael's death in 1945. Thus it was from Casson that we learned that Carmichael's widow, Ada, stunned by her husband's death at the age of fifty-five, had kept the body of his work intact, refusing to sell or, at times, even to show her husband's paintings. Hundreds of oil panels, canvases and watercolours, representing the bulk of Carmichael's artistic production, were stored by Mrs. Carmichael in their Willowdale home, precious souvenirs of their years together.

By 1957 our growing interest in Carmichael had produced an irresistible urge to telephone Ada Carmichael. Although I stressed my interest in her late husband's art and carefully avoided any suggestion that we might want to buy a painting, Ada Carmichael treated me with considerable reserve until I mentioned our friendship with Thoreau MacDonald, Arthur Lismer and the Cassons. The conversation warmed and she agreed to see me the following Saturday.

The modest but comfortable house on Cameron Avenue in Toronto's northern outskirts had been the Carmichaels' home since 1919, when the area was almost rural. By the mid-1950s, urban sprawl (typified by the huge Maclean-Hunter printing plant on nearby Yonge Street) had overcome much of the area. Yet the Carmichael home seemed quiet and undisturbed on its large lot. At the rear was a small wooden building, now silent — Carmichael's studio.

In her living room, Ada Carmichael began to talk in her soft but firm voice about the canvases which hung where her husband had placed them years earlier. In a large gallery they would have been arresting. In the small room the brilliant colour and design of these paintings was almost overpowering. Carmichael's paintings were richly textured, with the colour thickly applied. I was especially impressed by a panorama of jagged mountain tops with wisps of vertical cloud. The simplified cloud forms, which forcefully demonstrated the artist's remarkable design abilities, held my attention particularly.

From time to time, as she reminisced about the past and her husband's intense commitment to his art, Mrs. Carmichael stepped into an adjoining room, returning with an oil panel or watercolour. It soon became clear that the room must be the storehouse for most of Carmichael's work. It also became clear that Mrs.

Carmichael was the only person who would enter the shrine. As the little exhibition continued I found myself consumed by a raging curiosity. How many other treasures lay hidden behind that forbidden doorway?

Mrs. Carmichael had no intention of satisfying my curiosity. I had to be content with what she wished me to see, and that was considerably more of the artist's work than I had seen previously. It was still a struggle to subdue my collecting instincts. I felt a nagging desire to see if she would consider selling one or two, but discretion prevailed. I forced myself to be content with the opportunity to study the few sketch panels and the canvases on the walls while she prepared afternoon tea.

Ada Carmichael spoke of the couple's first home in Bolton and her husband's earlier employment as a carriage striper. Fondly, she recalled his letters from Orillia during their courtship. Almost always, they were illustrated with affectionate little drawings which she still preserved and treasured.

It was a day for listening and learning, not buying and selling. I discovered a great deal about a member of the Group who had been something of a mystery to us.

As I left I asked if I might visit again and bring my wife. I was pleased when she assured me that the welcome mat would be out for us. A week later, after a shorter than usual visit with Thoreau MacDonald in Thornhill, Signe and I drove five miles south through Yonge Street's Saturday shopping traffic to Cameron Avenue.

By mid-afternoon, Ada and Signe were in the kitchen preparing tea and exchanging recipes. In the living room I studied several more paintings which had emerged from the storeroom.

Over tea I asked Ada about Tom Thomson, with whom I knew Frank Carmichael had shared his first quarters in the Studio Building in 1914. At the mention of Thomson's name, Ada scurried into another room, returning with a smaller, framed panel. I knew immediately that the glowing oil sketch of snow-covered hills with rusty brown autumn leaves still clinging to distant hardwoods had to be the work of our legendary favourite. We discovered that the little oil had been a wedding present from Thomson to the Carmichaels in 1915. He had painted it in Algonquin Park only months before.

Ada Carmichael had many devoted friends both within and without the arts community, but she told us Thomson was the most thoughtful, genuinely considerate person she had ever known; a description of his character we were to hear repeatedly from others. She told us he loved to help her prepare dinner and that she came to realize that he was a very good cook. She also recalled that he would be the first to pick up a dish towel when dinner was over.

By this time, my desire to own another Thomson, in addition to the one we had, had become an obsession. Throwing discretion to the winds, I opened my mouth to plead for an opportunity to buy the magic little painting when I caught Signe's eye and a warning look whose message was clear ... don't ask! Blinded by my own desires, I had come very close to making an unpardonable and insensitive blunder. Mrs. C., as we had now affectionately named her, could only have been embarrassed by an attempt to buy one of the most treasured souvenirs of her marriage to Franklin Carmichael.

(The little panel was to have a far greater significance for us than we could have imagined that afternoon. It was the field sketch for *Afternoon, Algonquin Park*, our first Tom Thomson canvas, which we acquired two years later, but which at this time we had never even seen. Over twenty years later the field sketch would finally join the canvas in the McMichael Canadian Collection, a gift of the Carmichaels' daughter, Mary.)

A week later I brought Mrs. C. to Kleinburg for Sunday dinner. She told us Tapawingo took her back to the summer home her husband had built in the La Cloche Mountains north of Lake Huron and the happy years he had spent painting those towering hills and dense forests.

Our collection of paintings was modest — small works by Harris, Lismer, Jackson, MacDonald and Casson and our *Pine Island* sketch by Thomson. Lawren Harris's *Shimmering Water*, which I had acquired from the artist only weeks earlier, was our only large painting. Carmichael's absence was obvious. We made no effort to discuss purchasing any paintings from Mrs. C., but we did tell her about our dream that our home would one day be a public gallery for the Group and a few of their contemporaries. "I know you'll accomplish it," she told us. "I've never seen two young people more dedicated than you are."

A week later, on our next visit to Cameron Avenue, we were astounded when Mrs. C. took us at once into the forbidden sewing room. We could scarcely believe our eyes. Hundreds of oil panels and watercolours, the greater part of Franklin Carmichael's lifetime production, were carefully stacked in this one small room. No wonder we had seen so little of his work in either public or private collections!

With Mrs. C.'s delighted approval we took several stacks of

panels into the living room, where we spread them out like a picnic feast on the carpet. As each panel was revealed, whether of flaming autumn woods or a quiet summer pastoral, it became our immediate favourite. Then a glimpse of the next — an entirely different subject but equally striking composition — would deepen our awareness of Carmichael's virtuosity and force an immediate reconsideration.

Each panel had the same dimensions and, spread like postage stamps on the carpet, they seemed to meld with each other. Yet each was different — some were bold, some delicately subtle — they seemed to be competing with each other for our delighted attention.

I reminded myself that nothing had actually been said about selling. Then, with some trepidation, I asked her if we could buy some of the panels.

My fears were unfounded. Mrs. C. was indeed willing to sell to us and trusted that the seventy-five dollars each she had received for several panels she had sold earlier to Laing Galleries would be satisfactory. As to numbers, she felt we should have just enough to place her husband's work in proper perspective within our collection.

We were living a collector's dream but our immediate problem was to narrow our choices. The floor was covered but dozens of panels were still stacked at our feet. How could we be sure our limited selection would be the very best examples of Carmichael's work?

Mrs. C. made our task even more difficult. The scores of paintings represented every phase of her husband's work, but they were all old familiar friends to her and their value rested less on their worth than on the memories they brought back. Her memory for times and places was unerring and each had its own little story. One smaller panel we recognized as an early work because of its size. It was a painting of the channel near Go Home Bay and had been painted during their honeymoon in 1915 at Dr. MacCallum's summer home. A short time later, Carmichael had made a change to larger ten-by-twelve-inch panels from which he seldom varied.

The more we looked at the panels, the more intrigued we became, but we were also becoming visually and mentally drained by our efforts to see, to understand and to feel, let alone to choose. It seemed that every attempt to narrow our selection demanded the elimination of works whose appeal for one of us was so undeniable that agreement became impossible.

Mrs. C. saw our difficulties and with astonishing wisdom and generosity suggested that we take the entire body of works home with us so we could make our selection in private and at our leisure.

Days earlier we had wondered if we would ever be allowed into the sewing room. Now we were loading most of its contents into our little Volkswagen beetle. We would have been even more bemused if we could have foreseen that the hoard of over one hundred of Carmichael's finest small oil paintings would provide us with the foundation for the largest and most important collection of the artist's work.

That evening and through much of the following week Signe and I lived among the wooded hills of Bolton, in tiny Ontario villages, and in the sweeping panoramas of the La Cloche mountains. Through days and nights of studying, restudying and sorting, we finally settled on eight panels, including the early Go Home Bay "honeymoon" sketch and extending to works from Carmichael's last paintings of the Pre-Cambrian Shield; a small cross section of Franklin Carmichael's creativity. Although they had not been titled, we found ourselves referring to the paintings by "name"; *Dead Spruce*, *Scarlet Hilltop*, *Bolton Hills*, and so on.

Suddenly we found ourselves with more works by Carmichael than by any other artist! It was a stroke of good fortune but we had no idea then how fortunate. As I write these words in 1986, Carmichael panels, scarce and in demand, are selling for more than twenty thousand dollars each. Our six hundred dollar 1957 purchase would now be valued at more than one hundred and sixty thousand dollars, an amount greater than what we had spent up to that time for our entire collection, land and buildings.

Aboriginal peoples have been scattered across our vast Arctic regions for over five thousand years. For the past three thousand years they have been artists. Carved stone pieces from the prehistoric Dorset and Thule periods and the later historic period after the seventeenth century have been uncovered by archeologists and are displayed in museums across the country.

"Eskimo" art, as it is popularly known, is of much more recent origin. It was not until the middle of this century that Inuit art became recognized and sought-after by serious collectors in Canada and throughout the world.

After World War II and the development of air transportation networks and sophisticated communications systems, the people of our Far North who had lived for so long in isolation faced an abrupt transition from the Stone Age to modern times.

The Inuit's impressive ability to adapt to adverse conditions, to assimilate external influences, and to modify when circumstances demand, has never been more clearly demonstrated. In spite of the shocks and strains of this abrupt and inexorable change, the Inuit have maintained their identity and dignity and have responded by developing a new culture in which carving in stone and bone and the much newer medium, printmaking, have important roles.

Jim and Alma Houston were the first to introduce the ideas, the methods and initial equipment which launched the production of limited edition prints at Cape Dorset in 1957-58. It led to the formation of marketing co-operatives there and in most Inuit settlements, but for some time before their first visits a contemporary sculpture of unusually fine quality had been evolving. In the wake of a government-sponsored change from a nomadic life in tents and igloos to permanent housing in villages, new forms emerged. Steadily increasing contacts with white men, explorers, missionaries and government representatives introduced new influences to the intuitive and highly skilled Inuit carvers, bringing about a gradual transition over decades from the "historical" art to a newer contemporary expression. During this transitional period the Inuit sculptors developed conceptions which were quite different from those of their ancestors.

Soapstone carvings from this early contemporary period were brought out of the Far North by factors of the Hudson's Bay Company, who considered them to be interesting curios. These quality pieces, dating from before the 1960s, are now difficult to find. In later years, when their value was recognized, they were snapped up by institutions and private collectors.

Our first Inuit carving joined the small paintings in Tapawingo's living room in 1956. For some years it was the only piece of Inuit art we owned. We put the enchanting, eleven-inch figure of a parka-clad woman with the enigmatic smile of a northern Mona Lisa on a low bookcase across from our massive fireplace. In the flicker of firelight, the beautifully balanced lines of the little sculpture continually beguiled us, not as a primitive Arctic curiosity but purely on its artistic merits. We felt that its harmonious form and its unified composition would have done credit to any Western sculptor of world renown. Yet because few records were kept of this early work, we did not know its point of origin, much less the name of its carver. We did know, however, that it had given great pleasure to its creator. The sheen on its surface could have come only from the loving rubbing of human hands.

I first saw our Inuit carving in the office of David Garfield, a picture dealer who did not regularly handle Native art. He had acquired it in the estate of a clergyman who had once been a missionary in the Arctic. Fascinated, I asked the price, only to learn that the piece was not for sale. Garfield apparently liked it as much as I did. My disappointment was only slightly eased when he agreed that I should have first refusal if he ever decided to part with the little lady.

Months later I visited Garfield again to see two A. Y. Jackson panels he was offering for sale. Once again I asked if he would let me have the Inuit carving as part of a package deal with the two panels, which he seemed anxious to sell. (As I write this, I have to chuckle. Imagine asking a dealer to sweeten the pot to ensure the sale of two prime Quebec Jacksons. How times change!) Garfield's business must have been very slow since, albeit reluctantly, he did agree to sell the little Inuit lady along with the Jackson sketches of *Murray Bay* (1923) and *St. Pie Church* (1913) for a total price of just over five hundred dollars.

Perhaps because we had paid such a modest price, even by 1956 standards, we framed and hung the panels and placed the carving on our bookcase without much fanfare. Years later we recognized our "modest" purchases at the tiny Garfield Gallery as a major turning point in our collecting.

Among the hundreds of very fine Inuit pieces now in the Collection, there is none we treasure more than our first small piece by that unknown carver. The two fine Jackson panels were also to prove very significant. They were our first acquisitions of the work of an artist whom we were to meet only a few weeks later; an artist who became a profound influence on our collecting and our lives.

As if all these blessings were not enough, the two Jackson panels, still among our favourites in the Collection, were both painted on their reverse sides. Years later, after they had been expertly split by a conservator, we were able to display two more good paintings from the artist's great period in his favourite painting area, the tiny villages of old Quebec.

Signe and I do not fit the public stereotype of collectors. We are neither rich acquisitors nor conscientious members of families with a tradition of support for the arts, so we are often asked how we got started and what made us choose our particular kind of collection. We have a standard answer — that, like most Canadian children, we had been exposed to reproductions of work by the Group of Seven from the time we started school — and there is some truth in it. Of course, the real reasons that we, and others, became serious collectors are much deeper, more complex, and usually buried in the past. They are often difficult to pinpoint.

Most of us like to surround ourselves with objects that please us, but many influences and events, often fleeting, contribute to the decision first to purchase and then, as passion grows, to collect. The origins of collecting fever often lie buried in memory, like information on a silicon chip.

Scanning our own memories, Signe and I cannot remember a time when we were not in love with fine art — particularly the Canadian art that has contributed so much to our sense of national identity. With that abiding interest it was probably inevitable that we would become collectors of the Group of Seven and that we would then turn our attention to the totemic arts of the Indians of the Northwest Coast.

The transformation of our interest in acquiring fine Canadian art into true collecting fever came during a brief business trip to Vancouver in the autumn of 1957.

As it turned out, business came in a poor third on this trip. I renewed an acquaintance with Bill Reid, a Haida Indian whom I had met in Toronto when he and Signe were both working at Toronto radio station CKEY. I also came face to face for the first time with the man who had been the driving force behind the formation of the Group of Seven — Lawren Harris.

Reaching Bill was easy. He was a CBC announcer in Vancouver and when I called and reminded him of our Toronto meeting, told him of my interest in Northwest Indian art and asked if we might get together, he told me to come right along to the CBC studios in the Hotel Vancouver, where I was staying.

Minutes later I joined him in a small soundproof studio. He was wearing a headset and speaking enthusiastically into a microphone about Duke Ellington, but as the recording spun he pushed a little lever, removed his earphones and settled back to talk about Northwest Indian art. When the music stopped, without missing a beat, he switched on the microphone and again talked about jazz or read a commercial. I thought it was a virtuoso performance.

When the broadcast was over the disc jockey gave way completely to the Haida artist. Since it was obvious that my interest in Native art greatly exceeded my knowledge, Bill said he would take me to one of his favourite haunts. We would see objects from the cultures of all the Northwest Indian peoples and I would gain some insight into the stylistic differences in carvings of every type, from tiny decorative clothing buttons to massive totems, as well as the ceremonial masks that were my particular interest. (Even masks, I was to learn, ranged in size from tiny images which could be held between thumb and index finger to huge representations, some more than five feet in length.)

We headed for the campus of the University of British Columbia — a spectacular site of mountains and forest on a shimmering Pacific inlet — and the basement of one of the buildings, where the Department of Anthropology was housed. Reid seemed as familiar with it as with his own home.

Judging from its spartan quarters, anthropology was the low discipline on the university's totem pole. The basement rooms looked like a shelf-lined warehouse, with tiny offices and lecture rooms here and there among bins, racks and drawers overflowing with Northwest Indian artifacts. As my interest had developed, I had read books and visited museums, but neither had prepared me for the extent and richness of the Northwest Indian culture. For the first time I could hold in my own hands examples of the artistry that had been acclaimed by great museums and collectors in every part of the world. (Unfortunately, such appreciation was voiced more enthusiastically abroad than in our own country.)

I knew without a doubt that I had found another collecting passion, although I was still not knowledgeable enough to distinguish between Haida and Kwakiutl, let alone to differentiate among the treatments of the Tsimshian, Bella Coola, Salish and other tribal nations. Bill Reid was to be my first mentor. Unwittingly, I had sought out not only a ranking expert on Northwest Indian art, but possibly the finest living Haida artist.

To begin my education, Bill took me through the maze, picking up objects and examining them, sometimes with curiosity, sometimes with admiration, always with respect. With his vast knowledge of techniques and legends, he could single out the best, whether sophisticated or primitive. I had to learn from others, however, that his own designs and carvings, especially those in silver and gold, were considered by experts to be among the finest ever created by a Northwest artist.

Reid continued to examine minute details while my less knowledgeable eyes were dazzled by the flashier raven and thunderbird masks and the stump-sized fragments of ancient totems until, at the end of a long storage hallway, we came to an alcove where three people were drinking coffee at a table spread with artifacts. Two more mugs were quickly produced and I was introduced to a youthful Haida artist, Robert Davidson, his fiancée Sue, and Audrey Hawthorn, co-curator with her husband Harry of this extensive collection.

They abandoned their assessment of the rattles and masks on the table just long enough for introductions and now Bill joined in, offering fresh insights into these recent acquisitions. I felt that I was getting a graduate seminar from a group of exceptional scholars and knew I was fortunate to be welcomed into this little circle of experts. Not surprisingly, that unscheduled little gathering not only deepened my admiration for our native cultures and their superb art forms, it also stengthened my determination to learn much more and influenced my collecting in the years to come.

As we drank our coffee, we passed ceremonial masks, rattles and frontlets from hand to hand, and the treatment of eyes, nostrils, mouths and ears, as well as overall design and carving quality, came in for expert comment.

Yellow cedar was the most commonly used material but some smaller or particularly functional objects such as ceremonial spoons were carved in yew and other woods or in mountain goat horn. The materials were easy to identify but the type of paint and supplementary materials such as ground-up stone or potash, whether native raw material or commercial, were also carefully noted. The introduction of decorative substances such as fabric, abalone shell, tree bark and various metals was recorded and described along with precise measurements, but the greatest interest centred on design and the total impression the piece made on the viewer.

Subject matter fell into two broad categories: animal or humanoid, often in combination. All were abstractions, purposely distorted or exaggerated to produce greater impact. Some of the finest were bizarre combinations based on the human face but incorporating a stylized eagle's beak, the ears of a wolf, or the distinctive circular mouth of a mythological being known as Tsonoqua, the wild woman of the woods. Still others combined the humanoid face with the figure of a wild creature, usually mounted above it and often moveable, on a wooden axis controlled by the wearer. The most startling of the masks were carved with moveable parts designed to heighten the drama in a ceremonial dance or on a festive occasion.

Lower jaws, the most commonly hinged portions, are moved in unison with participants' chanting. Other parts, like fins and wings, also move, simulating swimming and flying to heighten the realism and excitement of the celebration. In the complex transformation masks, portions of the mask move away to reveal a second, entirely different being. The greatest of these masks are far more than mere artifacts. They deserve the eminent position they now hold among great works of art in the world's most important museums.

As the informal session concluded and Audrey Hawthorn made notes summing up the discussion, I felt that my eyes had been opened and I had been given a glimpse of an extraordinary society and the power and beauty of the art forms it had created.

At the Hawthorn home that evening, Bill and I feasted on Northwest Indian dishes, including whipped soapberries for dessert. When Professor Harry Hawthorn proudly displayed the magnificent masks which he and Audrey had collected over the years, I announced my intention of doing the same. Still, since I lived half a continent away from the source, without the Hawthorns' knowledge and contacts, I felt privately that my chances of acquiring even one good piece were very limited. Yet, my sincerity must have impressed Harry because he invited me to come to his office in the anthropology department the next morning, saying that he might have something which would interest me.

When we met the next day, he told me that his department's budget for acquisitions was almost nonexistent, so the only way he could buy the exceptionally fine pieces they were offered from time to time was to sell artifacts from categories in which they already had several good examples. At that time, they had an abundance of Kwakiutl raven masks created for use in the Hamatsa ceremonies and he said they were prepared to part with one.

When I was shown a striking black raven mask with an enormously extended beak and flaring nostrils, I was impressed by its sheer size and the strength of its features, brilliantly accentuated by classic white and red — a formidable figure of legend, almost four feet in length. It had been carved perhaps fifty years earlier in the remote northern sector of Vancouver Island by Kwakiutl carver Dick Price.

I could hardly believe my good fortune and quickly wrote a cheque for three hundred dollars. Weeks later, a Canadian Pacific Express truck pulled up at the entrance to my Avenue Road studio. The wooden crate was as tall as the delivery man and inside was the nucleus of what would become, many years later, an outstanding collection numbering hundreds of works — a tribute to the artists of the tiny villages of our Pacific Northwest.

There was still more excitement in store for me on that trip. In an earlier letter, I had written to Lawren Harris of my desire to meet him. Now, after my telephone call to him, Lawren Harris had agreed to lunch at my hotel. This was our first meeting, but I was familiar with much earlier photographs and found no difficulty recognizing him even though his hair, short and dark in the pictures, was now a flowing silver.

His old friends, Alfred Casson and Thoreau MacDonald, spoke often of the eager, enthusiastic artist who was always searching for new ideas and new places. He was co-builder of the famous Studio Building and had led his painter friends to that other historic locale, Algoma, in the railroad boxcar he had rented. It was probably in his mind, and certainly in his home, that the Group of Seven was formed in 1920.

At that first meeting I found a witty, urbane intellectual whose buoyant personality had undoubtedly mellowed over the years. He had an air of fulfillment, yet there was no hint of self-satisfaction or complacency concerning his past achievements. The Group years had been an interesting phase of his life, but his searching mind had carried his art from the merely modern of the 1920s through a more abstract transitional period to the later, boldly painted canvases whose forms were rooted, not in the natural, but in the spiritual and metaphysical. At that time, my own tastes and understanding were lagging nearly forty years behind his profound thinking and the non-objective work that he had produced recently.

When I mentioned our new friends Alfred Casson and Thoreau MacDonald, his thoughts went back to the years when they were together.

"How is young Thoreau?" he asked, still thinking of the youngster whose portrait he had painted many years earlier. "He's a remarkable young man, you know. Years ago, when he was still at the Studio Building, I wrote to him, asking a little favour. At the time, my painting and my life were going through change. I felt I was entering a new phase and that my work from the old phase should be left behind... forgotten. So I asked Thoreau to burn all my old sketches at the Studio Building. We were in the Depression anyway... and few people could afford paintings.

"It was years later that I told my wife Bess about it. She was furious. I had gotten rid of nearly all the oil panels I had painted up to the time I left Toronto in 1934. At that time it seemed to me the right thing to do, 'though I must admit that I also had some regrets about my rather impetuous decision.

"Bess just couldn't accept that everything I had done during our Group of Seven days was gone...except the few I had sold or given away.

"Well, she decided to write to Thoreau, hoping that some might have escaped the fire, and a short while later we received a hand-written letter from dear Thoreau.

"I told you Thoreau was a remarkable young man...and he is. When he had received my letter asking him to destroy my things he was shocked, and convinced that I was being foolish. So, with his own hands he built a storage cupboard and with his own meagre funds, bought a padlock for it. He saved everything from my old studio! Isn't that remarkable?"

I told him it was exactly what I would expect Thoreau to do.

"Well, I can't tell you how delighted we were to hear from him. I wrote, offering to pay the costs of his work and to compensate him for his good sense. But he would not hear of it. He said his costs were small and long forgotten. He refused to accept any payment, but arranged to have the whole lot shipped to me, collect, here in Vancouver."

"Knowing Thoreau," I told him, "it's a wonder he didn't insist on paying the shipping charges."

It was a true horror story. Virtually every magnificent oil panel from as far back as his earliest visits to Georgian Bay and the Laurentians through Lake Simcoe, Algonquin Park, and above all...Algoma and Lake Superior...the great early Rocky Mountain things and the Arctic paintings would have gone if it hadn't been for Thoreau MacDonald. Even the first picture in our collection, *Montreal River, Algoma*, would have been lost forever.

I told him that we were hoping to buy and preserve as an historic building Tom Thomson's shack behind the Studio Building and of some minor difficulties in negotiating the sale with its present owner, Gordon MacNamara.

He sighed. "I know MacNamara! When I sold the building to him, he promised that Alex Jackson, the last of our old Group living there, could stay as long as he wished and would never be asked to move. But he found ways of getting Alex to leave. I hope you'll be able to save the old shack. Tom Thomson was the finest painter this country has ever produced."

As lunch came to an end I thought I might now get to another purpose of my visit. "We recently bought one of your Algoma oil sketches, *Montreal River,* from Roberts Gallery. We're very fond of it, but we're also very anxious to have one of your earlier canvases. Do you still have any with which you would be willing to part?" I ventured.

"We have a few of the older things," said Harris. "Why don't you come out to the house tomorrow afternoon?"

The following day was momentous both for me and for the world: I acquired the first canvas in our collection and the morning radio news announced that a man-made satellite had rocketed into space and was orbiting the earth, sending out a beeping radio signal. It was the Soviet Union's *Sputnik*. Privately, I thought my news was more exciting.

When a taxi dropped me at Harris's Belmont Avenue home, I found the artist watching the World Series on television. From his seat on a sofa in the large, airy living room he beckoned me to a comfortable chair and my eyes fastened at once on a magnificent canvas in the glowing colours of autumn in Algoma. "That one's not for sale," he said firmly.

From a large closet nearby, he carried in two unframed canvases on stretchers. One I judged to be about thirty by forty inches, the other slightly smaller. Neither had the brilliant colour of the first I had seen, but both were from the early Group period which I favoured at the time. He remained silent but I found myself being drawn to the larger one — perhaps because its size was more appropriate for our large living room.

Aware that I lacked his fine judgement, I asked Harris how he felt about my choice and was relieved when, after a moment's consideration, he said, "It's a good solid picture." That settled it. I told him I wanted to buy it.

His response was characteristic. "Fine, I hope you'll enjoy it. The price is eight hundred dollars. I would prefer that you send me a cheque later on, dated for early next year. My accountant tells me I have sold as much as I should for this year. Also, I feel it needs relining to give it permanence. I will arrange to have this done in Ottawa and have the National Gallery people send it to you. It will probably be two or three months. Oh, incidentally, I will pay for the restoration work."

The few days I had to spend in Edmonton, Calgary and Winnipeg on the way home seemed endless as I waited impatiently to tell Signe that we now had our first Indian mask *and* our first canvas.

Within less than a year after meeting the artist, we added to our collection two more Casson panels which had not been among those we viewed during that first selection. One was a delightful main street scene painted in 1929 — of Kleinburg. So little had the three village stores changed over nearly thirty years that we felt the panel could have been painted the day we bought it. During our entire lifetime, almost nothing had changed; the removal of a four-foot pole, a hitching post, had been virtually the only change in "beautiful downtown Kleinburg". A typical Casson, charming, yet precise. His brush and pencil had lovingly recorded more of southern and central Ontario's backroads heritage than have those of any other artist.

Our next Casson acquisition was the most satisfying of all. By late 1957, our first canvas, Lawren Harris's *Shimmering Waters*, had arrived at Tapawingo after being relined by an expert conservation laboratory then simply but effectively framed. It was a proud addition to our modest collection and at thirty-two by forty inches it dominated all our other pictures, making them look even smaller in our big log living room. We badly needed another canvas of about the same size for balance.

In the more than two years since our first meeting in 1955, the Cassons had become close friends with whom we shared almost weekly visits.

"Who owns the original canvas of that blowing pines picture of yours that we see everywhere?" I asked him one evening when we were visiting him and Margaret. He knew at once the picture I meant. It was widely known because of large silk screen reproductions which had proven extremely popular with the Canadian public. Now it could be found in schools, offices, libraries and banks all over Canada and had become one of the country's best-known landscapes. In its foreground, wind-blown pines are growing among huge lichen-streaked rocks, standing like sentinels against an expanse of blue water which reaches a distant mountain horizon. The sky is flecked with clouds borne on a westerly wind.

Cass smiled and pointed to Margaret. "She owns the original watercolour sketch. It's a tiny thing which I used as a guide to do the silk screens for the large reproduction. I've never made a large painting of it."

I was astonished to find that the picture I had always thought of as a reproduction of one of his most popular paintings simply did not exist as a large original. My obvious question was, "Have you ever thought of making a large painting of it?"

"It's crossed my mind at times but I've just never got around to it." Then with an impish grin, "Maybe I was saving it for a special occasion." I knew he was fully aware of what I had in mind but he would never initiate a sale, even to us. I would have to ask.

"Is our collection a special enough reason? I've always loved the feeling of that picture in silk screen and I'm sure it would be magnificent as an original canvas. If you ever decide to do it, I'd like to have first crack at it."

The conversation moved on and nothing more was said.

About three weeks later the Cassons arrived for one of our regular dinner dates. As I helped him unload a cardboard package which took up most of the car he said with a twinkle, "I hope Signe has my favourite roast pork for dinner. I've brought something you may like as much as I like her cooking."

The roast pork had to wait.

Cass removed the cardboard and masking tape and revealed a glowing canvas, just two inches shorter than our large Harris. His best-known reproduction, *White Pine*, was now a breathtaking major canvas, its pigment not yet fully dry.

Signe and I were almost speechless when we realized it would be ours!

"In the silk screen," Casson explained, "I had a large, dark grey mass of flat cloud filling the upper portion of the sky. It seemed right for the silk screen and certainly simplified its production. Here I felt free to add fleeting white cirrus clouds which give a breezier, more windblown effect. I was pleased with it. I'm glad you are."

Always reluctant to discuss prices, Casson waited until, cheque-book in hand, I asked, "How much do we owe you?"

"Does three hundred dollars sound all right to you?"

"It sounds far too low."

"A dealer would probably ask more," he said, but with a tone of finality, "That's my price if it's all right with you."

Since our first meeting with Alfred and Margaret Casson in 1955 we have shared uncounted visits and weekend travels, enjoying each other's company, sharing our interest in art, becoming ever-closer friends. Cass is a skilled storyteller and we can never hear enough of his anecdotes about the lives and art of the remarkable Group. His memories of names, dates and places remain as crisp and clear as his paintings and although he has a keen appreciation of the humour in any situation, his stories never ridicule and always show people in the best possible light. Whether his subject is a fellow artist, a struggling beginner or student, a dealer or an important collector, Casson is sympathetic if at all possible, and often downright charitable. Rarely, even when he is talking about those who are patently dishonest, does he have anything more critical to say than "I decided I didn't want to have anything more to do with him."

As our friendship grew, Cass became our closest adviser, confidant and friend. In our bleakest moments, he was our most encouraging supporter. Fortunately there were also times when we were able to offer help and advice in return.

As the years passed, the Cassons came to think of Tapawingo almost as a second home. Nearly every season, often for weeks at a time, they would come to stay. With our ever-willing black Labradors, Sam and Inky, Cass walked the hills and woods, making oil sketches of our rural scenes and capturing for all time the beauty of our still unspoiled township.

During our frequent and long absences between 1959 and the late 1960s, our New York years, Alfred and Margaret Casson tended Tapawingo as their own; companions and "baby" sitters for our dogs and "picture" sitters for our treasured collection.

We always thought of Tom Thomson as a heroic figure — a Canadian Paul Bunyan who had traded his axe for a paint brush. In splendid solitude his brush had literally chopped and carved paint onto wood panels with an intensity and sureness which has no parallel in Canadian art. He was never content merely to interpret and amplify. Instead, his pictures reveal the very essence of untamed nature — more powerful impressions of trees, rocks and even deadwood than could be gained from the forest itself. He was not merely familiar with his landscapes; he was one with nature itself.

The sentimentality of so many of the traditional Canadian landscape painters was absolutely foreign to him. His eye and hand moved with fury to reinforce strong elements and ruthlessly eliminate extraneous detail on the small birch panels that captured the live spirit, the very soul of his true home, the Canadian wilderness.

Arthur Lismer put it best. In a 1950s discussion he said, "I've been with Tom in the woods when I've got the definite feeling that he was part of them, when the birds and animals recognized something in him that they had themselves. That's why I say that the rest of us were painting pictures; he was expressing moods. He was simply a part of nature."

Lismer was one of a small minority who fully appreciated Thomson's uncanny abilities. As late as the 1950s, when we purchased our first Thomsons, recognition of his genius, his singular qualities and his greatness was still confined to a relatively small number of astute collectors and fellow artists. Today, auction rooms overflow with rich and hopeful collectors when a Thomson panel is offered, even when prices as high as one hundred thousand dollars are forecast.

In 1958, of course, we had no inkling of today's prices — merely a determination to acquire a Tom Thomson canvas to add to the four birch panels we already owned and loved.

It was from our friend Thoreau MacDonald that we learned that a Thomson canvas had been purchased during World War I by painter Marion Long, at that time a temporary occupant of A.Y. Jackson's quarters at the Studio Building.

Following this lead proved surprisingly easy. A telephone call was all that was needed to set up an appointment. The following day, Marion Long, a quiet gentle woman, still attractive in her seventies, welcomed me to her pleasant midtown Toronto home.

One reward was immediate. Above the mantle of an unused fireplace in her living room was the Tom Thomson canvas, *Afternoon, Algonquin Park*. My second reward was an afternoon of vivid reminiscence and recollection as her thoughts went back over forty years to her friendship with Thomson and her purchase of the painting.

"In 1915, I was living at the Studio Building and occupying Mr. Jackson's studio during the time he was overseas in the Canadian Army. Mr. Harris kept the rents very modest and I was glad of this, since I had finished art college just before and was beginning my career in a profession which paid very little, in fact, often almost nothing in those days.

"One day I met Tom Thomson who lived, and painted, in the little shack behind the building. He impressed me as being very shy but offered his help with any chores or problems I might encounter as a new resident in the building. We came to know each other quite well, especially during the winter months. He was usually away in Algonquin Park from mid-spring until late in the fall.

"I remember asking him one day what kind of pen he used to draw in India ink the little illustrated quotations from famous writers like Robert Burns which I have one of," she said, pointing to a small framed drawing in a corner of the room.

"Anyway, Tom replied that he made his own quill pens by cutting turkey feathers in a bevel with a sharp knife. The next day I was surprised to find two turkey-feather quill pens at my studio door. He was a very thoughtful and generous person."

Turning her eyes to the Thomson canvas, she continued, "It was wartime, of course, and the war charities had assembled an exhibition of paintings donated by various artists, including this one given by Tom. The exhibition travelled to several Canadian cities, and at each, people were asked to fill out a little piece of paper with their names and addresses and a price they were willing to bid for one of the paintings. Tom was the only artist in the show whom I knew and I was very fond of his picture. I had very little money and didn't think I had a chance. But, almost for the fun of it, I wrote my name and address and a bid — it seems ridiculous now — fifty dollars.

"A month or two passed and, as expected, I heard nothing, so I more or less forgot about it. Then one day a letter came saying that mine was the high bid for the Thomson picture and asking that I bring a cheque to their office and pick up my painting.

"I hung the painting in my studio. One day I met Tom on the stairs and asked him to come into the studio to see it. He was quite surprised that I had bid for it and had my bid accepted.

" 'The picture's all right,' Tom said, 'but if you see anything of mine in the shack downstairs that you like better, just exchange it anytime.'

"It was a generous offer but I never thought seriously of changing it. I've enjoyed this one through the years, but of course I must admit that I often wonder if I shouldn't have exchanged it for one of his later, more forceful paintings. Many of those he painted in the next two winters were very strong and very large, I remember, so it wouldn't have been fair to trade one of those for my smaller picture. And besides, I never would have had the space to hang one of the large ones. Anyway, I've always loved this one."

As we talked I felt she was impressed by my interest in Thomson and the knowledge I'd gained from long talks with his sisters and brothers, his fellow artists and friends such as Arnold Mason and Thoreau MacDonald. No doubt she was perfectly aware that I wanted to buy *Afternoon, Algonquin Park*, but I felt that to make an offer at this early stage would be a mistake. If there was a hope of getting the picture, it would be only after she knew us better and had come to understand our hopes and plans for Tapawingo.

From the beginning, Signe and I had admired Thomson more than any other artist. Anxious to learn more about this shadowy figure who left few letters, personal documents or photographs of his short life, I grasped every opportunity to talk with those who had known him, particularly those who knew him during his most serious painting period, so brief as to be measured in months. Much of his time between 1914 and his death in July of 1917 had been spent alone, or almost alone. Those who had known him during his four winter months in Toronto and the smaller number who were in touch with him in Algonquin Park between April and December were becoming fewer and fewer as the years passed.

Aside from the Group members I knew personally, Marion Long was the only person I knew who had been an occupant of the Studio Building in those years. Casson and Holgate had never known Thomson or had studios in the building. The others — Jackson, Harris, Lismer and Varley — were mostly away from Toronto during those years. Jackson, Harris and Varley were in the Canadian Armed Forces and Lismer was in Halifax as principal of the Victoria School of Art and Design from the summer of 1916.

Unknown to Marion, and living just a few blocks away in an apartment on Avenue Road, there was another woman we had searched out who had known Thomson during the summer months of 1915 that she spent with her ailing husband at Algonquin Park's Mowatt Lodge. We found that Daphne Crombe also had vivid recollections of Thomson's life in Algonquin and his mysterious disappearance and death.

Both Marion and Daphne welcomed me repeatedly to their homes and, as they talked, I made notes of their impressions of Thomson and of incidents, often small and unimportant, which helped to flesh out my mental portrait of him. When these impressions were added to the recollections of Ada Carmichael, Thoreau MacDonald, Arnold Mason, park ranger Bud Calligan and Thomson's sisters and brothers, I began to feel that I was getting past the legend to know Tom Thomson the man.

I found a man who had appeared shy and reserved, who spoke no more than was necessary. He was thoughtful of others: Ada Carmichael recalled how he had always insisted on drying the dishes after dinner at their home. He was unselfish almost to a fault: a genuine expression of appreciation for one of his sketches would usually result in a gift of the admired work. He cared little for money as long as he had enough for paint and food, although one anecdote relates that he was so delighted with the money he received for his first important canvas — two hundred and fifty dollars — that he cashed the cheque in one dollar bills and tucked all of them in the wainscotting around his room, so he could see what that much money really looked like.

Behind his shy exterior he concealed a mercurial temperament. He was occasionally prone to bouts of utter despondency; at other times he soared close to euphoria. To more than one close friend he confided that he didn't expect that most people of his own time would appreciate his art. Yet, he was quietly and absolutely confident that at some future time it would receive full recognition and acclaim.

After two informative visits with Marion Long, I invited her to Sunday dinner at Tapawingo. As an added inducement, I offered to pick her up and deliver her home since she did not drive.

The thirty or so paintings we owned at that time could hardly be regarded as an important collection. Yet we were delighted that Marion's discerning eye appreciated their quality and we believed she saw and understood our dedication to Thomson and the Group.

By this time we had completed our downstairs gallery. It was panelled with silvered old barn boards and had the same floor space as our large log-and-stone living room. The art was in two gallery rooms with glass end walls that offered panoramic views of forested hills and valleys. As Marion walked slowly through our rooms and the adjoining halls she began to share our vision of the joys of art and pride of country Tapawingo could bring to countless others in the future. We were delighted to find that our ideas and plans for the future were infectious.

I felt we were now sufficiently close that I could broach the subject of *Afternoon, Algonquin Park*. Hoping I wasn't rushing things, yet fearful that a commitment might already have been made, I asked Marion if she had given any thought to its eventual disposition.

"Yes, I have," she replied thoughtfully. "And it worries me. I have no close relatives and I'm afraid it would be accepted as just another picture by the Toronto Art Gallery or the National Gallery. They already have so many."

It was a heaven-sent opening. I could feel my heart thumping.

"We would like very much to buy your picture," I told her, "and would never part with it except to make it part of the public collection we feel sure this is going to become."

It seemed like an eternity before I heard the words I had been hoping for: "It seems like the perfect solution."

Hesitantly, I asked about the price. Marion reminded me that she had paid only fifty dollars for it.

"But that was over forty years ago," I said. "Its value has certainly increased. We bought a little Thomson panel two years ago which was probably sold originally for twenty-five dollars and we paid Laing Galleries a thousand dollars for it. Since his canvases are even rarer, your painting might be worth a hundred times what you paid for it."

She was truly astonished. But I assured her it would be worth at least five thousand dollars, and suggested she get an independent valuation.

I shall never forget her answer. "No. If you're sure you're not offering too much, I'd be very pleased to accept five thousand dollars for it."

After examination by an expert conservator, a light cleaning and a very light coat of varnish, *Afternoon, Algonquin Park* was hung in the central position on a long log wall in our living room, always within view during happy hours in our favourite room.

Through the years we kept in touch with Marion Long, who was always delighted to learn of the progress we were making towards the realization of our dream. She was almost as pleased as we were when, eight years later, the collection was formally opened as a public gallery. By then we had acquired twenty-six Thomson oil panels, watercolours and drawings but *Afternoon, Algonquin Park* was still our only canvas.

We marvelled at those magnificent little panels and derived great pleasure from the medium-size *Afternoon*, which had been painted in 1914-15. Nevertheless, we were now obsessed with our desire for a major Thomson work. Most of them had been painted in the last two years of Tom's life and only a precious few remained in private hands. Not one had been offered for sale publicly in the past twenty years. More than another decade would pass before another Tom Thomson canvas came to Kleinburg.

In the late 1950s Signe and I met M. F. Feheley and his wife Kay. Bud Feheley was president of T.D.F., a large commercial art firm. His eclectic tastes were revealed by his home, which was filled with magnificent art ranging from the sculpture of Henry Moore to the brilliant abstractions of Jack Bush. Yet, his first love was Inuit carving. To walk through the Feheley living and dining rooms, the den, and even the bedrooms, was to tour a museum of the Arctic. Tiny ivories, giant narwhal tusks and sculptures in stone (most from Cape Dorset on Baffin Island) were everywhere. When Eskimo art was first becoming widely accepted Bud had befriended the manager of the new West Baffin Co-operative, Terry Ryan. Through Terry and periodic trips to the Arctic he had met such outstanding print makers and carvers as Pauta, Pitseolak and Kenojuak as well as a host of promising younger artists.

In those days transportation in the High North, although greatly improved from the days of A.Y. Jackson's visits, was still tenuous. Aircraft landing strips had been built on the permafrost but they were perilously short and very rough. That did not deter Bud Feheley from periodic flights in a chartered DC-3 to Cape Dorset, where Ryan would invariably have assembled a display of fine carvings. I envied him these first-hand dealings with the Inuit people but, in spite of his urging, I was never able to join him — our expanding American business made it impossible for me to be out of touch for a week or more at a time.

I had become a member of the Canadian Club of New York, whose clubrooms were located in the Waldorf Astoria Hotel, two blocks from my office. At least once a week I enjoyed dinner there with other expatriate Canadians like J.A. Boyle, who managed the Toronto Dominion Bank's New York agency on Wall Street. One of my earliest friends in New York, Ben Boyle told me in glowing terms of a gigantic new project, the Toronto Dominion Centre, which was to be erected in the heart of Toronto's financial district and was then in an advanced planning stage. I was impressed when Ben assured me it would be bigger than Rockefeller Centre, where I had my office, but had no idea the project was to have any personal significance.

One of the things I did not know was that, without fanfare, Toronto-Dominion had appointed a small committee charged with assembling an outstanding collection of Eskimo art which would be a spectacular feature of the top floor when the new Centre was completed. Two principal members of this committee were my good friends, art collector Charles S. Band and Bud Feheley.

Bud continued to make frequent visits to the Arctic and to add to his personal holdings of Eskimo art, but after his appointment to the committee he made scrupulously certain that the best pieces he was offered found their way into the Toronto-Dominion collection.

Like most true collectors, Bud found it impossible to pass over any really good work. At the conclusion of one visit to Baffin Island, he supervised the loading of his Arctic treasures, fastened his seat belt, and settled back as the pilot revved up the engines and positioned the twin-engined cargo plane to take advantage of every inch of Cape Dorset's short runway. Engines at full throttle, the aircraft lumbered down the runway with steadily increasing speed. Suddenly there was a screeching of brakes and the smell of hot rubber. With only a few feet of runway remaining, the DC-3 came to a shuddering halt. Sweat poured down the weathered face of the pilot as he turned to Feheley.

"You and your damned statues," he said. "You've got this thing so full of stone I can't get it off the ground!"

Reluctantly Bud oversaw the unloading of several major pieces, including the stones that made up a seven-foot-high Inuckshuk, the ancient direction-pointing figure erected in the Arctic for many centuries to guide the sleds of hunters on the windswept tundra.

After another of his forays into the Far North, Bud put a large group of stone carvings before the bank committee, expecting the usual almost routine approval. Seals, narwhals, walruses, birds and human figures in green, grey and black soapstone and a number of snowy owls and polar bears in grey or glistening white quartzite were only part of the display. There was also a two-foot-tall polar bear which had been masterfully carved by Pauta, the well-known sculptor, who had an uncanny affinity for the mighty beasts which roam the polar regions. Bud was justifiably pleased, particularly with the acquisition of the Pauta bear, and waited for the approval and applause he felt the distinctive series merited. Then a senior member remarked, rather gloomily, "Don't you think we already have too many bears?" To Bud's astonishment the other committee members agreed! He found himself with a masterpiece he could ill afford after the purchases he had made for himself on the trip. The logical course would have been to consign the magnificent piece to a dealer, yet Bud felt strongly that Pauta's powerful bear deserved a special home.

A few days later I was invited to Bud's T.D.F. office — always more like a studio than a place of business. On a desk littered with small soapstone and ivory carvings, a telephone, the only non-Eskimo object, stuck out like a sore thumb. On the walls, lively Cape Dorset prints provided a fitting background for the principal occupant of the floor space, a bear rampant and snarling through four spear-like ivory teeth. I was bowled over.

"Isn't he a beauty!" said Feheley. It was not a question but a pure statement of fact. I nodded.

"He's yours, dad...for a thousand bucks." I agreed! As always with exciting new acquisitions, I could hardly wait to get the beautiful bear to Kleinburg. Still, I recognized my limitations. I could hardly move two hundred pounds of stone, let alone carry it to my car. Never one to be deterred by a problem in transport, Bud summoned Adam, his muscular handyman-chauffeur, from a nearby workroom. Pointing to the heavy bear Feheley asked, deadpan, "How are your knockers, Adam?" Without a word Adam lifted the bear to his chest, cradling it like a baby!

At Tapawingo the graceful lines of Pauta's polar giant, our largest carving, were an arresting sight in our living room. We felt that where size was concerned we'd "gone about as far as we could go," little knowing that a decade later our second Pauta bear would make the first seem tiny by comparison.

3

When construction of the new Studio Building for Canadian Art was completed in 1913, it was the hope of Lawren Harris and Dr. James MacCallum, who financed the undertaking, that in providing studio facilities for a number of artists with apparently common interests, they could encourage the development of a truly indigenous school of painting in this country.

Three quarters of a century later, the building in the quiet Rosedale Ravine, a short distance from the bustling intersection at Yonge Street and Davenport Road, still houses art studios but it was those original occupants, several of whom lived as well as painted there, who were to change the course of Canadian art.

Without adequate and affordable places to work, the small band of painters might well have become disheartened and dispersed. But when Harris moved into his own studio and offered Thomson, Carmichael, Jackson and MacDonald similar spaces, a close association was formed which laid the foundations for the most significant art movement Canada has yet known.

For a brief period Tom Thomson shared a studio with Frank Carmichael in the modern Studio Building, but apparently he always had a hankering for the old wooden shack behind it, which reminded him of rangers' cabins in the north country he loved. When Harris agreed to rent it to him for a dollar a month he made it his studio and home. With the addition of interior beaverboard walls, a wood stove and spartan furnishings it became his winter living quarters and here he set up the homemade studio easel on which he painted *The West Wind, The Jack Pine* and the other great canvases which date from the three years before his death in 1917.

The shack had been on the site for many years and was used as a tool storage shed during the construction of the Studio Building. It is believed that it was originally an outbuilding, possibly a saddlery for Bloor's Brewery, whose dray horses are known to have been pastured in the ravine.

Never one for ostentation, Thomson furnished the simple cabin with a cot on a raised balcony, for maximum warmth during long winter nights, a table and chairs, and a cupboard for clothes and his few personal belongings, above which were open shelves for dishes and cooking utensils. The ever-present oil panels were loosely arranged against the surrounding baseboards. A few unusual stones picked up on northern trails and his own handmade fishing lures could usually be found on the window sills.

During the last years of his life, Tom Thomson set out each spring for Canoe Lake, Algonquin Park, but with the onset of winter he always returned to the small wooden building to paint up his summer's sketches into the monumental canvases that we know so well. After Thomson's death and the end of World War I, Frederick Varley painted in the shack for a brief period. Later a mining prospector, Keith MacIvor, who, like Thomson, spent much of his time in the North, made it his home when he was in the city, but it was always known as "Tom Thomson's Shack".

A wiry man of slight physical stature, MacIvor spent much of his life searching for mineral deposits in the wilderness and was comfortable in the most primitive shelter. He was also handy with tools. Years later, he told me he had jacked up the shack's foundation on stones to allow better drainage and prevent damage from mud slides from the steep hill above. He had also replaced much of the beaverboard which lined the interior.

It was Keith who, in the early 1930s, guided A. Y. Jackson into virgin areas where he was prospecting and where the painter found rich material for sketching. When the two returned to the city it became a ritual for them to have breakfast together in Tom Thomson's Shack every morning.

Keith, though he spent much of his time in the wilds, nevertheless appreciated things cultural and enjoyed entertaining artists, sculptors, musicians and writers, many of whom became his friends. Informal parties in the shack often included Alex Jackson and other artists of the Group as well as sculptresses Frances Loring and Florence Wyle, who were always affectionately known as "The Girls", and the legendary manager of Eaton's Bookroom, Norah DePencier. When he finally married he chose Edith, a daughter of University College's well-known professor of English, W. J. Alexander.

During his parties Keith often encouraged his artist friends to participate in a "paint-in" to produce a communal painting directly on the shack's beaverboard walls. The old building still displays some of these tempera paintings by A. Y. Jackson, Lawren Harris, Thoreau MacDonald and Langley Donges. In earlier years a large and buxom nude known as "Helrosa", by Fred Varley, adorned the walls, but shortly after their marriage it was removed at the insistence of the new Mrs. MacIvor.

Huddled against a steep hillside in the shadow of a still quite modern Studio Building, the humble wooden structure looked abandoned and forlorn when Signe and I first saw it in the fall of 1956.

Construction crews were working a mere hundred feet from its grey weathered walls, at the opening of a dark tunnel from which the city's new subway trains would dart into open-cut daylight. Glass and chrome glinted from new highrise buildings beyond the subway. By then the old shack's board and batten sides had withstood nearly a century of rain and snow but "progress" was certain to overtake it before long. Historic it might be, but the old shack was dying a slow death among the city's new towers of glass and steel.

Through the late 1950s and early 1960s our fascination with the art and life of Tom Thomson approached an obsession. Not only did we continue to have long talks with his sister and brothers, his fellow artists and others who had known him, we also began to keep written notes recording the little-known facts we gleaned from those who had been closest to him. We made notes about the shack and its furnishings based on the recollections of those who had visited it during Thomson's time and again and again we found ourselves drawn back to the little building — deserted since Frances Gage had last used it as her sculpture studio in 1960.

From time to time, articles and letters had appeared in the press urging that Tom Thomson's shack be maintained and preserved as an historic building. Since these brief flurries were always followed by indifference and inaction, we began to wonder if it would be possible to move the shack to our property at Kleinburg, where it could be restored and, later, opened to the public. Yet, sensitive to the outcry which might follow an attempt at removal, we were reluctant to take the first steps.

We did learn that the shack had been included in the sale of the Studio Building and its property by Lawren Harris and was now owned by two men in partnership, Gordon MacNamara and Charles Redfern. We had been cautioned by several people who knew him that MacNamara might flatly refuse to permit the shack's removal for fear of the adverse publicity which could result. Except for that reservation, it was believed MacNamara would be delighted to see the old building removed and preserved.

We were also told that MacNamara was not a man who changed his mind — his first response would be final. If we were to have any hope of success we would have to approach him through someone who knew him well and with a good measure of tact. We felt that our good friend Paul Duval, a resident of the Studio Building, was the ideal person for this assignment and he agreed to approach MacNamara on our behalf.

We accompanied Paul to this meeting so that, if the owner was favourably impressed by our proposal, any assurances he might require could be given on the spot. After Paul's brief statement of our wishes and intent it appeared that MacNamara might be willing to consider our proposal favourably if we were able to agree to certain terms he had in mind. He was very definite about what these would be and there was no room for misunderstanding and little for negotiation. MacNamara was a painter by choice but a lawyer by training.

These were his terms: eight hundred dollars cash payment, a written undertaking that there would be no publicity which could make it appear that he was anxious to get rid of the shack or that he was insensitive to its historic importance, and finally, that after the shack had been dismantled, the site would be cleaned up and landscaped at our expense so it would be almost impossible to see that the shack ever had been there.

Although we were surprised at some of his conditions, we nevertheless agreed to them. It would now fall to our trusted contractor, Buck Bayliss, and his crew to carefully dismantle the old building, board by board, and re-assemble it on new foundations at Kleinburg.

Following our purchase, we photographed the shack systematically inside and out so that Buck and his men would have excellent reference prints during the dismantling and reconstruction periods. Windows, doors and other components were numbered to match corresponding numbers on the photographs and sections which had deteriorated beyond re-use were noted so they could be replaced by weathered but solid materials from old barns and houses near Kleinburg which were slated for demolition.

Many of the rotted floor boards were replaced, and the shack received a new roof of tar paper, identical to the old. Most of the original exterior walls were incorporated into the rebuilding as were the windows and sagging doors which were stiffened with the addition of half-inch plywood. New but very similar beaver-board lined the interior except for the areas where the artists had painted their pictures. These were removed with great care and restored by conservator Percy Smith of Oakville, then reinstalled in their original positions.

When reconstruction was completed in 1963 the change of location from the bottom of one hill in Toronto to the top of another in Kleinburg gave the old shack a somewhat different aura as did the straightening of its sagging roofline and walls which, over the years, had gone badly out of plumb. Yet essentially, the old building was still Tom Thomson's Shack.

During one of our Saturday visits in 1960 Thoreau MacDonald mentioned a telephone conversation he had had that week with an elderly lawyer, Frank Erichsen-Brown, who years earlier had counselled his father and some of the other painters on various legal matters. As a result, he had acquired a few small paintings. Now living on a very modest fixed income and feeling the pressures of inflation, he had confided to Thoreau that he wished to sell his Tom Thomson paintings, if possible to an institution, alternatively to someone who would fully appreciate them. He had been in touch with Martin Baldwin, director of the Art Gallery of Toronto, but had received little encouragement. He had also made discreet enquiries of a well-known art dealer as to values.

By now, we had learned that following up any lead, even those dropped in casual conversations, was the best means of ferreting out long hidden works by the Algonquin artists. Such hints sometimes came from older people, especially those who had some interest in the arts or whose work or social activities had brought them in contact with one or more of the painters, but rarely were such leads as promising as this one appeared to be. It seemed to us almost too good to be true. I experienced a real feeling of panic at the thought that if Mr. Erichsen-Brown was so anxious to sell, someone might already have beaten us to him.

Thoreau grinned at my nervousness and assured me the phone call had been just the day before. "Don't worry," he said reassuringly, "I'm sure he still has them." I was not going to take any chances. Number in hand, I rushed to the phone and after a number of rings was about to hang up when a precise, dignified voice said, "Erichsen-Brown."

"Hello, Mr. Erichsen-Brown, my name is Robert McMichael. I have been speaking with Thoreau MacDonald and he suggested I call you about some paintings which I believe you discussed with him."

"Yes, he mentioned that you might be interested."

There was no beating about the bush.

"Indeed I am. Could I arrange to meet with you...perhaps even this afternoon?"

A slight pause. "I don't see why not. I'll be home if you'd like to come down." He gave me directions through the maze of streets and crescents which make the Rosedale district of Toronto one of the most confusing in the city. As I hung up with a deep breath, Signe smiled at my intensity and Thoreau said drily, "Better take a cheque with you...he's no youngster, you know."

Following directions, we finally drew up in front of a large red brick Victorian house on a quiet street shaded by huge elms and maples. It seemed an improbable hiding place for the treasures we hoped to find. I couldn't help wondering how many other unremarkable doors in the city also concealed the unique paintings we sought. Perhaps, in classic detective fashion, we should pretend to be plumbers, electricians, telephone repairmen or visiting nurses whose normal duties take them behind otherwise unrevealing facades.

Frank Erichsen-Brown was a tall teddy bear of a man on whose slightly bulbous nose perched horn-rimmed glasses through which his soft, mildly watery eyes quickly surveyed us. Without preamble, he led us into his Victorian parlour. Here, immediately recognizable in their 1920s art deco Boughton frames, hung the three identically sized small panels we had come to see. Even through forty years of accumulated grime and discoloured varnish they were unmistakable.

Oil sketches by Thomson and MacDonald, painted on panels of the same size, at roughly the same time, and with similar subject matter, are frequently so alike at first sight that attribution has at times challenged the judgement of experts. In this case, with a little prompting from the owner, I realized that two of the panels were in fact by Tom Thomson, the third by J.E.H. MacDonald.

Paying for Tapawingo and financing my still marginal American business made it difficult, sometimes even impossible, for us to add to our collection during the 1950s, but we could never bring ourselves to pass up a Tom Thomson. Though further borrowing placed a strain on our precarious finances, we justified these expenditures by our certain knowledge that opportunities to acquire his rare works would never come again. Things that other people considered essential — appliances, cars or even interior finishing work at Tapawingo could wait. These paintings could not!

Erichsen-Brown had a figure of three thousand five hundred dollars in mind for the two Thomsons and although we admired the stunning MacDonald panel of a rocky Algoma stream, we knew that the Tom Thomsons must be our first priority. It was obvious that Thoreau had given him a clear idea of what we hoped to accomplish and that he approved, but he told us he had obligations to meet and that he could not shave the price. We assured him we neither expected nor wanted him to cut his price. Pulling a tattered cheque from my pocket I wrote the agreed-upon figure, signed it and passed it to him with a handshake.

Thanking us, Erichsen-Brown walked to the little pictures and took a long wistful look at them, then removing them from the wall, he placed one on Signe's lap and one on mine. A few minutes later, as we stood in the doorway preparing to leave with our purchases, the old man returned to the living room wall, removed the MacDonald sketch and handed it to me.

"I want you to have this one too, as my gift."

One day, later that year, Thoreau and I were studying a book with illustrations of some of J.E.H. MacDonald's most important paintings. He asked if I knew Dr. Arnold Mason who also lived in Thornhill. We knew Dr. Mason's name because it always appeared as a credit under reproductions of our favourite MacDonald painting, *Leaves in the Brook*, but we had never seen the original nor had we met its owner.

"The doctor is a friend of mine," Thoreau said. "I don't think he'd mind showing it to you, if he's home." Following a brief telephone call, we walked from the MacDonald house to a more recently built-up section of the village.

A tall silver-haired man whose rimless glasses didn't conceal a welcoming twinkle met us at the front door of a white clapboard house overlooking a natural duck pond — the town's skating rink each winter. Clearly Dr. Mason was pleased by this rare visit from Thoreau. "I wish more of your friends would like to see my pictures. Maybe then I'd see you more often," he said happily, motioning us to a sofa by the fireplace over which hung the dazzling canvas, *Leaves in the Brook*.

During the many years that Dr. A.D.A. Mason was Dean of Dentistry at the University of Toronto, he lived in the city's fashionable old Rosedale district, a fifteen minute walk from the campus and not far from the Studio Building and Thomson's Shack. Often, while walking home he stopped in at Severn Street to chat with Tom Thomson in his rustic shack, or the others in their studios. Once, while visiting Thomson, he had noticed an unusually small oil panel apparently discarded, lying on the floor. Half the size of the usual panels but richly painted in the artist's unmistakable slashed-on style, it showed a logger's flume in deep forest. Intrigued by his glimpse of the little work but puzzled by its apparent rejection, Mason had picked up the post-card-sized painting to admire it.

Thomson smiled, "I made that little runt one day when I was running short of painting materials and had to start cutting my regular panels in half. It's just a quick impression, but if you like it you can have it."

Embarrassed that Thomson might have thought he had been looking for a gift, Mason reached for his wallet with a mumbled offer to pay for the little painting which had caught his fancy.

"No," said Thomson, "it isn't really worth anything. I had fifteen minutes of fun doing it. Put it in your pocket."

Arnold Mason had a rich fund of such stories. Seeing Signe and I enraptured before *Leaves in the Brook* he sensed that he had an enthusiastic audience for both his art treasures and his anecdotes.

"I can see you like my favourite picture," he began, "Thoreau knows it was given to me by his father in payment for a dental bill. Even forty years ago, I felt it was far too much ... but Mr. MacDonald insisted that I accept it. Now I can't help but feel that was the most expensive dentist's bill in history."

While his housekeeper and companion, Clara Ramsay, made coffee, Dr. Mason led us through room after room hung with pictures. An eight-and-a-half by ten-and-a-half inch Thomson panel as well as the half-size sketch he had found years earlier on the floor of Tom's shack now hung in the hallway. In the dining room, there was a powerful Frederick Varley landscape with figures flanked by two of Varley's West Coast panels. Mason recalled that Varley always seemed in desperate need of money, especially during the thirties. "But I guess most people were ... Fred often dropped into my office in Toronto and wrote to me during his years in Vancouver, always hoping that I would buy a painting. I felt that at his best he was among our few really great painters and I got some nice things from him. Those terrible Depression years. Varley was actually begging me to buy his things for less than seventy-five dollars. In hindsight, of course, I have regrets that I didn't buy more. But I was living on a teacher's salary and raising a family."

When we returned to the living room for coffee I could hardly take my eyes from *Leaves in the Brook* and I noticed that Thoreau still admired his father's marvelous colour and the feeling of motion conveyed in the lyrical, swirling flow of an Algoma brook carrying away the gold and red leaves of autumn. MacDonald's unfailing sense of design and composition and his oneness with this colourful little world had combined to produce a true master work.

A.D.A. Mason was an intellectual, but also a warm person with a barely concealed, playful sense of humour. Modest in the extreme, he established in minutes a rapport with those near him that others might not achieve in years. Our brief social call became an event and, we hoped, the beginning of a much closer friendship with this remarkable man.

Thoreau sensed our fascination. "You should get to know the doctor better," he told us on the way home. "I can tell he liked you and he'd like to see what you're doing in Kleinburg. Maybe you'd even get *Leaves in the Brook* some day."

"Not so fast, Thoreau," I said. "Even if we never see his painting again, I'd like to know him better and hear more of his recollections. His memory is fantastic!"

"The doctor's always been a good friend and I like him," Thoreau went on, "but the dental work he mentioned didn't do much good. Maybe it was too late because a short time later my father had to have all his teeth removed." Thoreau's memories of long ago years were also very clear!

A few weeks later, Signe invited Dr. Mason and Clara Ramsay along with Thoreau and Julia to dinner at Tapawingo, suggesting that they come in the afternoon so there would be lots of time to see our paintings and take a walk in the woods, always a favourite feature of Thoreau's visits to Kleinburg.

The history of the Group of Seven is familiar material, but as Thoreau and Arnold Mason studied and chatted in the present tense about historic paintings and painters, I felt a distinct intimacy with those bygone times when Canadian art history was in the making.

Looking at a Varley, Mason enthused, "Fred sure knows how to introduce a mystic quality into his paintings." And contemplating a Jackson, "Alex never fails to get the spirit of the place ... especially Quebec. Look at those marvelous old houses, the snakey road ... and the rhythm in those hills." Then, remembering Thomson, "Tom told me that he wasn't disturbed by the criticism, or the indifference that he experienced. He felt sure that someday most people would appreciate his paintings and recognize that they were true."

Unfortunately, this was before the days of the miniature tape recorder, but I hung on to every word that could increase my understanding of the painters, particularly Thomson.

Like Thoreau, Arnold Mason became a close friend. Our frequent visits with him were happy times, and his quiet enthusiasm added to our increasing perception that in our modest collection we had not only treasured possessions, but a solemn trust. Arnold Mason combined the best qualities of the academic and the country philosopher — astute judgement and an incisive intelligence, with a discriminating, but kindly and open mind. During the too few years from our meeting in 1958 until his death in 1962 A.D.A. Mason profoundly influenced both the development of our collection and the direction of our lives.

One evening, after one of my visits with Arthur Lismer in Montreal, Arnold Mason was with us at Kleinburg to share the excitement as we unwrapped several paintings I had acquired from the artist who was now my friend.

Among the packages we opened was a large rolled watercolour, a more recent version of *Pine Wrack*, a subject which Lismer had painted earlier, in oils on canvas, and submitted as his diploma piece when he was elected to the Royal Canadian Academy. As we carefully unrolled the heavy paper, almost two feet by three feet, there was an audible sigh as the powerful work was revealed. The subject was the tormented pine wreckage in the Georgian Bay Islands which so fascinated Lismer. It was painted in deep, bold colours and with a directness and power not usually found in watercolour. Other early landscapes emerged from the large corrugated cardboard package I had insisted on carrying with me on the plane. Among the larger works was an unusual, almost mystical canvas of a female nude seated on a rocky promontory, framed by twisted pines and bathed in moonlight.

Staring intently at our new-found riches, Mason gasped, "You've uncovered a treasure. I think I've been at almost every Group of Seven showing over the past forty years but I've never seen a more striking and unusual assortment of Lismer's work."

I told him how my friendship with Lismer had developed and that, even though he and Mrs. Lismer had never been able to visit Kleinburg, I felt he was genuinely interested in our project. Mason was still fascinated by the nude. "What did he have to say about this?" he asked. "It's so unusual for him."

"I'm sure he was speaking with tongue in cheek when he told me that it was painted one day when he was trying to be Fred Varley."

Mason chuckled, "There might just be a grain of truth in that. They both came to Canada from Sheffield, you know, and there appears to be an early interplay in their painting. Not a rivalry, but still some interaction between two artists with similar backgrounds and training."

One anecdote invites another and so, with some misgiving, I repeated a story Lismer had told me that involved Varley, Lismer and Dr. Mason himself. One day in the early 1920s Fred Varley had come into Arthur Lismer's studio and admired a twelve by sixteen inch panel he saw there. Looking at the work intently, Varley became quite lyrical in his praise of the work and stated to his slightly embarrassed fellow artist that the picture was having a profound effect on him; so much so that he could not tear himself away from it. Surprised, but nevertheless pleased by the accolade, Lismer promptly presented his sketch to an overjoyed Varley.

Some weeks later Lismer was seated in the waiting room of his dentist Dr. Arnold Mason. On the wall was a Varley oil panel — but there was something unusual about it — it was twelve by sixteen inches, the size of his own sketches, rather than Varley's usual twelve by fifteen. In a flash he knew the answer. Lifting the picture from the wall he found on the reverse side his own sketch which Varley had admired so enthusiastically. Fred Varley had been in desperate need of a blank panel so he could paint a picture that would settle his dental bill with Dr. Mason!

Mason laughed until tears came to his eyes. He remembered the two-sided Varley panel but had never thought to question the unsigned painting on the verso side.

It was typical of Arthur Lismer to enjoy a joke on himself. He will be remembered not only as a fine painter but as the resident humorist-punster of the Group. Scores of topical cartoons emerged from his witty and ever-ready pencil. Many of them, excellent likenesses of his fellow artists and associates, are in the McMichael Canadian Collection. Though drawn in a matter of minutes, sometimes on a paper table napkin, and always in fun, the cartoons are now taken very seriously by art historians and gallery directors as perhaps the best, and in many cases the only, visual record of historic situations.

In one of the cartoons, Lawren Harris is sneaking a look through an archway in the old Art Gallery of Toronto. A crowd of visitors is viewing pictures on one wall but no one is looking at his great mountain painting, *Isolation Peak,* on the opposite wall. The cartoon's caption is "The artist having an isolation peek".

Some of the greatest pleasures that our frequent get-togethers with Dr. Mason provided were the intimate glimpses of life and times during his association with the artists of the golden age of Canadian art.

One evening, at his home, he showed us an early Tom Thomson panel painted on canvas-covered academy board. Inches smaller than the familiar eight-and-a-half by ten-and-a-half inch panels, it had been painted about 1912 or 1913 and though somewhat laboured and lacking in the vivid qualities of the later work, it showed the promise that would be fulfilled a few years later. I was fascinated to see it, and since Dr. Mason had apparently chosen not to hang it among his other works I reasoned that he might be willing to make a trade, possibly for one of our many Lismers. We admired the work of all the painters in the Group, but works by Tom Thomson had special significance for us. Because of their rarity and cost we had been able to acquire only four panels, in addition to the medium-size canvas, *Afternoon, Algonquin Park*, which we considered to be the cornerstone of our collection. Treading carefully, I reminded Dr. Mason that Signe and I were intensely interested in Tom Thomson and everything he ever did. Then, taking the plunge, "I think you like the mystical Lismer nude canvas we have. We might be willing to swap it for this little Thomson if it's not one of your particular favourites."

"It's pleasant, but it is not a first-rate Thomson by any means," Mason replied. "I bought it with some other things a few years ago but as you see, I haven't hung it. Yes, I'd be more than willing to trade it for that Lismer, but I think I'd be getting the best of the bargain. I know Tom's work is scarce but the Lismer is a large ... and I think, fine work by a major artist. Maybe you should give a little more thought to it before you decide."

I looked again at the little Thomson sketch, the size of a large post card. "Though it's small and much earlier than his best period, its importance to us can't be measured entirely by size or period. Eventually, we hope to build one of the best Thomson collections, so its significance for us is disproportionate to its actual value."

Later that week I wrote to Arthur Lismer advising him that we had made the exchange with his old friend Dr. Mason and hoped that he would have no objections. I had written to him earlier about one of his smaller British Columbia paintings which I had sold at cost to my Kleinburg neighbour, Pierre Berton.

Feeling, as we did, that Lismer was selling us his paintings as much because of his interest in our plans for our collection and out of friendship as for money, we felt it was important he know that any we parted with were going to owners of whom he would have approved.

Through the years, Arnold Mason often referred to his paintings and their ultimate disposition. With a mischievous twinkle in his eye he would tell us that if we behaved ourselves some of his pictures might come to our collection.

In the last year of his life he suffered from the recurrence of a serious internal infection which he had contracted some years earlier while vacationing in Spain. No longer teasing, he told us that he had instructed Clara Ramsay to turn certain paintings over to us if and when she felt certain that he was dying. On the day before his death we received a telephone call from Mrs. Ramsay asking us to come to the Mason house in Thornhill to pick up some paintings. Among them was J.E.H. MacDonald's *Leaves in the Brook*.

From Thornhill we drove to the hospital where A.D.A. was lying in an oxygen tent. He reached through a fold in the plastic and took both of our hands, holding them firmly. Then he smiled and gave us a final puckish wink.

Between our early purchases of two small oil panels by Tom Thomson and Lawren Harris and our collection's growth to over two thousand pieces twenty-five years later, we met hundreds of people who shared our dedication to Canada's national art. A few became our closest friends and allies, helping us to make our small nucleus grow into a significant national art centre. Among them, none was a closer or more willing supporter than Robert A. Laidlaw.

Our friendship with Bob Laidlaw began when Oakley Dalglish, president of Pitney-Bowes, knowing of our interest, invited us to a private showing of works by Tom Thomson, J.E.H. MacDonald and Lawren Harris at his company's head office on Yonge Street, coincidentally located within a few hundred yards of the Studio Building and the original site of Tom Thomson's shack. The paintings had been borrowed from the private collections of the Laidlaw brothers, Robert and Walter, and it was at this little exhibition in the late 1950s that Signe and I first met Robert.

A year later, following a downtown meeting of the Conservation Authority Foundation, of which we were both members, Bob Laidlaw invited me to accompany him to his nearby office at King and Bay Streets. His small sixteenth-floor suite had a dramatic view of the heart of Toronto's towering financial district, but even this panorama paled in comparison with the breathtaking little pictures which surrounded his desk. Laidlaw was obviously amused as I stared in awe at his array of Tom Thomsons and J.E.H. MacDonalds. With advice from his friend Lawren Harris, Bob Laidlaw had acquired these little jewels more than forty years earlier from the artists' estates, long before they had been picked over by the collectors, galleries and dealers who surfaced as the fame of the two painters grew.

One of his favourite golfing partners at Lambton Golf and Country Club in the early 1920s, he told us, had been Lawren Harris. One day after a round, Harris suggested that Bob come to the Studio Building to see some paintings by an artist friend who had tragically drowned. Harris said he was the finest of all Canadian artists. (The bulk of Tom Thomson's works had been stored at the Severn Street building and most were still unsold.) Laidlaw was very excited at the prospect of seeing works by an artist for whom Harris had such high regard.

As an executive in his family's lumber business, Laidlaw was no stranger to the forests of northern Ontario. In his first glimpses of Thomson's little oil panels he recognized a profound empathy with the wilderness, an uncanny ability to grasp its very essence.

"When I first saw Thomson's pictures at the Studio Building there must have been almost two hundred of these little panels," Laidlaw recalled that day. "They were arranged in piles, each about a foot or so deep. I looked at each one, sorting out those which most appealed to me. It was very difficult to make a final selection because I liked almost everything I saw. Anyway, I finally bought about twenty. I'm glad I got as many as I did, but now I wish I'd bought all of them." It was probably the largest single sale of Thomson's paintings ever made. Years later he acquired a number of J.E.H. MacDonald's panels of identical size through the artist's son, Thoreau.

By this time I had spent several years tracking down every possible work by Thomson, especially those which were privately held. Most were not for sale but we had managed to acquire ten, including three pencil drawings and our flagship canvas, *Afternoon, Algonquin Park*. Eager to have Laidlaw see them at Tapawingo, I gave him a pressing invitation. "Our collection is not as impressive as yours but we do have ten works by Thomson and even more by MacDonald. We'd be delighted if you would come out to Kleinburg to see them ... and perhaps join us for lunch some day soon."

Two weeks later, on one of those heaven-sent southern Ontario summer Sundays, Laidlaw drove to our door in his silver-grey Rolls Royce. As always, he was dressed impeccably — dark blue blazer with gold pocket crest and flawlessly pressed grey flannels. His penetrating blue eyes and silver hair were accentuated by his normal ruddy tan, the product of winters in the Barbados and summers in the Canadian sun. Hollywood would have cast him instantly as a wealthy captain of industry and sportsman — which he was.

It was typical of Bob Laidlaw to sense that Signe and I felt underdressed in our casual pants and sports shirts. He peered up at the sun in the brilliant blue sky, asked if he might remove his blazer and strolled towards the massive log walls of Tapawingo in his shirtsleeves. It was the beginning of a real friendship.

Laidlaw became a regular visitor, often directing his chauffeur to detour by Tapawingo when he was en route to his summer home at Roches Point on Lake Simcoe. He seldom missed even minor changes or additions to our collection and would stroll very slowly through our rooms, viewing each painting with intense interest, as though seeing it for the first time. After an hour with the pictures he would relax with a pre-luncheon Scotch and water, and hold us enthralled as he recalled the early days when he had first discovered his favourite artists.

Norah Thomson DePencier lived in a charming old stone house high on the hill whose slopes form the basin of Owen Sound's natural harbour. The road bordering her hundred acres wended its way past the farm where Tom Thomson grew up and into the tiny village of Leith where he is buried in the cemetery of a small church.

The walls of Norah's living room were a veritable gallery of paintings by her favourite artists, including three striking oil panels by Tom Thomson. Many people thought she was a relative because she was born Norah Thomson, yet in spite of the remarkable coincidence of name, location and interests, Norah was no relation of the artist's family.

We met Norah through our good friend Yvonne McKague Housser. Yvonne had known her since the early 1920s when, as Norah Thomson, she had been manager of Eaton's Bookroom, then Toronto's best bookstore, frequented by artists and other members of the city's cultural community. Like a benevolent despot she presided over the Bookroom, offering unfailingly knowledgeable assistance to customers, which won her many lifelong friends. Not the least of these were Lawren Harris and A. Y. Jackson.

Next to books, Norah's great passion was art and she was so impressed by the work of Harris and Jackson that she regularly set aside a portion of her very modest salary to purchase their paintings. She was also an admirer of the then little-known painter, Emily Carr, and later, in 1936, visited the West Coast to seek out that extraordinary woman and buy one of her major canvases.

In Emily Carr's personal journals, published after her death under the title *Hundreds and Thousands*, the artist writes:

> *July 8th, 1936. I'm just whizzy. Sold four pictures, one from Vancouver Gallery,* Shoreline, *one paper sketch, one French cottage, one Victoria. What a help to finances! Mrs. DePencier of Toronto bought the first and her daughter the other three.*

From our first meeting Signe and I were enchanted by Norah. She had the regal bearing of a grand duchess, under which, nevertheless, was a rare warmth and vivaciousness and an untiring sense of humour. Her silver hair, usually held in a soft bun, framed a serene face which became beautifully animated when she found things or people that interested her.

During the late 1950s and early 1960s, weekends away from New York were short and precious, and on the whole I preferred to stay home and enjoy Tapawingo. Nonetheless, Saturdays often found us coming and going between Kleinburg and Leith. Frequently we would arrive at Norah's home in time for lunch and a full afternoon of good conversation while she reminisced of art and artists during the years when the young rebels of Canadian art were her friends. Every third or fourth week we would pick Norah up at Leith and bring her with us back to Kleinburg where she and Signe would spend the following week enjoying visits with old friends — Keith and Edith MacIvor, Barker Fairley, Florence Wyle and Frances Loring, Thoreau MacDonald, A. Y. Jackson, Bob Laidlaw and A.D.A. Mason, who had become frequent visitors to Tapawingo. She knew them all.

Naturally, conversation at these gatherings often centred on art. Norah loved to talk about the paintings she had been fortunate and foresighted enough to purchase years earlier. Though outwardly modest about her remarkable ability to see worth in the work of artists who were relatively unknown at the time, she knew very well how fine her choices had been. Keeping herself appraised of current values through auction reports, she was amazed and quietly pleased that her choices of decades earlier had risen like the richest cream to the top, at least by art market standards. But the dollar values of her possessions held little interest for her. Her joy came from understanding and feeling what the artist felt and conveyed in a painting.

When hung together, her collection of twelve panels and five canvases made an impressive Group gallery which could not fail to excite the most blasé collector or curator. Yet Norah had no desire to impress friends or visitors with her collection and, in fact, her paintings were seldom, if ever, all on her walls at the same time. Instead she would have two or three casually propped on a sofa or chairs so they could be moved to a more favourable distance or into variations of natural or artificial light for individual study. I think she felt that each had a soul of its own which came from the creative force of the artist and she preferred to look on each separately.

Signe and I recognized in Norah's perceptiveness the deep, intimate relationship which grows between a beloved work of art and its possessor. Our own infant collection was growing, usually one painting at a time, and each was given all the love and endless hours of appreciation that should come to any new addition to a family. We never saw our paintings as fibre and pigment objects. They were spiritual expressions and moving experiences of which we never tired, and for which our love grew deeper with passing time. The only reward for prolonged absences from them was the joy we felt at seeing them again.

Because Norah felt about her pictures as we felt about ours, we loved to hear her tell the story behind each of her acquisitions. One of our favourite paintings was purchased in the early 1930s. Norah told us its story. When visiting with her friend Alex Jackson at his studio, Norah told us, she had been immediately attracted to two canvases, *Grey Day, Laurentians* and *Indian Home*, which Jackson had worked up from sketches of old buildings in very different mountain landscapes.

As its name indicated, *Grey Day, Laurentians*, like many of Alex's best paintings of old farm buildings, had originated in the familiar rolling hills north of Montreal in the depths of winter snow. Usually the curves of the hills, buildings and sky created a sprightly rhythm. A radically different mood appeared in this picture; the rhythms were harsh and the colours dark and sullen. The gaunt shapes and angular roofs of the barns added to the threatening atmosphere. In the hands of a lesser artist the daring composition could have been melodramatic. Jackson's brush, however, had faithfully captured its lonely, sombre spirit.

Accompanied by Group member-to-be Edwin Holgate and anthropologist Marius Barbeau, in 1926 Jackson travelled to British Columbia's Skeena River. On a midsummer day in the western mountains he came upon an Indian dwelling. In the oil sketch he made of the house, the walls, which had been painted an exotic green, seemed bent on outdoing the colours of the giant skunk cabbages in surroundings cleared of all but two spindly fir trees.

In the later canvas Jackson added considerable drama to that first impression. The distant horizon of mountains moved forward like giant pyramids and the pole-like trees became bird-topped totem poles. Three small figures, a mother in a brilliant red dress and two children, drew the eye to the centre of the canvas, the doorway of an acid green *Indian Home*.

Norah was anxious to purchase both canvases but she learned that she was not the only person who had admired the two striking paintings. Another of Jackson's close friends, painter Isabel McLaughlin, also wanted to buy them. Such competition among buyers was rare for the painter in the lean years of the Great Depression but he could do only what he considered fair. Norah got *Grey Day, Laurentians*. *Indian Home* went to Isabel.

Years later, as part of Walter Stewart's gift, the original oil panel for *Indian Home* came to the McMichael Collection. Isabel still counts the canvas among her personal treasures.

One visit with Norah I shall never forget came on a long weekend late in the summer of 1963. I had left my car parked at Toronto

International Airport five days earlier so that on my arrival from New York on Friday I could drive directly to Norah DePencier's farm where Signe had been spending the week. We intended to stay over Friday night and return to Kleinburg sometime Saturday afternoon. After a pleasantly uneventful flight I pointed my red Volkswagen bug due north on Highway 10 and by a minor miracle missed the expected heavy traffic which traditionally plagues Friday evening driving. Two hours later I turned into the gravelled lane which went through Norah's apple orchard and past the barn to her handsome house with its welcoming country gardens, the first love of her housekeeper, Mrs. McPhall.

Like most people, Signe and I looked forward to Fridays, but our anticipation was doubled because I was in New York for the five weekdays. From the warmth of my welcome through the tall, cool before-dinner drink which we enjoyed on the screened porch in the glow of a Georgian Bay sunset, through dinner to a long, relaxed evening before an open fireplace which drove away the chill of an unseasonably cool summer evening, that Friday evening seemed special.

I had put my head back in an easy chair and let my eyes wander to three paintings which now seemed like old friends when I noticed that Norah was doing the same, deep in thoughts of the paintings and the memories they kindled. I knew they had been among her few prized possessions during her working years when she lived in a furnished room in a boarding house in Toronto's old "ward". Much later, during her married life, abbreviated to two years by H. P. DePencier's sudden death, they had been the focal point of the DePencier home.

Now they were old friends who had given joy and inspiration, solace and comfort through years of happiness and sorrow. There are times for silence and it was a measure of our closeness to Norah that we felt no need for conversation.

Inevitably, my thoughts turned to our dream and the gallery we were now confident would be brought into being. Of course, Norah knew all about our hopes of enlarging the collection and our home, so a McMichael gallery would become both a practical and an artistic success. She also knew that we hoped to see our dream a reality while people like her were still living so they could be assured that if they put their most cherished possessions in our keeping they would be lovingly displayed and cared for in perpetuity.

Norah believed in that dream, and in us. We knew that. But we had not realized that she was ahead of us. She had already decided that we would be assured of success if, at this critical yet indeterminate stage of development, our collection were to take a major step forward. It was true that our log and stone gallery in the idyllic Kleinburg setting ran counter to all accepted notions of what and where a gallery should be, but the time was ripe for innovation and daring. Our friend Tom Patterson had actually managed to mount a major Shakespearean Festival in a tent in an Ontario railway town!

Looking back, we think that all of this was going through Norah's mind when she suddenly turned to Signe and me and said, "If you could have any five of my pictures, which ones would you choose?"

I thought the question was rhetorical and was about to treat it as a joke when a warning look from Signe caused me to say cautiously, "I love most of your pictures, Norah, but I think it is quite natural for the mind to play games within itself. A collector's mind asks ... 'If I had the choice of any painting, or five paintings ... not for money but just for myself, which would I choose?' Maybe I shouldn't admit it but my mind has often played that fantasy game with your paintings."

Her eyebrows arched in mock surprise. "It has? With my paintings? That seems almost naughty ... but since you've already made your selection an answer should come easily. But let me go one better. My mind has also played games, as you say, and I've tried to guess which of the pictures, given the chance, you would choose. I'm interested. Go ahead."

Still not entirely certain where she was leading, I said, "My choices may surprise you. First would be ... Jackson's *Grey Day, Laurentians*". Norah seemed surprised. "Second," I continued, "would be the little Thomson sketch which I call *Purple Hill*."

She winced slightly and then smiled.

"Really, my third choice is equal to either of the first two ... Emily Carr's *Shoreline*."

A broad smile of agreement.

"Possibly just because I'm a rabid fan of Tom Thomson, my final choices would be the other two beautiful little Thomson panels."

Her eyes, looking a little misty, lifted to gaze at these two on her wall. "Your order surprised me a little, but your choices are almost exactly what I had guessed."

Then calmly, but very seriously, Norah said in a firm voice,

"I want you and Signe to have those five paintings for your collection and I want you to take them with you when you go back to Kleinburg tomorrow."

Sighing softly she placed her hands on ours in silent benediction for the passing over of her most beloved possessions. No one spoke. The tears in our eyes said it all.

We now had a successful advertising business in a midtown Manhattan skyscraper and an art collection in a Kleinburg log cabin. By the spring of 1963 both were booming!

We had difficulty finding a name such as "Travel Pak" which had not already been registered or copyrighted in the United States, so our American corporation was named simply Robert McMichael, Inc. By the spring of 1963, our new medium was distributing millions of drug and toiletry products annually and in addition to our New York staff, we had full-time employees in Los Angeles, Denver, Chicago, Atlanta and Boston. I found myself constantly on the go — visiting our regional people and calling on our major clients. We now had thousands of distributors all over the United States. The market seemed bottomless.

The company had become very profitable and new opportunities for diversification and expansion were presenting themselves regularly. Growth was the name of the game, a game which I found very enticing. I liked New York and never tired of my constant round of brief visits to the West Coast, the deep South, the Midwest and New England.

With my new base came new friends, most living in New York and nearby Connecticut and New Jersey. With typical American hospitality they welcomed me into their homes and treated me as one of the family on family occasions like Thanksgiving Thursday when I could not be in Kleinburg.

My closest friend became Charles B. MacDermott, a business associate who was vice-president of Winthrop Laboratories Division of the giant Sterling Drug Company. Mac lived downtown near Washington Square. My apartment was on East 57th Street near Sutton Place in midtown. One evening during one of our frequently shared dinners, a thought struck us almost simultaneously. Since we were both out of town many days each month and, when at home, spent a lot of long evenings alone, wouldn't it be a good idea to share a larger and more comfortable apartment? The financial advantages were obvious and we were also excited at the prospect of companionship. We wasted no time and within a few months we were living in a large apartment, high above traffic, with a walk-out balcony overlooking the city from First Avenue at

55th Street. It was within walking distance of both of our offices.

Mac was an excellent cook and we both enjoyed having more dinners at home. We had spent too much time living out of suitcases to enjoy restaurant meals. While he prepared dinner, I busied myself dusting and steering a vacuum cleaner. Our cleaning woman, whom we seldom saw, did a thorough job each Wednesday and Sam Lee's laundry on Second Avenue saw to our clothes and bedding.

Between our frequent travels, Mac and I enjoyed attending art exhibitions. Many of the best galleries were within a ten-minute walk to 57th Street or Madison Avenue. Broadway shows were usually saved for weeks when Signe planned to be in town.

We both joined the Art Students' League, a venerable school, where we spent one evening each week immersed in drawing. My work posed no threat to the professionals, but I did learn to appreciate more fully the dedication and skill that must go into a fine drawing or painting. It was an added pleasure to remember that over forty years earlier, David Milne had attended the same school. Our homework assignments were to draw everything in sight, from ourselves, each other, and our rooms and furnishings to the more conventional still lifes of vases with, or usually without, flowers. Of course we were not serious about becoming artists, but it was astonishing how much our drawing improved with night after night of practice. The school took note of our improvement. They moved us from "ghastly" to "not bad".

On summer evenings we often sketched or just sat in a tiny parkette at the end of 57th Street overlooking the tugboat traffic on the busy East River. We could not help noticing a frequent visitor to a nearby bench. She was always alone, an inconspicuous woman in casual slacks, her eyes concealed behind large sunglasses and her hair hidden in a nondescript kerchief. She seemed to enjoy watching the river tugs and their following scows as much as we did, but we never spoke to her or invaded the privacy of the neighbour whose apartment was directly across the street from ours—Marilyn Monroe.

I became a member of the Museum of Modern Art, which was located near our offices. One bonus of membership was the top-floor cafeteria where you could get a better-than-average light lunch for a modest price. My noon-hour gallery visit seemed a pleasant throwback to the Avenue Road days of searching through dealers' galleries. While the cafeteria provided food for the body, Monet's *Water Lilies* or Picasso's *Guernica* (then still in MOMA's possession) and my favourite, Van Gogh's *Road With Cypresses*, provided plenty of visual and intellectual nourishment. Often in good weather I spent a few minutes on a bench near Henry Moore's *Family Group*. It pleased me enormously that a Canadian totem pole held its own in such august company. Good, but not old or historic, it had been carved in British Columbia for the San Francisco World's Fair. When the fair was over it was moved to New York.

My favourite art museum, however, was not among the city's largest. Uptown, at the corner of 70th and Fifth Avenue, facing into Central Park, was a mansion built by Henry Clay Frick, the American tycoon who had left his handsome house and magnificent collection of European art for the enjoyment of all. I usually reserved my visits to the Frick for the few Sunday afternoons I had to spend in town. It was also a must on the weekends Signe was in town because the Frick, an oasis of peace among the Fifth Avenue highrises and bustling traffic, was also her favourite. We found in this, and other small galleries and museums we discovered, a warmth and intimacy that heightened our enjoyment of the treasures on display.

Even though the Frick home is large, the scale of its rooms, except for a few planned for the display of large paintings, is not. An afternoon stroll through these halls and rooms designed for graceful living allows the visitor to feel relaxed and close to the man who had so admired the genius of the old masters. Yet one visit is never enough. We found we were not the only ones who returned again and again to this inviting haven. Rembrandt's *Polish Rider*, El Greco's *Expulsion from the Temple*, or the Holbein portraits of Cromwell and Sir Thomas More would have alone brought us back, as would many of the other master works on view. Best of all, we found we could always be sure of seeing our favourites. The paintings are hung permanently and none is ever loaned out.

One of our favourite areas of the Frick was a room whose walls are made up of eleven enchanting Fragonard panels. The four largest of these romantic paintings, which are known as *The Ages of Life*, were originally commissioned by Louis XV of France in 1770 as a present for Mme DuBarry. It is said that she never accepted the gift because she considered one of them too forthright a comment on her relationship with the king.

Like the palaces of other turn-of-the-century financial barons, Henry Frick's classic mansion is opulent, yet it is easy to imagine the owner standing, as the visitor stands, in wonder and joy before the great masterpieces he had collected. Signe and I, at least, could also understand and applaud his recognition that he was, in a sense, merely a temporary trustee for these treasures and his decision to make them available to all after his death.

It is some years since I have visited 70th Street, yet I can recall many of the Frick's great paintings with amazing accuracy. I have spent at least as much time in more monumental galleries—the Louvre, the Hermitage, the Prado, the Metropolitan and others like them—moving purposely through their miles of display walls and corridors, yet I have difficulty recalling any one painting with that kind of clarity. These vast treasure houses, monuments to national pride (or sometimes, to national greed) certainly have their place, but Signe and I have always felt that there is much to be said for the smaller, specialized museums, often born of the passion of one collector for a particular period or kind of art. It has also seemed to us that some of the most memorable collections are found, like the Frick, in the former homes of dedicated collectors where they were lovingly and judiciously assembled, not by a professional curator, but by a self-taught and devoted admirer. To visit them is to experience the same intimacy and pleasure their owners must have felt. Dozens of these smaller art museums of exquisite quality in tiny as well as large communities can be found scattered across the United States and most European countries. In 1963, Canada had none.

During business jaunts I seldom missed an opportunity to visit art museums, especially those which had been established by an individual or a family. An outstanding example on the West Coast is the Huntington Library and Collection at San Marino, California. About the same distance from Los Angeles as Kleinburg is from Toronto, the former home of H. E. Huntington was built in the grand manner of an English country estate. The most famous works in its impressive collection are Gainsborough's magnificent *Blue Boy*, and its facing companion work, Lawrence's enchanting *Pinky*. As a perfect, if imaginary, couple they are much more endearing than any to come out of nearby Hollywood.

Other favourites we discovered were the Clarke Museum in Williamstown, Massachusetts, which has many fine works by the French Impressionists, originally collected by the heirs to the Singer Sewing Machine fortune. At Fort Worth, Texas, the Amon Carter Art Museum provides an ideal background for the work of Frederick Remington and other western artists.

In spite of my hectic schedule, our collecting efforts, rather than declining, actually intensified during my first three years in New York. In addition to the David Milne paintings I acquired from the artist's New York friend, James Clarke, I had been able to buy, from Robert Rourke in nearby Massachusetts, a Lawren Harris panel. This sketch for the great canvas *Mt. Lefroy* was to have considerable significance for us years later. I was also able to lay the groundwork for a later purchase—a fine Harris canvas nearly three by four feet in size, *Mountains and Lake*, with which Rourke was not quite ready to part at our first meeting. My pleasure in these purchases was heightened by the feeling that I was bringing these works by two of our favourite artists back to Canada. At home, I was almost equally delighted to be able to buy, from my friend Paul Duval, a glowing A. Y. Jackson canvas, *Sunlit Tapestry*, which he had repatriated from the United States.

Sunlit Tapestry was from the collection of International Business Machines, assembled by the company from the many nations in which it had business interests. Initiated by company founder Thomas Watson in the 1930s, the company's collecting activities were later abandoned and the paintings consigned to a New York warehouse. Learning of this, Duval was able, after considerable negotiation, to purchase many of the works, including all of those from Canada. Among the best of these was Jackson's brilliantly painted canvas showing a little pond at the base of a towering outcrop of glacial rock. Dominated by a mixed growth of tortured scrub trees whose struggling forms have taken on dazzling autumn hues, the scene is bathed in the sunlight of a crisp northern day.

During my weekends at home, Signe and I enjoyed many visits to a small church at 110 Glenrose Avenue in Toronto's Moore Park. It had been converted into a studio-home by sculptresses Florence Wyle and Frances Loring. We found our conversations with them almost as stimulating as the statuary which filled their wooden chapel to overflowing. Both were contemporaries and old friends of most of the Group artists and their work could be found side by side with Group paintings in homes, institutions and galleries.

During one of our visits to "The Girls", as they were affectionately dubbed in art circles, I spotted, in an obscure corner of their storeroom, an unframed oil panel darkened by years of grime from a nearby coal stove. Almost immediately I recognized it as the sketch for one of A. Y. Jackson's better-known paintings, one which I had always admired. The large canvas painted from it, which hangs in the National Gallery of Canada, bears the title *Algoma, November*. Even through the discolouration it was apparent that the much smaller panel had all the drama and design quality of the larger canvas.

A few minutes before I spotted the Jackson, I had bought one of Florence's most unusual pieces, a female figure carved in sumac wood. She had used the lines of the grain to such full advantage that they appeared drawn on the wood to form the muscles like those in a medical model. Seeing my astonishment as I handled the sculpture, Florence picked up a small uncarved sumac log from a nearby pile and pointed to spots where there had been small limbs and then to the circular grain showing on the cut ends. She told me, as though it were the most natural thing in the world, that by studying the grain she could get a feeling for the figure which would emerge from the log. She made it sound simple, but I am still awe-struck when I look at this unique piece and my cheque for three hundred dollars seemed a very inadequate tribute to this unpretentious woman and her remarkable talent. In the face of that talent I was both astonished and saddened when Florence revealed that my modest cheque would relieve a very difficult financial situation because she had had so very few commissions or sales.

Now, looking at the Jackson panel, almost hidden by a small mountain of sculptures, I tried to think of some way that I could offer to buy it without implying that Florence was reduced to selling gifts from her old friends. There seemed no easier way than simply asking, so I said, in as businesslike a way as possible, "Florence, this is the sketch for one of my favourite Jackson canvases. I'd like very much to buy it from you if you could bring yourself to part with it."

As I had expected, she replied that she needed money very badly but could not risk offending Alex who had, indeed, given her the panel as a gift. By that time Alex Jackson was actively helping and advising us on our acquisitions so I was reasonably certain he would be happy to see another good panel come to us if Florence were willing, particularly since he was almost certainly aware of her financial problems. Confident that Alex's reaction would be entirely favourable, I suggested that I should then and there telephone Alex in Ottawa, stressing to him that the proposal was mine and that because of their long friendship Florence was naturally, and properly, reluctant to part with the sketch which he had given her. We agreed that we both knew Alex well enough to sense even the slightest reservation in his response.

Although Alex was slightly hard of hearing he usually heard telephone conversations with complete clarity. This one was no exception. Not only was he enthusiastic about the proposal, he also suggested a price which he felt would be fair to both parties. I then offered to increase it by fifty percent to seven hundred and fifty dollars, a high price for a Jackson panel in 1963, but it was after all a very special sketch.

After I handed the phone to Florence, the two old friends talked for a full five minutes and it soon became obvious that they were in full accord. Indeed, it was difficult to know which was more pleased.

In the previous year we had also bought three more of the finest J.E.H. MacDonald sketches, *Silver Swamp*, *Wild Ducks* and *Young Maples, Algoma*, from Thoreau, whom we now counted among our closest friends and whose enthusiasm for Tapawingo and the growing collection matched our own.

Two Tom Thomson panels, *Poplar Hillside*, from Roberts Gallery and *Rocks and Deep Water*, from Bud Feheley, brought to fourteen the number of works of our favourite artist which Signe and I now owned.

From Feheley we also purchased two strong Lake Superior sketches by Lawren Harris, which brought our Harris holdings up to an impressive dozen. Our paintings by Frederick Varley, while fewer, were fine examples and now included a male portrait acquired from his agent, Jack Wildridge, of Roberts Gallery.

In addition to many fine works which had come directly from the artist, our Lismer grouping now included another striking Georgian Bay panel, *Evening Silhouette of 1926*, from Paul Duval and the sketch panel for *October on the North Shore*. Both had been forerunners of major canvases. The second of these we bought from Napier Moore, the well-known writer and editor, who had owned it for years.

A few seasons earlier Tapawingo had seemed large. Now, even after completion of a large gallery room in its lower level and tight hanging in every room, we had again run out of wall space. Nor could we delude ourselves that our list of artists was complete, since our artistic horizons had broadened to include, in addition to the painters of the "Algonquin School", those two equally significant yet distinct Canadian artists, Emily Carr and David Milne.

Our affection for the Frick and other smaller specialized galleries had convinced us of the importance of having all of our treasures on permanent display. True, we had special favourites among the pictures, yet every one had been individually and lovingly selected and most had come to us only after a long search and extended personal effort. Each was a distinct and inspired expression with its own characteristics. Each deserved a permanent sanctuary where it could be viewed and appreciated. We knew we could never continue to seek out the work we loved if new acquisitions were going to consign cherished old friends to storage. Art, we felt, was meant to be seen, not hoarded, and even the prospect of a rotating collection would be, we felt, a betrayal of trust.

Once again, the previous winter, we had called in architect Leo Venchiarutti for discussions about the building of Tapawingo's first new wing which would alter its shape from the original L to a considerably larger T. By April of 1963 the frost was out of the ground and Buck Bayliss and his crew got off to an early start in the construction of a large log-and-stone-walled room with a high vaulted ceiling and nearly a thousand square feet of floor space. Beneath it there was to be another of the same size. Both were to have huge north windows looking into our forest of towering pines and feathery hemlock intermingled with the leaves of maple, beech and ash. It always gave us pleasure to know that we lived with a view much like a Group painting.

With this increase in size it was inevitable that our thoughts should turn increasingly to the next obvious step—Tapawingo's transformation from private home to public gallery.

Our convictions about Tapawingo's future were not just personal daydreams. They were reinforced and encouraged by friends who visited regularly. These included Group painters Jackson, Casson and Varley, and artists Yvonne McKague Housser, Thoreau MacDonald and Isabel McLaughlin.

In effect, all agreed that our lodge-like building, set in unspoiled woods and hills, was the perfect place to display Canada's best-known landscape painters. Sensitive collectors like Bob Laidlaw, Paul Duval, Arnold Mason and Norah DePencier, and other friends whose judgement we respected, gave us the same message.

Although at that time we never sought publicity, stories about our growing collection had appeared from time to time in newspapers and magazines. As a result, strangers began to appear unannounced on our doorstep, asking if they might see our pictures. Most of these visitors seemed to be nice people, so we found it hard to refuse their requests. As our reward we were often touched and pleased by their spontaneous comments, which we valued the more because, unlike our friends, they had no reason to tell us what we wanted to hear.

Then we began receiving requests from nearby schools for class tours of our collection. At first we were reluctant to increase our public activities, but we came to realize that children attending school in rural areas, unlike their city counterparts, were seldom, if ever, taken to art galleries. Overnight, Signe became an expert booking clerk, guide and lecturer.

Any doubts about the sincerity of the adults' reaction to our log cabin gallery were banished by the eagerness and interest we saw in the smiling faces of the youngsters in those early class tours from Kleinburg's public school.

By summer's end, new walls of solid old timbers and stone reached up to a steeply pitched roof of split cedar shakes. The new addition had been built so skilfully by Buck Bayliss and his crew that it looked exactly like the nine-year-old original (except for the shingles, which were an unweathered light orange colour). Rain, snow and sunshine would soon take care of the new-looking roof.

Our satisfaction with the new wall space was short-lived. Even with the most careful planning the handsome new wing could not accommodate our host of new treasures, including J.E.H. MacDonald's magnificent *Leaves in the Brook*, bequeathed to us by Dr. Arnold Mason.

In less than a year, Signe and I would have another new and much larger wing on the drawing board, a wing that would bring us closer still to our dream of Tapawingo as a "place of joy" for all.

We maintained our friendship and continued to visit with Ada Carmichael. She had begun writing a book about her husband and, working largely from memory, had recorded dozens of pages of their early experiences in longhand. One afternoon she asked me to read parts of her first draft which dealt with her husband's early employment as a carriage-striper in Orillia and, for a short time after their marriage, in Bolton. His father had urged him to stay with this dependable trade, but young Carmichael had his mind set on a career in the graphic arts and had already determined to set aside most weekends for his landscape painting.

Mrs. C. was completely familiar with every aspect of her husband's experiences and his mastery of not only watercolour and oil mediums but also of the tedious art of wood engraving. She was in a position to speak and write with an intimate knowledge of his beliefs and feelings, his highs and lows, but she found it difficult to be objective about either her husband or his art. Nevertheless, we felt she could make a priceless contribution of first-hand information about the relatively unknown Frank Carmichael and we tried to encourage her. Sadly, the book was never completed.

As our friendship grew, we visited quite regularly with her at her home and at Tapawingo. On at least one occasion we were delighted when she brought her daughter Mary, son-in-law Dick Mastin and their children to Kleinburg.

By 1963 we had been able to buy two more panels from her to help fill gaps in our Carmichael collection, but although we had managed to acquire canvases by Harris, Casson, Lismer, Jackson, MacDonald and Varley as well as *Afternoon, Algonquin Park* by Tom Thomson, we still did not have a large work by Carmichael. We were not, in fact, aware of any except the four that hung in his home and we knew they were untouchable.

Our growing collection of canvases did not escape Ada's notice. One afternoon, as we sipped tea in her home, she brought out two large canvases which had been rolled like wallpaper and stored away, she told us, long before her husband's death.

On our knees, Signe and I began slowly to unroll the bulky cylinders, placing handy objects as weights at their corners. The hairline cracks on their extremely dry paint surfaces started to show as, inch by inch, we carefully revealed the two largest Carmichael canvases we had ever seen. In spite of their brittle surfaces, the two long-hidden works burst forth with a power of colour and composition that left us overwhelmed.

One showed an approaching summer storm on a lonely northern lake in the midst of towering forested hills. The artist had used powerful contrasts of light and shadow to add impact to nature's performance, the tension created by a rapidly approaching funnel of dark cloud against a more distant blue sky in still-lingering sunlight. It struck us like a tornado.

The other, a vertical composition, was from the earlier years—a stunning tapestry woven in rich masses of carefully balanced colour. In the near right foreground a tall white birch extends an arm dangling with gold pieces over the precipice of a river canyon clad in masses of autumn copper and pumpkin orange interspersed with stately green conifers. Viewed beside its glowering companion from the later period, it was a bonfire.

Despite their fine cracks, discoloured varnish and frayed edges, I could see the canvases expertly re-stretched, cleaned, re-lined, framed and hanging in our big new dining room gallery—a dazzling addition to Tapawingo's increasingly impressive display.

The vision faded abruptly when I realized Mrs. C. had said nothing about her intentions. Were we to be allowed to buy or only to look? One look reassured me. Mrs. C. was smiling with the same satisfaction and purpose I had seen a few years earlier when she had first decided to sell us some of her husband's smaller paintings.

Once again she suggested prices based on her earlier dealings with Laing. They were, of course, several times those of the smaller panels but we thought her prices fair, even modest, although we knew the canvases would require expensive work by a highly skilled conservator. Months later, the canvases which we had titled *Summer Storm* and *October Gold* had been fitted on extra-heavy stretchers and re-lined, a process which strengthens the support medium and allows for the ironing out of fine cracks in the paint surface. Cleansed of offending dirt and discoloured varnish, the two major works glowed with all the radiance they had had when Carmichael first created them.

Sadly, Ada Carmichael did not live to see *October Gold* and *Summer Storm* restored to their original brilliance. She died in June 1964, the year before the McMichael Collection became the first major cultural facility to be owned by the Province of Ontario.

In the early 1960s we had built the first major addition to Tapawingo without additional mortgage money and were straining to finance our expanding U.S. business. Opportunities to purchase paintings that we knew we should have kept coming up, but we had to force ourselves to pass up pictures we felt sure we would not see again.

There also seemed to be periods of drought when we had at least some available funds but just could not turn up the exceptional paintings we were seeking. Then, as if to taunt us, two outstanding works by our favourite artists, often from different sources, would appear at the same time and we would have to choose between two very important pieces because we could not afford both. It was extremely difficult. The rare occasions when we felt forced to sell a picture we had purchased in order to buy one we considered to be even more indispensable were agonizing. Each of our paintings was a valued friend, unique and irreplaceable, from whom parting had to be accepted as final. One of our most difficult periods came when we were faced with the substantial cost of restoring our two major Carmichael canvases while we were still paying off our construction costs for the dining room gallery and providing the business with badly needed operating funds. With some temporary juggling of our finances, we felt we could just manage. It was a classic example of bad timing.

Just when we were most strapped for funds, our zealous missionary work, our enlisting the help of friends in a continuous search, was rewarded. Two irresistible opportunities with the possibility of buying three superb paintings, the once-in-a-lifetime kind, suddenly opened up. Both called for immediate decisions and cash.

Retired professor Barker Fairley, an artist who was a close friend of all the Group's original members, had returned from a vacation in England where, by chance, he had met a former University of Toronto colleague who had moved to Oxford more than forty years earlier. At Professor Sam Hook's modest country cottage, Fairley had spotted a Tom Thomson panel and one by J.E.H. MacDonald, even though both were badly discoloured by half a century of grime. Both were very fine works.

Now living on a meagre pension, the aged Hook was anxious to sell when he learned that the two panels might now fetch one thousand dollars in Canada. Our good friend Barker had called us first and our decision was immediate. Anything Barker thought very fine would be superb!

The other opportunity arose during our negotiations to purchase Tom Thomson's shack from lawyer-painter Gordon MacNamara, who now owned the Studio Building. Paul Duval and I had commented on a striking Emily Carr canvas which appeared somewhat out of place amid dozens of MacNamara's own paintings in his studio apartment. Then and there MacNamara offered to sell it for three thousand dollars.

Deeply moved by its sweeping green forest and swirling sky, I felt that *Reforestation* was one of the most compelling works I had ever seen by the great West Coast artist.

MacNamara's offer required a prompt response. Without permitting myself to ponder our delicately balanced cash position, I wrote a cheque and handed it to him.

We were overjoyed with Carr's *Reforestation*, which I had brought home with me, and the prospect of receiving the Thomson and MacDonald panels which were later entitled *Sunrise* and *Beaver Dam and Birches*. But sooner, rather than later, Signe and I had to come back to earth, a real world of bank loans and cash flows. The former seemed to be engulfing us while the latter had dwindled to a trickle. Over and above our budgeted living expenses and monthly payments on our construction loan, we had spent nearly ten thousand dollars on paintings, framing and necessary restoration work in less than a month—a huge amount when related to our net income at that time.

We took a long, hard look at our alternatives—there were not many—and reluctantly turned our attention to the two large Carmichael canvases which had just returned, beautifully cleaned, framed and ready for hanging. As much as we delighted in the rich decorative treatment of *October Gold* and the sweeping power in *Summer Storm*, we knew in our hearts that only one of them would hang at Tapawingo. The other would have to be sold.

One of my Canadian advertising clients, George Thompson, general manager of Shulton Inc., had recently moved his company's manufacturing facilities and offices into a new plant in Scarborough. Knowing of my interest in Canadian art, he had asked my help in finding a good and fairly large painting which would become the focal point of their lobby-reception area.

The horizontal format of *Summer Storm* and its strong cool colours would, I felt sure, provide the strength and excitement he was seeking in a single picture and though I've always hated to think of art in dollar terms, I knew the painting would be a good investment for its new owner.

As expected, George Thompson was very taken with the picture and received prompt approval of Shulton's board for its purchase by the company. *Summer Storm* was a focal point in Shulton's offices for more than a decade and the five thousand dollars that it brought reduced our crushing load of debt to manageable proportions.

It was the only major thing we ever sold and though *Summer Storm* had been only briefly at Tapawingo, we missed it. We consoled ourselves in the knowledge that its sale had not only eased a heavy financial strain, but had reduced a state of tension which was becoming both acute and harmful. We have never been comfortable owing very large sums of money. We felt sure Ada would have understood.

The story has a sequel. Twelve years later, in the spring of 1976, a visitor to the McMichael Canadian Collection introduced himself as J. M. Ferrin, chief executive officer of Shulton of Canada. Many years earlier and before his time, he explained, the company had acquired a fine canvas by Franklin Carmichael which now hung in the boardroom. He and other senior people in his company felt that this important painting should not remain in private hands but that it should be presented as a gift to the Collection.

Sometimes it is impossible not to believe in fate! *Summer Storm* rejoined *October Gold* and our many other smaller Carmichaels. It soon became one of the Collection's most popular works.

When the picture was officially appraised for tax purposes, I came to realize just how much Carmichael's work had appreciated in the eleven years since the Collection had been opened to the visiting public. The painting was valued at sixty thousand dollars.

October Gold also had its day. Joan Murray, the well-known scholar and critic, reproduced it in a full-page colour illustration in her 1984 book, *The Best of the Group of Seven*.

Many years after Ada's death, I heard a true story which verified our belief that her decision to sell to us was no hasty impulse but an honour, deliberately bestowed.

Paul Duval, then art critic for the *Toronto Telegram*, was acting for Lord Beaverbrook, who wished to acquire Canadian paintings for the new gallery the press baron was building in his beloved Fredericton, New Brunswick. Beaverbrook, notorious on Fleet Street for his autocratic ways, was visiting Toronto. As yet, his collection did not include a Carmichael painting so Duval telephoned Ada and asked if he might bring Lord Beaverbrook to see some Carmichael paintings. Ada readily agreed to receive the two men and before long Duval arrived at the Cameron Avenue house with his lordship in tow. Mrs. Carmichael brought out several paintings in addition to those already hanging. Lord Beaverbrook did not waste time. "I'll take that one ... and that one ... and that one."

"Oh, I'm sorry," said Ada, "I'm delighted to have you see my husband's paintings, but they are not for sale!"

Mrs. C. was not our only benefactor in the Carmichael family. After Ada's death we came to know her daughter Mary and her husband Richard Mastin well and to count them as our friends.

Over the years since her mother's death in 1964, Mary has sold few of the pictures she inherited. Instead, she has chosen to give them year by year to our collection. Her gifts have included the Tom Thomson sketch for *Afternoon, Algonquin Park* that we remembered so fondly and her father's canvas of mountaintops which had so impressed me earlier. Other magnificent canvases we had not formerly seen, choice oil panels, watercolours and hundreds of drawings, wood engravings and prints, plus the engraved wood blocks and fine tools with which her father's limited edition prints and book illustrations were made have also been among her gifts. This has enabled us to build on our original collection and to bring together in the McMichael Canadian Collection what is believed to be the largest and finest collection of Franklin Carmichael's work anywhere.

Late one chilly autumn afternoon in 1964 we received a telephone call from Bob Laidlaw. He was at his downtown office and asked if we could possibly join him there. With an urgency, unusual for him, he said he had something important on his mind that he wished to discuss with us. An hour later, driving in a gusty cold rain through the canyons of lower Bay Street, we had become both concerned and puzzled by the urgency of the invitation.

It was the end of the business day and workers were streaming towards the elevators as we entered his office in the Bank of Montreal building at the northwest corner of King and Bay Streets which was shortly to be demolished to make way for First Canadian Place. Seated on a comfortable sofa and deep in thought we found Robert Laidlaw looking from one to the other of the exquisite little paintings which, over forty years, had become his most cherished possessions. Suddenly, aware of our arrival, he broke into a grin and motioned us to sit beside him.

During the three years since we had first met, Bob had come to know and share our vision of Tapawingo as a public centre, a home for the national art that he so admired.

In fact, so intrigued had he become with what he saw emerging in Kleinburg that scarcely a day passed without a phone call, or a week without a visit. Like the four painters of the Group who had visited us in Kleinburg, he was stirred by Tapawingo and felt it would be a unique setting for Canada's distinctive national art. Like us, he saw the need for a gallery that would avoid the problems that most public galleries face because they must rehang paintings almost constantly to accommodate changing exhibitions. Of necessity their walls are usually neutral grey plaster or burlap, a versatile if uninspired background for many kinds of art. He knew that we intended the art at Tapawingo to be hung permanently against an enduring backdrop of natural timbers or weathered barn boards which would enhance and increase the impact of the paintings and carvings.

The reason for our summons soon became clear. Bob Laidlaw informed us that, as he was now eighty years old and his business responsibilities were diminishing, he had decided to close this downtown office and move his longtime secretary, Mrs. Shoemaker, with her files, desk and typewriter to one of the many unused rooms in his home on Jacques Avenue.

"I've made another decision which I think will please you," he continued. "A few of my paintings are for Rod, Nick and Kaye [his children] but I want you to have all the rest ... and I want you to take them with you now."

We were flabbergasted. Before we could find our voices, Bob Laidlaw went on, "These little paintings have given me endless pleasure. Now they should bring some of that pleasure to you and the many others who will someday enjoy them at Kleinburg. I know how hard you've worked; I hope this will give your collection a real boost and make you even more determined to achieve your goal."

Still speechless, I caught a glimpse of Signe, her eyes welling with tears. She had come to think of R.A. as almost a father figure and, overwhelmed, she threw her arms around his neck and wept unashamedly. Bob tried to make light of his own obvious emotion. "The pictures are the *good* news. But I expect to come and see them often so the *bad* news is ... you'll be stuck with me."

"But that's the best part of the deal," Signe exclaimed.

One by one the paintings came down from the wall. It seemed so unreal. Was this actually happening? These treasures were literally falling into our hands because Bob Laidlaw believed in us and trusted us to make our dream come true. With this unbelievable act of faith, he had stiffened our resolve to succeed. Now it was unthinkable that we could fail.

Still feeling as though we were in the middle of a magnificent dream, I groped for some way of converting this fantasy into tangible reality. We could not, I felt, simply load nine of the choicest Thomsons, thirteen of the finest little master works of J.E.H. MacDonald and four panels by Lawren Harris into our car with a heartfelt thank you and a handshake!

I suggested that Mrs. Shoemaker, who was in the outer office, should type a list of descriptive *pro tem* titles and sizes so we would at least have an informal signed record of this extraordinary day. Little oil panels by Thomson and MacDonald, unless they were sketches for a larger canvas, seldom had a title assigned to them. None of these panels was the sketch for a known canvas, so for present purposes Bob and I agreed on suitable descriptive titles, some of which had been used during the many years the pictures had been with him. Names such as *Windy Day* or *Evening Clouds* were obvious, others needed amplification to make identification unmistakable.

Carefully carrying a few pictures at a time, Signe and I made several trips to our car where we packed them carefully between newspapers to minimize vibration. As we emerged from an elevator, our arms full of paintings, we were a little embarrassed to meet R.A.'s son, Rod. "It looks like we're being plundered!" he said with mock severity, but his smile made it clear that he approved of his father's gift. Our last doubts disappeared when he offered to help us carry our precious loads.

Despite our pleasure we could not help wondering why R.A., whose health was good and who could expect to live for many years, had decided to part with treasured possessions which gave him so much pleasure. There was no possibility of financial gain or even tax relief and we know now that he or we might even have been penalized by the imposition of a gift tax. Serious and sincere as we were about our project, we were really just two private citizens who collected Canadian art; we did not even have the status of a private foundation. Although the pictures were not for sale at any price, the market value at that time would have run into the hundreds of thousands of dollars. Now it would be millions.

Moreover, we had reason to believe Laidlaw's two sons and daughter admired and quite possibly coveted the paintings. (He had given two to each before his call to us.) Some time later we were invited to Rod Laidlaw's home with the firm admonition, "I hope you'll enjoy my paintings, but please don't get ideas. They're not for sale—or giving."

We believe there is only one explanation. Bob Laidlaw had come to share our hopes and dream that Tapawingo was destined to become a centre of Canadian national art.

At the time of the Laidlaw gift, our collection numbered one hundred seventy-six paintings. Eleven were by Lawren Harris, twelve by Tom Thomson and twenty-six by J.E.H. MacDonald. Obviously these forty-nine would be enormously enhanced by the addition of another twenty-six prime works by the three great painters.

Our confidence soared. Arnold Mason, Norah DePencier and Yvonne Housser had already placed a trust on our willing shoulders. The Laidlaw gift, we believed, would make it possible to honour that trust. It would make the vital difference between an impressive private collection and a public treasure that could, and would, command public support. We knew we now must find the best possible way to join hands with a senior government to create a public collection which would survive in perpetuity.

We had long since made the firm decision to give Tapawingo and the art collection to some level of government which could assure its maintenance and successful operation as a public art gallery in perpetuity. It was now primarily a matter of which government... and when. Finally, we felt the point had been reached that our offer of a gift—with conditions regarding maintenance and the direction of growth and development—could hardly be refused.

Our gift would be final and irrevocable but we believed the conditions we intended to attach to it would ensure that the collection would grow in size and excellence during our lifetimes. While we knew our concept would be refined and that some change was inevitable, we were determined that it must not be watered down in any way that would diminish its impact as a national symbol.

To safeguard that vision we decided that during further development and improvement we should have to retain the inviolable right to direct and supervise the collection's aesthetic character for as long as it seemed desirable, and that we would have to stipulate rigid limits, not on its enlargement but on its broadening, after our deaths. To accomplish this we would seek an equal, indissoluble partnership in artistic matters between ourselves and the government which received our gift.

By the time of the Laidlaw gift in 1964, we were making discreet enquiries of various government bodies. At one point we gave serious consideration to the Metropolitan Toronto and Region Conservation Authority, which had been created to assure conservation of the area's river valleys and to implement flood control in the wake of Hurricane Hazel, ten years earlier. As a by-product of its principal purposes, the Authority had developed several large Conservation Areas which served as nature parks and were proving very popular for weekend outings. Since we were located on the Humber River's east branch in a natural wooded setting not unlike these parks, we thought the idea had merit. After serious private discussions with senior Authority officials, however, it became clear that their mandate did not include the operation of a major art gallery, nor were funds available to ensure its maintenance.

We looked into the possibility of becoming an arm of the National Gallery of Canada, only to find that its constitution, at that time, did not allow for satellite or branch galleries.

Inevitably, we turned to the Government of Ontario and what seemed to us a vast conglomerate of ministries, secretariats, departments, Crown corporations, authorities, commissions, committees, boards and regulatory agencies.

Where to begin? The route into this never-never land had not yet been charted for a proposal like ours. The Province made laws and levied taxes. It had responsibilities for public health, natural resources, welfare and transportation. But it did not own or operate even one museum or art gallery. (Creation of a Ministry of Culture and Recreation was many years away.) Who could make the final decision on such an unusual proposal? Who would have to approve the establishment of the first public art gallery to be owned by Ontario?

Our plans for Tapawingo were unique. If they were to be carried out we would need the co-operation and support of a powerful public figure who not only had a creative imagination but the power to act on it. After a long and thoughtful weekend of discussion in late autumn of 1964, we decided that a letter should be drafted to the Premier of Ontario, John P. Robarts.

The weekend ended, as usual, too quickly and I returned to New York where, paradoxically, I always found it easier to think and plan for the future of our cabin in the woods and its treasures. Seated by my Manhattan window overlooking the city's lights, I planned a letter which would briefly and sincerely state our desire to give away our most cherished possession ... our aptly named "place of joy".

As passionately as we felt about Tapawingo, nationalism and art I reminded myself that this letter had to be a serious, realistic proposal to a head of government we had not yet met and who had not seen or even heard of Tapawingo and our collection. It should express something of our hopes and beliefs to create a little excitement but it must be brief and offer a practical conception which would be worthy of serious consideration by a premier.

By the following weekend I had written, rewritten and condensed several drafts. The final version of this letter, undoubtedly the most significant we would ever send, travelled back to Kleinburg with me for Signe's approval and suggestions. I thought we could read and discuss it as we relaxed before dinner, but Signe was so anxious she had to be restrained from sitting down to read it in the airport lobby. We compromised. I promised to let her read it on the way home and she promised not to discuss it until we were sitting quietly with our before-dinner drinks so I could see her first reaction.

First impressions are often intuitive. Signe has always had the ability to grasp the sense, the strengths and weaknesses of a stated proposition. During our drive, deep in thought and oblivious to traffic, she read and reread my draft letter, occasionally gazing silently across the passing fields while pondering a particular phrase or thought. Not a word passed between us.

Sam and Inky's welcome reduced the tension, but it was not until I had changed into my well-worn blue jeans and pulled a stool towards the huge granite hearth that Signe quietly gave me her reaction. "Do you think it's a bit too brief? It's certainly to the point."

I wished I had brought my earlier drafts home—at first I had gone into some detail about the artists, the paintings and the buildings. Then, reading it over, I felt that it might seem prejudiced. I shortened it and left out the descriptions.

Signe smiled, "We're not prejudiced, of course!"

I reminded her that we had never doubted that everyone would love both Tapawingo and the pictures just as we did.

Again, she put her finger on the crucial point. "Perhaps you're right. I just hope *he* loves it—that he'll be willing to come and see it."

In a flash I remembered some advice I had received from veteran newspaperman and author Greg Clarke when I was a cub reporter: "Writers should never try to please the public. Please the editor, or you won't get a chance to please the public." Like writers, we too would have to please the "editor" before we could hope to please the public.

After we had agreed on a few desirable changes, Signe retyped our message to Premier Robarts and the following morning we mailed it from the post office in Kleinburg's general store.

A week later, on my return from New York, I was greeted by Signe with news that there had been a telephone call that day from Premier Robart's office. A Mr. Rohmer would like me to call. He had left numbers where he could be reached by day or night, even on the weekend.

During my years in the advertising business I had developed a formula called "Chances of Success"—which noted clients' reactions on a scale of one to ten. Timing and method of reply were two crucial elements. A quick reply by telephone rated a high score and the designation "most hopeful". When a caller asked to have his call returned day or night, it was even more promising. Negative responses do not make for an enjoyable conversation. They most often come by mail.

Everything about Signe's message from Mr. Robarts' office seemed promising. I gave it a score of eight, seated myself at my desk in our library, took a deep breath and dialed Richard Rohmer's number.

"Yes," answered a firm, controlled executive voice.

"Robert McMichael, Kleinburg. You were calling me." Equally firm, a bit less controlled.

"Yes, Mr. McMichael. Premier Robarts has your letter and would be pleased to meet with you at your home."

Desperate effort at control. "We'd be delighted."

"Would next Thursday about six-thirty in the evening be convenient?"

"That would be fine."

This dramatic initiative by Premier Robarts exceeded our wildest hopes. We had hoped to approach the top of the mountain. Now the mountain was coming to us!

We can never remember the day, or even the exact month, we

decided to give away our home and the possessions we loved most. The seed of the idea probably had been planted when we first laid Tapawingo's firm foundation. It was nurtured by the first little Canadian paintings we acquired and our budding acquaintance with the artists themselves. Certainly, from the first we had felt a consuming need to surround ourselves with the symbols we regarded as representing the spirit of our country.

As early as the autumn of 1956, our Kleinburg neighbour, author Pierre Berton, then managing editor of *Maclean's* magazine, had written:

> *After two years, the McMichaels have come to have an almost mystical feeling for their home. To them it is now more than a dwelling place; it is a link between the past and the present. This blending of two centuries is to be found in the pictures on the walls. Sketches by Tom Thomson, Arthur Lismer and Lawren Harris hang side by side with a schoolgirl's sampler, perhaps a hundred years old ... this house is neither a museum nor a museum piece; it simply points to a way in which authentic Canadian materials and traditions can be used in a contemporary fashion.*
>
> *The theme of the house, indeed, is to be found in a fragment from a speech by Joseph Howe, which Bob McMichael unearthed in an old schoolbook of his father's and had carved into a piece of weathered barnboard which now hangs in front of the entrance-way.*
>
> > *'In every village in our infant country we have the quiet graves of those who subdued the wilderness, who beautified the land by their toil and left not only the fruits of their labours, but the thoughts and feelings that cheered them in their solitude, to cheer and stimulate us amidst the inferior trials and multiplied enjoyments of a more advanced state of society.'*
>
> *That's how the McMichaels feel about their house, and if they have their way, it will still be around two centuries hence to cheer and stimulate a future world and act as a link between the ages. There's no reason why it shouldn't. It was built to last.*

After our early meetings with Yvonne Housser, Norah DePencier and Arnold Mason, we were consciously envisioning a publicly owned gallery and actively planning and collecting for it, convinced that Tapawingo would one day blossom into a distinctively

Canadian sanctuary that could be enjoyed by all.

Our enthusiasm had been infectious and persuaded many of those who shared our vision to give us their paintings. It was an extraordinary demonstration of trust that turned our plans from a personal desire for the fulfillment of our ideas to a deeply felt moral obligation to achieve political and public acceptance of Tapawingo and its growing collection.

Our meeting with John Robarts in October 1964 would be the most crucial in a chain of events which began a decade earlier. In the next few hours judgements would be made and decisions taken to determine Tapawingo's future — and ours. Would the years of dreaming, planning and working be politely dismissed or would Mr. Robarts be impressed by what he saw and our ideas for a unique Canadian art centre?

We felt apprehensive, yet confident, when two figures stepped from a long, gleaming limousine at the foot of our stone pathway that Thursday evening. Surely our visitors would sense our dedication and respond to Tapawingo's warm welcome! We bravely told ourselves that it would be largely a matter of the how's and whereas's.

John Robarts' easy manner as he sat by the fireplace convinced us that he would give sensitive and sympathetic consideration to our proposals. He wanted to hear about the feelings behind our extraordinary proposal almost more than he wanted to know about the actual gift.

Signe and I had invited Warren Jones, property administrator of the Conservation Authority, to join us for this meeting. He had been aware of our plans for more than two years and had helped us with land acquisition and reforestation as well as off-the-record advice on government and public affairs. Warren decided that as a neutral observer he was the best one to open the discussion. He began:

"Mr. Robarts, it's been my pleasure to know Robert and Signe and to follow their progress over the past few years. I have had many talks with them and I know the single-mindedness with which they have developed their lands, built their buildings and assembled their fine collection of Canadian art. They are an extraordinary couple. I know that they are completely sincere in the proposal they wish to place before you this evening."

John Robarts smiled at us encouragingly and responded with mock formality, "You have my undivided attention."

"Mr. Robarts," I began.

"If I'm to call you Robert, please call me John."

That simple suggestion dissolved my tension and set a tone of informality for the rest of the evening.

"John," I began again, more confidently, "over several years, Signe and I have built this place and a collection of some of Canada's finest national art. It may seem an unusual idea for a public art gallery, but that is the way we have always thought of it — a centre for a distinctively Canadian art and heritage—in an equally distinctive Canadian building and setting. The area is rural but close to the centres of population and main highways. It is a short drive from the city but has no parking or pollution problems. It's beautiful but it's also practical. We believe it could become a major centre of Canadian culture, which everyone could enjoy as much as we do. Signe and I want to give the land, buildings and collection to the people of Ontario and Canada. We have only one major stipulation and a few other provisions. The major one is an absolute assurance that Tapawingo will be well maintained in the future and the grounds, the buildings and the collection will retain the spirit we have set for all time. The minor provisions are that we continue to live here for the rest of our lives to oversee the growth and aesthetics of the site and the collection. That's it!"

Robarts grinned broadly, then adopting an almost fatherly attitude, he looked at us searchingly and said seriously, "I'm curious to know why any young couple would be willing to give up all this. You appear to have it made ... you have exactly what you want right here. Why are you willing to give up your ownership now? I emphasize 'now' since I assume that's what we're talking about."

I assured him "now" was correct. The reasons why were harder to explain, but I tried.

"Assume, for example only, that we willed it all to the Province and that we died within a year. To begin with, we're not even sure the Province would want our gift ... or would know what to do with it. Much as we love Tapawingo, it is questionable whether the buildings and the collection are large enough at present to be practicable as a public institution. Certain public amenities would have to be installed ... a proper roadway and parking facilities ... washrooms and other things. And then there's the maintenance and security." (Why, in heaven's name, was I dwelling on these apparently negative points?) I pressed on, "We feel if we are given average life expectancy, this place can be built into the finest centre of Canadian national art in the country. Canadians are finally beginning to appreciate their own artistic heritage ... in ten years it could become one of the most popular art museums in the nation.

But we also believe that it could reach this stature only if its unique ambiance is maintained and we are able to continue adding to the collection and devoting our full time to encouraging others to do the same. It would be very difficult for others to step in, try to make the collection grow and also maintain the present atmosphere. We believe we can preserve the unique atmosphere of Tapawingo, and further develop the collection for the enjoyment of all."

By now I was in full flight. "We have already received gifts of paintings. We believe that many more people would contribute to the collection if it were recognized that it was publicly owned and maintained.

Finally I tossed in what I hoped might be the clincher. "I've recently negotiated the sale of my American company. We feel that the proceeds, properly invested, will provide enough income for us to live comfortably for the rest of our lives. [I couldn't foresee the inflationary pressures that were to come.] We are both willing to work full time, without any remuneration, to bring the collection to a point of complete public acceptance." I concluded, "I hope that's an offer you can't refuse."

"It would be difficult, I admit," Robarts said. "Can we take a little walk around the other rooms, while I catch my breath?"

As we strolled through room after room, pausing frequently before pictures, John was reminded of areas he had explored with rod and gun. "They sure caught the moods and spirit of the country," he enthused. "Somehow in these paintings I see the forests and lakes with a greater clarity than when I was right there." He had echoed our feelings with an enthusiasm approaching our own.

"In our travels, Signe and I feel that we now see these scenes more clearly through the artists' eyes. We often point out to each other ... a Carmichael sky, a Jackson hill or a Thomson pine," I agreed.

Robarts was no art expert, but looking at the pictures I think he sensed, as he often did, how most Canadians would feel.

"I think most people still find it difficult to truly enjoy and love great art, unless they understand it. Some of these things might be termed 'modern art', but they are completely understandable and as moving as great art can be for most of us," he said as we rejoined the others back at the fireplace.

"Bob, I'm still puzzled by your willingness to give up what most people only dream of possessing," John continued as we settled before the fire. "You should know that I am not aware of any way in which the government could even extend income tax relief to you for such a gift. It's possible we could pay you a salary to look after the place and oversee its development ... but you've made it quite clear you don't expect that sort of thing. If you and Signe were a lot older and it was a bequest I could understand it better. I assume you have no serious health problems?"

"I hope not," I replied. "Certainly not any that we're aware of."

He persisted, "I can assure you both that the Province would be grateful for such a magnificent gift. I believe it could, and most likely would, become an important public institution for the preservation of the art we see here and I have no doubt that it could grow to be even more impressive. But what does that get for you?"

Richard Rohmer and Warren Jones had remained discreetly silent as Robarts continued to probe into our motives, an honest attempt to dissuade us from an action we might later regret. From our point of view, however, the discussions were proceeding exactly as we had hoped. The Premier had unequivocally stated that the Province would be willing to accept the gift and our terms and that he believed the collection would grow and be well received as a public art centre. Wasn't this all we had hoped for?

But John was not yet satisfied. "How old are you, Bob?"

"Forty-three."

"That's young, by any standard, but very young to be contemplating this kind of thing. I don't wish to appear overly inquisitive, but did you inherit a considerable amount of money to help pay for this?"

"No," I replied. "Although we both had wonderful parents and I'm happy to say my father is still living, neither of us has inherited any money."

"You mentioned earlier that you were selling your New York company. Is this a company that you started? What kind of business are you in?"

"Advertising and public relations," I told him and gave him a brief synopsis of our unique merchandising ideas. Our company was now operating throughout the United States with offices in Los Angeles, Denver, Chicago, Atlanta and Boston. The corporation had proved to be profitable beyond our most optimistic forecasts, but five years of commuting had taken its toll. We were tempted to settle in the United States but Kleinburg was our home and I had welcomed the purchase of our company by an American syndicate.

After a pleasant dinner and more discussion of art and the Canadian image, it was a shock to see that it was after eleven o'clock. I realized that Dick Rohmer's quiet visits to the telephone during the evening had been to cancel or postpone Premier Robarts' other plans for the evening. As promised, we had held his undivided attention!

Over coffee by the fireplace, John had let his gaze wander from our log walls to the frieze of pioneer implements, small sculptures in themselves. Then he began again, "I trust you will forgive my cross-examination ... by the way, who is your lawyer?"

We told him our friend Thomas Sylvester, Q.C. attended to our very simple legal requirements.

"Tommy Sylvester!" Robarts beamed. "Small world ... would you believe I articled under Tommy Sylvester! A great guy, who is wise enough to maintain a small practice he can attend to personally."

"You're right," I said, "but I don't think we need him here. If we are to achieve a meeting of minds — and it seems we are — success will depend entirely on good faith between the parties. We have implicit trust in you and the Ontario government. We hope that we will earn that same confidence from you."

The premier was still hesitant. "You're a hard man, McMichael, a rugged individualist with your own very definite ideas, not willing to stop, or be stopped short of your goals. God knows, we need more self-starters! But, having said that, I must caution you ... to my knowledge, there is no precedent, at least in this country, for a gift such as you are suggesting.

"What you have proposed to me this evening is bound to have a very profound effect on your lives. I hope you will never regret it. After all, if we complete our arrangements, you would never again be able to call this beautiful place and these beautiful pictures your own ....

"In my opinion it will take at least a year ... maybe more ... to make the arrangements and prepare an agreement which will serve both you and the Province well. As I said earlier, it is unprecedented. But I feel sure we could achieve it. Unlike taxes and so many disagreeable matters we must deal with every day, this would be fun!

"Sleep on what we have discussed. Take all the time you wish. If then, or anytime in the next year or so, you have changed your minds, let us know. If you are determined to go ahead, I promise that I will personally do everything possible, with the help of Richard here and others, to prepare with you the best possible arrangement between yourselves and the Province of Ontario."

After Robarts and the others had departed, Signe and I sat silently staring into the dying embers. The premier's acceptance was everything we could have hoped for but... inexplicably, we felt a sort of emotional letdown. The tensions that had built, especially in the preceding months, were suddenly relaxed—so suddenly, it seemed, that we were unable to grasp that Tapawingo, and our concept for its development, had won admiration and acceptance at the highest level.

That Sunday I returned as usual to New York, determined to expedite the company's sale. One condition that the purchasing syndicate was being quite emphatic about was giving me the most cause for concern. They wanted me to carry on for another five years as chief executive while, with their approval, I chose and trained my successor. I felt this was out of the question. We expected that in about a year our collection would become public property and I could not tie myself to a contract of sale which would force my continued absence from Kleinburg for several years. Finally after months of negotiation a compromise was achieved. I would give the company my full time during 1965 and every other week in the following two years and we would select and begin training a successor as soon as possible.

For the next year, while I ran the business and travelled all over the United States, I still managed to set aside a morning each week to meet with Dick Rohmer, who was preparing the detailed agreement under which Tapawingo and our collection would become the first cultural facility to be owned by the Province of Ontario. We also found time to continue our purchases.

A few years earlier I had come to know J. J. Vaughan, whose estate in Toronto's Bayview area adjoined the grounds of the mammoth Sunnybrook Hospital. He and I had spent many pleasant hours with his collection of Canadian art, which was so large that even in his huge house not all the pictures could hang at one time. Many were stored, unframed, in specially designed padded drawers. He kept two pairs of white gloves always at hand so we could cover our hands before we touched the MacDonald, Jackson, Harris and Carmichael panels which filled a large cupboard in his main picture room. Over the years he had pursued many of the artists we were seeking but his considerable fortune had allowed him also to buy important works through the best dealers, at prices still beyond our own reach.

In 1965, during our period of transition, I had a telephone call from Vaughan's son-in-law, Eddie Bond. Mr. Vaughan had died. Since his family was not particularly interested in art, his pictures were to be sold. Before his death Mr. Vaughan had requested that we be informed and given the first chance to purchase. Blair Laing had been asked to do an estate valuation of the art.

I felt sad that the collection so lovingly assembled and cared for was to be broken up but I knew this often happened when a private collector died. It had been a factor in our decision to protect our own collection.

I met with Eddie Bond in the familiar room where I had so often enjoyed exchanging thoughts on pictures and artists with J. J. Vaughan, but this was not a time for sentimental memories. Bond was pleasant but businesslike. Handing me typewritten lists of names, sizes and prices, he suggested I match his lists with the hanging pictures as well as those, mostly unframed, which were propped against the surrounding baseboards.

Studying the lists, looking up occasionally at one of my favourites, I realized that the one I had admired most was missing and did not appear on the lists.

"There was a small painting by J.E.H. MacDonald," I said diffidently, "of the artist's home, with apple trees in the foreground."

"Ah," he replied. "You like that one too. Mr. Laing said it was the most beautiful little picture in the collection, so my wife and I have arranged with the estate to have it for ourselves ... in memory of Mr. Vaughan."

Disappointed, I continued to study the pictures and their prices. For estate purposes, Blair Laing had valued them at prices a dealer might expect to pay if they were liquidated by the estate in one wholesale lot. By retail standards the prices were reasonable, but there was no way we could afford to purchase all, or even most of them.

Finally I began making a list of those I had always liked best and that would fill significant gaps in our collection. Vaughan had been particularly fortunate to acquire J.E.H. MacDonald panels from Thoreau, long before I knew him, and had also bought several fine David Milne canvases from the 1920s. These had probably been acquired a few years earlier from a Laing Gallery sale from the extensive collection of Vincent Massey. There was also a large 1922 Lismer canvas, *Forest, Algoma*.

After several hours of looking and list making I made the largest purchase Signe and I had ever undertaken. Tomorrow, I knew, I would have to pay a visit to our friendly bank manager. But our collection was enriched by panels by Lawren Harris and J.E.H.

MacDonald, two canvases by David Milne and Lismer's *Forest, Algoma*.

A few years later, after Eddie Bond's death, I received a gift for the Collection from his widow—J.E.H. MacDonald's exquisite little panel, *Artist's Home and Orchard*.

A few years earlier, in 1961, during one of A. Y. Jackson's week-long stays at Tapawingo, we were chatting about early Group days when I asked a question I thought he might not, or perhaps could not, answer.

"Of all the paintings that you ever made, which is your favourite?"

He pondered the question carefully. I would not have been surprised if he had named *Red Maple* in the National Gallery, or *The Red Barn*, which was owned by Montreal art dealer William Watson, or any of the canvases which are on public view elsewhere in Canada, but after a few moments he turned to me smiling and said slowly, "I think *First Snow, Algoma* is my favourite."

Surprised to hear the name of a painting I was quite sure I had never heard of, I said, "That's not in the National Gallery, is it?"

"No."

"I know it's not in the Toronto Gallery. Is it in one of the larger galleries out West?"

"No," said Alex, "it's not in any gallery ... It's privately owned by a man in Preston, Ontario ... Percy Hilborn."

I was naturally intrigued and overjoyed when Jackson said he felt certain Mr. Hilborn would be delighted to have us see the painting.

A few days later, after Alex Jackson's return to Ottawa, I reached Percy Hilborn by telephone. He sounded pleased when I told him what Jackson had said and insisted that Signe and I join him for dinner at his home, Blue Heron Ridge, near Preston.

A few days later, we swept up the circular drive of Blue Heron Ridge to be greeted by a tall, well-tanned man with steel grey hair who introduced himself as "Hilborn". Once inside, he led us to the living room and the long wall facing the fireplace where Jackson's great work of forty years earlier, *First Snow, Algoma*, was hanging.

Compared to many Jackson canvases, it was a large painting. But this panorama of a gaping canyon, seen through a column of burnt tree skeletons at the edge of a sheer precipice, seemed even larger, threatening to burst from its restraining frame. Scarlet mountain ash saplings struggle from between rocks to form a precarious foreground, beyond whose sudden lip is a yawning, brilliantly forested chasm which extends to the infinity of a horizon dark with forbidding mountains. A thin sky hangs low with threatening clouds, giving almost theatrical lighting to the vast abyss which seems to open at the viewer's feet. Adding to the feeling of vertigo, the first huge flakes of winter snow drift lazily over the dizzying space.

I knew why it was the artist's favourite. We were standing before a Canadian masterpiece.

Percy Hilborn had bought the painting years earlier at the urging of his wife Gertrude, who was now dead. It had been purchased directly from Jackson and in the intervening years a friendship had grown up between artist and collector.

After dinner that evening, Hilborn, an avid conservationist, drove a few miles with us to a large parcel of undeveloped land straddling the boundaries of Preston and Galt (now merged to form the City of Cambridge). He had bought this land and planted it with a wide variety of trees and shrubs, with the thought of giving it as a natural park in what would eventually be the city's centre. As we walked through the property, Signe and I were reminded of our similar efforts at Kleinburg and the parallel between Hilborn's hopes and our own. Once again our passion for art had brought us to know someone who shared our concern that Canadian treasures be preserved. If such meetings were becoming the means by which we acquired capital works for the collection, new and enduring friendships were equally rewarding dividends.

Over the next few years Percy enjoyed many visits to Tapawingo, often when Alex Jackson happened to be staying with us, and Alex's enthusiasm for our project was soon matched by Hilborn's. When we talked of our plans — and at such times we talked of little else — we now had the self-assurance of those who were discussing practical realities. During the year following our first meeting with John Robarts, there was never a question of *whether*, only of *when*.

With the approach of autumn 1965, it appeared that John Robarts and the government's legal experts had finally produced a unique agreement which clearly embodied Signe's and my wishes and conditions while allowing for the continuing growth and development of the property and the collection. We felt we were about to become partners with the Province in a very exciting new concept for a public art centre. November 18th was to be the big day.

In addition to John Robarts and several of his cabinet members, it had been arranged that Norah DePencier, Yvonne Housser and

Bob Laidlaw would be present at the legislative buildings in Queen's Park to witness the signing of an impressive wax-sealed and beribboned document, enclosed in parchment, which would assure in perpetuity the care and public enjoyment of Tapawingo, its lands and its art treasures.

The assembled media representatives, members of the legislative press gallery, chuckled frequently at John Robarts' lighthearted introductory remarks.

Following the signing and lunch in the cabinet dining room, Signe and I drove the twenty miles to Tapawingo. Our weather-worn log walls and tall dark pines welcomed us back silently. We fancied they realized that they were no longer ours alone and that their days of quiet privacy were coming to an end.

We were saying our goodbyes to Tapawingo. We were also silently celebrating the birth of a place where Canadians could come to absorb the images and spirit of their nation. We knew its rebirth would cheer and stimulate poor and rich, young and old, farm-hand and financier, student and teacher, who would be brought together by a common love of their land and the artists who had first celebrated its beauty in a uniquely Canadian way.

In spite of our ideals and hopes for the future, other feelings were already setting in during the bittersweet time of transition. Change would be gradual. It would also be inexorable.

We had a melancholy nostalgia for the simple things we had treasured, yet taken for granted. In the years ahead we might never again know the joy of seclusion in our wild and peaceful valley with its soft green hills etched against the dreaming silence of a changing sky. We might never again, in quite the same way, smell the deep woods and the fresh scent of wildflowers, hear the distant tinkling of cowbells or sight a timid deer on the crest of our quiet slopes.

The Right Honourable Vincent Massey is best remembered as our first Canadian-born Governor General, an outstanding Canadian, whose achievements in the diplomatic and academic fields led to his appointment to Rideau Hall. Less well known is his interest in Canadian art and that he was an early collector of works by Tom Thomson, David Milne and members of the Group of Seven.

Vincent Massey was born into one of the families that founded Canada's largest farm machinery company, Massey Harris. In the 1920s he became very active in the development of the University of Toronto's student centre, Hart House, a family gift in memory of his cousin, Hart Massey. He was especially interested in the development of the House's fine collection of Canadian art and came to know personally many of the men who were introducing a new movement and style into that art—the Group of Seven. A lifelong Liberal, he later served as Canada's first High Commissioner to Great Britain and then as our first Ambassador to the United States where his First Secretary was prime-minister-to-be Lester Pearson. As might have been expected, he brought a new style to the position of Governor General. Unlike his British predecessors, he travelled to all parts of the country, including remote areas of the Arctic.

Towards the end of his life Massey was instrumental in the founding of Massey College for graduate study at the University of Toronto. He is well remembered as chairman of the Massey Commission, which resulted in the founding of the Canada Council and whose recommendations still guide much of the Canadian government's policy on arts and culture.

Our first personal contact with Mr. Massey was in 1965 and came about as the result of a casual conversation A. Y. Jackson had held with him. Massey was then living in retirement at his beautiful home, Batterwood, near Port Hope, Ontario. Knowing of his intense interest in everything connected with the Group, Jackson mentioned us to him and described us as a Kleinburg couple who were seriously interested in collecting their work.

He said he was sure we would welcome a visit by him to our collection. A few weeks later, during one of his week-long stays with us at Tapawingo, Jackson reported this conversation and told us that Mr. Massey would very much like to see both our paintings and our home. He urged us to telephone Mr. Massey and issue an invitation, perhaps for lunch. Signe and I were hardly in the habit of picking up the phone and asking distinguished national figures to lunch, but Alex Jackson insisted that his friend Vincent was not at all the formidable person we imagined but a fellow collector who would enjoy an opportunity to talk about shared interests.

I dialed the number Alex gave me and felt a little more at ease when Mr. Massey assured me he would be happy to come to lunch a week or so later. Nevertheless, Signe, in charge of our luncheon arrangements, and I, planning the best way to interest our visitor, were decidedly apprehensive by the time a chauffeur-driven black limousine arrived. Coming up the walkway we saw a small man in a dark suit and coat and matching dark Homburg who looked every inch the gentleman of distinction. Still, the genuine warmth of his smile did much to soften this rather austere appearance.

It was a short walk to our front door but I sensed that his eyes missed nothing — the trees, the valley, even the black iron rooster on our roof. He paused to examine the massive hewn logs and to study the hand-split shakes of the roof. I extended my hand. "Hello, Mr. Massey," I said warmly. "Welcome to Tapawingo. I hope you didn't have any trouble finding us."

"Not really," he replied. "Your directions were good, but I must say you are well hidden back here in the woods. How did you ever find this place? It's more like the north country, yet so close to the city ... and these old timbers seem to fit right in."

He shook hands with Signe and continued, "Your husband called this Tap.... What was that again?"

"Tapawingo," she said with a big smile. "It's an Indian word meaning 'place of joy'. We're so happy to have you share it with us because it really is a place of joy."

"If the art is up to the surroundings, it must be just that. How on earth did you ever find these lovely old timbers? I'm sure they weren't cut here," he said, sensing, I think, that we loved our own trees too much to consider them as lumber.

"You're right," Signe said, "but it's a long story and someday we'll tell you all about it."

The skilled diplomat had put us so quickly at our ease that we felt as relaxed with him as with an old friend. When he doffed his coat we saw a slight man who gave an impression of controlled energy but whose eyes missed no detail of the small paintings and artifacts in the hallway. Without further introduction he began concentrating on each little landscape picture, then, putting on horn-rimmed glasses, his attention became riveted on a small J.E.H. MacDonald and then a Tom Thomson painting. We knew what he was feeling — no matter how many paintings we saw, our pleasure never diminished and, in fact, intensified to pure, child-like wonder at these artists' capacity to create a more powerful impression than even nature can provide.

Mr. Massey exclaimed, "I'm stunned each time I see the extraordinary power of these artists to extract the very essence from subjects we have all seen. How much more clearly we see it and feel it through their marvelous interpretations. How they could compress the feeling of a vast forest or a single tree onto a pocket-sized panel with such force has never ceased to astonish me."

When he had absorbed the paintings in our living room we moved on to the dining room with its dramatic display of our favourites — Varley ... Jackson ... Harris ... Milne ... Thomson ...

"Yikes," said the dignified Mr. Massey. "My eyes and I need a rest. Each painting is like a special treat, but it's easy to get indigestion if you take too many at once. I like to savour such delicacies, just a few at a time."

It seemed a good time to head for the Quebec platform rockers in front of our large fireplace and a glass of pre-luncheon sherry. As we all relaxed before the crackling fire I heard with misgiving the familiar sound of dog claws and watched in horror as Sam and Inky shot across the oak-plank floor and made directly for our distinguished guest. Before I could intervene they had placed their huge paws in his lap and were giving his hands a slathering welcome. I knew his face would be next.

"Down, down ... out, out!" I shouted, hoping that for once I would get instant obedience, but they paid no attention whatsoever. Instead they had quietly set their heads in Massey's lap and were already enjoying our guest's confident stroking of their ears.

"I think they know something that you don't," said Mr. Massey with a smile of satisfaction. "I have two black Labs called Beau and Nash almost exactly like them and, I would judge, about their age." Then, as he looked down at the heads in his lap, he said, "I'm sure they know."

Even after all my years in photography I seldom have a camera handy, but I would have given a great deal to record that moment when the heads of Canada's most famous native dogs were affectionately stroked by the first Canadian-born Governor General.

With the dogs settled contentedly at his feet, Mr. Massey's gaze rested on a painting by Fred Varley and he told us of an incident that had occurred more than thirty years earlier.

"We had arranged for Fred Varley to do a portrait of my wife Alice at our home," he said. "During the first few sittings Varley sketched outlines in charcoal but perhaps by the third session he was beginning to paint various areas. He didn't try to complete any particular section such as face or dress but instead preferred to place a few dabs here and then a few strokes there. At one stage of the sittings he had finished sections in the face such as the eyes but only parts of the nose and lips. I must say that at this juncture the work appeared quite grotesque and when Alice and I peeked at his progress on the easel one evening she was very upset to see parts of her face apparently disembodied in blank space, or, rather, not quite blank, since the charcoal lines were there. But where the cheeks and forehead would eventually be he had streaked the canvas with greens and mauves, giving an impression of dissipation. She was naturally tempted to be critical at the next sitting but I dissuaded her because I was quite sure that these colours were mere underpainting and would be blended and overpainted to form effective skin tones. More important, I had remembered another lady who had had similar feelings while Varley was painting her portrait. Apparently she had been critical of his use of certain colours which she felt were too violent. Furious about criticism, Varley approached the canvas with palette knife in hand and slashed his work to ribbons. The happy ending in our case was that Alice said nothing to Varley and he finished a beautiful portrait of her which I treasure to this day."

Massey did not mention the portrait of himself by Varley which is in the collection of the National Gallery of Canada and which is regarded as a very fine example of Varley's extraordinary talent.

After lunch we showed Massey the early David Milnes which I had been fortunate to get from James Clark in New York, and then our guest asked to see the new wing which Buck Bayliss and his crew were constructing. Work had begun in late summer and by then, late October, the roof was on and the crew was installing interior stud walls in what was to be our living quarters in the first area of the gallery to have a third floor. The stairs had been completed though I was a little apprehensive about taking our distinguished visitor over a sawdust-covered obstacle course littered with nails and boards. He assured us he had overseen the building of his own home and he would enjoy nothing more. Nevertheless, as we began to climb the stairs Mr. Massey took a firm hold on my arm.

"I hope you don't mind," he said, "I have a touch of the same problem that bothers Alex Jackson, the inner ear thing which affects my sense of balance." My grip tightened.

Work stopped for a few minutes while I introduced our construction crew. Our visitor had a firm handshake for each and steered the conversation to carpentry about which he was quite knowledgeable. The workmen were as pleased as they were surprised.

Although we felt Mr. Massey had enjoyed his visit with us and he made us promise to come to lunch at Batterwood sometime, we thought this was mere politeness. However, several months later in early 1966, we were pleased and surprised to receive a telephone call from him at Port Hope.

"May is coming up," he said, "and my gardens will be in bloom again. I hope the two of you will come for lunch on the seventeenth."

We needed no urging, even though the official opening of the McMichael Collection in July was only weeks away and the buildings and grounds were crawling with men and machines working to complete the new facilities, roads and landscaping.

Buck Bayliss and his men had finished the new gallery wing in February and they were now building another log and stone building to house public washrooms, and a maintenance workshop next to a large area where bulldozers were levelling and filling the base for a parking lot and a new winding approach road, the first pavement at Tapawingo. Our wilderness was preparing for an invasion that would eventually be counted in millions.

The adjoining wheat fields, still cultivated by Cecil Mitchell until just a few years earlier, had been purchased by the Province as part of our agreement and were now undergoing dramatic changes. To the south of the new roadway the land was essentially flat and a subdivision of homes had been built up to the south boundary line. To provide a separation from the gallery lands and a measure of privacy for residents of the subdivision it was decided to build extensive berms and man-made hills over the half-mile area from the highway to the new parking lot and gallery. This had been a gravelled laneway and our original right-of-way.

Fortunately County Road 7 (now Islington Avenue) was being straightened to the south of us and, as part of this construction work, thousands of tons of clay and precious topsoil were being scraped from farm easements to accommodate the new and wider highway. Arrangements were made to transport mountains of this earth to the land at our new entrance where they would form a long line of grassy hills planted with thousands of native trees. Most of the trees would come from Department of Lands and Forests woodlots a few miles northwest in Albion and Caledon Townships. It was there that, clad in blue jeans and windbreaker, I spent many happy hours tramping through deep woods with the local zone foresters. Most of the trees were to be dug and balled by hand so we were generally restricted to those not more than four feet tall. We were anxious to have them grow into a mixed wood which would appear natural but which would have a good selection of the northern trees painted by the Group as well as more indigenous varieties. We placed a heavy emphasis on white spruce and pine as well as maples, our national tree. Two species we wanted very much proved a little more difficult, but not impossible, to find — the tamarack and jack pine — immortalized in paint by Tom Thomson.

Through the Metropolitan Toronto and Region Conservation Authority we had access to a wondrous new machine known as a tree saver. It looked like some prehistoric animal whose gigantic hydraulic spades formed a large circle and were capable of slicing into the earth around a tree fifteen feet tall or more and lifting it with a compacted lump of earth weighing tons. Machine and tree could then be pulled by tractor to the tree's new location where the earth was placed in a previously excavated hole exactly the same size. Before the tree was moved, a ribbon was wrapped around its trunk with the bowknot on its north side so that it could be planted facing in the direction it had grown. The tree would hardly know it had been moved. Such moves were expensive and were confined to trees available within two or three miles but they produced an immediate result in a few highly visible areas of our grounds.

Bayliss had built our log garage back in 1955. Now it seemed strategically located for maintenance and security purposes. An Ontario cabinet committee on security had recommended that a couple should join Signe and me as permanent residents on the grounds. Leo Venchiarutti, who had drawn up plans for the garage, now designed a log house addition to it that looks like a part of the original building. It became home for our first employees, Stuart and Estella Wright, our maintenance man and gallery housekeeper.

Even with all this activity we looked forward to visiting Vincent Massey and seeing his fine art collection, about which we had heard and read so much in past years, so on May 17, a beautiful late spring day, we were happy to play truant and head for Port Hope.

Batterwood was located off a little-travelled rural road. As we approached the mature trees surrounding it, we could see well-tended, formal gardens leading to a wide stone piazza and the steps to the main entrance. "Elegant" was the word that came instantly to mind and we felt a little intimidated as we approached the massive oak doors. The ivy-covered stone walls and leaded window panes would have been completely at home in the English countryside.

The butler admitted us to a hall panelled in oak with a massive carved oak stairway. Mr. Massey greeted us warmly and led us to a favourite room, his den-library. It was filled to overflowing with books and the mementos of a long, illustrious career. At the time, he was working on a second volume of his memoirs, a sequel to *What's Past is Prologue*. Shuffling a handful of notes, he told us that he intended to include his visit to Tapawingo in this second book.

Then, as if on cue, two black Labradors came bounding into the den. To our delight there was a replay of Sam and Inky's welcome to Mr. Massey. Beau and Nash were about the same age as our two and like ours they settled down contentedly as we kneaded their heads and rubbed their soft, floppy ears.

Mr. Massey had been full of praise for our home and we were happy to be able to tell him how beautiful we found Batterwood and to compare it favourably with an English manor house.

"Some people seem to think it's too English," he said, "but I find no inconsistency in my love of England and my patriotism for Canada."

Two little Jackson oil panels hanging on the wall led the conversation to art. Modestly he said, "I don't have anything like the collection you have at Kleinburg, but I'm very fond of what I have. Perhaps you would like to see a few of my things now and we can save those upstairs for after lunch."

Adjoining the den was a very large living room, decorated in muted colours and comfortably furnished for relaxed enjoyment of the major paintings on its walls. It was a liveable art gallery — the same effect we had been striving for at Kleinburg. By any measure it was a gallery of art, but the pictures would not have been nearly so appealing away from the charming and relaxing room.

We were immediately drawn to *Ludvina*, the well-known and captivating portrait of a young girl painted by Edwin Holgate of Montreal who, in 1930, became the eighth member of the Group of Seven. In this picture, which has been widely reproduced, Holgate has departed from traditional Canadian subjects to capture a winsome little immigrant. We soon recognized that all the paintings in the room were fine examples of the work of the same artists we had so lovingly collected. Among a number of David Milnes, Massey's favourite painter, were outstanding compositions by J.E.H. MacDonald, Frederick Varley and A. Y. Jackson. The total impression was stunning, almost overpowering. It was the most concentrated display of canvases we had ever seen by "our" artists. Seen individually, each would have produced a high level of excitement. Seen together they were literally a feast for the eyes.

Massey had made direct and intimate contact with the artists at the peak of their powers and his judgement had been unerring. He watched our wide-eyed admiration with quiet satisfaction until the announcement, "I believe lunch is ready", brought us back, with a jolt, to reality.

Lunch was served at a beautifully carved walnut dining table. As we sipped our white wine we were surprised to see that the butler had apparently neglected his employer. A moment later he reappeared with a bottle for our elegant host — a pint of Old Vienna beer!

After lunch it was suggested that we might like to see the pictures in "The Queen's Room". This was the room Queen Elizabeth and Prince Phillip had occupied during their visits to Batterwood. Although the room was not particularly large, it was beautifully furnished, undoubtedly fit for a queen. Yet it was not royalty that made it important for us but a group of little panels, as splendid as any I have seen, by Tom Thomson and J.E.H. MacDonald. The small paintings were perfectly scaled for the room but their sheer power and colour overshadowed everything else in it.

Though I have seen and closely examined hundreds of these little gems by Thomson and MacDonald, each one produces the spine-tingling sensation I experienced when I saw my first. The pure colour and absolute sureness of their brushes combined with a strength of composition and feeling for their subjects produced such astonishing effects that the viewer can only marvel.

"Some of these are painted on both sides," Mr. Massey remarked. At once I asked permission to take them down so I could see both paintings. "Certainly," said Mr. Massey courteously and then, in a slightly nervous tenor, "I know you'll be very careful."

One by one I examined the magnificent Thomson panels, each a magic distillation of Algonquin. The paint had been laid on heavily and with unerring sureness, to give the main elements, such as trees, an almost three dimensional, sculptured effect. The paint was thrust on the small board with axe-like chops.

As I expected, there was very little writing on the reverse sides but as I also expected and hoped, two of the panels were fully painted on both sides, not unusual for Thomson when his supply of panels was short. Frequently, the paintings on both sides, though entirely different subjects, are so nearly equal in quality and appeal that it is difficult for an owner to decide which to frame facing outward. I agreed with Mr. Massey's choices but the two with faces to the wall were, I felt, permanently hidden little master works.

With motives that were not entirely disinterested, I could not resist telling Mr. Massey of a master conservator we knew who was capable of splitting such panels even though they are only three-sixteenths of an inch thick. He then mounts the two wafer-thin sections of wood onto supports of well-seasoned half-inch plywood.

"We have had this done with Jackson and Thomson panels of our own with excellent results," I said, "and never a miss ... indeed, I believe that the resulting panel, skilfully remounted on a much heavier support, is less prone to possible warping and checking." Warming to my subject, and seeing an opportunity to acquire two beautiful Thomson panels for our collection, I proposed, "We could have these two panels split and I feel absolutely certain you would be delighted with the results. I am so confident of a completely successful result that, in the most unlikely event of damage resulting to your favourite side, I would offer you in exchange your choice of one of the Tom Thomson panels Signe and I have recently acquired — we own them personally. After the operation has been completed at our expense, we would be delighted to pay you one thousand dollars each for the backside panels."

Mr. Massey had listened very carefully to my proposal, but from his expression I knew that he had misgivings. Screwing up his face like a frightened boy, he said, "I'm skeee...rt."

We understood and let the matter rest.

In room after room we looked at more fine paintings until our host suggested a walk in the gardens. The three of us, with Beau and Nash closely to heel, strolled from box-bordered flowerbed to flowerbed, each overflowing with bud or bloom. At last we came upon a small formal plot almost totally filled by a dozen or so squared stones set into the earth. Each carried a name — Rover ... Laddie ... Rex.

"I've loved every one," said Mr. Massey with the sadness only another dog owner can understand. "If I have any regret it's that I discovered the Labradors last." He bent to stroke Beau's ears as Nash hastened over for his share of petting.

We left Batterwood bathed in late afternoon sunlight. It had been a memorable day.

From our first meeting in October 1964, John Robarts made it clear that there were no provisions in the federal *Income Tax Act* which would make our proposed gift tax-deductible, nor could he see any way in which his government could promise any form of tax relief to us. We appreciated his forthrightness and felt it was an unfortunate omission in our tax laws, but we never for a moment reconsidered our intention to give our collection and Tapawingo to the Province of Ontario. I could not, however, help contrasting our situation with that of similar donors in the United States, whose gifts were fully tax-deductible.

Later, I was surprised to learn that gifts to Her Majesty in Right of Canada, that is, to the federal government, were entitled to tax credits. It was gifts to Her Majesty in Right of Ontario (or any other province) which were not. Under the Charitable Gifts section of the *Income Tax Act*, a donor could deduct an amount equal to ten per cent of his income annually for gifts to churches, hospitals, community chests and other charities which held certificates issued by the Department of National Revenue. In our case this would have been almost meaningless since our annual income in 1965 was approximately thirty thousand dollars and a three thousand dollar deduction would have resulted in a tax saving of about a thousand dollars for a gift worth over a million dollars. In any case, the calculation was meaningless since the Province of Ontario, hardly a charity, did not hold the required certificate.

Thus, when we signed the formal agreement which transferred our ownership of Tapawingo, its lands and collection of art to the Province of Ontario on November 18, 1965, we knew we could not expect a penny of tax deduction. Nevertheless, even as we were signing, Buck Bayliss and his men were building a new wing onto Tapawingo at our expense. When it was completed in mid-1966, we had four important new galleries on the main and lower levels and modest living accommodation on its third floor.

Our gift of the land, buildings and collection was unique. Tapawingo became the first public cultural facility to be owned by the Province of Ontario. The Agreement which Dick Rohmer had laboured over for more than a year — a year of almost weekly meetings with the premier and then with me — was unprecedented. The final Agreement was put together with the help of some of the government's best legal talent and was something of a pioneer effort. The premier was determined to make it clear and workable, and above all to be certain that its intent, and the concept which we had envisioned for the collection, could never be compromised. Week by week, section by section, the Agreement was written and rewritten with the help of senior crown counsel, David Bernstein. "Duke" MacTavish, legislative counsel, put it into the final form that represented full consultation among Dick Rohmer, the premier and me. In effect, the Province and the McMichaels were to be partners.

Richard Rohmer's role was particularly interesting. Unlike the others, who were government employees, Richard Rohmer, Q.C., was an independent barrister who enjoyed the premier's confidence and was engaged to handle special situations for the government, particularly for the Office of the Premier. During late 1964 and through 1965, we met at his Bay Street office on Monday mornings before I flew back to New York. Each meeting brought forth new clauses or reworded clauses which had been reviewed with the premier and senior members of the Attorney General's staff. Since Signe and I had felt it unnecessary to involve a lawyer of our own, John Robarts and Dick Rohmer, as his representative, made a concerted effort to make sure the Agreement would be understandable, fair and secure for us. Although the Agreement eventually contained thirty sections, filling twenty legal-size pages, we were given ample time to study and approve each section. Throughout the weeks and months of preparation there was never any serious disagreement with the manner in which it was being constructed. We all felt that with good faith on both sides the final Agreement would serve both parties well.

When the final document was produced, we felt absolutely certain, as I am sure John Robarts did, that the words, the intent and the spirit of the document were so clear that future legislation, or even a change of government, could not alter the fundamental principles governing the Collection's future development and artistic direction. The premier's integrity was beyond question, but there was further reassurance, if any had been needed, in the fact that he would be signing our Agreement as premier on behalf of Her Majesty in Right of Ontario. I believe everyone involved shared our certainty that whatever the future held, no government, civil servant, committee, board or appointee could change the aesthetic concept that had governed the collection from its inception.

In summary, the Agreement included covenants covering our giving, and the government receiving, the lands, buildings and collection, all of which were accompanied by surveys and detailed lists. The main terms of the gift agreement were to be carried out through the creation of an Advisory Committee which would consist of Signe and me, two government appointees, and a chairman chosen by, and acceptable to, all four members. The committee could (among other things):

— Approve the design and location of any new building to be constructed either by the McMichaels or the Crown on the lands of Tapawingo;
— Approve repairs, alterations or additions, now and thereafter situated on Tapawingo, prior to such repairs being undertaken; and
— Approve or reject for inclusion in the Collection any work of art. (This was the part of the Agreement which we felt was the most important.)

Though it became a formal public entity as the result of the Agreement, the Collection did not have corporate status. It could not, for example, have its own bank account or engage in certain contracts in its own name. Signe and I had suggested to John Robarts that the Metropolitan Toronto and Region Conservation Authority, with whom we had excellent relations and whose headquarters was located in nearby Woodbridge, might serve. (It had, of course, corporate status.) The Authority could pay our staff and other bills from monies the Legislature would approve for the Collection's operations. For this reason the Metropolitan Toronto and Region Conservation Authority became a third party to the Agreement with the written proviso that the Crown might make such further or other arrangements as it deemed necessary to carry out its obligations.

Section 13 of the Agreement stated:

The Crown shall, with the advice and assistance of Robert McMichael and Signe McMichael, establish, develop and maintain in perpetuity at Tapawingo a collection of art reflecting the cultural heritage of Canada; the said collection shall be known as the "McMichael Conservation Collection of Art", and shall be comprised of paintings by Tom Thomson, Emily Carr, David Milne, A. Y. Jackson, Lawren Harris, A. J. Casson, Frederick Varley, Arthur Lismer, J.E.H. MacDonald, Franklin Carmichael, and other artists as designated by the advisory committee, who have made contributions to the development of Canadian art.

The clear intent of this section was to limit the scope of the Collection for all time to the artists named, with provision for the addition of a few others whom the advisory committee might decide were complementary to the original group and whose work had been produced mainly during the first half of the twentieth century. We also intended to include, at a later date, the art of our aboriginal peoples, the Indians and Inuit, whose work we considered to be basic to our theme. We agreed to include the right to designate other artists beyond those named because the Collection did not, at the time, own works by three of the Group of Seven and other very closely related painters.

Our conviction that the particular theme of our collection should, and would, be maintained in the public Collection was embodied in section 16 of the Agreement:

> *The McMichaels agree to donate to the Crown, for inclusion in the Collection, all works of art hereafter acquired by them and deemed by them to be suitable for permanent inclusion in the Collection.*

We have never regretted this lifetime commitment. During the months in which the Agreement was being prepared we added continually to the Collection inventory list. In 1965 alone we were able to purchase important paintings by David Milne, J.E.H. MacDonald, Arthur Lismer, Lawren Harris, A. Y. Jackson and Tom Thomson and in almost every year since the Agreement we have continued to purchase new works, including those of members of the Group who were missing from our collection in 1965. Other gifts we made to the Collection in the sixties and seventies were additional works by Tom Thomson, David Milne, Emily Carr, J.E.H. MacDonald, A. Y. Jackson, Arthur Lismer, Lawren Harris, Lemoine Fitzgerald, Franklin Carmichael, Frederick Varley, A. J. Casson and Edwin Holgate, as well as some fine Eskimo carvings.

Section 23 of the Agreement was extremely important to us. It designated Signe and me as curators of the Collection "for as long as they [that is, we] deem advisable" and assured our "entitlement to reside at and occupy Tapawingo for the rest of their [our] lives". In full it read:

> *In consideration of Robert McMichael and Signe McMichael advising and assisting the Crown in its establishment of the Collection, agreeing to serve upon the advisory committee, and continuing for as long as they deem advisable to act as curators, advisors and supervisors of tours for the Collection without remuneration, the Crown hereby agrees that the said Robert McMichael and Signe McMichael shall each be entitled to reside at and occupy Tapawingo for the rest of their lives, subject however to any right of the Crown, the Authority and the public to enter upon and use Tapawingo under the terms of or in consequence of this Agreement.*

Premier Robarts and the Ontario government's lawyers reminded us frequently that the Agreement was unprecedented and as such was breaking new ground. With hindsight, we see now that section 23 covered too much important ground. It became mired in *non sequiturs* which apparently were considered to be politically attractive at the time.

Tapawingo was our home, our only home. While we had no intention of relinquishing our right to live in it, we had every intention of sharing it to the full with members of the public who would come to enjoy great Canadian art in a warm and inviting atmosphere. Living there was simply a retained interest in our gift. Our commitment to the public was underlined by our gift of the new wing of galleries which put our bedroom and kitchen well out of the public's way on the third floor.

As a condition of the gift, Signe and I were appointed curators of the Collection for our lifetimes. We offered to work without remuneration to avoid any hint that we had made what we hoped would be a precedent-setting gift only to ensure that we would have lifetime access to the public trough.

John Robarts and his lawyers, we believe, felt the Agreement would make Signe and me lifelong curators of the Collection and would ensure our right to reside at, and occupy, Tapawingo. Unfortunately, we now see that these important conditions were couched in terms, and carried inferences, which did not follow from the premises on which we based our gift of the lands, buildings and collection. These unsuspected chickens came home to roost some fifteen years later when Premier Robarts, his lawyers and his staff had long since departed the government.

Section 25 of the Agreement dealt with public attendance and reiterated our permanent positions as curators. It stated:

> *Members of the public shall be admitted to Tapawingo for appropriate cultural or recreational purposes at such reasonable times as are designated by the advisory committee, subject to such reasonable arrangements as may be established with the McMichaels as resident curators.*

After November 18th, 1965, Signe and I could have pursued our collecting while also continuing to enjoy the solitude and privacy of Tapawingo. The government neither expected nor urged that Tapawingo's doors be thrown open to the public. The Crown had undertaken to maintain the grounds and buildings and those involved in bringing about the Agreement would, I believe, have been content to see the already impressive collection of Canadian art grow under our guidance, with the expectation that on our deaths it would pass completely into public hands. In the meantime we could have retained the quiet enjoyment of the home we had lovingly created. For the government, the Collection was a good investment in the future and there would have been no quarrel had we chosen to spend our lives in the contemplation of art and nature, strolling the hills and valleys with Sam and Inky and perhaps sharing our idyll with the public on special occasions.

We had worked very hard for many years, several of which had necessarily been spent apart from each other. Through that hard work we had achieved the financial success that made it possible to build Tapawingo and our art collection. With the sale of my corporation in the United States, we felt we had enough money securely invested to assure a pleasant, though simple, life. We were young and in good health.

Establishing a unique centre for Canada's national art which would make it possible for all Canadians to enjoy our collection had been our dream. Creating an environment that would enhance and complement the work of a small group of selected artists and the art of the Native peoples was a part of that dream that had been realized just as we had planned. The Collection was displayed in a building that combined the inviting warmth of a ski chalet and the rugged coziness of a pioneer home. At Tapawingo we had created a gallery in which the soft golden glow of primitive pine furniture was set against massive logs and barnboards weathered to silver grey by a century of sun and storm.

The rough, homespun surface of the hewn walls, softened by wind and rain, formed a muted backdrop for the brilliant colour of the paintings.

A feature writer for *The Canadian*, a national weekend rotogravure newspaper supplement, headlined his seven-page colour-illustrated article of March 1966, "The Group of Seven Gets a New Home ... Not Just a Home but a Place of Joy — Back in the Woods — and Out in the Open. You'd Think the Paintings Were There First".

All of this was part of our dream; a life of leisure was not. Section 7 of the Agreement, which created the advisory committee, was very carefully prepared to ensure that our partnership with the two government appointees on the committee would be maintained on an equal basis even when one of us died. It stated:

In the event of the death or incapacity of either McMichael then the other McMichael may appoint a member in substitution therefor.

To make even more explicit our intention that the Collection should be confined for all time to the artists and art we had specified, section 19 stated:

The Crown agrees that upon the death of the survivor of Robert and Signe McMichael, additions to the Collection shall be confined to works of art by the artists specifically named in section 13 above or designated by the advisory committee pursuant to the said section 13.

Finally, anticipating the possibility of the Collection being turned over to a corporate entity established by the Province of Ontario, as indeed it was seven years later with the creation of a Crown corporation to be named The McMichael Canadian Collection, the Agreement concluded with section 30:

Notwithstanding any of the foregoing provisions of this Agreement, in the event that the Province of Ontario establishes a foundation for any of the general purposes of preserving, maintaining or developing lands, buildings and collections of art for the public benefit, the Crown may assign the whole of the lands and premises and collection vested in or subsequently acquired by it pursuant to this Agreement, including all its rights, powers and privileges and subject to all its obligations in connection therewith, to the said foundation; provided that the Crown agrees not to make such assignment until the said foundation covenants to be bound by the provisions of this Agreement to the same extent as is the Crown herein.

The original pages of this unique Agreement were elaborately bound in heavy parchment with traditional blue ribbons that intersected with a red-wax impression of Ontario's coat of arms. The calligraphy on the cover was black, gold and red. Impressive as the binding was, the Agreement itself was of far greater significance. In addition to establishing the first Ontario-owned art gallery it guaranteed Signe's and my right to play a major role in maintaining the Collection's theme, ambiance and content, not just for our lifetimes but even beyond.

It seemed that we were fully protected and covered by an air-tight agreement. Fifteen years later we found we were not even decently clothed.

Photographs of the two of us and Premier Robarts signing the founding instrument at Queen's Park appeared with the story on the front pages of many Canadian newspapers. Afterwards, we received dozens of congratulatory letters, telegrams and calls. One telephone call was from my friend Bill Withrow, director of the Art Gallery of Toronto. Our lengthy conversation led to several thoughtful meetings with him and, later, with both him and the Toronto Gallery's president, Ed Bovey.

At that time the Art Gallery of Toronto, like most others in the province, received only modest financial grants from the city council and provincial or federal sources. With limited revenues and steadily increasing costs, the Toronto Gallery, as well as civic galleries in cities such as Hamilton, Windsor and London, was experiencing financial difficulties which not only ruled out expansion of its facilities but also threatened its continuing operation.

Thus, the Art Gallery of Toronto was hard pressed for operating funds and was badly in need of modernization and improvements to its structure and facilities. The gallery had remained virtually unchanged for several decades, and massive aid, running into millions of dollars, was now needed. It was Bill's hope that since the Province had demonstrated its willingness to fund the operations of its newly acquired gallery in Kleinburg, it might also be persuaded to provide the needed funds for the Toronto Art Gallery. Bill believed Toronto to be a special case since, although it was owned by its members, the gallery was open to the public and could properly claim to be the senior art institution in the province.

Bill put this proposition to me during one of our lengthy phone discussions. I agreed that the Toronto Gallery could be considered special, but I pointed out what seemed to me to be the political realities of the situation. With so many galleries in financial distress, I suspected that if Toronto were singled out for massive aid, many members of the legislature would soon receive protests from their constituents in other communities whose galleries needed similar help.

The chances of success would be vastly improved, I told Bill, if the city label were removed from the gallery. Could he persuade his board and, if necessary, the membership, to change the gallery's name from the Art Gallery of Toronto to the Art Gallery of Ontario? I warned him that the change would necessarily give the Province an important measure of control through provincial board appointments, perhaps based on a formula similar to the one that had been created for our own advisory committee. If these two conditions could be accepted, the Gallery might then be perceived as a provincial institution rather than a civic facility and criticism from other centres would, at the very least, be greatly diminished.

At the other end of the wire there was a moment of silence following my radical suggestion but, after brief reflection, Bill responded, somewhat to my surprise, that the Gallery's board and members might not find these changes too difficult to accept if the end result was the assured stability and growth which a provincial accord could guarantee.

A short time later, when the board had reached general agreement on the changes which were so necessary if they were to seek the Province's support, I called my friend Dr. Keith Reynolds, chief of staff in the Premier's Office, and two days later at Queen's Park I introduced Bill Withrow to him. Keith was sympathetic, as was the premier.

I followed the resulting negotiations with a good deal of interest but, of course, my primary concern was with our own transition from private to public status. Friday July 8, 1966, the day the Ontario legislature was prorogued, turned out to be a momentous day for both galleries. On that day, the *Ontario Art Gallery Act* received royal assent and the McMichael Conservation Collection of Art officially opened its door to the public.

Passage of the *Ontario Art Gallery Act* provided the new AGO with a grant for operating expenses, but it was generally agreed that some special reason would be required to open the legislature's pocketbook for the much-needed capital grant for improved buildings and facilities.

For some time, two of the Toronto Gallery's important benefactors, Sam and Ayala Zacks, had been planning to give the bulk of their fine collection of modern art to the Gallery. At the same time they were negotiating with world-renowned sculptor Henry Moore in the hope that a major portion of his personally-held works could be secured for Toronto. Two such magnificent gifts coming almost simultaneously would do much to justify a large capital funds grant for the newly created Art Gallery of Ontario.

In pursuit of the Moore donation, Sam Zacks brought Ed Bovey and Bill Withrow to a meeting with Henry Moore at the artist's home near Much Haddem, Herfordshire. At this meeting Moore indicated that he was indeed willing to give a vast collection of his works to Toronto but only on condition that they would be housed in a huge new gallery room that would be a part of a much-hoped-for rebuilding of the Gallery.

The Toronto delegation was more than agreeable to this condition, but in order to make possible a great new gallery building with a special gallery to house the world's finest collection of Henry Moore's works, they knew they would require the concurrence of the premier and the Ontario government.

The gallery group, now joined by Toronto architect John C. Parkin, learned by pure coincidence that Premier John Robarts was visiting London on government business. The delegation moved quickly to seize this golden opportunity and arranged a meeting between the immensely popular premier and the soft-spoken, charismatic sculptor over a lengthy, talk-filled dinner the following evening. To the relief of the gallery foursome, the two took an immediate liking to each other which did much to smooth the way for a proposal in which they would be the key players.

In his final act as premier, before turning the leadership of the government over to William Davis in 1971, John Robarts announced that the Art Gallery of Ontario would receive the necessary capital funds to greatly enlarge and modernize its venerable old building on Dundas Street and that the new building would include a large section dedicated to the works of Henry Moore. The new AGO would soon be ranked among the continent's finest galleries.

To this day, I find it hard to pass over the words "Art Gallery of Ontario" without feeling a little like a proud godfather who has had a hand in naming the baby.

In the early part of June 1966, Stuart and Stella Wright had moved into the cosy log house which had been added to our garage. In addition to helping Signe maintain a much enlarged Tapawingo, Stella was responsible for maintenance of the new public washroom building and Stuart set up shop in the maintenance and supply area of the new log building. After regular working hours, most early evenings found Stuart and I mowing the large lawn areas which now extended beyond the new paved parking lot. By summer's end, the lawns, dotted with a thousand newly planted trees, extended a full half mile on Islington Avenue to a stone entrance wall and gates which Buck Bayliss and his crew were beginning to construct. Larger tractor-type lawn mowers and local students to operate them soon became a necessity.

The only other full-time staff member was Maria Van Dyke,

who, during her student days, had helped Signe on weekends. Now she was to be tour guide, secretary and receptionist, assistant picture hanger and invaluable aide for just about every other job necessary to our rapidly approaching official opening. We relied heavily on her judgement when we came to select young women to be weekend gallery guides and young men to mow our acres of lawn and act as parking supervisors. Most were students at Woodbridge High School.

Through Keith Reynolds, I asked Premier John Robarts to select a time at which he could be present for the official opening. We felt the premier's presence was essential on this historic day and knew that it would also give him an opportunity to meet and thank many of those who had helped to make it all possible. Bob Laidlaw, Norah DePencier, Yvonne Housser and Thoreau MacDonald as well as Group artists A. Y. Jackson, Alfred Casson and Frederick Varley would be among the nearly two hundred invited guests. Our first advisory committee chairman, Jack Brockie, committee members Dave Bernstein and Fred Wade, the Honourable James Auld, Minister of Tourism, and A. Y. Jackson were to be seated on the portable stage that would be erected on our front lawn. Early in June the premier told us he expected the legislature would prorogue for the summer on Friday, July 8, so the afternoon of the eighth would be ideal if everything could be in place at Kleinburg.

With a clear target date only four weeks away the pace quickened. Our road and parking lot were still sandy stretches waiting for two layers of pavement and striping. Only after that could border sodding be completed. Carpenters and painters were trimming the new workshop-washroom building and adding finishing touches to Stuart and Stella's new home while giant earth-compacting machines still roamed like pre-historic monsters on the further berms and fields, preparing them for a final layer of topsoil and grass seed. Maintaining a homelike atmosphere in a complex that would have to accommodate thousands of visitors required a great deal of thought and planning.

Maria and I gave a cram course to our guides-to-be. In addition to security (which was all-important) we stressed the importance of making the visitors feel welcome, and also emergency procedures in the event of fire, sickness or injury. We also gave several crash courses on our artists and the historical background of the paintings. There was no assigned homework for our courses but we developed our own private lending library to encourage further reading and we were proud when visitors later remarked on the courtesy and intelligence of our attractive young guides. On his first visit after our opening, A. Y. Jackson said with typical gallantry, "Even if the pictures weren't here it would be worth coming just to meet the guides."

Following the mailing of invitations, about two weeks before the opening I received a telephone call from Percy Hilborn in Preston. He said he would be delighted to be present and would be bringing his daughter Helen.

If his acceptance delighted me, his next words were nothing less than spellbinding: "I think you should have something special to commemorate, and perhaps even liven up, your opening ceremonies. I'm going to give you Alex's *First Snow, Algoma*."

I was quite literally speechless as he continued, "For some time I've intended to give it to you and your opening seems to me to be the most appropriate moment. When would you like to pick it up?"

The question brought me back to practicalities at once. The great Jackson canvas must play an important role in the ceremonies of the official opening ... especially since both donor and creator would be present. The following evening I drove to Preston in a van borrowed from the Conservation Authority and returned with the great painting which Jackson considered his finest. A day later it was in Ed Zakowski's hands for cleaning and had been measured for a new frame. We were determined that so great a picture should be at its dazzling best for its first public appearance.

July 8 was a perfect summer day. More than two hundred guests took their seats on the folding chairs on our front lawn before a bunting-wrapped stage for the event we had looked forward to for so many years. It was not until later that we realized how symbolically appropriate the time and day had been — on the same date and at the same hour in 1917 Tom Thomson had paddled his canoe away from the little dock at Canoe Lake, never again to be seen alive.

During brief introductions by Jack Brockie and some fitting reminiscences by A. Y. Jackson, Signe and I gazed out at a host of familiar faces. These friends, we felt, should also have occupied seats of honour on the small platform: Bob Laidlaw, Norah DePencier, Margaret Tweedale, Yvonne Housser, Thoreau MacDonald, Percy Hilborn, Alfred Casson, Keith and Edith MacIvor, Florence Wyle and Frances Loring and so many others. We thought, as well, of two who would have cherished the moment but who could be present only in spirit — A.D.A. Mason and Ada Carmichael.

No summary could possibly do justice to Premier Robarts's brief speech. Spelling out, in the clearest possible terms, the objectives and intent that we, and the Government of Ontario, shared for the first art gallery to be owned by the Province, he said:

Mr. Chairman, may I preface my remarks by saying that the privilege of participating in the official opening today of the McMichael Conservation Collection of Art is an honour to be cherished throughout the years. It is one of those rare occasions which truly transcends all partisan considerations and can, therefore, be enjoyed to the utmost by all of us. However, let me add immediately that we would not be assembled at Tapawingo for this happy event were it not for the selfless devotion and generosity of two remarkable Canadians, Signe and Bob McMichael.

In preparing my remarks for today's official opening, I reviewed again the course of negotiations which led to the gift of Tapawingo to the people of this Province and nation. I went back particularly to an evening in the Fall of 1964 when, at the invitation of the McMichaels, I came to Tapawingo for a quiet discussion of their proposal and, equally important, my first view of their magnificent collection of Canadian paintings. Any of you who have enjoyed the privilege of a visit to Tapawingo with the McMichaels can predict the result. Despite the fact that no precedent existed for the arrangement envisaged, the conclusion was inescapable — we must proceed at once.

Consequently, just one year later in November of 1965, the land, premises and art collection were officially transferred by the McMichaels to the people of Canada.

In my view, the major objectives of Mr. and Mrs. McMichael can be set out in three parts. The first is to collect and display in an appropriate setting the works of ten eminent Canadian artists — Tom Thomson, Emily Carr, David Milne and the renowned Group of Seven, composed of J.E.H. MacDonald, Lawren Harris, A. Y. Jackson, Arthur Lismer, F. H. Varley, Franklin Carmichael and A. J. Casson. I might say that we are greatly pleased and honoured to have with us today three members of that famous group — A. Y. Jackson, A. J. Casson, and F. H. Varley. The second is to preserve forever for the people of this nation this outstanding collection of Canadian art. The third is to encourage, by example and by the provision of full assurance of permanent care and display, the enhancement of Tapawingo's galleries through the donation of additional art treasures by others whose love of their country, its history and its art is akin to that of the McMichaels. Furthermore, the establishment of the McMichael Conservation Collection of Art may very well inspire the creation of similar galleries and treasures of Canadiana elsewhere in this Province and nation.

Clearly, the first two of these objectives have already been achieved. The first by the dedicated efforts of Signe and Bob McMichael, and the second through the signing last November of the formal agreement with the Province of Ontario. Shorn of its legal phraseology, the agreement provides a lifetime interest in Tapawingo, its grounds and its galleries for the McMichaels; an inviolable obligation on the part of the Province to maintain the land, premises and art collection in perpetuity; assignment of responsibility for the operation of the programme to the Metropolitan Toronto and Region Conservation Authority; and an assurance of public access to the Collection on a planned and reasonable schedule.

The third objective, a continuing one, is being realized in a most impressive fashion. Mr. R. A. Laidlaw, of Toronto, has augmented the Collection in a very substantial way with the gift of a group of twenty-six paintings by Tom Thomson, J.E.H. MacDonald and Lawren Harris. Moreover, within the past few days, a most exciting and important addition to the McMichael Conservation Collection of Art has been provided by Mr. Percy Hilborn and his family in memory of the late Mrs. Hilborn. Their gift to the Collection, A. Y. Jackson's First Snow, Algoma, *was painted in 1919 and is acknowledged to be this distinguished artist's most important work. So clearly does this gift exemplify the ideals and ultimate success of the McMichael Conservation Collection of Art that it was agreed, in consultation with Signe and Bob McMichael, to symbolize today's official opening by the unveiling of this magnificent painting.*

May I express again to Mr. and Mrs. Robert McMichael, and to all who have supported them in this most worthy and demanding endeavour, the gratitude of every citizen of this great country.

I now take great pleasure, on behalf of the people and Government of Ontario, in officially opening the McMichael Conservation Collection of Art by unveiling the Hilborn family's gift to the gallery — Mr. A. Y. Jackson's First Snow, Algoma.

Signe and I felt the premier's remarks were all the thanks we could possibly want as well as the perfect preface to the climactic moment when he and A. Y. Jackson jointly unveiled the breathtaking canvas, *First Snow, Algoma*!

When the two hundred guests had been received, taken their fill of light refreshments and feasted their eyes on the paintings, most departed with words of praise. Metro Toronto's first chairman, Fred Gardiner (then chairman of its Conservation Authority) mentioned that the display gave him a new and greater appreciation for a small Thomson he owned. Then twenty of those who had had a part in the realization of our dream remained with us for an informal buffet dinner. Together for the first time, and sadly, the last, were almost all of those whose faith had made our dream come true. It is impossible to describe our feelings as we watched Bob Laidlaw chatting with Norah DePencier, the Hilborns with Yvonne Housser, and Thoreau, Jackson and Casson in earnest conversation with Premier Robarts whom, surprisingly, they had never met.

Later I noticed John Robarts and Dick Rohmer grinning broadly in a huddle with Percy Hilborn. The premier motioned me to join them and then revealed that Percy had told them of his wish to give a large, beautiful tract of land located between the nearly adjoining towns of Preston and Galt for the creation of a natural public park. Coming on top of his presentation of *First Snow, Algoma* just a few hours earlier, this was a gift to the Province of incredible generosity. This beautiful piece of unspoiled land became a park, a magnificent public sanctuary in the heart of the towns which are now merged to form the City of Cambridge.

As the sun set across the hills and valleys, our patron saints took their leave one by one and finally we said our farewells to a tired but happy premier who was setting out for his home in London in the familiar limousine bearing the licence plate ONT 1.

Reluctant to end such a perfect day, Signe and I relived the magic hours over a nightcap, both happy and sad that it would be the last time we would be alone in possession of Tapawingo. At our feet, Sam and Inky dozed, blissfully unaware that a new chapter was about to be written in their lives and ours. Tomorrow we would greet the first public visitors — the vanguard of those for whom Tapawingo and our collection had been created.

Saturday's newspaper and television news programmes carried glowing reports of a new and completely different kind of Canadian art gallery, a hilltop lodge of log and stone amid tall pines and sweeping valleys near the Village of Kleinburg, a pleasant half-hour drive from Toronto — open to all beginning this weekend. That was all that was needed to fill our huge parking lot to overflowing. The normally quiet main street of Kleinburg was overrun with the first explorers of the Collection, forerunners of the thousands upon thousands who would make the hamlet as well known as cities many times its size.

After the new AGO had opened, Alex Jackson and I were invited to join Henry Moore as head table guests of the Club of Toronto at the Royal York Hotel. It was a fascinating experience to be present at this historic meeting between Canada's senior painter and England's greatest sculptor. A few weeks after the luncheon we received photographs of the two engaged in happy conversation. Picking up one of the large photographic prints Jackson promptly turned it over and wrote Henry Moore — Sculptor, A. Y. Jackson — Painter. A few years later, when Signe and I were invited to visit Moore at his home in Much Haddem, I gave him the photograph with Alex's engaging inscription.

I shall never forget the lessons Moore taught us as we sat, all eyes and ears, in his rambling country home. As we talked, the great sculptor held the weather-bleached skull of a small animal between his thumb and index finger. Setting it down on a low table beside a small bottle and a pebble, he told us that he often obtained his ideas and forms from such familiar objects. He then led us to a small, adjoining, windowless room whose floor-to-ceiling shelves were crammed with hundreds of common articles ranging from earthenware vases to discarded tools and sea shells. Like a young lad among boyhood treasures randomly collected, Moore beamed at the countless shapes of these simple, everyday things like a king in his counting house. This treasury, he told us, was his idea room. Under Moore's discerning hand and eye, and guided by his unlimited imagination, some of these mundane objects would be transformed into world-famous works of sculpture.

Of course, the metamorphosis was not a simple process. It was natural and usual for him to begin, Moore explained, by making a miniature three-dimensional image of the form that he envisioned, small enough to be held in the palm of his hand. If the small piece proved interesting, an assistant would then make a copy in styrofoam, perhaps five times larger. The artist might then decide to make changes. After that, assuming that the form still appealed to him, the mid-size model would be further enlarged in styrofoam, possibly up to the monumental size of a major work.

In the garden, Mrs. Moore was pruning rose bushes and paused only long enough to give us a cheery smile as her husband led us through the grounds (the size of a golf course) which had been beautifully developed from a pig farm, hence the name "Hoglands". Not far from the house we approached a series of large glass structures, which appeared to be greenhouses standing on their ends. In these huge glass boxes men were working to shape enormous white plastic figures. One day, some of these would be cast in bronze and further refined, with files, by the sculptor himself before they were shipped off to sites in the world's finest parks, squares and buildings.

As we strolled further into the vast park, between clumps of large evergreens, we came upon dramatically placed bronze sculptured forms which struck us with a force that words cannot describe. These overpowering pieces were to be part of Henry Moore's legacy to his own beloved Britain.

Our time with the Moores was far more than a pleasant social visit. It was an opportunity to get to know the humble, yet heroic, man who has had such a profound influence on twentieth-century art and to contemplate first hand his incalculable contribution to our civilization.

In the spring of 1967, we began the task of recreating the ambiance of Tom Thomson's years of living and painting in the little studio cabin. During long talks years earlier with Dr. Arnold Mason, A. Y. Jackson and Thoreau MacDonald, we made notes of the things they remembered and particularly of features they recalled in common. All remembered the easel, the sketches strewn around, his bed on the small balcony and the wood-burning stove. It was Thoreau, whose life had been devoted to drawing old buildings, furnishings and artifacts in minute detail, who recalled the interior with such clarity that he was able to give us a detailed floor plan of furnishings, with which the older men concurred. He recalled the old iron stove so clearly that he was able to make a lovely little ink drawing which illustrated it charmingly and precisely. Paul Duval, who shared our interest in the project, used it to illustrate one of his weekly art columns in the *Toronto Telegram* when he devoted it to the restoration of Thomson's shack. The perfect little drawing was complete down to the model name in raised cast iron, "Pearl", and Paul asked his readers to help us find one of the same vintage.

Within a few days we received a telephone call from a Mr. Bruce Randall of Willowdale. His wife Peggy had read Paul's column and realized that they had an identical stove, a family inheritance, which they were prepared to donate to the Collection.

Tom Thomson had been a stickler for the finest quality in his painting materials and equipment. When he couldn't find or afford precisely the equipment he wanted he often made it with his own hands — as with the quill pens he made himself from turkey feathers. He had constructed his own large studio easel of heavy lumber, carving oak dowels with a penknife for insertion in holes which controlled the level of elevation of canvases of various sizes. On that rugged painting stand some of the greatest works of art created in this country's history took form. After his death, when the executors entered the shack, the sturdy easel held his last, and perhaps greatest, painting, *The West Wind*.

Upon his return to Toronto after his years as a war artist with Canadian troops in World War I, A. Y. Jackson arranged to have Thomson's easel moved to his own third-floor quarters in the Studio Building. From that time until his departure from Severn Street over thirty-five years later, all of Jackson's great canvases were painted on the firm painting frame which Thomson had built with such consummate care.

Jackson left the famous Studio Building after some disagreement with the building's new owner, Gordon MacNamara. Reluctantly, he departed for a small studio apartment near his niece's home in Manotick, a small village near Ottawa.

In January 1955, this last representative of the Group to still be living in the Studio Building had received a letter from Lawren Harris, who had sold the now historic structure in 1948. It read in part:

> *Dear Alex,*
>
> *Given the conditions of 25 Severn Street, I am very glad you are going to move....*
>
> *Your moving from the Studio Building marks the end of an era, the one era of creative art that has the greatest significance for Canada, and you were the real force and inspiration that led all of us into a modern conception which suited this country, and the last to leave the home base of its operations.*
>
> *Yours, Lawren.*

When Jackson left Toronto the old easel remained, perhaps because the artist, now in his mid-seventies, was confining his efforts to smaller canvases and also recognized the more confined space of his new quarters. He arranged to pass the great easel to a younger artist, Jack Nichols, whose work he admired.

A few years later, learning about our rebuilding of the shack at Kleinburg from his friend Keith MacIvor, Nichols called to say that he felt the easel which had played such a prominent role in the art of Canada should now be returned to Tom Thomson's shack.

Following Thomson's death in 1917, his sister Margaret had acquired his large studio palette. It was not merely a flat board with a thumbhole but a large classically shaped palette, bent into a rolling contour which allowed it to rest with perfect comfort over the artist's forearm. Made of the finest wood, it still held hardened globs of the oil pigment which had been used to create the masterpiece, *The West Wind*. Margaret wholeheartedly agreed that the handsome palette should join her brother's easel in the historic shack. Thoreau MacDonald then added some of Thomson's brushes which had been given to his father, J.E.H. MacDonald, by the grateful Thomson family after Tom's death. He also came up with several of Tom's handmade fishing lures, which he had inherited.

These fortuitous windfalls, key artifacts of Thomson's life as a painter, had been tended through decades by people who cared about him. Now they added a vital dimension to our project.

Today the restored shack consists of two rooms, each with an outside entrance. In Thomson's day, the larger was his home and studio; the smaller was used largely for storage and firewood. In restoring it, we attempted to re-create an atmosphere that was as close as possible to Thomson's. For example, a checked wool Mackinaw-type coat hanging on a nail is similar to one he wears in an early photograph. Nevertheless, we tried to remember that Thomson lived in spartan simplicity. We resisted any temptation to be cute.

Stacked casually against the walls are reproduction panels of a number of Thomson's oil sketches and on the easel, the size of the original, is a reproduction of his well-known canvas, *Northern River*.

The smaller storage room was finished in new pine panelling which we make clear to visitors is not of Thomson's time but *is* admirably suited for a display of photographs, drawings, letters, maps and newspaper clippings related to his life and times.

At times the whole project — the restoration and relocation of a derelict shack — seemed almost fanciful. But through the years our fancy has been vindicated by the thousands of Canadians who have felt closer to Canada's greatest artist through a glimpse of Tom Thomson's Shack.

Upper left, Franklin Carmichael. A master of design whose art was as varied as his wide choice of media.

Upper right, A.Y. Jackson with A.J. Casson. The great painting *First Snow, Algoma* forms the backdrop at Kleinburg for a birthday cake filled with ninety years of good wishes.

Bottom, Edwin Holgate and Frederick Varley. Two Group painters who placed people before the wild and untamed land.

Prime Minister Lester Pearson (right) and Mrs. Pearson during a tour of the McMichael Collection personally conducted by the old master himself, A.Y. Jackson.

Walter Stewart with A.Y. Jackson. Collector and artist reminisce over the signature sketch, *Red Maple*, the cornerstone of Stewart's unmatched gift of Jackson paintings to the Collection.

Lawren Harris with A.Y. Jackson. The leader and innovator, Harris possessed a sense of mission which propelled the Group into new realms, geographic and aesthetic.

Above, Premier John Robarts, the godfather of the McMichael Collection, chats with A.Y. Jackson during the opening day celebrations in July 1966.

Right, Dorothy and Charles Matthews with A.Y. Over sixty years ago Chuck Matthews hired Frank Carmichael and Alfred Casson at his commercial art firm. Most of his fine Group paintings were given to the Collection.

This page, Tom Thomson (with a good catch of trout). The legendary artist whose unrivaled paintings of unspoiled wilderness are at the heart of the Collection.

Facing page, left, J.E.H. MacDonald, an outstanding painter who along with his close friend, Tom Thomson, was among the first to capture a true Canadian spirit in his art.

Facing page, right, Arthur Lismer, artist and teacher, whose lively wit captured in cartoons countless amusing moments among his fellow painters of the Group of Seven.

The original Group of Seven at the Arts and Letters Club. Left to right: A.Y. Jackson, Frederick Varley, Franklin Carmichael (photographically inserted) Lawren Harris, Barker Fairley (a non-member friend) Frank Johnston, Arthur Lismer and J.E.H. MacDonald.

Norval Morrisseau (right) with A.J. Casson. Considered to be the father of contemporary Anishnabec art, Morrisseau, through his paintings, dramatically reveals the sacred legends of his people.

Below, Thoreau MacDonald. Shy, warm and sensitive, yet vigorous, talented and witty. Like his namesake, Thoreau was at one with nature and her creations.

Prime Minister Pierre Elliott Trudeau visited the Collection in Kleinburg, and recalled his boyhood days at Canoe Lake where he and his fellow-campers were practically brought up on the lore of Tom Thomson and the Algonquin school of painters.

Margaret and Bill Tweedale (right) with Norah DePencier. The youngest of Tom Thomson's sisters, Margaret inherited twelve magnificent oil panels from her brother's estate, which now form part of the Collection.

Norah DePencier with Naomi Jackson Groves. Another of our generous benefactors, Norah gave us her art treasures long before we achieved our dream of a public collection of Canadian art.

Upper left,
R.S. McLaughlin, a leading Canadian industrialist. Following an impressive gift of paintings to the McMichael Collection, "Mr. Sam" lived to celebrate his one hundredth birthday.

Upper right,
R.A. Laidlaw, one of our Collection's patron saints. His good judgement, his quiet determination and his love of life were as big as his bountiful heart.

Lower left, W. Garfield Weston. With an almost imperceptible wink towards his daughters he turned to me and said, "We will buy the picture for you." (Tom Thomson's *Woodland Waterfall*, $285,000.)

Lower right,
Dr. A.D.A. Mason gave J.E.H. MacDonald's magnificent *Leaves in the Brook* to the Collection. Given to him by the artist for services rendered, he felt the picture represented the most expensive dentist's bill in history.

4

Those who would become successful collectors must develop one skill very early in their collecting careers — the ability to see through dirt!

Most of the works we sought had been painted between forty and sixty years earlier. While this is not a long time as the ages of fine paintings go, it was long enough for paintings in city rooms, often hung over fireplaces, to give the impression that they were being viewed through smoked glass. Colours which were once brilliant and vibrant seemed murky and lifeless, appearing as unrecognizable monotones. Strangely enough, this gradual veiling often went unnoticed by the pictures' owners. Fortunately, Signe and I were both endowed with sufficient visual imagination that we could foresee the splendour which would emerge with a cleaning by an expert conservator.

As a result of endless research through old exhibition catalogues, discussions with the artists, their families and friends and, often just pure good luck, we were able to locate pictures (and their owners) long hidden from public attention. Close study of literally thousands of works in public collections, art dealers' showrooms and private hands, coupled with intense scrutiny of the artist's life, travels, changes of genre, favoured sizes and variations as well as the painting and support media used (and deviations from them) gave us confidence in our ability to distinguish authentic works from those that were merely "in the manner of".

Oil paintings usually have a light coat of clear varnish applied to their surfaces shortly after their completion. This varnish will absorb most of the atmospheric dirt which might threaten the painting, but the varnish itself tends to take on a light brown colour with age. In extreme cases the combination of dirt and discoloured varnish can make a painting unrecognizable. Fortunately, a competent restorer can quite easily remove all of the varnish, and with it the grime, without affecting the original oil paint.

Dirt on paintings did not bother us — we expected it and recognized it as an indication of age. Conversely, we were often suspicious of paintings of the early or pre-Group period which appeared to be quite clean. In most cases such pictures had indeed been cleaned, but not always with happy results. We learned to look closely for the telltale signs of an amateur restorer who would invariably leave traces of dirt, usually most noticeable on the shoulders of heavily impastoed paint strokes.

A more important and potentially disastrous clue was any sign of "scrubbing" — an incompetent attempt to clean which had removed paint, particularly in thinly painted areas, and scaled off the peaks of heavily painted strokes. If the painting had had any tendency to flake, an amateur restorer would have unwittingly removed loose areas of paint, often a complete desecration.

Such damage can be skilfully impainted by an expert conservator and usually the repairs will not be detectable to the naked eye. Nevertheless, the painting must be considered flawed to a degree dependent on the amount of original paint removed. The new paint can always be easily detected under a black light, an indispensable tool for most galleries and conservators.

In the tricky field of identification for authenticity, experts will almost always base a major part of their conclusions on their first visual impression of a work. Is it "right"? At first viewing an expert naturally looks at subject, composition, paint handling, colour and any number of known traits and mannerisms associated with the putative artist or an imitator whose works may bear similarities to the work in question.

If the question is, for example, whether a painting is by Tom Thomson or an imitator, the art detective's work becomes much more focussed. But with this hypothesis he should not lose sight of other fine artists who were associated with Thomson and could have been briefly influenced, perhaps even unconsciously, by the great artist. During Thomson's most important painting years, from 1914 to 1917, he and most of his close friends — MacDonald, Lismer, Harris, Carmichael, Varley, Beatty and Jackson — all painted on solid birch painting panels, identical in size, approximately eight-and-a-half by ten-and-a-half inches. In fact, it was Jackson who had brought this wooden panel size back with him after his student years in Europe. In these same crucial years the artists had all painted in Algonquin Provincial Park or in very similar country nearby. Their hills and lakes, rocks and vegetation often appeared much alike. Their composition and colour had inherent similarities. These were formative years and the young artists were all experimenting. Moreover, they subscribed to a common creed: they were all determined to break with European tradition and paint their country in a distinctively Canadian way. Almost all of them used unmixed pure colour directly from the tube. At the time this was considered a daring departure.

Even in the early years, from 1914 to 1920, the little band of painters had serious followers, reasonably competent painters who, consciously or unconsciously, were so excited by the new approach to Canadian art that they adopted it, sometimes slavishly. By the 1920s and 1930s countless aspiring painters, mostly amateur unknowns, but some with training and skill, were innocently producing panels in the manner of the Group and Thomson. Some of these were so similar that years later, in less than honest expert hands, they would be offered and accepted as original works of the Group.

Signatures on paintings, though quickly accepted by unsophisticated buyers, often mean very little. Thomson very seldom signed his panels and MacDonald, for example, frequently initialled his panels with a simple and easily forged "J.M.". However, MacDonald and some others frequently made notes on the backs of their panels in pencil or ink, usually indicating the locale and date, in their own handwriting. Such notes are invaluable evidence for the expert and seldom appear on pieces that are not authentic.

Shortly after Thomson's death in 1917, J.E.H. MacDonald, recognizing the possibility of confusion and misattribution in later years, designed a circular estate identification stamp bearing the initials "T.T." and the year 1917, which he affixed to as many of Thomson's panels as he could locate. Each panel was stamped on the back in ink and many have the stamp also impressed in the lower left corner of the painted side. In some cases, the paint was too dry and an attempt to impress the steel die left an unattractive, almost paintless circle of board showing. When this became apparent, MacDonald and his son Thoreau prudently discontinued marking the painting side except when they were quite sure that the paint was malleable. After J.E.H. MacDonald's death in 1932, Thoreau designed a similar stamp bearing his father's initials and year of death and marked many of the senior MacDonald's oil panels.

Admirable as the intent was, the indentification stamps were easily copied. During the 1950s and 1960s, some crude and some excellent forgeries of the stamps began appearing on forged or misattributed works offered as original Thomsons or MacDonalds.

Support media can be a giveaway clue. Through the early years Thomson, MacDonald, Jackson and others were known to use solid birch panels or panels of grey bookbinders' board, which they obtained from the firm of Warrick Brothers and Rutter Limited. Panels purported to be Thomsons or the early work of other Group members, which are painted on plywood, are immediately suspect. Yet even this evidence is not conclusive, since the expert who has done his homework knows that Thomson, MacDonald and Jackson briefly experimented with quarter-inch plywood in 1914. (They soon rejected it when its surface was seen to be prone to checking, probably as a result of the imperfect lamination techniques which were used for this newly developed product, or because the wood veneer had been improperly cured.) The relatively few authentic oil panels that have survived from this period usually have fine, straight check marks through the paint surface and can be dated 1914 with reasonable certainty.

Notwithstanding strong physical and visual evidence, a perfect, or at least good, provenance (the picture's history of owners through the years back to the hand of the artist) is virtually indisputable evidence of its authenticity and is of paramount importance in authenticating a work, especially one which may be atypical of the artist's known works.

An outstanding example of this is a fine canvas in the Collection entitled *Gambit No. 1*, painted by Franklin Carmichael. It is a totally abstract, non-objective painting consisting entirely of geometric shapes, and is completely unlike any known work by this member of the original Group. It was painted very near the end of Carmichael's life and is undoubtedly the only full-size, non-objective work he ever completed. It was presented to me, acting on behalf of the Collection, by the artist's only child, Mrs. Mary

Mastin. Needless to say, despite its complete lack of Carmichael's known mannerisms, its authenticity is not in doubt.

I have been asked many times how a person buying a work of art can be quite certain that the work is authentic. Unless they are acquiring it from a living artist or the artist's family, I have always recommended that purchasers should deal only with art dealers whose reputations are known to be impeccable and that they should ask for the provenance of the work. If this is not readily available, the purchaser should, at the very least, be given the name and address of the immediate past owner. This may not prove conclusive but it does provide a starting point from which to pursue the history, and possibly establish the authenticity, of a prospective purchase.

After that first meeting with Margaret and Bill Tweedale years earlier when Tapawingo was just beginning, Signe and I returned again and again to the Tweedale house on Glenlake Avenue. After 1959 we remained frequent visitors to their new home, a modern bungalow in a newly developed section of Etobicoke, then the city's most westerly suburb. Although he was partially crippled with arthritis, Bill could still drive his car and their new proximity to a major road to the north, Highway 27, made visits to Kleinburg much easier.

Margaret's twelve magnificent oil panels by her brother Tom Thomson were more than ample reason for our frequent visits to Etobicoke. We soon realized, though, that our growing collection of paintings by Thomson and his fellow painters was becoming equally fascinating to her as she approached her eighties with undiminished vigour. Margaret's memories of her famous artist brother, his personal traits, his love of nature and many of the events surrounding his mysterious disappearance and death were as vivid and clear as though they had been recent events.

Margaret had many fond recollections of Tom, the second oldest among nine sisters and brothers, of which she was second youngest. The family was widely scattered, but several members were still living and through her we came to know her oldest brother George, then in his nineties, who lived in Owen Sound, and Fraser, the youngest, who worked in a Toronto haberdashery.

With Margaret and Bill we made several visits to Owen Sound, which was not far from the family's original home at Leith. After visits with old friends, many of whom had known Tom, and a call at the old Thomson farm and the graveyard at Leith, we usually made our way to George's home for a hearty dinner and long talks with the old man. George was a well-known and prolific painter of considerable competence whose pictures sold widely through Toronto dealers. By both age and inclination he was probably closest of any of the family to his brother Tom.

In July of 1917 it was George who had travelled by train to Canoe Lake, Algonquin Park, when the great wilderness artist was reported to be missing. It was also George who, a week or so later, made arrangements with the undertaker to have Tom's body brought to Leith when he learned it had been hastily interred in a tiny cemetery at Canoe Lake.

When I visited Tom's grave at Leith with his sister and brother, George told me how he had made the small tombstone and pointed out how he had filled the letters etched in the stone with lead because he felt that was the material which would be most impervious to erosion.

For years that seemed about as close to a discussion of Tom's death and burial as George, Margaret or Fraser were prepared to go. Whenever the conversation strayed close to the subject, Margaret would grow quiet and gently remind us of the anguish which the Thomson family had suffered in 1917 over her brother's mysterious disappearance and death. That pain, she said, had been greatly exacerbated by the rumours, charges of foul play, doubts about the burial place and, above all, speculation and newspaper reports about her brother's "murder".

A four-inch bruise or gash on the right side of the temple had been used to support theories that Tom Thomson had been struck with a canoe paddle by an unknown assailant. The fact that one of Thomson's paddles was missing was put forward as further evidence of foul play. When the body was recovered on July 17, 1917, eight days after Thomson had been last seen, it was reported that fishing line had been tied many times around his left leg and that there was no water in his lungs. To make matters worse, there was also a controversy about Thomson's true place of burial.

Thomson was not yet forty years old and apparently in good health, an expert woodsman and canoeist, and a good swimmer. Inevitably, his death on the lake he knew so well gave rise to considerable suspicion and speculation. It had all the ingredients for a mystery which would eventually become part of the country's folklore.

All of these mysteries should be considered against the background of the times. Without telephones, Algonquin Park in 1917 was considered to be very remote and communications were correspondingly slow. It was summer and facilities were primitive so it is hardly surprising that Thomson's body had been buried at Canoe Lake just hours before his family's instructions to send it to Leith were received. When George learned of the burial he arranged for a man named Churchill, an undertaker from nearby Huntsville, to disinter it and it was duly shipped to the family. Yet the story that Thomson was really buried in a tiny hilltop cemetery at Canoe Lake persisted. One reason for this persistence was the statement by Mark Robinson, a local park ranger who was a friend of the artist's, that he had not known of the exhumation until he had seen a casket loaded on the train. Shannon Fraser, proprietor of Mowat Lodge, was known to have taken the undertaker and casket to the grave site in a horse-drawn carriage at sunset and returned at the undertaker's request to transport undertaker and casket back to Mowat Lodge later that evening. Robinson and Fraser maintained that since Churchill had worked alone, by lantern light, the body could not have been removed and transferred to the casket in such a short time. Neither had seen the actual exhumation and both insisted they knew no one who had.

These speculations were widely discussed and through the years came to be accepted as something between fact and legend. The macabre story surrounding Thomson's burial place refused to die.

In her 1935 book *Tom Thomson*, the first biography of the artist, Blodwen Davies concludes somewhat melodramatically:

> *And so mystery laid its imprint upon the seal of Thomson's death — and the seal has not yet been broken. All that was earthly of Tom Thomson was lowered into a sandy grave in the country that he loved and the broken turf was covered with wild flowers. No one who knew Tom Thomson ever looked upon his face again. Legend in the north says that he still lies on the brink of the hill overlooking Canoe Lake.*

Blodwen Davies was not the only author to accept Shannon Fraser's theories as fact. During the 1920s, Fraser repeated the story of his visits to a number of people and confirmed it to Judge William T. Little in 1930. In 1953 Mark Robinson taped his recollections (apparently confirmed by his meticulous diary for 1917) in which he stated his belief that the body had never been moved.

The unearthing of a skull, with a hole at the temple, and metal casket hardware from the tiny cemetery at Canoe Lake in the autumn of 1956 by a group which included Judge Little was reported in newspaper articles across Canada. Once again there was speculation that Thomson's body had not been removed from Algonquin Park in 1917.

On October 19, 1956 the Toronto *Globe and Mail* reported under the headline "Bones at Canoe Lake Not Those of Artist":

> *... Scientific investigation has established that a skeleton dug up by amateur artists in an unmarked Algonquin Park grave was not that of the great Canadian painter, Tom Thomson, who died thirty-nine years ago. Attorney General Roberts said yesterday it had definitely been determined that the remains were not Thomson's but those of a male Indian or half-breed of about thirty years of age...."*

Yet far from putting the mystery to rest, this publicity added fuel to the fires of speculation and re-opened old wounds for the remaining Thomson family members.

In 1970, publication of *The Tom Thomson Mystery*, by William T. Little, gave the burial controversy new credibility. The respected judge, for years a summer resident at Canoe Lake, deals briefly with Thomson's life and art and his mysterious death. The greater part of the book is dedicated to what the author perceives as the second mystery, the location of Thomson's final resting place. Surprisingly, Judge Little suggests in his conclusion that Thomson's grave at Leith should be opened. More surprisingly still, he states:

> *The mystery attending Tom Thomson's death and subsequent burial will never be solved short of an official opening of the Thomson family plot at the United Church Cemetery at Leith. In this grave lies the secret surrounding not only the location of his body, but possibly the facts regarding his premature death. Regardless of whether this action is ever taken, a large number of Canadians will feel that he was a man dedicated to portraying the truth and beauty of his adopted home, Algonquin Park. Many of them will be satisfied that his remains are located where he would want to be — in a simple grave in the Park.*

Had William Little attempted to interview any of Thomson's surviving sisters or brothers on the subject of the long ago interments, he would undoubtedly have met the same stoical silence and distaste that Signe and I sensed whenever conversation threatened to approach the painful subject. Accordingly, one evening in 1968, after dinner at the Tweedale's, we were astonished when Margaret deliberately brought up the subject herself.

Very calmly she told us that she and her immediate family had strongly resented the rumours and malicious stories, particularly those which cast doubt on the fact that Tom was buried in the church cemetery at Leith. Her parents and her sisters and brothers had always known for certain that Tom was buried there and had steadfastly refused to be drawn into any discussion of what they felt was a very private family matter. They hoped that by refusing to comment they would lay the rumours to rest and bring to an end the speculation that seemed determined to make more of Tom's death than of his remarkable life.

The evening before Thomson's burial at Leith, she told us, his coffin was placed in the family parlour by an Owen Sound undertaker. In addition to Tom's parents and four of his sisters and brothers, Elizabeth, Margaret, George and Fraser, a neighbour and close friend, John McKeen, was present.

John Thomson, Tom's father, asked that the coffin be opened. Although the undertaker was reluctant to do so because the body had been in the water for eight days, Mr. Thomson insisted.

A solder seal was broken and the coffin was opened in the presence of Tom's father and his friend John McKeen. Both men readily identified the body and, although shaken, John Thomson expressed relief that Tom's body had come home. From the time the casket had been opened briefly, Margaret recalled, an unmistakable, musty odour pervaded the room.

Several years after Margaret Thomson Tweedale's death in 1979, I learned that the facts she had recounted had been independently corroborated by two Owen Sound women who had been childhood neighbours of the Thomsons. Misses Agnes and Margaret McKeen recalled clearly Thomson's burial in 1917 and the circumstances of the opening of his coffin and the positive identification of the body which had been reported to them by their cousin, John McKeen.

In 1969, both women made a statement which corresponded exactly with the one Margaret Tweedale made to Signe and me and which was recorded by their niece, Catherine McKeen, also of Owen Sound.

During the fifty years from her brother's death to 1967, Margaret turned down innumerable offers for any or all of the twelve magnificent Tom Thomson panels she had inherited. They had been painted by the artist at the peak of his career. There were times in the more than ten years that we had known her well when I had been sorely tempted to try to negotiate a sale with her, since I felt ours was a unique situation. With hindsight I realize how wise Signe was to dissuade me from anything that might have caused Margaret embarrassment and cast a shadow over our friendship.

By 1966, the Collection was open to the public and was proudly displaying no fewer than twenty-six Thomsons, including those we had received from Bob Laidlaw and Norah DePencier. Instead of being satisfied with this impressive showing, I became obsessed with a desire to acquire still more of my favourite artist's paintings. I was determined that one day we should present at Kleinburg the largest permanently hanging exhibit of Tom Thomson works to be seen anywhere. Margaret's twelve panels were, I knew, the key to achieving that goal, and as the years passed I began to worry about her long-range plans for the works.

Even though she and Bill had no children, people of their generation usually felt very strongly about family ties and Margaret had many nieces and nephews as well as great-nieces and great-nephews. During our long chats it was almost inevitable that talk would turn to the future of the panels, but nothing definite ever emerged. We were not sure, in fact, that Margaret even had a will. She did tell us how disappointed she had been to learn that the sons and daughters of her now dead sisters and brothers had almost all sold the panels by Tom that they had inherited. While she recognized their right, and sometimes even the necessity, to make these sales, such dispositions made her realize that there was little use in trying to keep some of the artist's best work in family hands.

We agreed with her conclusion but had no inkling what her solution to the problem would be until one evening in November 1966, when we had settled in the living room after one of Margaret's excellent dinners. With the same calmness with which she was pouring tea, Margaret said very quietly, "I would like you to pick out your favourite of Tom's pictures to add to your collection."

I caught a slightly mischievous twinkle in her eye. She knew she had taken me completely by surprise.

"I can't part with this one yet," Margaret continued, indicating the *Wildflowers* panel, "but I'm sure after all these years you must know the one you like most among the others."

She was right, but years of looking at the panels, all hand-picked from the finest work of Thomson's last great years, had not fully prepared me to make a single selection instantly. I could see that she and Bill were enjoying my confusion as I looked from one stunning panel to another. Yet I found my eyes returning again and again to the one that Signe and I had always said we loved most, *Black Spruce in Autumn*.

The stunning landscape embodied everything we admired most in Tom Thomson's work. Soaring dark silhouettes of ragged spruce stand as gateposts on jutting headlands which form a narrows in the long lake. Beyond, like a vast stage bathed in full light, stretches a densely forested autumn hillside resplendent in crimson-orange. Above all is the overwhelming sky. Immense billows of stratocumulus cloud reach hungrily upwards, their enormous masses threatening to devour a patch of sunlit blue. The ominous approaching wall of cloud has its own swirling energy in paint, trowelled with a broad, paint-loaded brush onto the board.

Seen by few until Margaret Tweedale donated it to the Collection, *Black Spruce in Autumn* became one of the artist's most admired panels. In 1970, it was selected to be the frontispiece for Peter Mellen's *The Group of Seven*, the most important book on the lives and art of the Group ever published. In 1977 that other magnificent panel, *Wildflowers*, which by then was also in the McMichael Collection, was selected for the same position of honour in the most important book published on Tom Thomson, *The Silence and the Storm*, by Harold Town and David P. Silcox.

After my permanent return from the United States and to an even greater degree after our collection was opened to the public in 1966, we made no attempt to separate our private lives from the joys and demands of the Collection. Most of our close friendships had come about through our passion for Canadian art. The Cassons, Thoreau MacDonald, Norah DePencier, Bob Laidlaw, the Tweedales, Yvonne Housser and Isabel McLaughlin were frequent visitors, as were sculptresses Frances Loring and Elizabeth Wyle, and former occupants of Thomson's shack, Keith and Edith MacIvor.

Others, like media personality Betty Kennedy, sales executive Jennings Young and senior government official Dr. Keith Reynolds became friends and, in turn, serious Canadian art collectors, as did our niece Penny and her husband Dr. Jack Fenwick of Montreal. A. Y. Jackson was a house guest for several days each year although we had as yet no inkling that he would one day be a member of our "family".

All of these friends were, of course, aware of our search for a major Thomson canvas as were Thomson relatives and his fellow painters. We searched old records, books and catalogues and enlisted the aid of art dealers, public galleries, longtime collectors and anyone else who was willing to listen or whom we thought might have a lead.

Repeatedly the same names came up, a short list of people who were believed to own a Thomson. Yet locating the paintings brought us only one step closer to ownership since nearly all were held by individual collectors or private organizations who, we felt, were unlikely to part with their treasures for any amount of money. To add to our difficulties, by the late 1960s, dealers, collectors and galleries from St. John's to Victoria were competing for Thomsons and the other Group paintings, offering prices that were, until then, unheard of for Canadian art.

One of the most avid and determined collectors was Toronto financier Allan Manford. In the mid-1960s, when I first met him, he had already begun collecting works by Thomson, Milne and members of the Group. Although he had few direct connections with the artists, their families or very early collectors, he made it known through the Canadian art grapevine that he was prepared to pay the highest prices for the paintings he wanted. He told me very frankly that his collecting strategy was based on his successful stock market manoeuvers — he was always prepared to offer more money than other bidders. As news of his purchases spread, he was offered paintings which we had been told were considered sacrosanct by their owners. (One such painting was the major J.E.H. MacDonald canvas, *Rowanberries*, from the collection of the Right Honourable Vincent Massey.)

From time to time Signe and I were invited to cocktail parties and dinners at the Manfords' home in Toronto. It was hard not to be envious when nearly every visit showed us new acquisitions — almost always works by our favourite artists. Manford's strategy was hard to fault but impossible for us, with our limited budget, to copy.

At one point, to flush out hidden owners, Manford prepared small anonymous advertisements offering to buy privately owned works by members of the Group of Seven, Tom Thomson and David Milne. One such ad in the *New York Times* prompted an answer from Charles McDermott, with whom I shared my New York apartment. He had no intention of selling, but was curious enough to respond and to confirm, as I had believed, that the advertiser was Manford.

This advertising programme actually did pay off. One letter came from a little old lady who claimed to have a Tom Thomson canvas. Manford was skeptical but followed through anyway — and hit the jackpot. The lady did indeed have a small eighteen by twenty inch Thomson, obviously authentic. Manford bought it at once. This single response more than justified his advertising programme.

For some time I had known that the Hamilton, Ontario collector, Roy Cole, had at least one Tom Thomson canvas, *Woodland Waterfall*. Cole lived alone and kept most of his collection in a bank vault. Though we'd made discreet enquiries, we'd never managed to view it.

We were, therefore, astounded when an invitation to cocktails at Manford's revealed that he was now the owner of *Woodland Waterfall*. As we studied the picture and the unerring strokes of Thomson's brush, we realized it was of the same monumental scale as his best-known master works, *The Jack Pine* and *The West Wind*. Our admiration for the painting was mixed with envy and apprehension because we believed this might well be the last large Thomson to change hands in our time.

We felt sad that we might never acquire a major canvas by the painter we most admired. At that moment we made a decision. We would follow up every Thomson canvas on the list that we had so painstakingly prepared until we had a definite yes or no to each offer.

Like millions of others, we celebrated our country's one hundredth birthday with a visit to Expo '67 in Montreal in the summer of 1967. There being literally no room at the inns we were happy to accept an invitation to stay with Penny and Jack Fenwick.

Even on holiday, the Collection was never far from our minds, so we took this opportunity to get in touch with a Quebec family, the Porters. From an old exhibition catalogue we had learned of a canvas that had been purchased many years earlier from Toronto's Laing Gallery by Porter which we believed was still owned by his widow. She was listed as living in the family home at St. Andrews East and we were able to phone and arrange to see her at her home the following Sunday.

Alma Porter and her son Tupper welcomed us to their large country home. Their extensive collection of paintings by the Group and their contemporaries was hung in several rooms that seemed almost like a private gallery. After a brief tour we settled into their comfortable living room. Above the mantlepiece was Tom Thomson's canvas, *Saplings*.

Until that moment we had seen only that small black and white reproduction of *Saplings* in the catalogue. The original hit us with the full force of Thomson's magic — his uncanny ability to transform a simple, unlikely subject into a powerful work of art. A clump of hardwood saplings on a wilderness slope had become the linear elements of a forceful and controlled composition, a living mass of crimson, gold and green, firmly structured around a tensile screen of young, skeletal tree forms. That the artist should have chosen to paint such an apparently mediocre thicket seems surprising. Yet his tough sense of design, combined with a self-assured, aggressive application of pure colour, had wrung a work of visual intensity from the uninspiring copse. It was little short of astonishing.

The Porters were aware that we had opened our gallery to the public a year earlier, so they were not surprised at my special interest in their painting. Over the years, they told us, dealers and other serious collectors had been interested, but until recently they had not seriously considered selling their most important picture. In fact, they were at that moment considering an offer from a large corporation which had been made through a well-known Montreal dealer.

From our discussions it became clear that Tupper Porter was in charge of negotiations and that he favoured a sale of the painting. It was equally clear that the time for dealing was now. After a fifteen-minute huddle with him I obtained a thirty-day option with the understanding that I would leave him a cheque which would cover the price of the painting in the event of loss or destruction, or be payment in full if our option was exercised. This was because we would be permitted to take the picture to Kleinburg for the option period. My hand shook as I filled out a cheque for fifty thousand dollars, praying silently that our bank manager in Toronto would accept a telephoned pledge of collateral the following morning.

Now I faced a real dilemma!

Although I had a bird more or less in hand, there was another in the bush. There was another major Thomson canvas on our list which I had always believed to be the finest of those not owned by public institutions. Since the possibility of purchasing it seemed remote, we had not yet really pursued it.

One thing was certain. If by chance, the particular canvas we had in mind could be bought, there was no way we could afford it and *Saplings* too.

The magnificent canvas, *The Birch Grove, Autumn*, was owned by the Hamilton Club, whose art committee had purchased it for the club's private quarters about twenty years earlier, when prices were still depressed. We believed they had paid about six thousand dollars.

Now we knew the price would be at least that of our option price for *Saplings*, if not more. Acquiring either one would be the largest single financial outlay on art we had ever made. Either purchase would put a great strain on our personal financial resources, an expenditure that we would certainly never be able to repeat. Nevertheless, we were now fully committed — we wanted the best that money could buy.

I had always been reluctant to approach the venerable Hamilton Club, but in view of our new circumstances, it was now or never!

Suspecting that a head-on approach might be met with a curt refusal, I decided instead to talk with Joseph Pigott, chairman of the art committee which had purchased *Birch Grove, Autumn* almost two decades earlier. To my surprise, a telephone call to his office produced a prompt connection and an appointment to meet at his office in the Pigott Building in two days.

At this first meeting I gave my enthusiasm full reign as I outlined the concept and purposes of the Collection, now in its second year of growing pains under public ownership. I complimented him and his committee on the foresight that had led them to buy *Birch Grove* and made no attempt to depreciate its importance. In fact, I pointed out it was a national treasure which I felt should be viewed and enjoyed by hundreds of thousands of people, particularly school classes, not restricted to often casual glances by a select few.

I asked him whether he felt the Hamilton Club's executive might consider selling *Birch Grove* for the larger public benefit and told him that we would be willing to purchase it personally for permanent inclusion in the Collection, at a figure many times that of the original purchase price. This, I continued, would permit the Club to replace it with one or more fine paintings which would probably be equally enjoyed by the members.

Joseph Pigott looked thoughtful.

"Frankly, I don't think many of our members would miss it too much," he said. "It's very seldom mentioned. Some of them may realize it's important, but I'm inclined to think they wouldn't stand in the way of it going to a public art gallery ... particularly one devoted largely to Thomson and the Group. Also, new pictures might have considerable appeal for a lot of the members."

Then, getting down to practical considerations, we discussed price. He seemed surprised when I told him it would be worth at least fifty thousand dollars, possibly more.

He believed the painting was insured for much less than that and concluded that our offer might be very well received. I was happy to follow his suggestion that I leave the approach to him so he could discuss it privately with a few of the people who would make the final decision.

A few days later he called to ask for more detailed information about the McMichael Conservation Collection of Art. Our first catalogue, with a text by Paul Duval that included a brief history, had been published only a month or two earlier. I promptly delivered a copy and included a photocopy of the Agreement under which the Collection had been established as Ontario's first provincially owned cultural facility.

Our second meeting was brief, but I became convinced that Joseph Pigott was exerting all of his considerable influence to persuade his fellow Hamilton Club officers that *Birch Grove* should become a part of the Collection in Kleinburg.

In order to be able to answer other questions about the gallery, the following day Joseph Pigott and his wife Yvonne, an art enthusiast, came to Kleinburg.

The Collection building now consisted of four large gallery rooms on the main floor with three more, plus our library, on the lower level. We had added a second large addition to the building the year before. In addition to the four new gallery rooms it provided third-floor living accommodation, which inevitably became known as "the attic". Here we lived in two rooms, with a closet-sized kitchenette and even smaller bath.

Yet there were pleasant diversions. In the evenings, after our tiny staff and the visiting public had departed, we could stroll in the unspoiled woods with our black Labradors, Sam and Inky, or take a dip in our thirty-foot indoor swimming pool. The pool was more than a luxury. We had built it in the first (1963) addition to our home and it was designed to be a reservoir in case of fire as well as for its more obvious benefits. Also, instead of the usual exhaust fans to outdoors, a series of ducts directed to the gallery rooms provided ample humidity during the winter months.

The Pigotts explored every area of the gallery, frequently returning to linger over favourite pictures. By the time their visit was over, Joe Pigott had graduated from intermediary to advocate for our cause.

In the days that followed, Pigott met individually with members of the Hamilton Club's executive and art committee and then called a formal committee meeting. After several anxious days he asked me to come to his office again. He came directly to the point: "All the committee members, save one, favour accepting your offer. While I would like to have had unanimity, the overwhelming majority feel that the picture should be seen and enjoyed by a much larger number of people, as it certainly would be in your gallery. It will be on the agenda of the full committee meeting next Wednesday. In the meantime, I would appreciate receiving a formal offer to purchase in writing. We all felt your offer of fifty thousand dollars was very fair — I might even say generous. However, I'm sure you understand that we need something on paper before we can call for a vote."

Driving back to Kleinburg my spirits, like my car, were in overdrive. Two weeks before we had had an impossible dream. Now we needed only a formal majority vote for that dream to become a reality. And that seemed a sure thing!

That evening we talked into the small hours, trying to think of some way we could retain the lovely *Sapling* canvas, on which our option was running out, and also purchase the superlative *Birch Grove*. Acquiring the *Birch Grove* would be a notable victory. Obtaining both of these major Thomson canvases would be an unparalleled triumph!

We were tempted to discuss our dilemma with John Robarts, but we had assured him in good faith that the Province would not be called upon to provide funds for the purchase of paintings. We thought of calling Bob Laidlaw but could not bring ourselves to pick up the telephone. Although he had given his own cherished Thomson panels, it was quite another matter to ask for fifty thousand dollars, especially since, in 1967, we could not even offer a tax receipt as those were not available to donors of art. We came to a decision. We could not ask either of these benefactors to do more.

At the same time we knew our personal credit with the bank was now stretched beyond any former limits. We could not sell our remaining securities since we were dependent on them for our living expenses and we had given the Ontario government a firm commitment to work full time for the Collection without pay.

Nor, after our enthusiastic persuasion, could we expect the Porter family or the Hamilton Club to wait in limbo with the hope that in a year or two we could raise the necessary money from small donors.

Reluctantly we came to a painful conclusion. We were willing to bite deeply into our personal resources for the fifty thousand dollars to pay for *The Birch Grove*. But there was no way we could donate both paintings. *Saplings* would have to be returned to the Porter family. (We were sure they would have no trouble finding a buyer. Very shortly after, it was snapped up by dealer Blair Laing, who had originally sold it to Mr. Porter. He acquired it for his private collection, with no intention of reselling, and to this day it hangs on the wall of his Toronto apartment.)

While we waited for the Hamilton Club vote we often took an evening stroll from one gallery room to another, full of happy anticipation as we surveyed the walls, seeking the most prominent location for *Birch Grove*.

Wednesday and the vote finally came. After our weeks of discussions and waiting, the day seemed to drag out. Even though we considered our acquisition of the picture a virtual *fait accompli*, I found by late afternoon that I could think of nothing but the expected telephone call.

When it finally came, I was immediately apprehensive. The voice was unfamiliar.

"Mr. Joseph Pigott has asked me to call you." Now I was certain that something had gone wrong. "The Hamilton Club committee met this afternoon to discuss your proposal ... and nearly all of our committee members favoured its acceptance."

A slight pause. I waited for the axe to fall.

"However ... one committee member, Mr. Roy Cole, whom I believe you know, has made a rather startling counter-proposal, which I feel certain you will realize is almost impossible for us to refuse ... he has made an offer to buy the painting at the same price as you have offered and to then present it to the Art Gallery of Hamilton."

My response was stunned silence. Then I asked, "Will he present it immediately?"

"That same thought occurred to us. The committee intends to make it a written condition of the sale. Mr. Pigott and I honestly can't see any way the club can refuse ... unless of course you might wish to increase your offer substantially ... in which case he naturally expects to have the opportunity to match your new offer ... I'm awfully sorry...."

Sick at heart, I said I would call the next day.

Even hearing only one side of the conversation, Signe knew something had gone seriously awry. The details hardly mattered. That evening we reviewed the problem from every possible angle, but no amount of discussion could change the facts.

We were living on five percent interest from the government bonds in which we had invested our savings. Two or three years earlier, our capital and income had seemed ample for a comfortable, if not luxurious, life. Now, with accelerating inflation, it appeared much less adequate. We had asked to be appointed unpaid curators of the Collection. While it was an arrangement we never regretted, we were working full time and more. There was no extra hour, even on weekends, for gainful employment. It didn't take an accountant to show us we could really not afford a fifty thousand dollar painting. Certainly we were in no position to become involved in even higher bidding.

There was another compelling consideration. Although we had put the wheels in motion for the sale of *Birch Grove*, Roy Cole had made an apparently selfless offer which would make the painting available to the public but keep it in Tiger Cat territory. Even if we could afford to raise the ante, there was no assurance we would win the prize. It might appear that we were merely determined to make Roy Cole's gift more difficult.

Our frustration was compounded because we knew that Cole had sold Tom Thomson's *Woodland Waterfall* to Allan Manford, presumably to pay for his donation of *Birch Grove* to the Hamilton Gallery in memory of his parents.

It was devastating to realize that in little more than a month three major Thomson canvases which might have been ours had changed hands, possibly for the last time. And we had come up empty-handed.

From the very outset we have always thought of the rugged-hewn log and stone structures on our woodland hilltop as a home, designed to display — in the most appropriate of settings — a special few of Canada's painters and Native artisans whose creations were inspired by our nation's earth and the distinctive natural forms that sprang from it. In the midst of this unabashed tribute to our nation, we wanted also to present periodic exhibitions of younger artists who were making contributions to our culture. Accordingly, we set aside one of the gallery rooms that had recently been added to Tapawingo for this purpose.

Our first such exhibition featured magnificent watercolour paintings of birds by a young West Coast artist, Fenwick Lansdowne. Fen, and our friend Bud Feheley, visited with us in Kleinburg many times in the 1950s and 1960s and we believed that this largely self-taught artist had a very special talent. (Signe and I had, in fact, purchased three of his paintings five years earlier.)

When he was a child, Fen suffered a bad bout of polio, which left him paralyzed from the waist down. Barred from so many normal activities of childhood when he was growing up in Victoria, British Columbia, he had started to draw birds. His extraordinary powers of observation led him to a very personal style characterized by the perfection of its ornithological detail. Using the "skins" of birds which had died striking the windows of friends' and neighbours' homes, Fen was able to study the sizes, colours and shapes of feathers, beaks and talons. He also grasped every opportunity to visit nearby woods and meadows to observe the birds in flight or perched within range of a treasured pair of inexpensive binoculars.

The resulting impressions were produced with enormous attention to detail in the figure of the bird but with little or no background. Fen's birds were in flight or perched on limbs, foliage, rocks and stumps which also were used to their fullest artistic values. So detailed were his birds that admirers remarked that you could not only feel the feathers but the individual hairs of the feathers. The lifelike realism of Fen's work soon attracted buyers among his friends and neighbours who were happy to pay small sums for his paintings. Unfortunately, the Lansdownes were in very modest circumstances and the meagre return for pictures that often took a week or more to complete did not even cover the cost of fine watercolour paper, much less painting materials and Fen's everyday expenses. It appeared inevitable that the young artist would have to find a regular job, thus curtailing his painting and the daylight hours he could spend observing birds.

Around 1958, a few of Fen's paintings came to the attention of Bud Feheley. Bud visited Lansdowne in Victoria and saw at once the difficulties he was facing. He immediately set up a contract, which took the general form of a partnership agreement. Briefly, the arrangement guaranteed Fen a better regular income than he was likely to earn at other work, as well as assuring him of painting materials and the funds necessary to travel to observe his subjects in their natural habitats. In return Bud was to have reproduction rights and the right to mount fine art sales exhibitions for Lansdowne's paintings. This agreement proved so beneficial to both parties that it continues to this day — as does our friendship with both.

An exhibition of magnificent paintings of native birds was a natural complement to the works of Canadian artists who had painted the land. Visitors were fascinated by Lansdowne's birds and the show received considerable publicity in the media, a welcome boost to the artist and the Collection — both in the early stages of their development.

Some years later we mounted a second Lansdowne exhibition, considerably more extensive, which included very large life-size works depicting the great owls and other birds of prey. We also let it be known, discreetly, that some of these were for sale. Our neighbour, Grant Glassco, who owned a large cattle farm of several hundred acres adjoining the Collection property, paid a visit to the Collection and was enchanted with a small painting of a saw-whet owl. He asked if I would make the necessary arrangements to purchase it for him so that he could pick it up the following Saturday. Grant, president of the Canadian-owned Brazilian Light, Heat and Traction Corporation, a man at the height of his career, was dying of cancer. The painting was to be an anniversary gift to his wife Willa. The following Saturday, he telephoned me to ask if I could bring the little painting over to him because he could no longer make the short trip to the Collection. I went at once. The little painting was his second last gift. The last, which he and I had discussed in considerable detail through the years, was a gift of his wooded farmlands to the Province of Ontario. This magnificent gift added enormously to both the size and value of the Province's holdings adjacent to Tapawingo.

In the late sixties, another young wildlife artist called to show me some extremely realistic paintings of snarling grizzly bears, howling wolves, playful squirrels and other critters including colourful snakes. Glen Loates, a somewhat shy but obviously devoted painter was barely out of his teens, but he impressed me with his treatment of animals in some form of natural action which usually involved a second creature. One work that I remember was an impressive depiction of a bear swatting at bees over whose broken hive his left paw rested in a pool of honey. Our Loates exhibition in the late 1960s was his first showing in a public gallery. Since that time several books devoted to his works have been published and his print reproductions have found wide international acceptance.

Of course, our special exhibitions were not confined to wildlife painters. Other artists with widely varying styles and subject matter who were given exhibitions lasting from one to three months included Ron Bolt, Tom Chatfield, Mac Sloan, Frank DeMatais, Rod Prouse and master photographer Bud Watson.

An exhibition of old maps, mostly of Canada, which dated back to the seventeenth century, proved of great interest to visitors. Regular lectures on weekends by the collector, Joe Armstrong, who described some of the unusual mapping difficulties encountered by early explorers and cartographers and, hence, the distortions which arose, were a popular feature of this showing.

In 1969, during one of our frequent visits to western Canada, I met the Winnipeg sculptor, Leo Mol, whose busts of Frederick Varley and A. Y. Jackson had already impressed me. At his home and studio Signe and I were able to see a great variety of his work ranging from figure maquettes to commissioned portraits of world leaders such as President Eisenhower and Pope Paul. We purchased bronzes of Jackson and Varley for the Collection and determined that we would present an exhibition of Mol's work a year or so later at Kleinburg.

In spite of his international reputation, this would be Mol's first major exhibition in a public gallery in Canada, the country he had adopted some twenty years earlier. It was also our first sculpture exhibition and it brought Mol's work to the attention of the public and the media who were surprised to find that a Canadian who had received such important commissions was almost unknown to them.

About eight years later, in 1979, we presented a second Leo Mol exhibition. While this second exhibition at Kleinburg was in the planning stage the sculptor was in Germany overseeing the casting of a commissioned bust of Pope John Paul II which was to be unveiled at the Vatican in September 1979. (The commission arose from the Vatican's satisfaction with the earlier bust of Pope Paul and Mol had again lived at the Vatican while he was completing it.) Mol asked for, and received, permission to display the second cast of this fine bronze — the one every sculptor is permitted to make as his own copy — on the condition that it not be shown before the unveiling of the original in Rome.

When I heard about it, I had what I thought was a bright idea. We would open our exhibition with a simultaneous unveiling in Kleinburg, possibly by the popular new cardinal, Emmett Carter. After discussions with Father Brad Massman, his executive assistant, I wrote Cardinal Carter, inviting him to unveil Mol's bust of John Paul II at Kleinburg on the same day as the Vatican unveiling. The following week I received a letter from Father Massman accepting our invitation for Cardinal Carter and himself in which he added, "We are both looking forward to meeting you, and viewing Mr. Mol's work, which certainly is a tribute to the artist and our country."

On September 21, a group of special guests joined the public visitors to the gallery. Among those we had invited to attend the unveiling were Maple Leaf hockey star Frank Mahovlich and his wife Marie, Ontario ombudsman Arthur Maloney and his wife Lillian and the world-famous author and scholar, Professor Marshall McLuhan of the University of Toronto and Mrs. McLuhan.

The ceremony was scheduled for three o'clock and, as planned, Cardinal Carter arrived at two-thirty and was taken to our private quarters. We found him a man of great natural warmth who put us immediately at our ease but — was it my imagination? — I thought I detected a slight lack of enthusiasm. To bridge the awkward wait for the ceremony I gave him a catalogue of the Mol exhibition, with a fine colour photograph of the bust of the pope on its cover.

The atmosphere immediately changed. "Is this it?" asked the cardinal, his face lighting up. "I saw a picture in the *Globe and Mail* which was taken from one side and made it look positively ugly! This looks great!"

Cardinal Carter then turned to Father Massman and dictated a telegram to Pope John Paul telling him of his pride in the simultaneous unveiling of the second cast at Kleinburg.

Later, when the ceremonial shrouds dropped from the bronze figure of John Paul II, I could see that Cardinal Carter, who of course knew John Paul personally, was both moved and delighted by the extraordinary half-length likeness. He and the Honourable Tom Wells, who had spoken for the Province of Ontario, gazed in silent amazement at the likeness and many of the onlookers were so affected they automatically made the sign of the cross.

At the reception following the ceremony, Tom Wells pulled me to one side.

"Bob," he said, "the government is planning a major dinner to honour Cardinal Carter's appointment. We've been at our wit's end for a suitable gift. This bust is it! Couldn't we arrange to purchase this cast and present it to him?"

I told him Leo was still in Germany and I had no idea of the protocol surrounding a papal bust, but I did promise to try to reach the sculptor by phone.

The following morning, I called an associate of Leo's in Winnipeg and learned the name of the foundry near Munich where Leo was still working on a series of special bronze castings. To avoid the delay I knew my rudimentary German would cause I had one of our guides, who spoke the language fluently, place the call. It was a great anti-climax when we found Leo was out and we had to be content with leaving an urgent message.

When the return call came an hour or so later it was on a very bad line. I did hear Leo say that he could not, and would not, sell the second cast. Trying to make myself heard through noises which sounded like sharks gnawing at the undersea cable, I was finally able to explain that the Government of Ontario wanted to purchase the bust of the pope for presentation to Cardinal Carter and that it would be held permanently by the Roman Catholic Church. That was different! Leo immediately assured me he would ask Rome for the necessary approval. Two days later he relayed that wholehearted approval and suggested what I considered to be a very modest price.

More than a thousand people attended the dinner honouring the cardinal in the Harbour Castle Hotel's enormous ballroom. Several hours before, Signe and I had arrived bringing the blanket-wrapped bust in the Collection's station wagon. The gift was to be a surprise, so in classic cloak-and-dagger fashion we loaded our heavily disguised four-foot package into the freight elevator and had it trundled on a dolly to a specially constructed booth on the ballroom's stage. Walter Bourassa, Ontario's chief protocol officer, was waiting to unwrap it and ready it for presentation.

At the appointed hour, Cardinal Carter, flanked by dignitaries who included Premier William Davis and several cabinet members, took his place on stage at the centre of the head table and the magnificent evening got underway. Signe and I watched it all from a rear table where we had been placed so as not to give a hint of the surprise to come.

Following dessert, the lights were lowered and a giant spotlight picked out a single piper of the 48th Highlanders of Canada, piping the opening strains of Amazing Grace to a hushed assembly. Then, behind the piper, the huge moveable wall, controlled by a giant motor-pulley arrangement, began to part noiselessly as a flood of coloured lights rose over an entire pipe band which paraded toward the platform, dividing ranks as the pipers marched down the aisles between the tables. At centre stage the lead piper turned and now two columns of pipers were moving in opposite directions in each aisle while the skirl of the pipes sent thrilling shivers throughout the crowd. As if out of nowhere, kilted lassies twirling huge silver batons suddenly appeared at all four corners, the glint from their spinning maces creating a shower of reflections on the walls and ceiling and flowing over the enthralled guests.

The premier's executive assistant, Claire Wescott, turned to me and whispered wryly, "If this is our tribute to his elevation to cardinal, what will we do if he becomes pope?"

As the pipers retreated, the spotlight fell on Premier William Davis who made a short speech of congratulation and then handed Cardinal Carter the drawstrings so His Emminence could unveil the hidden bust. It was a dramatic moment and even from our distant table I thought I saw a mist over the cardinal's eyes when the beautiful sculpture was revealed.

Later that evening in his hotel suite Cardinal Carter assured us that the gift had been a complete surprise and that he was already thinking where it should be located so it could be seen by the greatest possible number of people after the Mol exhibition closed.

Several weeks later, after a special column had been created, the bust was unveiled again to a smaller gathering of church, government and lay people who saw it in its permanent location at the Roman Catholic Church's Toronto headquarters, where it would be seen by a steady flow of clergy, nuns, and lay people in those busy offices.

In his short speech the cardinal said, "Most of you have seen this beautiful image in other locations, but I don't think the Holy Father would mind — after all, he is a travelling man. Still, this is the third time I have had the honour of officiating at its unveiling," and then smiling directly at us, "By now the McMichaels and I are going steady."

One evening while I was watching a hockeyplay off game on television I was struck by the similarity between the brightly coloured and imaginatively designed face masks that were used at that time by NHL goaltenders and the equally colourful masks which had long been used in ritual dances by our Northwest Indian peoples. Of course, the fibreglass hockey masks, made to fit closely to goalies' faces and usually painted to resemble imaginary creatures, were primarily protective. Those carved in wood by Indian artists had a symbolic function linked to their ageless traditions. Yet in appearance, size and often in design, they were astonishingly similar. Why not, I asked myself, exploit that similarity in an unusual exhibition? The pictorial and public relations possibilities of such an event were, to say the least, exciting.

Without delay, I set out to make my idea into a reality. To my delight, all of the NHL teams provided us with pucks bearing their individual logos and many of the goaltenders were willing to lend their masks since most had a spare in case of breakage. Hundreds of pucks were mounted on our walls to form a background for the hockey masks and they appeared to be flying toward the masks which had been designed to deflect them.

Greg Harrison of Brampton, Ontario, who designed and made most of the masks for NHL goaltenders, was particularly helpful in the assembling of the exhibits and Rob Harris of Burlington, Ontario, another young maskmaker for the pros, also contributed to the show.

From wooden Northwest Indian masks in the Collection, we selected several to be mounted and labelled amidst the plastic goalie masks. The visual resemblance was striking.

Soultenders and Goaltenders was an exhibition which caught the imagination of television stations and newspapers across the entire country was well as the interest of thousands of young would-be hockey stars and older but equally enthusiastic fans of the game. They came to Kleinburg in such numbers that all our attendance records for a single exhibition were shattered.

By the spring of 1967 the Collection had grown modestly and, although it was open only four afternoons each week and closed during December and January, public attendance was showing a steady, if not dramatic, increase. School classes came regularly for morning tours and lectures by our guides and, on some busy mornings, by Signe or me. It was apparent that more space for picture galleries and a library was required and although Signe and I were happy in our snug little three-room apartment, it was hardly suitable for even modest entertaining, not to mention official guests and potential donors.

I talked about this with Dr. Keith Reynolds, chief of staff in the premier's office, who had become our most important liaison with the Ontario government. During our get-togethers from time to time I showed him the conceptual drawings which I had asked Leo Venchiarutti, our architect, to produce. These informal plans envisioned a three-storey wing forming the crossbar of a T with the new wing Signe and I had constructed in 1965. It would provide four small galleries on the lower level and two on the main level as well as one large main-level gallery of over twelve hundred square feet. The third-floor addition would have two large rooms and one bedroom with bath, all of which could be used by the Collection in what we hoped would be the distant future, when we no longer lived at Tapawingo. The wing would straddle the hogback ridge. Large window areas at the ends of each floor would provide striking views of the broad river valley and intimate glimpses of the wooded hillside. The natural shape of the land continued to be a deciding factor in the building's design. We wanted to accommodate the hills and trees, not remove or change them.

Eventually Leo Venchiarutti produced a more detailed set of plans for the wing which provided over eight thousand square feet of usable space. Buck Bayliss and I poured over them for several weeks and finally arrived at an estimated cost of just over one hundred thousand dollars, modest even by 1967 standards, so Keith Reynolds was able to get approval for the necessary funds.

By early autumn, Vaughan Township's building and fire departments had carefully scrutinized and approved the plans while Signe and I were again rounding up any available hand-hewn timbers on our travels through rural Ontario.

At that time, heating by electricity was being touted as the system of the future. Ontario Hydro convinced us it was not only economically feasible but also cleaner than gas or oil and that it would enable us to maintain a higher degree of relative humidity in winter since no combustion would be involved. Ontario Hydro's engineers designed the system. Most areas were radiant heated from a network of low heat wires buried in the plaster ceilings which provided evenly distributed heat, thermostatically controlled, in each room or hall area. Later, when construction was completed, Ontario Hydro used colour photographs of the building in their advertising to show that "Ontario Lives Better Electrically".

By August, construction of our Centennial project was underway so we could have a roof over the unfinished wing before winter. Once again, Venchiarutti purposely overdesigned structurally, and Bayliss overbuilt to ensure the structure could support floor loads much greater than the attendance figures of the early days warranted, and in keeping with the timeless durability of the enormous hewn timbers and the granite and concrete foundation.

Massive log walls and stone columns rose steadily during the autumn and by December the roof decking was in place, temporarily covered in layers of heavy polyethylene, which would be replaced by split cedar shakes the following spring. Through the winter months Bayliss and his crew, electrical contractor Joe Beedham and other tradespeople ranging from plumbers and plasterers to welders and painters worked steadily while we began to plan and schedule the opening of the wing for the late spring or early summer of 1968.

That year, several events occurred which were momentous both for the Collection and for Signe and me, which made it seem that our expansion had been preordained. Without the additional gallery walls and living space in the wing, the Collection's growth and our lives might have followed a very different and much less stimulating course.

In four months, beginning in April, Parliament amended the *Income Tax Act* making gifts to a province deductible, the Collection acquired the three largest gifts of art it was ever to receive, and A. Y. Jackson came to make his permanent home with us at Tapawingo.

Almost a year earlier, George McIntyre, a senior official in the Ontario Treasurer's Department, had asked me and a department official to go to Ottawa for a meeting with Mitchell Sharp, then Minister of Finance. At that meeting Sharp questioned the official very closely about gifts by citizens to the Province of Ontario. He could not recall any gift paralleling ours but felt that others might be more likely to follow our example if gifts to a province were treated for tax purposes in the same way as a gift to Her Majesty in Right of Canada — fully deductible from the donor's taxable income, and spread over two or, in some cases, more taxation years if necessary.

The disparity between the tax status of gifts to the federal and provincial governments went back beyond the beginning of World War II, when the federal government became the collector of all income taxes, which had formerly been shared with the provinces. This change, apparently a temporary wartime measure, became permanent after several somewhat contentious federal-provincial conferences on revenue sharing. Although major issues such as tax splitting between the two senior levels of government were eventually resolved, lesser matters such as the deductibility of gifts to a province had been either overlooked or given little or no consideration.

Mitchell Sharp asked me an obvious question, "Since you intended your collection to be for the benefit of all Canadians, why didn't you give the collection and gallery to the Government of Canada, through the National Gallery?" Then, as if to answer his own question, he said, "Ah, I seem to remember some discussion I had concerning this. At the time your gift was being contemplated, the *National Gallery Act* did not allow the Gallery to maintain satellite or branch galleries."

Throughout the meeting I was more interested in the possibility of the government amending the *Income Tax Act* to recognize gifts to a province and thereby encourage donors to the provincially owned McMichael Collection than I was in a possible retroactive tax treatment for Signe and me. We had long since made our gift and any possible tax benefits would, at best, be modest, since our income was very modest in relation to the appraised value of our gift. But we hoped our example might prod the federal government into changing the rules in order to provide a real incentive for those who owned major works of Canadian art to give them to

Ontario's only provincially owned art gallery — in Kleinburg.

The Minister of Finance promised us that he would discuss the subject with his cabinet colleagues and about two weeks later I received a telephone call from him. He told me that, after considerable thought and discussion, the government had come to see that our gift was for the benefit of the entire country and that it would be treated for tax purposes as a gift to Her Majesty in Right of Canada.

I thanked Mr. Sharp for the good news. The decision resulted in a modest tax saving for us. It was a step in the right direction. In fact it was the precursor of legislative action which the Government of Canada would take in the not too distant future.

In April of 1968, Finance Minister Sharp introduced a budget in the House of Commons. It contained an amendment to the *Income Tax Act* dealing with gifts to a province. This amendment to the *Income Tax Act* went as far as the government could prudently go toward giving credit to unselfish people who had a sincere desire to pass on their personal treasures for the benefit of the nation.

The significance of the amendment to the *Income Tax Act* and its probable effect on the growth of the Collection did not escape us, but it received surprisingly little comment in Parliament or in the media and, in fact, was little known or understood at the time even by tax lawyers and accountants, let alone potential donors to the Collection. For many years, we still found potential donors who knew nothing about it and in some cases, it was the deciding factor in a decision to give. However, most of our donors continued to be collectors who had been early patrons of the Group of Seven and the other artists we were showing and their gifts came to us because of our special focus rather than as the result of tax planning. They wanted their pictures to be permanently hung (both during their lifetimes and beyond) for the enjoyment of all Canadians.

When the budget had been passed I went to see Robert Bryce, Deputy Minister of Finance, and J. Gear McIntyre, Deputy Minister of National Revenue in Ottawa, as I was anxious to understand completely the procedures which the Collection would be expected to follow under the new legislation. In those meetings with Bryce and McIntyre and their tax and legislative experts we reviewed hypothetical cases and it was decided that a valuation committee composed of two or more members of the Collection's advisory committee and including at least one professional art dealer should be formed to determine the fair market value of gifts to the Collection.

Methods of valuation and possible problem areas were also discussed. How, for example, would a difference of opinion among committee members be resolved? (Usually by calling for expert advice from outside the committee and reasonable compromise.) What about possible conflict arising from future gifts by members of the committee such as Signe and me? (Donor committee members would absent themselves from discussions and valuation of their gifts.) How would valuations be arrived at when committee members were unfamiliar with the market value of a gift? (Through a call for expert advice for the committee's consideration.)

One point on which the Ottawa people unanimously agreed was that when there were honest doubts as to the fairness of valuation the committee should try to reach a figure satisfactory to all members and should lean toward a figure which might be as much as five or ten percent above a known, but possibly out of date, market value. It was recognized that Canadian art was going through a period of dramatic escalation and that a valuation based on the price of a similar item, established several months or even a year earlier, would probably err on the low side. Inflation stalked the economy and it was entirely possible, even likely, that by the time a donor received his receipt a new and higher price for such an item would have been established. After all, the donor was receiving a tax credit worth only fifteen to fifty percent, depending on the tax bracket, of what would have been received from a sale.

On my return from Ottawa I invited Jack Wildridge of Toronto's respected Roberts Gallery to join our valuation committee. The Roberts Gallery was the exclusive agent for Frederick Varley and A. J. Casson of the Group, and Jack was very knowledgeable about the quality and market values of Canadian art, most particularly the works of the artists in the Collection at Kleinburg. Years earlier, Signe and I had purchased our first Group of Seven painting, Lawren Harris's *Montreal River,* from him.

Jack seemed pleased to join the committee as an unpaid volunteer, like the other members. He was to prove not only expert in the field of valuation but also helpful when we had to determine the quality, authenticity and desirability of paintings which were offered to the Collection during the next decade.

Since the federal government's revision of our own tax status we had hoped that the same privileges would be extended to the major donors who had shown so much faith in our vision that they had made their gifts before our gallery-home became a public institution. To its credit, the Department of National Revenue did not hesitate. It issued receipts to Yvonne Housser, Bob Laidlaw and Norah DePencier. A receipt was also issued to Percy Hilborn for his magnificent gift of A. Y. Jackson's *First Snow, Algoma.*

Edwin Holgate was a gentle, soft-spoken man with a twinkle in his eye, who usually managed to see a humorous side to even the most disconcerting of situations.

During my first get-together with him at his home in the village of Morin Heights in the Laurentians in 1967 he pointed to a large painting he had made to form a permanent section of wall when his house had been built many years earlier. One day, he told me, an insensitive art dealer from Montreal whom he had never liked much, had arrived on the Holgate doorstep uninvited. After quickly surveying the living room his eyes rested on the painting, which had been a fixture of the Holgate home from the time it was built.

"I have a client who'd love that one," the dealer gushed. "I'll take it!"

"But I can't sell it," Edwin replied. "It's part of our home. It's permanently screwed to the wall."

"So get a screwdriver!"

Chuckling as he recalled the incident the artist, who had become the eighth member of the Group of Seven in 1931, led us to comfortable chairs in his library. On the walls were several of his favourite small oil panels. Continuing to reminisce, he told us of another unpleasant incident which now made him smile. A voracious Group collector from Ottawa who was visiting had been shown a book of Edwin's favourite drawings, assembled and beautifully hand-bound by the artist to make a unique volume. While Edwin and his wife were preparing tea and cookies in their kitchen, the collector in the library had brazenly removed pages of drawings from the treasured volume. When the Holgates returned they all but dropped the cups and saucers they were carrying. Standing and holding several of the prized drawings loosely in his hand, the collector said, "I'd like to have these. How much do I owe you?" For an answer he was ushered to the door and told never to return. Time had mellowed Edwin's distress and he was now able to chortle, "We've never seen him since."

Born in Allendale, Ontario, Edwin Holgate grew up in Montreal where he began his art education at an early age, studying under William Brymner at the Art Association of Montreal. He lived in Paris for a number of years both before and after World War I but returned to Montreal and opened his own studio and also began teaching wood engraving at the Ecole des Beaux Arts. In those early days he often went sketching with A. Y. Jackson and several of the artists of the city's Beaver Hall Group. Unlike his friends Jackson and Albert Robinson, Holgate was more interested in figure painting than landscape, but many of his best-known works combine the two. He often interposed the burly figures of lumberjacks and woodsmen into natural river and forest settings and was a true innovator, painting the female nude against the rocky, forested backdrop of the Laurentians. His portraits, like the one of humorist-scholar Stephen Leacock, are more conventional, yet they have a vigour and freshness whose appeal has rarely been surpassed in this country.

At that first meeting in 1967, while Frances Holgate served tea and cookies, Signe and I found it difficult to tear our eyes away from the mostly small but very striking paintings which were hung in groupings on the walls of the comfortable living room. Side by side with oil panels of nearby rural Quebec were strongly defined paintings of Northwest Indian villages with colourful totems — products of Holgate's wanderings with A. Y. Jackson forty years earlier. Among these memories of past years there was only one small portrait, a white-turbaned woman's head against a brilliant red background. When I stepped over to examine it more closely Frances, who was the subject, told us that one day she and Edwin had been working together laying a stone and concrete patio in their garden. Knowing that her hands would become coated with wet cement and fearful that she might unconsciously spread it, she had wrapped her long hair in a white towel. When their work was finished, her husband suddenly recognized that her face, framed by the impromptu turban, made an unusually interesting persona and quickly reached for his paints and brushes.

The result was the penetrating study which he had simply called *The Head*. Edwin seemed amused as I returned to it again and again, marvelling at the strength which came from its extreme simplicity. "Someday," he chuckled, "I may give you *The Head* in memory of both of us."

When we left that day I had a small oil panel tucked under my arm. It was a nude figure painted in 1922, the first Holgate painting to join the McMichael Collection.

In the decade between our first meeting and his death in 1977, Edwin Holgate visited Kleinburg several times, often staying overnight to reminisce into the late hours with his old painting pal and travelling companion, Alex Jackson.

During one of his visits his memory went back to a large canvas he had painted of a prominent woman musician which was entitled *The Cellist*. Since he referred to it in the present tense I began to wonder if he still owned it. He did. The problem was, he confided, that it was a life-size portrait, far too large for their home, so he had had to roll it up and store it in their basement.

By this time (the early 1970s) the Collection had acquired at least one major canvas by each Group artist except Holgate. Would he sell *The Cellist* to me and fill the gap? (I was particularly excited because I was sure that, while he was still actively painting, none of his more recent works were on the large scale he was describing.) Holgate had obviously not seen the painting for some years but he seemed pleased, and even excited, at the thought of having it re-stretched so we could view it together. A short time later Signe and I were gazing with excitement at the impressive figure of a black-skirted musician seated with her bow stretched across the strings of a gleaming cello.

In one of our largest galleries, which we set aside for major canvases of Group artists, it is the only work that is not a landscape. We have no regrets about that. On the contrary, we have always felt *The Cellist* is far more appropriate as a representative of Holgate's work than the land — only his second love.

Following the arrival of this, Holgate's largest work, in the Collection, other important Holgate paintings, including a fine figure study, *Mother and Daughter* (1926), a gift of Syd Hoar of Vancouver, and *Fishermen's Houses* (1933), a gift from Bruce Gill of Montreal, as well as several smaller pictures came to Kleinburg, greatly increasing our representation of this important artist.

In April 1974, Edwin Holgate made his last visit to Kleinburg. With Alfred Casson, the other surviving Group member, he was an honorary pallbearer for his old painting pal, A. Y. Jackson.

A year before his death in 1977, I visited Edwin and Frances in the Montreal apartment to which they had moved because of his failing health. That day, artist and subject made a joint presentation to the McMichael Collection which would, indeed, become a memorial to both of them — *The Head*.

It had been announced in late 1967 that A. Y. Jackson would be invested as a Companion of the Order of Canada, the second Group member after Arthur Lismer, to receive the honour. The investiture would take place at Government House, Ottawa, in the spring of 1968. Ten days earlier Jackson arrived in Toronto to attend to some unfinished business and spend a few days with several old friends in the city, winding up with four days at Kleinburg.

Just before his arrival I had received a telephone call from an official of the North York Board of Education who knew that Jackson was a regular visitor at Tapawingo and that he would be with us later that week. North York was building its largest high school and the borough wished to call it A. Y. Jackson Secondary School. The official said he understood Dr. Jackson was quite hard of hearing and that he would appreciate it if I could explain the situation to Jackson and, he hoped, receive approval for the naming.

Shortly after his arrival I cornered him. "Alex," I asked, "how would you like to have a school named after you?"

"I always thought it would be nice to have one of those little red schoolhouses named after me," he said.

"This won't be a little red schoolhouse," I continued, "but a very big schoolhouse in North York." I went on to explain the request from the Board of Education and encouraged him to accept the honour.

"Tell them it's okay with me, Bob," he said with a twinkle in his eye, "and that I hope to be around to see the building finished."

Alex had always been a lively and gregarious guest who loved to join the gallery guides in their after-work dips in our indoor pool. During this visit he was unaccountably quiet and, it appeared, tired. He went to bed shortly after dinner and we missed the long evening chats we had come to expect. At first we thought he was just tired after a strenuous week in Toronto but, although he was always an early riser, he had to be wakened for breakfast on the second day and settled for a rocking chair instead of the walk Sam and Inky had come to expect. He seemed inexplicably distant, even confused.

Signe and I had a long talk that evening. Though Alex had always described himself with mock humour as indestructible, he was in his eighty-sixth year and still living alone on the ground floor of an older house on Ottawa's McLaren Street, which had been converted to flats. We worried that if he were to have an accident or be taken suddenly ill, no one would know. (We learned sometime later that he *had* been taken ill and as a result had fallen in his bathroom, receiving a nasty bang to his head.)

We had known A.Y. for over twelve years and during his many visits we had enjoyed his company and the knowledge that he always thought of Tapawingo as his home away from home. We felt comfortable with him and he with us ... like members of a family. Now, our new wing with its ample living space was nearing completion. Should we not ask Alex to make his home with us in Kleinburg?

On Sunday afternoon, knowing that he planned to leave for Ottawa the following morning, I took him into the partially completed living area, its floor still deep in sawdust, and pointed out the magnificent view of the woods from the unfinished windows and exterior balconies.

"Alex," I said, "we know you are indestructible, and a carefree bachelor who has always lived alone ... but Signe and I enjoy your company ... and after all you're here so often ... well, we'd like to have you live with us at Tapawingo. You can see we'll have lots of space and frankly we think you shouldn't be living alone."

He thought awhile. "That would be very nice, Bob, but I think Naomi [his niece] would hate me to leave Ottawa. She's alone since Walton died and we're in touch with each other almost every day. Anyway it's nice of you and Signe to ask me. I'll think about it and talk with Naomi."

During that afternoon and evening the old artist was unusually quiet, shuffling from room to room, occasionally picking up a book which in the past would have occupied him for hours but which now held his attention for no more than minutes. He seemed to be trying to focus his thoughts and actions, apparently with some difficulty.

Suddenly, in a burst of clarity he said, "Bob, I finished that canvas of Great Bear Lake for the country club. I was able to borrow back one of my old sketches to work it up from. It's the biggest thing I've done in some time and it looks okay. I've arranged for it to be packed and sent in care of you ... and it should be here in the next week or so."

The message was clear, but he brought it out as if he suddenly felt he had to finish a piece of business which was on his mind but which had been hard to remember. As if relieved, he put his head back in his easy chair and dozed off.

The large canvas had been in my thoughts from time to time over the past months, but I had not wanted to appear to be rushing him or to embarrass him if he had not yet started it. Some months earlier, the Metropolitan Toronto Board of Trade Country Club's art committee, of which I was a member, had asked me to extend to Jackson a commission for a large canvas, the choice of subject to be his. I had told him about this offer and he seemed delighted, not only because of the freedom of choice but also because the painting would hang in the club's dining room where he had enjoyed many meals as our guest.

Now with the painting finished and soon to be delivered, I called Bernie Stevenson, chairman of the art committee to tell him the good news. Delighted, the chairman insisted I ask Jackson to be the guest of honour at a dinner where the painting would be unveiled for the club's members and assured me they would set the date for the artist's convenience.

A few days later it became clear that the unveiling dinner was not to be. But the painting hangs prominently in the club's dining room and Jackson returned many times to see this last canvas of his long career.

Knowing that nothing we could say would dissuade Jackson from returning to Ottawa on Monday morning, since he was to receive the Order of Canada two days later, I asked him if he would be willing to fly instead of taking the long bus trip and if he would like me to go with him. We did not want to upset him, but we were deeply worried by his unusual behaviour. He would have none of it. He would take the bus, he insisted, and there was no need for me to accompany him ... just be sure we got him to the bus station on time the next morning. In fact, Reg and Jean Dowsett were coming to dinner at Tapawingo that evening and he was planning to spend the night with them so they could deliver him to the bus terminal at Bay and Dundas Streets early Monday morning.

We had never consciously concerned ourselves with A.Y.'s comings and goings. After all, he had travelled the barren lands, the Arctic and the mountains on foot, by dogsled and by canoe, most often alone. Yet after Jackson had left with the Dowsetts I found Signe in tears.

"I feel I may never see him again," she sobbed, "and I feel so helpless to do anything for him. Maybe you don't know it Bob, but he's been almost like a father to me."

That did it! I picked up the phone and dialed Naomi's number in Ottawa. Since Naomi was partially crippled by illness in her childhood it took seven or eight rings before I heard her cheerful voice. I minced no words.

"As you know, Alex has been with us for the past few days ... and we're terribly concerned. He's just not himself. He's slept much of the time and frankly, Naomi, he seems very confused ... almost in a daze. We don't think he should be living alone any longer and we have asked him to come and live with us at Kleinburg."

"Oh Bob," it was almost a wail, "you know I can't look after him ... and I have to be away because of my books and lectures so much of the time ... [A fine arts Ph.D., formerly a professor at Hamilton's McMaster University, Naomi Jackson Groves has published major books on the great German sculptor Barlack as well as best-selling works on Canadian art.] "But Bob," she continued, "I love that old Unky Punk of mine so much that I don't know if I could stand having him live away from Ottawa. He and I talk almost every day when we're both in town and I would miss that so much. Perhaps he just needs to rest more ... I'm always telling him he shouldn't travel so much ..." Her words trailed off.

"I know how close you two are, Naomi, and Alex feels the same way as you do ... but we are really concerned. We know he has that inner ear problem which affects his balance ... but this seems much more to us ... and he's precious to us too. We'll soon have much more living space here and I urge you to consider very carefully the possibility of his coming to live with us. You can be sure he would get lots of loving care ... which we believe he needs."

"I know how fond of you he is and I'm sure you feel the same way, but ..."

"Naomi," I said, "we're not going to resolve this now with a telephone call, but promise me you'll meet him tomorrow when he arrives on the bus. Your decision will probably be all important and final for Alex. Above all, make sure Bob Starrs [his doctor] sees him ... and spends some time with him ... Signe and I will be anxious to know what you and Bob Starrs feel after seeing him. Please keep us posted, dear."

After the six-hour bus trip on Monday, Jackson made his way by taxi to his McLaren Avenue apartment and in a short time Naomi arrived to welcome him back. After a warm hug, Alex suddenly collapsed. Dr. Starrs and an ambulance were soon on the way.

Though conscious, A. Y. Jackson was confined to Ottawa General Hospital in a very weakened condition. It was clear he would be unable to go to Rideau Hall two days later to receive the highest honour which can be bestowed on a Canadian, so Naomi was designated to receive the Order of Canada on his behalf from his friend, Governor General Roland Michener. During the reception which followed, world champion skier Nancy Greene, long admired by A.Y. for her athletic prowess and winsome personality on TV, learned of the weakened condition of her favourite artist and asked if she might visit him in hospital. Within the hour Naomi, carrying the Order of Canada medal, and Nancy, carrying her bouquet of red roses, arrived at Jackson's bedside. The visit seemed to raise Alex's spirits momentarily, but after the two women had left the hospital he feel into a deep sleep and then into a coma which was to seem endless and which the doctors reluctantly diagnosed as terminal.

So deep was our love of Tapawingo and its lands, that years earlier we had expressed our wish that at the time of our deaths we should be buried somewhere among its lovely hills and trees. Those wishes had been included in the 1965 Gift Agreement and had apparently caught the attention of A. Y. Jackson. In 1967 we had been somewhat surprised to receive a letter from him in which he stated that although his birthplace was Montreal, he was concerned with the developing political situation in Quebec and, indeed, feared that Quebec might not always be a part of Canada. Could we find a grave site for him, somewhere near Kleinburg?

Although he hadn't mentioned Tapawingo specifically it was apparent he had it in mind. I wrote a rather noncommital reply telling him I felt sure that the Ontario government would find such a request appropriate and that I would follow up on the necessary approvals. A few months later, while A.Y. was visiting us and Alfred and Margaret Casson were also guests, he and Cass brought up the subject again. It was clear that Casson shared Jackson's view and that he and Margaret also felt Tapawingo would be an appropriate final resting place. The more they talked the more they enthused about a memorial ground on the gallery property for all the members of the Group of Seven. The idea of a memorial cemetery now began to take shape. A few days later I mentioned the proposal to Dr. Keith Reynolds, our senior liaison with the Ontario government, and he promised to look into the whole idea.

In those spring days of 1968 with Jackson gravely ill in Ottawa, the need for a burial ground at Tapawingo became pressing, but as far as I knew no formal action had been taken. I called Keith Reynolds and explained the seriousness of Jackson's illness and the urgent need for whatever actions and approvals would be required. Keith was in a position to get swift action when necessary. Within an hour I received a call from the director of the Cemeteries Branch, who told me that one of their officials would meet me at Kleinburg to survey the proposed cemetery and that documents officially consecrating the ground as a permanent cemetery would be forthcoming. He asked if the ground had been staked out and the acreage determined. I mumbled something about it being taken care of and only then realized that we had never given the exact location or size of the cemetery any serious thought.

Some considerations were obvious. It should be easily accessible on foot from the roadway or parking lot, yet it must be quiet and dignified, away from the main flow of pedestrian and motor traffic. It must be on high and dry ground and should, if possible, command a view of the woodlands and valleys similar to many in the artists' paintings. We knew our lands. Almost inevitably our thoughts were drawn to a grassy knoll about one hundred feet north of the main driveway and two hundred feet west of the parking lot. The top of this rise offered sweeping views of the river valleys, the woods and Tom Thomson's shack, and in the distance, the roofs of the gallery.

When two men from the Cemeteries Branch arrived with their surveying equipment we prepared a plot plan for graves. Later we arranged to have the then Department of Highways bring carefully selected slabs of granite, blasted during road building in the painters' beloved north country, to the site. These rough-hewn stones would become appropriate grave markers. On each would be carved the name of one of the Group with the years of his birth and death.

As Alex continued to lie in a coma we received daily phone calls from Dr. Starrs and Naomi, who reported little change but that the old painter seemed to be resting comfortably; his heart was strong. After the fourth day, Bob Starrs began preparing us for the death he considered inevitable, and Naomi and I began painful but apparently necessary discussions about the funeral arrangements, choice of minister, (Ottawa or Kleinburg) pallbearers and other details which must be attended to when a life is coming to an end.

At Ottawa General Hospital a team of young neurologists had been observing Jackson. Studying the nurses' charts, they noted that when the patient, who was frequently turned to avoid bedsores, was lying on one side there was no sign of motion, but when on the other side, minor twitches could be observed. From this they reasoned that there must be fluid pressure on the brain which was shifting as his position changed. Fortunately there was a new electronic instrument which, when strapped around the head, could scan the cranial area to detect clots. Within the skull they detected a scab-like formation, probably the result of a severe concussion, which was attracting moisture and creating a pool of water which was placing considerable pressure on Alex's brain.

The young doctors discussed their findings with Jackson's physician, Dr. Robert Starrs, and asked his approval to operate immediately. Starrs felt sure there was nothing to lose and a good chance of winning. When he called Naomi, she too grasped at this last chance and gave her permission for an operation to remove a subdural haematoma. That evening, the surgeons cut a dime-size hole through the top of Jackson's skull, removed the clotted formation and drained off nearly thirty c.c.s of fluid.

By the following morning A.Y. had regained consciousness, and though weakened and somewhat wan, he smiled and was able to speak a few words. Dr. Starrs, holding his old patient's hand said, "The worst is over, Alex. Now you've got to get stronger so we can take you down to Kleinburg."

With just the slightest quiver in his voice Jackson asked, "Do they still want me?"

A few weeks later on a warm June day in 1968, Dr. Robert Starrs and his wife Rita, an accompanying nurse, and Naomi Groves drove A.Y. to Tapawingo. We watched the old painter as his eyes looked once more through pine and spruce to our hills and our log home. We felt he knew he was home.

And his home was ready.

Recognizing that our old friend would require considerable care we had advertised in all the local weekly newspapers for a "nurse-companion for an elderly gentleman living in the Kleinburg area". The patient's name was not mentioned. We hoped to find two women who would be willing to spend half a week each, day and night, as Jackson's nurse, cook and companion. Knowing as we did Alex's restlessness and energetic temperament, we thought it was likely he would require more holding down than holding up.

Signe interviewed all of the applicants and finally selected Zita Wilson, who lived with her parents in the tiny community of Loretto, Ontario, and Dora McLean, who lived nearby in Kleinburg. Both proved to be ideal choices. Together they, and later Phyllis Cooper, were responsible for providing care and bringing comfort, happiness and love into the remaining years of A. Y. Jackson's life.

Alex Jackson had always been a roamer. Someone once said that if red dots were placed on the map to represent each place he had painted it would appear that Canada had a rash. He could make his home wherever the night found him — on forest boughs, a tent in the Arctic, a farm home in rural Quebec or a suite in Montreal's Ritz-Carlton Hotel. Moving from Ottawa to Tapawingo, he settled in at once. After all, for years he had considered it his second home. Within a few days the rapport between A.Y. and his "staff", Dora and Zita, was so close it seemed they had been together for years.

Some problems, minor and natural, yet potentially critical, were quickly solved by the women's combination of common sense and a little ingenuity. Jackson had always lived alone and like most people his age found that during the night he had to visit the washroom. We knew it was probable, however, that it was such a visit, when he was still groggy with sleep, that had led to his fall and, in turn, his recent illness. So that they could assist him, Zita or Dora slept while he did, in a nearby bed, and tried to impress upon him that he should not visit the washroom alone. Either out of kindness or sleepiness, Alex refused to do this. Finally, in desperation, the nurses fashioned a ten-foot long leash of elastic tape with wrist-size loops on each end. When Alex went to sleep they slipped one loop over his wrist and the other over their own. The first night this ingenious system was in place, Alex got up in the dark and was startled when he felt the tug of the leash. Dora said it felt as though she had a fish on the line. Fortunately, they both saw the humour of the situation and burst into laughter. But the simple idea worked and the probability of a nocturnal accident was greatly reduced.

Other problems, usually unforseeable, were not disposed of quite as easily. After a few weeks, his strength returning, Jackson asked for the paints and easel which had been sent down with his books and other personal items from Ottawa. From his cartons of art supplies he removed a blank, stretched canvas about eighteen by twenty-four inches in size and placed it on his easel. With a panel he had painted a few months earlier propped up nearby, he began painting, oblivious to everything around him. Dora went to our adjoining dining room to make herself a cup of coffee feeling that he might prefer to paint alone. After about half an hour she returned to find Alex bent forlornly over his easel, trembling from a fit of sobbing which seemed almost like a seizure.

Fearful that her patient was suffering a relapse, Dora darted to the nearby intercom. Her anxious words, "Mr. McMichael, please come immediately", left no doubt there was an emergency. Moments later I stood by the easel. Alex kept his head turned away, but I could see that his cheeks were wet with tears as he looked dejectedly back and forth from the small panel to the roughed-in canvas before him. I saw at once that his distress was mental, not physical.

Following his gaze from sketch to canvas I saw that the outline of an old barn on the canvas was grotesquely out of scale and perspective. Alex looked at me with a mixture of futility, terror and the extreme anguish which had come with the sudden realization that he had lost his skill, perhaps forever.

The lump in my throat made it almost impossible to speak, but I tried to rally him by saying, "We all have our bad days at one time or another, Alex," as I lifted the stretched canvas from the easel and placed its still-wet face against the nearby wall.

Forcing her best smile, Dora took his arm firmly and helped him to get up. "How about joining me for a cup of coffee?" she said cheerfully. The tension of the moment was broken. The trauma would remain.

One day a letter arrived from one of Alex's closest old friends, artist Anne Savage. She said that she was concerned that Jackson might be in difficult financial straights and that she would like to help. Almost forty years earlier she had purchased, for about one hundred and fifty dollars, a fine Jackson canvas, *Valley of the Gouffre River*, which she still treasured. Since it would now have a greater value, she wished to sell it and arrange to have the proceeds turned over to Alex. Her offer was simply phrased, but every word spoke of her unselfish love for the man she had painted with, and idolized, through long years.

When Signe and I had invited Alex to live with us we had not the slightest idea of his financial position, nor did we care. After his arrival we learned from Naomi that Canada Permanent Trust in Ottawa managed his portfolio, accumulated through years of frugal living, and that, prudently used, his funds were sufficient to cover his personal and medical expenses for an almost indefinite period.

Our Special Art Fund, derived largely from the sale of postcards and our first modest Collection Catalogue, was limited. Although I had seen only the small snapshot of the canvas that came with Anne's letter, I wrote her at once telling her how much we appreciated her most generous offer and assuring her that Jackson's living costs were well within his modest means. Nevertheless, the Collection would very much like to purchase the canvas and that after consulting with our committee we were prepared to offer five thousand dollars for it with the understanding that she would keep the money for herself. She replied that she was overwhelmed by the amount and accepted our offer. After its arrival and the necessary cleaning and reframing, the magnificent painting of rural Quebec was hung in the centre of the long wall in our living room. It was now rapidly becoming the Jackson room and on most weekend afternoons, seated in a favourite rocker, he revelled in the admiration of visitors to the Collection.

As summer drifted into fall there were many happy times. Old friends like Alfred and Margaret Casson, Reg and Jean Dowsett and Chuck and Dorothy Matthews were frequent visitors with whom Alex could reminisce. Newer and younger friends such as skier Nancy Greene and radio commentator Betty Kennedy and her husband Gerrard also visited, and were often amazed at Alex's grasp of current events and his instant recall of places and events. Hockey star Frank Mahovlich, a Sunday painter, and his wife Marie soon became friends.

Alex was an avid hockey fan and he enjoyed watching the Saturday night hockey games on television, particularly in the late 1960s when the Toronto Maple Leafs and the Montreal Canadiens were considered the top teams in the National Hockey League. One or the other was always a contender at playoff time. One year, during a final game between the two arch rivals for the Stanley Cup, Jackson and I were glued to the set when toward the end of the third period, with Toronto leading by one goal and one minute left to play, a face-off was called. The tension was terrific. Alex turned to me, "If I were the Leafs' coach I'd simply pile my six players up against the goal like cordwood," he said firmly.

Another friend of long standing was Charles Matthews, co-founder of the highly regarded commercial art and printing firm, Sampson-Matthews. Through the years Chuck had been more closely associated with the painters of the Group of Seven, as friend and employer, than anyone we knew. Both Franklin Carmichael and A. J. Casson had been longtime members of his staff in earlier years and he numbered all the other members of the Group among his close acquaintances.

A man of great energy and restless imagination, in 1941 Chuck Matthews had conceived the idea of making silk screen reproductions, the size of canvases, from the works of Canadian painters to relieve the monotony of the barracks and mess halls that housed Canadian service men and women in stations throughout the world. He persuaded Group artists Casson, Jackson, Harris and Carmichael and others to produce special works for this project and also persuaded sponsors to cover the cost of printing. Then he arranged with officials of the armed services and government to provide suitable distribution. The prints were so popular that after the war ended they enjoyed a second round of popularity in schools, libraries, offices and banks across the nation. Naturally, Chuck also had a fine personal collection of the Group of Seven with particular emphasis on the work of his closest friends Casson, Jackson and Harris.

We had known Chuck and his wife Dorothy for many years, so

we knew and understood his reluctance to part with any of his beloved paintings, and particularly not with those by his friends. Yet he was an enthusiastic booster for the Collection and had made it clear on several occasions that he thought his paintings should be in Kleinburg. One evening during one of our frequent get-togethers Chuck told me that he wouldn't rest easily until he was satisfied that his pictures would be part of the McMichael Collection. He asked if he might give them immediately and then borrow them back for the remainder of his life. Winking, he said, "I'm touching eighty you know." The advisory committee happily approved the proposal which would one day bring many fine paintings to the Collection and Chuck and Dorothy continued to enjoy the treasures they had collected. Years later in 1985, at the Christmas of his ninety-sixth year, we visited Chuck. He was still enjoying the pictures, happy that other Canadians would share his enjoyment in the future.

Toward year's end Jackson had regained most of his earlier strength. His voice did not have its former clarity and his writing was shakier, but both were usually quite understandable. One Sunday afternoon he was writing Christmas cards and handing them to me to be folded, put into envelopes and stamped. I could not help noticing one addressed to his old friend Roland Michener, then Governor General of Canada. He had penned a brief personal message which even I could not decipher. "What did you write?" I asked him as I handed it back. He looked at the message for a long puzzled moment then shrugged, "I really don't know — but Roly will be able to figure it out."

As it is in most Canadian homes, Christmas was a magic time at Tapawingo. We always looked forward to having my father with us for the decorating of our Christmas tree. On his first Christmas Eve with us, Alex joined Dad, adding whimsical but artistic touches to the tall spruce which reached the peak of the soaring window wall of our living room. When the last bauble was set, Dad and Alex joined us in front of the fire. To the strains of "Silent Night" from our record player the two old men chatted of bygone days while Signe and I reviewed a year which had brought many blessings.

Retiring early, Alex and Dad placed colourful presents, which Zita had been wrapping for them in great secrecy during the evening, under the tree. Later that night, our niece Penny and her husband Jack Fenwick arrived with their little daughter, Debra, and infant son, Craig, after a long drive from Montreal to complete our family Christmas circle.

It seems that on Christmas morning the youngest are always the first to rise, but the oldest are not far behind. As dawn was breaking Alex was looking sleepily out of his bedroom window when the naked figure of little Debra Fenwick came streaking in one bedroom door and out the other. Springing to a bolt upright position in bed and rubbing his eyes, Alex called to Zita, "What did I have to drink last night? I swear I just saw a little naked cherub run through here."

I've always hoped that some day I'd uncover a small oil painting signed "Zuppa". There probably are no more than five of these in the world, if indeed that many still exist.

Among the first to feel the adverse effects of the Great Depression were artists, most of whose works were considered non-essential luxuries. Although fifteen years had passed since the Group's first exhibition in 1920 and their fresh approach to painting was slowly gaining a measure of acceptance, their works were not selling consistently. Even with his always frugal lifestyle, Jackson was reduced to counting pennies.

One day he visited the studio of a friend, former Group member Frank (by now his name was changed to Franz) Johnston, who had developed a very realistic style resembling brilliant colour photographs. His appealing landscapes had proven so popular that even in the very restricted market for paintings his works were in considerable demand. Jackson found the prolific artist working systematically on several paintings of various attractive subjects all at the same time. Economizing on his labours, the painter moved from picture to picture adding a few daubs of blue here, and then on another pass adding a dash of red there from generously loaded founts of colour on his painting table. When a number of pleasing paintings on his little assembly line were completed, they would be moved to a low-heat oven in order to hasten surface drying in readiness for their delivery to Eaton's College Street store the following day. During conversation, Jackson sensed Johnston's impatience at being disturbed in his painting routine. It was a busy day of producing what he referred to as the potboilers so necessary to his economic well-being.

Alex returned to his own studio on Severn Street, broke and desperately needing to earn a few dollars. He resolved to paint some little pictures, not in his own characteristic style, but similar to earlier European landscapes: misty, traditional and sentimental. Bridges, canals and ancient buildings in the manner of nineteenth century salon painters were, he knew, still extremely popular.

Sure enough, when the little pictures, European and murky in appearance and sombre in colour, were offered for sale they were enthusiastically accepted. For the time being, Alex knew where his next meal was coming from. Nevertheless he never again was purposely tempted to paint old canals in that melodramatic fashion — it was anathema to him.

Reminiscing toward the end of his life, Alex confided that this little ruse was the only occasion on which he had resorted to the use of a nom de plume in his painting. He had carefully signed each little picture "Zuppa", which is the Italian word for soup.

Our close friend, painter Yvonne McKague Housser, liked to entertain at small cocktail parties in her home near the village of Markham. At one of these gatherings in 1960 she introduced us to her friend and fellow painter Isabel McLaughlin. Isabel was a talented artist, one of five daughters of the founder of General Motors of Canada, Colonel R. S. McLaughlin. After the death of Yvonne's husband, Fred Housser, author of the first comprehensive book on the Group of Seven, *A Canadian Art Movement*, she and Isabel became frequent travelling companions. (Housser's first wife was Bess Larkin. After their divorce she became the wife of the Group's moving spirit, Lawren S. Harris.)

We admired the work of both artists, but our friendship was based on their fun-loving spirits. Isabel, like Yvonne, was a fount of amusing stories — often of early painting trips and discussions about art with members of the Group, most of whom she had known well from the twenties and thirties.

Isabel lived in Toronto near Hogg's Hollow but spent many weekends at Parkwood, her father's Oshawa estate. Colonel McLaughlin was then in his late nineties but was still amazingly alert and maintained his excellent physical condition through a rigorous programme of nutrition and exercise. In fact, he was still able to visit his private salmon-fishing camp near Cap Chat, Quebec and his winter home in Bermuda. It was during one of his southern trips, while Yvonne was staying in Oshawa with Isabel, that Signe and I were first invited to Parkwood.

Parkwood was situated in a private park in the heart of the city of Oshawa. The house itself, with its handsome portico of columns, could only be described as a mansion, but to Isabel it was simply her childhood home. She treated it as a nice place for nostalgic visits but not a place she would any longer choose to live. Still, she took a natural pride in showing it to first-time visitors like ourselves.

Strolling on velvet lawns through groves of ornamental trees past beautifully tended beds of flowers, we found it hard to remember that we were in the centre of a thriving industrial city, not far from the assembly lines of General Motors. But the best was yet to come — the sunken garden. Standing on the stone patio behind the house we looked over a recessed boulevard of formal stone pools with dancing fountains which seemed to stretch the distance of a city block, to a marble-columned building which seemed to have been magically transported from ancient Greece. Sculptured walks bordered the pools on either side and then gave way to immense slopes covered with brilliant flowers. At dusk the fountains were illuminated with ever-changing lights.

For all its size, Parkwood was no decorator's showcase but a comfortable family home if, of course, you can imagine a family home whose main hallway ceilings displayed murals by Frederick Challener. On our tour we passed through the beautifully panelled library and dining room and eventually, at the north side of the house, reached a huge conservatory-greenhouse which was connected to the house by a doorway leading into the exercise area which included not only a squash court and indoor swimming pool but a full-scale bowling alley. It was in the bowling alley that we first saw a major part of Colonel McLaughlin's collection of Canadian art.

Crowded together and compressed into that long narrow space, works by Tom Thomson, Emily Carr and the other artists of the Group were almost overwhelming. Commanding our startled attention at such close range we saw Lawren Harris's *Pic Island*, flanked by Emily Carr's strong and brooding *Old Tree at Dark* and A. Y. Jackson's *Radium Mine*. Franklin Carmichael's compelling *Northern Tundra* was cheek by jowl with A. J. Casson's splendid watercolour, *Pike Lake*. This astonishing collection went on and on.

Colonel McLaughlin had acquired most of these paintings in 1940, with the help and advice of his old friend A. Y. Jackson. At that time works by members of the Group and, in fact, virtually all Canadian artists, were going begging and the sale must have been a real boon to the artists.

As they were no longer entertaining on a grand scale, in 1940 the McLaughlins had decided to redecorate and refurnish their large ballroom while the family was spending a winter vacation at their home in Bermuda. Alex suggested to R. S. McLaughlin that the room would make a fine art gallery and that he, Alex, should assemble some paintings for the McLaughlins' approval upon their return. Naturally, Alex's selection was made largely from works by his painter friends. It included such major canvases as J.E.H. MacDonald's *Forest Wilderness* and Lismer's *Bright Land*, as well as his own more modest *Radium Mine*.

After personally attending to the hanging, Alex was at Parkwood on the day of the McLaughlins' return, anxiously awaiting their reactions. Mrs. McLaughlin was the first to come in from the car. As she walked through the room she seemed far more interested in the effect of the redecorating than in the paintings which dominated all four walls. When she left without comment, it seemed to Alex that the pictures had held little appeal for her. His heart sank. Moments later Colonel McLaughlin stood in the archway, beaming with excitement as he saw the display. He moved slowly from painting to painting, absorbing the impact of each one, his excitement building as he questioned Alex with growing curiosity about each artist, when Mrs. McLaughlin returned.

"Adelaide," he exclaimed. "have you seen these exciting paintings that Alex Jackson has brought for us?"

Sensing her husband's enthusiasm, Mrs. McLaughlin gallantly rose to the occasion. "Yes, Sam, I'm sure they are very fine," she said austerely.

As Colonel McLaughlin continued to study the individual paintings Jackson began to breathe more easily. Colonel Sam was about to become the owner of a fine collection of Canadian art.

After his wife's death in 1958, R. S. McLaughlin lived alone with his memories, his paintings and his gardens at Parkwood, watched over by a loyal cadre of servants and his secretary-companion of many years, Betty McMullen. The years had reduced his business and social activities, but his mind was clear and he still visited his office at General Motors of Canada almost daily. On his door was the gold-lettered title, Honorary Chairman of the Board.

Back in the living room, relaxing with Isabel and Yvonne, Signe and I tried to assimilate all we had seen, but we found this brief *tête-à-tête* was to be merely an intermission between two major exhibitions.

Isabel led us up the great staircase to a large sitting room next to her father's bedroom suite and we sensed by her excitement that this room was to be the climax of our tour. The entire area was carpeted and decorated in muted greys, a perfect setting for the scores of small paintings in equal-sized frames which surrounded us. It was a major art collection within a collection — the fifty-four magnificent illustrations which had been created by the great

Quebec artist, Clarence Gagnon, for the famous 1933 Mornay Edition of Louis Hémon's classic French-Canadian novel, *Maria Chapdelaine*.

The pictures ranged in size from a tiny frontispiece of a wilderness lake which measured less than three inches, to illustrations of *habitant* life, the largest slightly over ten inches. Executed over a five-year period between 1928 and 1933, these magical little paintings are, in the opinion of many, the finest series of illustrations ever produced by a Canadian artist. Gagnon's familiarity with and love for rural Quebec and its people, his meticulous attention to detail and his daring use of light and shadow make them unforgettable. Colour, at once rich and subtle, gives each of these little master works a jewel-like quality. Each picture was strikingly mounted in a hand-striped matte frame on which McLaughlin had commissioned a calligrapher to letter a short related passage from Blake's English translation of Hémon's classic. We have never forgotten the exhilarating day when we were first privileged to see these national treasures.

Isabel told us how her father had come to buy the series. After Clarence Gagnon's death in 1942, his wife Lucille offered to sell the fifty-four exquisite little paintings to the Government of Quebec and then to several public institutions with the stipulation that the series must be kept together forever. For reasons that are not entirely clear, she was unable to sell the works as a series until a friend suggested that she approach R. S. McLaughlin. McLaughlin promptly agreed, not only to her asking price but to her stipulation that the precious series never be broken up. Madame Gagnon knew that R. S. McLaughlin's word was his bond.

First published in 1913, *Maria Chapdelaine* proved to be an enduring classic about a young French-Canadian woman and her life in the Lac St-Jean area of rural Quebec. The book was translated from the original French and published not only in English but also in nineteen other languages and Braille. Various editions have been illustrated by distinguished artists such as Thoreau MacDonald and Suzor-Côté. The story has also been made into a stage play, a motion picture and a television drama.

Nevertheless, by far the most important and impressive edition of *Maria Chapdelaine* was produced by Mornay Press of Paris in 1933. Gagnon was commissioned to create the colour illustrations. This lavish limited edition (two thousand and eighty numbered copies) featured colour reproductions of the fifty-four paintings with such superb quality that the volume has long been among the most sought-after by rare book collectors and has commanded prices at auctions in excess of three thousand dollars. On the coffee table in Colonel McLaughlin's private viewing room was his own copy of that special edition.

After our first visit to Parkwood, Isabel became a frequent visitor to Tapawingo and we saw her often in her own home as well as at Yvonne's. Our second invitation to Parkwood, for afternoon tea, was special because we were introduced to her father. We found him alert and chipper, delighted to show us the prize blooms in his conservatory and to share his memories of the gardeners who had developed his cherished gardens, or to praise our mutual friend, A. Y. Jackson, who had been a frequent guest.

In later years Alex would chuckle over an incident that occurred during one of his weekends at Parkwood.

"We were having breakfast on Sunday morning and I mentioned to Colonel McLaughlin that my friend Bill Beatty had an art school during the summer months at Port Hope, about twenty miles away. I said that I would very much like to visit him and asked if there was a bus or train connection. Colonel Sam told me not to worry about a train or bus, he would see that I got to Bill's school in Port Hope.

"After breakfast, I was taken to the front door and installed behind the McLaughlin chauffeur in a sixteen-cylinder Cadillac limousine, the biggest car I had ever seen.

"When we arrived at the school, Bill Beatty walked out to meet this unexpected and obviously important visitor. The chauffeur stepped out, opened the back door, and I stepped out.

" 'My God ... Alex,' Beatty exclaimed, 'you must have sold a painting!' "

Colonel McLaughlin took great pride in his best-known painting, *After the Bath*, by Paul Peel as well as works by European old masters, but there was little doubt that his deepest affection was reserved for the collection of fifty-four exquisite little paintings by Clarence Gagnon, which he kept close to him in the large sitting room next to his bedroom.

Although he was somewhat shorter than my own six feet, even in his nineties, Mr. Sam, as he was affectionately known, gave an immediate impression of wiry energy. He told us with some pride that he did fifty push-ups every morning — perhaps a slight exaggeration — but his alertness and memory would have done credit to someone half his age and his interests still went far beyond the business and finance that still occupied him daily. Whether he was salmon fishing at his Quebec retreat or dealing with fine horses at his thoroughbred stables north of Oshawa, no significant detail escaped his attention. He also scrutinized carefully the public and charitable causes which commanded his interest and generosity.

Bob Laidlaw told us a story about his term as first chairman of the then new Toronto Hospital for Sick Children. During the capital fund-raising phase, Laidlaw visited Sam McLaughlin in Oshawa and explained the details of a new and very advanced unit which the hospital hoped to install — a critical area known as "intensive care", monitored by wondrous new computers. McLaughlin was fascinated with the revolutionary new concept and after plying his friend with penetrating questions finally came to the crucial question, "How much will it cost?"

"A million dollars," said Bob, hoping for a sizeable lead donation.

"I'll pay for it," McLaughlin said quietly.

A more personal project was his gift of the McLaughlin Planetarium to the Royal Ontario Museum. While it was under construction he attended many meetings and sessions and no detail, from overall design to optics, escaped his attention. He was always searching for, and demanding, the best.

As he delighted us with his anecdotes that afternoon at Parkwood we had no inkling that two years later, R. S. McLaughlin would play an important part in the growth of the McMichael Collection.

After our first viewing of Colonel McLaughlin's collection I often thought of those great paintings by our favourite artists and the magnificent little works by Clarence Gagnon. The Colonel continued in good health, celebrated his ninety-eighth birthday, and as far as I knew, the paintings were still not committed to any public gallery nor had he any plans to build a public gallery to house them. Would they be divided up among his heirs when none, except Isabel, had a special interest in art?

One evening, at a small party at Yvonne Housser's, I drew Isabel aside for a few minutes hoping to get some answers to my speculations and possibly enlist her help. I felt that if her father consulted anyone about his plans for his collection it would almost certainly be Isabel.

"I hope you won't think I'm being too forward, Isabel," I began as tactfully as I could, "but I can't help wondering whether your father has made any definite plans for his art collection."

"Not ... that ... I ... know ... of." Then, with a mischievous twinkle in her eyes, "There's only one way to find out. Ask him!"

That was not at all what I had in mind. I continued, "I was

hoping that you might help by telling him about the Collection in Kleinburg and perhaps encouraging him to visit us. Maybe even..."

"I know what you're thinking, Bob, but Dad has a mind of his own. I wouldn't presume even to suggest what he should do. If I were to ask him it would only annoy him and probably lessen your chances. I can't play any part except to suggest that if you wish to talk with him, you should call his secretary and make an appointment."

"But does he even know of the Collection?" I asked nervously.

"I think he does ... he reads the papers and I believe I gave him one of your nice little catalogue books." After a moment of reflection she continued, "I would strongly advise that you approach the matter on a businesslike basis and on its merits. He knows that you and I are friends, of course, but it would be better if my name is not mentioned. He is a strong man with a very strong will and admires people who will stand up to him. Remember that!"

I am as likely as the next person to put off 'til tomorrow any formidable challenge, but how many tomorrows are there likely to be when a man is ninety-eight years old?

I wasted no time in calling R. S. McLaughlin's secretary at General Motors to ask for an appointment, fully aware that the meeting could be a major turning point in the Collection's history. Later that day the same polite, precise voice called me back to say that Colonel McLaughlin would see me in his General Motors office at nine o'clock on the following Wednesday morning, less than forty-eight hours away!

Except for Tapawingo and our own collection, this would be the most significant gift the Collection had ever received if I could bring it off. I had arrived at a rough valuation of approximately one million dollars, but it was less that huge sum than the quality of the McLaughlin collection that excited me.

To overcome my nervousness I tried to place myself in Colonel McLaughlin's position. He had not visited the Collection in Kleinburg and it would be difficult, nearly impossible, for me to do it justice. If only he could visit Kleinburg, I was certain he would see it as exactly the right place for his paintings, but I also knew that he saved his energies for visits to places and things in which he was intensely involved. He would, for example, allow himself to be taken to Woodbine Race Track, when one of his own horses was running in the Queen's Plate.

There had to be a better way of securing the McLaughlin

collection than walking in and asking, or more accurately, begging for it, but the harder I tried to think, the more difficult the problem became. Finally, seeing my anxiety, Signe suggested that I go for a walk in the woods. As Sam and Inky bounded among the trees and I strolled somewhat aimlessly through ferns and wildflowers, a new and seemingly foolproof approach to Colonel McLaughlin came to me.

Most collectors are flattered to be asked to loan their prized art to a public gallery for special exhibitions. I realized that if I were to approach Colonel McLaughlin for a loan of some of his pictures for a special exhibit over a period of possibly two or three months he would probably agree and, more important, be interested enough to visit the exhibit and the rest of the Collection. Seeing how well his pictures looked in this unique setting he would ...

My mind was made up. I got a good night's rest. The next day I met R. S. McLaughlin and Jack English, his extremely shrewd accountant and personal financial advisor, in the office of the Honorary Chairman of General Motors.

Following perfunctory pleasantries the two men sat in silence, ready to give their full attention to my proposal. Confident that my request to borrow a major part of his collection for a special exhibition would be well received, I made a little speech. "Colonel McLaughlin," I began formally, "like most things you have accomplished in your distinguished lifetime, you have succeeded in creating an extremely fine collection of Canadian art. At Kleinburg we have established a unique art gallery which is now owned by the Province of Ontario and which is dedicated exclusively to presenting the works of Canada's national school of artists, the Group of Seven and a few of their fellow painters ... exactly the same fine painters whose works make up most of your collection. We are almost ready to open an important new wing at the gallery. We would be honoured to mark the occasion by hanging a large part of your collection, if you would consent to loan it for two or three months." I paused, confident that I had made a request that would be received with pleasure and waited for what I was sure would be a graceful acceptance.

Suddenly stiffening as he leaned forward on his elbows across the massive, hand-crafted desk, Colonel McLaughlin said bluntly, "Why should I? I love those pictures. At my age I won't have too much longer to enjoy them. I don't see why I should be expected to loan them for even a few days. Time is very precious to me and two months is a very long time." In the circumstances, his reasoning was flawless. My brilliant strategy had failed to anticipate this natural, human, and now completely understandable reaction. My prize was slipping away.

Isabel's words flashed before me and I shifted gears. To reverse — and then fast forward.

"I understand your feelings, Colonel McLaughlin. In similar circumstances I would feel exactly as you do. In fact — we have given our pictures away, but we continue to live with them. You should do the same! You should not lend, but give your pictures to the Collection in Kleinburg, while continuing to enjoy them in your own home for the rest of your life!"

"Why should I give them?" the Colonel was not easily swayed.

"First, and most importantly, you should make sure that the great paintings which you love so much are cared for permanently so that they can be admired by future generations. Our gallery was conceived to hang a collection specially dedicated and limited to a small number of great artists who interpreted our country in a distinctively Canadian manner ... the same artists that you and we have admired most. The Collection is not a rotating exhibition like most other public galleries. It's a permanent full-time display. For the first time in Canada, a public gallery, owned by the Province of Ontario, has been established to present a very important part of the nation's art on a permanent basis. All your paintings would be on view at all times in the future. Each would have an attractive brass plaque bearing the artist's name along with your name as donor."

"A most interesting idea," he said cautiously. "But I've been around a great deal longer than you and I've found that things have a habit of changing with time. Original good intentions are so often forgotten. What assurance is there that after you and I are gone, someone won't change the plan?" Perhaps his thoughts were going back to one of Canada's best-known automobiles, the "McLaughlin Buick". With the outbreak of World War II, production of consumer automobiles was halted and for several years General Motors became an important part of the Arsenal of Democracy. After war's end and the resumption of civilian production, McLaughlin had retired from active management and the hub caps of one of Canada's most popular cars bore only the single word "Buick".

"Fortunately, the Ontario government has foreseen that possibility in advance," I said, handing him a copy of our 1965 Agreement. "You may keep this copy. In it you will find that only ten artists — all of them also in your collection — are designated.

Any further designations must be nominated and approved by the advisory committee. My wife and I are two of its four members and it has a chairman who must be approved by us. In order to maintain this balance, in the event of one of our deaths, the remaining partner may appoint a member to substitute for the other McMichael. When we are both gone, the Collection is specifically confined by this Agreement to those artists that have been designated by the advisory committee."

The old master of business, well aware of human and government frailties, began reading the ten-page document and then quickly leafed through to the final page on which he read the words, "HER MAJESTY THE QUEEN IN RIGHT OF ONTARIO, represented by the Honourable John Parmenter Robarts, Premier of Ontario", over the bold signature of John P. Robarts. Under this appeared Signe's and my signatures, and that of the Honourable J. R. Simmonett, Minister of Energy and Resources, acting as witness.

I pursued what I hoped was a slight softening. "Designation of other artists is necessary on a very limited basis to include certain other members of the Group of Seven and three or four of their very close contemporaries such as Clarence Gagnon, although we haven't yet a single example of his work. But to these few additional designations and works by our Indian and Inuit peoples, the Collection will remain strictly confined. Your paintings would be on display at all times."

"I'm impressed with the thoroughness with which the government and you people appear to have set this up," McLaughlin said.

"There's one more point which I should mention," I went on. "Your paintings would be evaluated at present market values and you would receive an official receipt, the amount of which would be totally deductible from your taxable income."

Smiling at English with an expression of futility, he replied, "That's all very nice. But I've always donated more than the government will allow me to deduct and this year's no exception."

"Please let me explain," I said. "Your gift to the McMichael Collection would be a gift to Her Majesty in Right of Ontario. Parliament has recently enacted an amendment to the *Income Tax Act* which makes such a gift totally deductible from income without reference to the limitations which apply to charitable giving. As I stated, the value of your gift will be one hundred percent deductible from your income."

Turning to his advisor, McLaughlin asked, "Have you heard of this, English?"

"No, I haven't, Mr. McLaughlin."

"Are you sure of your facts, young man?"

"Yes, I am, sir," I replied confidently. "I can have an official copy of the amendment on Mr. English's desk by nine o'clock tomorrow morning."

"You're sure of your facts," he smiled. "I don't need the money, but I'm pleased to know that the government has at last learned how to say thank you. Now, young man, how soon can we complete this gift?" Half jokingly he added, "We may not have much time."

'I can be at Parkwood in fifteen minutes," I said, smiling, "and if your secretary can lend me a tape measure or a yardstick I can list the paintings. I can deliver a gift agreement for your signature, along with a copy of the amendment, to Mr. English tomorrow morning."

"That's prompt attention," he replied. "Let's get on with it."

I pushed my luck a little further, "Colonel McLaughlin, do you intend the Collection to have its choice of all your Canadian pictures ... including Gagnon's illustrations for *Maria Chapdelaine*?"

There was a pause. "Leave the Maria Chapdelaines. I'd like to think about those," he answered. My luck had run out.

Pausing just long enough to try to express my gratitude, I lost no time getting to Parkwood. Betty McMullen met me at the door and, bursting with excitement, I told her my news and asked for a ruler and some paper. In spite of my initial confidence, in my fondest dreams I could not have imagined the events of the past hour or that there would be an urgent need for measuring, cataloguing and preparing a formal agreement of gift.

Minutes later I was in the bowling alley busily assigning descriptive titles to the McLaughlin paintings and measuring their dimensions with great care. Merely touching these great paintings and knowing that some day they would be part of the Collection in Kleinburg made my heart pound. As I moved from Jackson to Harris to Casson and to Lismer's monumental *Bright Land* I felt sure the artists would be pleased when they learned that these outstanding examples of their work would be hanging one day in "their" gallery.

About noontime Betty McMullen stopped by to ask how I was getting along and to tell me that Colonel McLaughlin had returned from his office and was expecting me as his guest for lunch.

Seated at the head of the dining room table, R. S. McLaughlin re-introduced "Nursey" and Betty, who were having lunch with us, and asked me to be seated on his right. Recalling my earlier suggestion, he asked how I felt about Gagnon's illustrations for *Maria Chapdelaine*.

"What can I say?" I answered, not very originally. "The paintings are each a tiny master work. Together ..., and I feel they must be kept together ... they are truly a national treasure! They should always have a room to themselves where people can study and marvel at them and also see them in the context of the book they were so lovingly created for ... sort of a little shrine."

"Would you be prepared to set aside such a room for them in your gallery?"

I felt my pulse race. "Yes, we would. As a matter of fact, my wife and I have recently built a new wing which contains a perfect gallery for them. It's over fifty feet long and is finished in weathered barn siding ... not unlike the textured silver-grey of the rural houses described in *Maria Chapdelaine*."

"I'd like to see that room sometime," he mused. Then, as if wanting to give the matter more thought, his mind turned to another subject. My pulse returned to normal and I settled down to enjoy my lunch and the Colonel's reminiscences of the early days of the auto industry.

"Sixty years ago," he began, "almost every family had a horse and buggy. I was in charge of our family's business, the McLaughlin Carriage Works. I grew up in the little village of Inniskillen, not far from here. At that time, a new invention called the automobile was just beginning to appear on the roads ... and I was very interested in it. But a group of my competitors, mostly friends of mine in the carriage business, were afraid that the new contraptions, as they called them, might seriously cut into their business. They'd decided to band together into one larger company which they felt would make them stronger in opposing, or at least competing against, the automobile. They approached me with a proposal to join them, to merge our works into the new and much larger company. This would have been a big move for me and I asked for twenty-four hours to consider their proposition. When they returned next day, I told them that I felt I couldn't join them but that I'd be willing to sell our carriage works to them so that it could become part of their new company. I guess they were puzzled, but anyway, they were delighted to be able to buy our company and readily agreed to terms. The day after the sale I was on the train to Detroit where I met with Willy Durant and purchased the Canadian rights to the Buick engine. That was the beginning!"

"And the rest is history," I seconded. The story had undoubtedly been told and retold many times, but for me it was utterly fascinating to hear of the beginnings of General Motors of Canada from the lips of its founder.

As our green Buick station wagon purred its way along the Macdonald-Cartier Freeway toward Kleinburg, I prayed, not entirely altruistically, that the grand old man of Parkwood would live to celebrate a remarkable century of achievement.

That evening, Signe and I checked and re-checked the Agreement of Gift and the detailed lists of works appended to it. As we read the names, *Pic Island* by Lawren Harris, *Silver Birches* by Tom Thomson, *Forest Wilderness* by J.E.H. MacDonald and dozens more, we became more and more excited as we realized that, with a stroke of the pen, R. S. McLaughlin was about to make possible our greatest single advance.

The following morning, I was again in Oshawa. I gave Jack English a copy of the new Income Tax Amendment, as promised, and reviewed the terms of the gift agreement which we had prepared along with the attached lists of paintings covered by the agreement. He said he would have it signed that day and assured me that he felt certain he would soon be in touch with me again concerning some of Colonel McLaughlin's other pictures.

A few days later English telephoned to say that the signed and witnessed gift agreement was ready to be picked up. Always the keen accountant, he asked, "How much do you think Colonel McLaughlin's series of paintings for *Maria Chapdelaine* would be worth?"

I hesitated, recognizing that McLaughlin would not concern himself with dollar values related to something so emotionally important to him, but that his watchful accountant would. Trying to place a value on this unique series would not be easy and I did not want to leave any impression that I was setting even an unofficial value on it. But I also knew that English was probably in a position to influence the final decision and I didn't want to offend him by turning away his question.

"I can't place a value on the paintings," I said shortly, "but knowing the value of small Gagnon landscapes which are frequently on the market, and recognizing that each of the fifty-four pieces is in a very different and special category from available landscapes, I would hazard a guess ... and that's all it is, that the total series should be worth over a quarter of a million and perhaps as much as a half million."

"That's a wide spread. You can't give me a closer idea?" he asked.

"No, I really can't, and I must stress that the figure is only my personal opinion. It may be low or high. I can tell you that the value is very substantial."

"I'm sure you understand, Mr. McMichael," English continued, "that my concerns are always for Colonel McLaughlin's financial affairs and that's the only reason I asked. I am authorized to tell you that he has decided, regardless, to give the *Maria Chapdelaine* pictures to your collection."

He made the statement softly, almost casually, but my heart began pounding. "Can I ask you to repeat that, Mr. English?"

With a slight chuckle, "I am authorized to tell you that Colonel McLaughlin has decided to sign over the *Maria Chapdelaine* pictures to your collection. He wants to keep them for a while, of course, like the others." Then with a bigger chuckle he said, "Colonel McLaughlin asked me to tell you he won't keep you waiting too long." At ninety-eight, the Colonel's sense of humour was still in good repair.

"Now that the decision has been made, what would you like me to do?" I asked.

"I think it would be best if you prepared another agreement covering the *Maria Chapdelaine* pictures as an additional gift to the ones which he has already signed over to you. Bring it to me in Oshawa just as soon as possible." Then he told me that Colonel McLaughlin had just left for his estate in Bermuda but that the documents would be forwarded for his signature.

Almost as an afterthought, Jack English said, "Colonel McLaughlin was quite surprised when he studied the first gift agreement that you hadn't included in your selection his favourite picture *After the Bath*. He wondered if you knew that he intended you to have it as well as the other Canadian pictures."

The offer of this fine painting put us in something of a quandary. The beautiful, almost life-size picture of two little children warming themselves before a fireplace, glowing flames reflecting on their naked little bodies, was quite possibly the best-known painting ever created by a Canadian artist. For generations it had been widely reproduced and was a sentimental favourite in countless homes. I remembered well the strong impression a print in my grandmother's home had made on me as a youngster, and Signe recalled seeing a reproduction during her childhood years in the remote Peace River district of northern Alberta. It would unquestionably be a popular drawing card for the Collection.

After the Bath was painted in France, where Canadian artist Paul Peel, a native of London, Ontario, was living in 1890. The painting is reputed to have been a favourite of Sarah Bernhardt, who at one time had considered purchasing it. She was not alone. The painting had endeared itself to people of all ages all over the world, not the least of whom, I knew, was Premier Robarts.

Yet could this famous painting by a Canadian artist be considered in the oeuvre of the artists of our "national school"? Signe and I had always insisted the Collection be dedicated to the pioneers of our artistic nationalism and we, and the government, had agreed it would be confined to their art. The fame and captivating qualities of this unique painting gave us pause and tested our commitment.

We were almost overpoweringly tempted to take the famous and enchanting *After the Bath* into the Collection, but our decision was never really in doubt. We knew in our hearts that accepting it would change the Collection forever. It would no longer be a memorial to our truly national art. This gift would open the doors to other fine works, older or newer, but quite removed from the spirit in which our collection gallery had been conceived.

After the Bath was a classic and it should be held and preserved by the province of its creator's birth for the enjoyment of all. But it did not belong at Kleinburg.

Jack English must have wondered at my indecision when I concluded our telephone conversation by telling him that we would prepare a gift agreement for the *Maria Chapdelaine* pictures promptly but that I wanted to give some thought to *After the Bath*. A decision could not be long delayed since English was sending the agreements to Bermuda within the next few days and Colonel McLaughlin had every right to expect an answer concerning his favourite painting. An outright rejection would be difficult for him to understand.

Some time earlier, John Robarts had given me an unlisted telephone number which should be used only when I felt it was absolutely necessary to reach him directly — and in a hurry. Using his hotline for the first time, I heard after three rings a gruff, familiar voice, "Robarts."

"John, this is Bob McMichael." I said. "I'm sure you know of Paul Peel's famous painting, *After the Bath*."

"I sure do. Peel was born in my home town, you know, and it's always been one of my favourites."

"How would you like to receive it on behalf of Ontario, as a gift?"

"I'd love to." Then, a little cautiously, "What do I have to do?"

"Just say so."

"All right, I'd love to."

Robarts had already been briefed by Keith Reynolds about R. S. McLaughlin's magnificent gift to the Collection and I explained as briefly as possible the situation as it appeared to us at the moment, saying that I felt it would be entirely appropriate for the famous picture to hang in the Ontario Legislative Buildings, perhaps even in the office of the Premier of Ontario.

"You're a devil, Robert," growled John. "Tell Colonel McLaughlin we'll hang the painting wherever he wants it to be hung. Thanks for calling ... and keep me posted ... I'd like to write to him myself."

Arranging an appointment with English, I arrived in Oshawa the following morning carrying with me two gift agreements, one covering Gagnon's *Maria Chapdelaine* illustrations for the McMichael Collection, the other referring only to *After the Bath* for the Province of Ontario. After telling English of my conversation with Premier Robarts, I stated that we felt that the great painting should not be within a collection which, as I had pointed out to Colonel McLaughlin, was meant to be confined to a defined national theme, but that with its very broad appeal it should be in a place of special honour in the province ... perhaps the Ontario legislative buildings, or as Mr. Robarts had said, "wherever the Colonel wants it to be."

Jack English seemed satisfied and, moreover, impressed that Premier Robarts was taking such a personal interest in the picture. He would send the agreements to Bermuda and relay our thoughts and the premier's proposal to his boss. He felt that Colonel McLaughlin would probably view the slightly amended proposal favourably and expected it would be about two weeks before the agreements would be returned to him from Bermuda.

Those were two of the longest weeks in our collecting lives. After what seemed an eternity, English telephoned from Oshawa to say that he had both signed gift agreements ready for me to pick up.

In a letter accompanying the agreements, R. S. McLaughlin had written:

"I am glad the collection of Gagnons is going to the McMichael Gallery at Kleinburg as that undoubtedly is going to be a great art centre for Canadian paintings."

I knew what it must feel like to win the jackpot in a lottery, and Canada had been the big winner.

When we first met A. Y. Jackson back in 1956, he was making fairly frequent visits to Toronto, where he liked to stay with congenial friends like Walter and Jane Stewart, and Reg and Jean Dowsett.

The Stewarts' friendship with Alex Jackson dated from about 1920, when the Group had its first exhibition at the Art Gallery of Toronto and Walter, then a reporter for the University of Toronto's student newspaper, *The Varsity*, interviewed the young rebel painter at the Studio Building. As a result of that first meeting, Walter Stewart became an ardent admirer of Jackson's painting and a frequent visitor to the third floor of the Studio Building, which was also Jackson's home. A close friendship developed between the young student and the thirty-eight-year-old painter and Walter could usually be counted on to turn up at the studio for an enthusiastic preview whenever A.Y. returned from a sketching trip.

Like most young people, Walter lived on a limited budget, but it was inevitable that he would develop collector's fever and long to possess an A. Y. Jackson of his own.

Six years earlier, during a sketching trip with his friend Tom Thomson on Algonquin Park's Oxtongue River, Jackson had painted a beautiful little panel from which he had made an enlarged canvas, *The Red Maple*. Walter had managed to scrape together only twenty-five dollars, so he had no hope of buying a major canvas, but since A.Y., when asked if he still had a particular picture, always joked that he "had all of them", Walter hoped the original birch panel of *The Red Maple* might be available. It was. Still, the artist was reluctant to part with it. The larger canvas had been purchased by the National Gallery of Canada and was destined to become one of the country's best-known paintings — almost a Canadian symbol — but Jackson felt the small panel was better than his larger canvas and was reluctant to part with a work that he felt was very special. Finally, he gave in and Walter paid his twenty-five dollars for the first of what became a most outstanding collection.

Through the years, Walter, and after his marriage, his wife Jane, remained two of Jackson's closest friends. His insurance agency prospered and Walter was able to afford more choice panels and canvases. As a frequenter of the Studio Building he was fully aware of the work being done by the other artists in the building and could have acquired a fine Group collection, but he steadfastly continued to collect only works by his friend.

Our introduction to the Stewarts came through Alex's friends, the Dowsetts. We came to know the Dowsetts well during our many trips to their Lawrence Park home, the first of which was to pick up Alex for a visit to Kleinburg. They had, in turn, known how much we would have in common with the Stewarts — in-laws of their son John, who had married the Stewarts' daughter Maxwell.

When Signe and I were first invited to dinner at the Stewarts' in the mid-1950s we were delighted to be shown the legendary little panel that was everyone's favourite, but we soon realized that it was only the most famous work in an outstanding collection. Walter Stewart's good eye and his special relationship with the artist had filled his home with a unique treasury of Jackson's finest works. The walls, even those in the bathrooms, were crowded with canvases and panels. The collection overflowed into storage drawers containing very early watercolours and drawings. Walter also owned the whimsical tongue-in-cheek Jackson self-portrait, *Père Raquette* (Father Showshoes).

Like many Jackson paintings, *Père Raquette* had an interesting history. Years earlier, the Arts and Letters Club of Toronto had held a competition among its artist members. Each was to paint a self-portrait and submit it to a club exhibition for judging. After this challenge to all painters in the club, Alex Jackson returned to his studio and in the time-honoured fashion of painters of self-portraits, set up a mirror beside his easel. Still dressed in his "go-to-meeting" clothes — vest, white shirt and tie — he began a portrait of himself in the best academic tradition. A good likeness began to emerge and with all the care that he would have lavished on an important commission he continued with background detail and the calculated flourishes of an academician, right down to a mantel clock whose hands were nearing midnight.

Stepping back to view the barely completed portrait, Jackson found he was chortling to himself almost derisively. He was taking himself too seriously. Without hesitation, he turned over the large board on which he had been working and began painting a near-cartoon of himself, as he imagined he appeared when he was making a quick sketch on the snow-covered hills of rural Quebec. In this second painting, Jackson is wearing his tattered old army greatcoat and fur helmet, his feet firmly resting on bear-paw snow-shoes. His unmistakable nose emerges in semi-profile. His brush is recording the image of a decrepit barn on the hill's horizon.

This was the real Jackson ... this was Père Raquette! The nickname, appropriately, was given him a few years earlier by his fellow painter and travelling companion, Edwin Holgate.

The whimsical but unmistakable self-portrait was submitted for the club's show. Recognizing that it was precisely the image they had of A.Y., his fellow members awarded it first prize and years later it was selected by Jackson's publisher to illustrate the cover of his best-selling autobiography, *A Painter's Country*. The well-conceived, more serious portrait remains on the picture's verso side.

In half a century, Walter Stewart had gathered a fine retrospective selection of Jackson's work which traced the artist's life and travels — his boyhood home, his student years in Europe, his pre-Group and Group periods and his years of often solitary journeys from the Arctic and Indian villages of the Northwest Coast to the outports of Newfoundland. It was unquestionably the finest private collection of Jackson panels and it was crowned by superlative canvases depicting rural Quebec and the North.

Over the years our friendship with the Stewarts extended to their children, Sally, Walter Jr., Maxwell and Wendy, who grew up regarding "Uncle Alex" as a member of the family. In the summer of 1968, the entire family shared our joy that the aging artist had accepted our invitation to come to Kleinburg permanently. We, in turn, shared their sorrow when Walter Sr. was found to be terminally ill with cancer.

One warm July day, I received a telephone call from Walter, asking if I could join him on a walking tour through the McMichael Collection; Jane and Signe, he suggested, could join us or perhaps just have a cup of tea and a good chat.

I was delighted, although somewhat embarrassed, that he'd had to ask — and offered him a private tour, knowing that he could provide me with valuable background material, particularly on the Jacksons.

Walter thanked me for the offer of VIP treatment but characteristically said he'd rather see the gallery when it was open because "we can always learn a lot by seeing other people viewing art".

On the summer afternoon that Walter and I joined the other gallery visitors he told me without a trace of self-pity of his illness. Then, abruptly changing the subject, he began pointing out the obvious gaps in our Jackson holdings. Although we had twenty-two small, but very choice early panels and drawings and five important canvases, in order to have a truly retrospective representation, the Collection needed a lot of filling out; with examples from areas and periods of a very long lifework, which it did not yet cover.

Finally, when Walter had had time to assess both our strengths and our weaknesses, he turned to me without preamble and said, "Bob, I'd like to fill a lot of the gaps. When can you come down to the house?"

I was torn between joy — for the prospective gift — and sadness about the illness that had prompted it. "Walter, you may have a lot longer time to enjoy your pictures than ..."

But Walter was a realist. He wanted to see his pictures in our gallery and he had no time to waste. We made a date to review his collection the following Wednesday and he was pleased when I suggested that I bring Reg Dowsett, now chairman of the advisory committee of the McMichael Collection and a mutual friend, with me.

Walter was in high spirits when we arrived at his home in East York. We were hardly seated before he moved across the living room to his most famous little painting, *The Red Maple*, and removed it from the wall.

"I know you've always had your eye on this little fellow, Bob, so let's get off to a good start by putting it first on your list," he beamed, placing the framed panel in my hands. "Now it's yours to look after." His voice was not so steady.

I was too moved to speak as I held the little work which I had always felt to be nothing short of a national icon.

Reg Dowsett spoke for me, "You can be certain, Walter, that it will be well cared for and that it will always be given a place of honour."

Walter's incredibly unselfish performance continued. One by one he removed the very finest of his Jackson panels and canvases. As each was placed against the wall or on the sofa he said a few words about it as though he was saying a final word of farewell to friends of a lifetime. Jane wept silently and in our hearts Reg and I wept with her.

It was Walter himself who tried to lighten our mood. "Come on, Bob," he said cheerfully, "you should be helping me with this! Which of your favourites have we missed?"

By now, something over twenty works had been set out and I assured him he had more than filled the gaps.

Walter would have none of it. "You haven't any of Alex's Arctic paintings or his few works from the Rockies. He didn't care for the Rockies very much, you know ... but he did some nice things there." With that he left the room, returning with the powerful canvas, *Skeena Crossing*, which shows a majestic mountain rising beyond the totems of a tiny Indian village. Then, as if remembering something very special he had almost overlooked, he asked Jane to go with him to another room. They returned carrying a very large canvas almost five feet wide. It was *Above Lake Superior*.

"Alex painted this back in the early Algoma days and Jane made an exact copy of it as a hooked rug for our summer place at Cawaja Beach," Walter explained. "A.Y. often stayed with us there during the summers and several times he said that he liked Jane's tapestry better than his painting." Then, looking fondly at his wife, "I don't think he was joking."

When Reg Dowsett and I left the Stewart house that day there were twenty-two marvelous little oil panels and seven outstanding larger paintings, including *Père Raquette*, neatly padded and packed in the rear of the station wagon, signed gift agreements covering them in my briefcase. Walter Stewart, Jane and their children, who had given his decision their enthusiastic support, had filled many of our gaps and made a most significant contribution to our Jackson holdings.

Our primary object now became our determination that Walter should see his magnificent gift in place at Kleinburg. Time was our enemy. The next day, after each had been measured for new frames, the paintings were delivered to Ed Zakowski, the excellent conservator, for a thorough cleaning and new varnish, with instructions that he and our framemaker give the work the highest priority. They did just that, and a few weeks later we were able to hang the Jackson paintings in our newly opened wing. Each bore a bronze plaque with the inscription, "A. Y. Jackson, 1882 — Gift of S. Walter Stewart".

A special weekend in August was arranged so the entire Stewart family could be present for the formal presentation of the paintings. Jackson now lived at the gallery and would be present and we hoped to have John Robarts with us as well. Unfortunately, the premier had a previous commitment to be at Lakehead in far northwestern Ontario, but we felt that, in the circumstances, the opening should not be postponed, although Walter had always been a staunch Conservative and it was fitting that the government to which he had given much of his volunteer energy and the province to which he had made his gift should pay tribute. Fortunately, former premier Leslie Frost was willing and happy to be present as the key speaker. Following his tribute to Walter and his family we held the first reception in our much enlarged living quarters while downstairs a steady stream of visitors caught their first glimpse of the new acquisitions, many of which had never been shown publicly.

One of our prizes, however, was not yet ready to appear in public. The largest painting in the Stewart gift, *Above Lake Superior*, painted in 1924, is rich in psychedelic colour, quite unlike Jackson's characteristic style. For many years it had hung above the fireplace at the Stewarts' summer home Chez Nous on Georgian Bay. After several decades of wood smoke it required not only thorough cleaning but also the more complex treatment known as relining. The conservation work on it was not completed in time for the special August showing.

Weeks later, when years of dirt had been removed and the relining and framing completed, we contracted to have the large canvas moved from the conservation laboratory in Toronto to Kleinburg in the van of a company that specialized in the transportation of works of art. Knowing that Walter's deteriorating health made it unlikely that the Stewarts would be able to visit Kleinburg again I made special arrangements to have the truck stop at the Stewart home en route. The drivers carried the big picture into the Stewart living room and set it before an astonished Walter and Jane. They thought it had been almost completely repainted! Reassured that no new paint had been added, and that the vivid colours were as the artist intended they were somewhat chagrined to realize that Jane's prized tapestry was in fact an exact copy of a painting darkened by smoke!

Now they were seeing it exactly as it had appeared many years ago when, as a young couple, they had first gazed at its richness, in their cozy Georgian Bay retreat.

After those memorable first visits with Lawren Harris in 1957, when I had purchased our first canvas, I saw him only twice during the next eight years ... and on those occasions we met only briefly. Most of my travelling took place south of the border, but whenever I could return from the Coast via Vancouver I made it a point to call at the Harris home. Yet even on these infrequent occasions, it was not always possible to see the man who had become one of my idols.

I knew, of course, that Harris was not deliberately avoiding a meeting. After suffering a heart attack he had undergone by-pass surgery and his wife Bess was, understandably, trying to shield him much of the time from all visitors except his family and doctor. She had engaged a nurse-companion who accompanied Lawren on daily exercise walks and relaxing drives to nearby Point Gray. I had never seen myself as a nurse-companion, but I certainly envied this devoted practitioner her hours of conversation and comradeship with the charming and witty artist-philosopher. Her attention to Harris's needs, however, made it possible for Bess and I to have long chats and, sometimes, lunch. On one visit she introduced me to one of the artist's sons, Howard, who lived in Vancouver and also to the surgeon who had performed the successful by-pass operation, Dr. Jack Parnell. Over the next few years both became good friends who entertained Signe and me nearly every time we visited the West Coast. When they and their wives came to the Toronto area they were our guests at Kleinburg.

One evening, years later, at the Parnell home on Rabbit Lane, high on a mountain overlooking Vancouver, Jack showed us a fascinating little sketchbook filled with drawings interspersed with lengthy hand-written notes about the sketches and the artist's daily activities. In effect, it was an illustrated diary. We immediately recognized the words and illustrations of a book published by Clarke, Irwin & Company in 1953 under the title *Pause*. We had both read this enchanting, light-hearted record of Emily Carr's confinement to a sanatorium in England in 1903 and delighted in her humorous drawings of herself, her nurses, her doctors and her pets, which included a nest of newly hatched thrushes.

As we turned the pages of notes and sketches in pencil we could hardly believe that we were holding the original manuscript of the well-known book, written and drawn over half a century earlier. Both our delight and our familiarity must have been obvious to Parnell for he then told us that he had felt for some time that the sketchbook should be in the hands of a public institution which had a special interest in Emily Carr. He had watched with approval the steadily increasing number of her works being displayed at Kleinburg, and now felt that the Collection was the right place for this unique illustrated manuscript.

Although he was unable to make such a long trip, Lawren Harris was pleased that his wife, Bess, and his daughter, Peggy, could travel together to Montreal for Expo '67. It was unfortunate that Signe and I chose to visit Expo at the same time, so it was only on our return that we learned that the two women had paid a visit to Kleinburg in our absence. On that visit they would have seen only two of Lawren's canvases, our first larger picture, *Shimmering Water*, and a fine, slightly smaller one given by Yvonne Housser, *Lake Superior Island*, among a dozen of his oil panels including our very first purchase, *Montreal River*.

There had been times during talks with Bess over several years that I had the impression she was skeptical about the Collection and our motivations and intentions. She was not the only one with doubts during this early period of our development. Even though our collection, land and buildings had been given to the Province there were many who could not understand, much less accept, what we had done as being purely altruistic. Given that we were neither wealthy nor old, such skepticism, especially among those who had not yet visited Kleinburg, was disappointing but understandable. We could only hope that even in our absence the two women closest to Lawren Harris had been impressed with what we were attempting to achieve.

A year later, in October 1968, when I was at last completely free of any further responsibilities to New York, Signe and I made another visit to Vancouver. We visited with Jack and Juanita Parnell and Howard and Lynn Harris and were welcomed, it seemed, with open arms by Bess and Lawren Harris for a long and very satisfying afternoon at their home.

During earlier visits Bess had discussed her hope of having a book published which would deal with her husband's art and philosophy, with special emphasis on his final period of abstract painting, which was not yet being well accepted by galleries, critics and collectors. By this time the book, which she was coediting with R.G.P. Colgrove, was almost ready for publication and she proudly showed us a dummy paste-up and read aloud some of Lawren's writings which were to be included in it. We felt she was anxious to receive our comments and I'm certain she could feel our enthusiasm for the book which, though not a biography, would provide an insight into Lawren's intellectual interests as well as a rich sampling of good colour reproductions of some of his outstanding paintings from the early houses of 1910 through the Group period and, reaching a climax, his last quarter century of abstract painting.

Other than those on his walls, most of the paintings Lawren had kept were stored in racks in a basement room to which I had never been invited. Now, to my great joy, Bess led us to this room, which few except family members had entered. Perhaps she sensed somehow that this would be our last visit to Belmont Avenue.

From our talks together over the years, and her viewing of the Collection in Kleinburg the previous year, Bess was aware that our preference was for the paintings Lawren had produced between 1912 and 1932 when the Group disbanded and he moved toward pure abstraction. Within this earlier period we had been most attracted by his stylized, but quite literal interpretations of Algonquin, Algoma, Lake Superior and the Arctic. True, we had moved cautiously into a few works which might have been classified as semi-abstract but, like most galleries and collectors at that time, we had not yet ventured into Harris's non-objective compositions.

The canvases in the racks which surrounded us in the basement storeroom were mostly from the later non-objective years, after the mid-1930s. To my surprise, I found several of the abstracts exerted a strong appeal. One in particular, *Migratory Flight*, I withdrew from its rack for a second and more searching study. I also found myself drawn to works from the transitional period — when Harris was departing from abstract realism and moving steadily toward the totally non-objective.

Speaking of this period, Harris had said: "Our people who pay attention to the development of our art view transitions from one phase to a deeper phase sometimes with misgivings.

"There is always something given up in every change, and this means, perhaps, a little regret.

"Each new phase constitutes a new experience, a fresh revaluation, readjustment, and alteration of emotional values that at times may prove trying."

One smaller section of racks contained earlier works. Among these was the richly painted *Billboard* (1922) and the very early *Houses on Wellington Street* (1910) as well as several other major works predating the non-objective paintings.

In Harris's mountain and Arctic pictures of 1930, painted with incisive line and great simplification of detail, his continuing movement toward the total abstractions of a few years later can be sensed. I was so strongly drawn to one of these large canvases, *Mount Lefroy*, that I asked if we might move it to a larger room for proper viewing.

Surprised at my obviously deep interest in such a stark picture, Bess said teasingly, "I didn't think your tastes would ever move this far beyond the representational things — the early houses and Algoma. They're all you've talked about in the years I've known you."

"You're absolutely right, Bess," I said, "but it took Lawren over twenty years of painting to reach this stage. I've had only twelve years of collecting to catch up to him."

She burst into laughter.

Standing back from the powerful canvas, now in better light, I felt the full impact of a stark, soaring pyramid of rock and snow reaching upward to an ethereal ringed sky and one pronounced cloud formation, whose flatness makes it more symbolic than literal. In the painting, the great mountain peak becomes a symbol whose spear-like thrust all but stabs beyond the upper limits of the canvas. This impact is heightened by the elimination of the mountain's base, which remains unseen, an infinite distance below. The peak's vertical snow-covered face is formed of smoothly rounded symmetrical stripes, almost as if a giant hand had squeezed circular ribbons of white paint directly from the tube. Exposed rock sections resemble molded pylons and cylinders of rich earthy brown, highlighted by raking back lighting.

It is a portrait of a gigantic and timeless mountain, but its conception owes as much to the spiritual as to the representational. Painted in 1930, *Mount Lefroy* stretches the literal very nearly to its limits and presages Harris's imminent departure from realistic painting.

Nearly mesmerized by the compelling canvas, I was suddenly released from the spell by Bess's soft-spoken but definite announcement that it could not be sold at this time. It had yet to be photographed for her upcoming book and also because of strictures imposed by tax planning, I would have to wait for at least another year. She did, however, assure me that she was pleased with my choice and that we should have the right of first refusal. As Signe and I reluctantly carried the large canvas back to its rack, Bess suggested that I should write to her in about a year if we were still interested in the picture. I had no need to get out my calendar. I knew that was one date I would not forget.

While we had been spending two exciting hours with his work, Lawren had taken his prescribed afternoon nap and when we joined him again in the living room he appeared refreshed and happy to see us again. Bess told him of our new appreciation of his more recent work, how excited we were by the large *Mount Lefroy* canvas, and how we hoped to acquire it for the Collection in Kleinburg.

Lawren gave us a wry smile. "That sounds like progress," he said dryly.

Lawren was naturally interested in news of A. Y. Jackson who, he knew, was now living with us at Kleinburg, and he seemed delighted to hear that Alex appeared to be getting back his strength after a bout in the hospital some months earlier. We told him that Alex went for walks on our grounds almost every day with his nurse-companion and often painted sketches of the nearby hills and valley.

Talking of his old friend, Lawren recalled that he and Alex had travelled together by boat in 1930 to the Arctic and that in the same year he had painted the canvas *Mount Lefroy* from sketches made a few years earlier. He told us in a modest way that he had considered the picture quite successful but that he had taken some good-natured joshing about it from Alex and some of his painter friends.

His own painting style, he told us, was going through a change which tended to emphasize strongly defined geometric shapes. *Mount Lefroy* was basically a huge geometrical cone but the snow on its sides, so evenly applied in a series of symmetrical ridges, had reminded Alex of nothing so much as whipped cream. And, he chuckled, Alex had named the well-defined area of lemon yellow near the peak "Mount Jello"!

We were enjoying this glimpse of days gone by so much that we did not notice that Bess had left the room until she returned carrying some panels. To our astonishment and pleasure she then told us that, in anticipation of our visit, she and Lawren had selected three oil sketches which they had decided should be given to the McMichael Collection. The trio of small paintings had been carefully chosen to represent Lawren's wide-ranging travels and painting in Canada.

From the mountains of western Canada came *South End of Maligne Lake* (1925), from the East, *Newfoundland Coast* (1921) and, between the two in both time and place was *Algoma Canyon* (1923). Signe and I were brought back to the real world by Bess's gentle question to Lawren, "Shall I make us all a nice cup of tea, dear?"

"Hell no," said Harris, "this is a celebration. Let's have whisky!"

During the next twelve months we met Bess's co-editor, R.G.P. Colgrove, on several occasions as the Harris book moved towards its publication by Macmillan Company of Canada in Toronto. We felt honoured when the publisher and the Harrises asked us to arrange the official launching at Kleinburg on October 22, 1969. Appropriately, the date was the eve of Lawren's birthday. He would be eighty-four. We decided the book-launching party would be held in the largest gallery room of the new addition which had been completed a year earlier. For this important occasion, the large room would be temporarily rehung with major Lawren Harris paintings. Unfortunately, except for my earliest purchase from the artist and another smaller canvas from Yvonne Housser, all of our holdings were sketch size, approximately twelve by fifteen inches, some slightly smaller. We felt a more dramatic display was needed so we arranged to borrow *Isolation Peak* from the University of Toronto's Hart House, *Above Lake Superior* from the Art Gallery of Ontario and *Mount Lefroy* from Lawren and Bess. Seeing these three works together was an unforgettable experience. Two would, of course, be returned immediately after October 22, but we hoped that we might be allowed to keep *Mount Lefroy*, on loan, until such time as we could purchase it.

When the first copies of the book came out of the bindery, packaged in an attractive outer sleeve, one was handed to Bess's lawyer, Thomas Ladner, who happened to be in Toronto at the time. He delivered it to Bess and Lawren in Vancouver the following day. Another copy was delivered to us by hand from the publisher's Toronto office.

I immediately wrote Bess to congratulate her on the fine design, brilliant and faithful reproductions and impressive text. I felt certain the book would be a sell-out. I also took this opportunity to remind her of our discussions concerning *Mount Lefroy* and told her that now, seeing it strikingly illustrated in the new book, we were more anxious than ever to purchase the painting for the Collection.

As I wrote, I could imagine the joy Bess and Lawren would feel as they saw her labour of love, a summary of sixty exciting years, in its final splendid form.

During that night Bess suffered a severe heart attack and was rushed to hospital. The following day Dr. Jack Parnell had the sad duty of telling Lawren that Bess's work was finished.

I was sad to realize that my heartfelt letter of praise could not have reached Bess before her death, but I learned later that it was read by Peggy, Howard and Lawren P. Harris, her trustees. I felt confident they would do everything possible to honour her wishes.

Less than a month later, more than one hundred invited guests from art and media circles, as well as close friends of the Harrises and Lawren's two sons, joined co-author Pete Colgrove to celebrate the book's launching at Kleinburg. Lawren's daughter Peggy had moved into Lawren's Belmont Avenue home to be with him in his grief and could not be at the launch, but Harris's painter friends A. Y. Jackson, A. J. Casson and Barker Fairley were there to see Pete Colgrove cut into a huge cake decorated with a very realistic copy, in coloured icing, of *Mount Lefroy*.

Half a century earlier the young modernists of the Group of Seven and their supporters had been locked in bitter controversy with the Royal Canadian Academy over the selection of paintings which would represent Canada at the British Empire Exhibition, held in England at Wembley in 1924. Primarily because of firm support from Sir Edmund Walker and Eric Brown of the National Gallery of Canada, members of the Group and Tom Thomson were well represented in the show, which earned much favourable comment in the British press. It was a major turning point which gave the Group international status and, eventually, recognition at home. It was also one of the skirmishes in a battle which might have been billed as R.C.A. vs Group.

Now in 1970, the Group's fiftieth anniversary, old antagonisms had long since vanished and the Royal Canadian Academy announced that special Academy medals would be presented to Group members still living and to the nearest relatives of those who had died. The ceremony was to take place at Government House in Ottawa and the presentations were to be made by His Excellency, Roland Michener, Governor General of Canada, on January 30, 1970.

Alex Jackson and Alfred Casson were the only two living Group members who were able to be present in Ottawa to receive their medals. On the day before the presentation, Jackson, with Signe and I and his nurse Zita, shared a hotel suite adjoining one occupied by Alfred and Margaret Casson. In other nearby rooms were the relatives of other Group members.

The night before this eagerly awaited event, some four months after the death of Bess Harris, we heard from Lawren's son Lawren P., whose flight had been grounded by inclement weather in Sackville, N.B., that his father had died in Vancouver.

On March 20, 1970, pine caskets containing the ashes of Lawren Harris and his wife Bess were buried in the small memorial cemetery on the Collection grounds. Nearby were the rugged granite stones bearing the names of Arthur Lismer and Frederick Varley. At graveside, a gathering of family members and old friends, including A. Y. Jackson and A. J. Casson, stood in silence as Lawren Harris's friend Dudley Barr delivered the eulogy. Harris's granddaughter Susan placed a white floral spray on one pine chest. A. Y. Jackson, gloveless even in the cold, placed the Group's symbol, a spray of white pine, upon the other. Just before the caskets were lowered into the earth side by side, Harris's grandson, Lawren Scott Harris, read from the Harris book some of his grandfather's own words, concluding with:

"And there is no finality, no final statement...everything remains to be recreated..."

Alex Jackson, unable to hear the service as well as he might have in early days, spoke up suddenly with the final word. "Look," he said, "the sun's coming out. The sun's coming out."

And so it was. As the sun broke through sullen clouds it created pools and streams of light across the valley. On the hilltop a stand of tall pines and birches stood etched against a flat grey skyline. Everyone agreed it was a Lawren Harris kind of day.

If, in earlier years, we had suffered doubts about Bess Harris's feelings for us and the Collection they were dissipated forever that day — when we learned from a representative of her co-executor, National Trust Company Limited, that in her final will Bess had bequeathed the funds remaining in the Bess Harris Agency Account, which represented almost all of her own assets, to the McMichael Collection. She had unselfishly stipulated that the nearly fifty thousand dollars, including accrued interest, could be used by the Collection "for the purchase of paintings, drawings or other works of art executed by any one or more of the Canadian painters known as The Group of Seven".

It was a generously broad stipulation, but Signe and I were certain that we knew what she would have wanted us to do. *Mount Lefroy* was still in our possession on loan. It was insured for fifty thousand dollars.

The complexities of settling two estates resulting from deaths only four months apart were not resolved for nearly five years. With the co-operation and necessary abatements by Peggy, Howard and Lawren P. Harris, the great canvas, *Mount Lefroy*, became a permanent part of the Collection in June 1975. The appraised value had increased somewhat, but the purchase was primarily made possible by the funds which Bess Harris had so thoughtfully provided.

During the years necessary for probate, *Mount Lefroy* hung proudly, though technically still on loan, at Kleinburg and, later, was joined by the drawing and oil panels which had been its genesis. In June 1971, Pete Colgrove gave the Collection an impressive oil panel of the mountain which had been given to him by the artist. Another very similar panel was purchased by the Collection from Bob Rourke of Connecticut two years later. To complete the grouping, Lawren P. Harris then presented a grid-lined drawing which, unlike the oil panels, included another background mountain and details of clouds and sky, much as they appear in the finished canvas. Just one month after the Harrises' burial at Kleinburg, we were also able to purchase from Bob Rourke, who had been one of Lawren P. Harris's teachers at Pickering College many years earlier, a fine canvas by the senior Harris which was entitled *Mountains and Lake*. (Lawren P. Harris is, of course, also a widely respected Canadian artist.)

This acquisition was made possible by the sale of four Harris panels which had been given by Bob Laidlaw. With his approval, money obtained from the sale was used to purchase the important larger work in his name.

In November 1971, my friend Spencer Clark, co-owner with his wife Rosa of Scarborough's famous Guild Inn, invited me to lunch at the Guild. I was overjoyed when Spencer and Rosa offered me, as a gift to the Collection, their great Harris canvas, *Icebergs, Davis Strait*. Four feet by five feet in size (approximately that of *Mount Lefroy*) and painted in the same year (1930), *Icebergs* had for some years hung in the main hall of The Guild. Like its sister, *Mount Lefroy, Icebergs* is a literal, but highly stylized, portrayal of towering natural forms. In spite of my pleasure I could not help wondering how Spencer and Rosa could bring themselves to part with it. In a sense, they couldn't.

Spencer and Rosa were torn between their sincere desire to see this important work in a secure and permanent home in Kleinburg and their own and their guests' pleasure in it at The Guild. Was there some way that they could have a "duplicate" made that they could keep?

I gave the problem a lot of thought. After a long talk with Alfred Casson, we decided that painter and illustrator Joe Gauthier, who had painted excellent portraits of each of our artists for several editions of the Collection handbook, could undoubtedly produce a faithful copy, with perhaps a little help and guidance from the old master, Casson himself. Spencer and Rosa readily agreed that the painting to be hung in The Guild should carry a brass plaque stating that it was a copy of the original which had hung in that location for many years and that, to avoid even the remote possibility of controversy or misattribution in future years, it should be painted a few inches smaller than the original.

When it was completed, the copy was so good that Casson and I found it slightly frightening. But it gave great pleasure to the Clarks, who installed it where the original had hung with an appropriately worded plaque mentioning that the original was now in the McMichael Canadian Collection in Kleinburg.

Following a visit with us the preceding July (1976), Howard Harris, the painter's younger son, wrote:

> *I do want to thank you both (belatedly) so much for all your hospitality when I spent the night with you on my way home to Vancouver. I had two tours 'round the galleries but didn't complete either of them. I made it about three-quarters of the way. Next time I hope to make it all the way 'round. Your*

collection is so extensive and excellent to really *see it all in one day is a very tall order... Hope to see you both again sometime after Thanksgiving. Thank you so very much for making my last visit such a pleasant and memorable one.*

Till October, all the best of everything. Howie H.

The visit was not to be. Howard Harris died suddenly in October 1976 and Signe and I lost a good friend.

Howard's favourite of the Lawren Harrises in his own collection was the monumental *Mount Robson* (1929). Approximately the size of our three other large Harris canvases (*Pic Island*, a gift of R. S. McLaughlin, had come to Kleinburg following Col. McLaughlin's death in 1970), it had all the power of *Mount Lefroy*, to which it was very closely related by the manner of its painting, although it was very different in composition. Howard had spoken many times of this gift from his father and always with the hope that some day it would join the others in the Collection. Now his executor, National Trust Company Limited, offered the Collection first refusal, subject to other competing bids. We negotiated its purchase through our Special Art Fund, which now received the profits from the Collection's popular gift shop. Although it reduced the balance in our fund to zero, we considered its purchase for one hundred and thirty thousand dollars to be a wise decision. Looking at present prices for Harris canvases at auction, it was a very fortunate purchase for the Collection.

Harris's great painting talent was not confined to landscape subjects. Some of his portraits, such as the one of the Rev. Salem Bland in the Art Gallery of Ontario, are among the finest ever produced by a Canadian artist. Yet he rarely accepted commissions, probably because he felt that he would be depriving other painters who depended on them for a living. Of the few he painted, one of his friend, Julia Holden, is in the McMichael Collection. It and a fine Emily Carr forest subject and other smaller Group works were a gift from painter Doris Huestis Speirs.

Harris painted a major canvas of *Maligne Lake, Jasper Park* in 1924, which is in the National Gallery of Canada. In the early 1940s he made a tempera painting of the same subject for his old friend Chuck Matthews, who was producing large silk-screen reproductions for distribution to Canadian Armed Forces bases. Chuck retained the original, which he presented to us as part of a larger gift in 1969.

Many of Harris's oil panels are, in themselves, major paintings which have a visual impact out of all proportion to their modest twelve by fifteen inch size. One, *The Sentinels*, presented to the Collection by the McEacheren family of Kleinburg, is the sketch for a major Lake Superior canvas. Like *The Ice House* (1923) and *Eclipse Sound and Bylot Island* (1930) and other smaller oils it is an extremely powerful work, with all the force of a much larger painting.

The first two Harris abstract paintings came into the Collection in the early 1970s. The first, a panel known simply as *Abstract Sketch* (1937) is from his transitional period and portrays quite literal mountain images dominated by a weaving of sharply defined, light, dark and shaded spiritual forms, a bridge between Harris's departure from stylized landscapes and his entry into his final non-objective phase. The second, a canvas known as *Autumn Rhythms*, a gift of Mr. and Mrs. Robert Manuge of Halifax, was painted twenty years later and is a nearly total abstraction of brilliantly coloured leaves over swirling waters. Although in this period most of Harris's works are made up entirely of abstract patterns, this one maintains a tenuous, if far removed, contact with the literal.

One day in the late summer of 1972 I received a telephone call, which intrigued me because of its brevity and directness. Hundreds of calls which come in concerning pictures are enquiries about paintings, drawings or prints, often inherited and about which the caller knows very little except for the signed name of an obscure artist. Others bearing the name of a well-known painter are usually framed reproductions. To follow up each with a personal visit would be nearly impossible, but we try in our conversations to get a verbal description of the picture, its size and, if possible, whether it is on canvas, paper or other material along with any other known information. A photograph, even a small Polaroid, can be helpful in making identification and to determine whether a serious follow-up should be undertaken.

But this short call was different from most. In a confident, businesslike manner a voice stated, "My name is Wood. I live on Glencairn Avenue in the city. I have a picture which I think you'll be interested in... Could you come down to see me tomorrow?"

I sensed a teasing, almost taunting, yet purposeful quality in the crispness of the message and the tenor with which it was delivered. I asked no further questions except for the caller's exact address and we set a mutually convenient hour for meeting.

At the unusually impressive white stone house in one of the city's loveliest residential areas, a tall man with silver hair and a mischievous smile introduced himself as Clare Wood and led me directly to his den.

In the doorway I stood gaping at a small, richly painted canvas in which a patch of water and distant blue hills could be glimpsed through a screen of richly coloured scrub maples and towering beeches. Although I had never seen it before, there was not the slightest doubt that it was a Tom Thomson and its composition seemed strangely familiar, as if I should have recognized it immediately. As I moved closer to the brilliant painting, which was about four times the normal panel size, I looked with mounting curiosity toward my host, who until then had remained silent.

"I think you have the sketch for it in your collection," he remarked. "I can understand your puzzlement, because there's quite a difference between the sketch and the canvas, which is much freer. He's bent the trees and eliminated a lot of detail. Now do you recognize it?"

My thoughts went immediately to a birch panel Signe and I had purchased years earlier from Frank Erichsen-Brown and which we had named *Algonquin, October*. True, Thomson's painting had become much looser between the time of the panel (1914 or 1915) and the larger canvas, perhaps a year or two later. The erect foreground trees in the sketch had become twisted and bent in the larger work and a dark pine had been added on one edge to pull the scene together into a less formal but improved design. But even with the considerable changes he had made there was little doubt that Thomson had used his panel, *Algonquin, October* as the inspiration for this lovely canvas.

"I bought the painting many years ago and I've had a full share of enjoyment from it. Now I think it should join its sketch along with all the other beauties you have out in Kleinburg," he said.

Without hesitation Clare Wood removed the painting from his wall and handed it to me. Then, almost before I could put together a few inadequate words of thanks he guided me into the living room. Hanging in the centre of the main wall was a magnificent, large canvas by Franklin Carmichael. I caught my breath as I stared at one of the most powerful Canadian paintings I had ever seen.

"I'm not quite ready to part with this one yet," Wood said. "I think it's the finest thing he ever did."

I agreed with his appraisal and so it was easy for me to understand his wish to keep and enjoy the magnificent panorama of mountains, forests and near incredible cloud formations in the artist's favourite painting area, the La Cloche Mountains to the north of Lake Huron.

Clare and his wife Frances became our good friends, often coming to the Collection for a stroll among the paintings. We marvelled at the intense appreciation the couple showed for art.

After Frances's death, I received another telephone call from Clare Wood, "I have a picture I think you'd be interested in."

I smiled at Clare's humorous repetition of his call of years earlier. This time I didn't have to wonder at his invitation to meet with him at his Glencairn Avenue home. With the same gallant casualness of old he helped me load the great Carmichael canvas *Autumn* into our stationwagon. Yet in his generous gesture I could sense a concealed anguish in parting with a dear friend that had through the years brought so much pleasure to a house that now seemed somehow empty.

Robert A. Laidlaw, whose early vote of confidence — the gift of most of his paintings — had meant so much to the Collection as well as to Signe and me personally, shared our joys and excitement as we continued to build what was to become the most extensive permanent display of Tom Thomson's art to be seen anywhere. Bob's warm friendship and boundless enthusiasm, not to mention his seemingly ever-ready chequebook, helped the Collection, particularly the Thomson section, for which he always had a special affection, to scale ever-new heights.

In April 1970, we learned of three very fine Thomson panels which had come into the hands of the Roberts Gallery and promptly made arrangements to bring them to Kleinburg on approval.

In the fifteen years since our first purchase of a Thomson panel and others that followed we had watched closely the prices being paid for works by Thomson and members of the Group. In the spring of 1968, following Sotheby's opening of a major auction division in Toronto, works by most of the best-known Canadian artists began to appear in their glossy catalogues. Waddington's and other Canadian auction houses soon followed suit. An awakening interest in Canadian art combined with a new Canadian affluence filled salesrooms to capacity. A much wider audience of aggressive collectors now began to vie for a finite number of fine paintings. The race was on and it soon became obvious that Tom Thomson and members of the Group of Seven were, far and away, the front runners.

Almost every sale set new price records which were promptly reflected, or sometimes anticipated, in dealers' showrooms or by private owners of prized works. New price levels, sometimes thousands of dollars higher, were often established in a single evening and soon became known throughout the art world as the media discovered that Canadian art had become front-page news.

I think Bob Laidlaw felt the same way we did about the appreciation of work by the Group — a combination of pride at judgement vindicated, yet disbelief at the accelerating prices.

When Signe called to tell him about the three paintings we had on approval from Roberts Gallery and to invite him to lunch on his way to Roche's Point the following Friday, he was not entirely joking when he enquired wryly, "How much will this lunch cost me?"

Signe was tempted to take the bull by the horns and say frankly, "Forty-four thousand dollars!" but discretion prevailed and she ducked the question. Still, she knew that was the price being asked for the trio of Thomsons: *Ragged Pine* (later the cover piece of our second catalogue of the Collection), *Rushing Stream* and a third, which was to be one of our all-time favourites, *Tea Lake Dam*.

The following Friday, as he lingered over the single Scotch and water he permitted himself before lunch, I could see that Bob was glowing with quiet admiration for the three small works by his favourite artist. When I finally told him the price, he asked for a second drink. Small wonder. The prices Roberts was asking were nearly two hundred times greater than Bob had paid for similar works years earlier. What's more, although inflation could account for an increase of ten or twelve times, most of the rise in prices reflected a real increase. It was a classic case of many dollars chasing a few treasures.

As Bob continued to study the three panels, I knew he was thinking back to the time, fifty years earlier, when he had paid seventy-five dollars for the work of artists who were begging for recognition and sales. Even in recent years he had insured paintings for five or six hundred dollars, each now commanding prices of fifteen thousand dollars.

Before he left us that day, R. A. Laidlaw had decided to purchase all three panels for the Collection. Signe and I were overjoyed. So was Jack Wildridge. He told us later that Laidlaw's purchase was the largest individual sale Roberts Gallery had ever made.

A few months later, another Thomson panel, *Autumn Colour*, painted with a wide, lively brush in pure colour approaching the bounds of abstraction, was offered to the Collection. Again Bob

Laidlaw came to our rescue and it was purchased for about the same price as the three from Roberts.

Robert Laidlaw lived to see both these four and another four outstanding Thomson panels hanging proudly with his first magnificent gift to the Collection. Long after his final purchase, his early judgement was futher confirmed. Just over ten years later another Thomson panel came under Geoffrey Joyner's hammer at Sotheby for one hundred and thirty-two thousand dollars.

Our luncheon with Robert Laidlaw was not an exceptional occasion — except in the results. Signe and I enjoyed giving small dinner parties at Tapawingo for those who had done so much to make our dream become a reality. We never tired of the pleasure of entertaining these friends or of bringing together people like Yvonne Housser, Thoreau MacDonald, A. Y. Jackson and Isabel McLaughlin with other friends like Arnold Mason, Keith and Edith MacIvor and Barker Fairley. As might be expected, such informal gatherings of people with an abiding interest in Canadian art were the beginnings of many close friendships.

Bob Laidlaw met Bill and Margaret Tweedale at Tapawingo on several occasions. Margaret always enjoyed her long talks with Bob and, like most people who met him, she felt both respect and affection for this remarkable man. For his part, Bob was both intrigued and delighted by his friendship with the sister of his favourite artist and with any opportunity to learn more about the personal and family life of the man he had known only through the work that had always held such fascination for him.

After Bill Tweedale's death in the spring of 1971, I became even more apprehensive about Margaret's intentions for the eleven panels still hanging in the Etobicoke home where she now lived alone. At eighty-seven, she was still a lively companion, but her increasing physical frailty was a cause for real concern.

Since they were unquestionably the most important collection of Thomsons in private hands, Margaret's paintings were now attracting increased interest, not only from relatives but also from dealers, wealthy collectors and, even more disconcerting for me, curators of other public art galleries.

Although it had been apparent for some time that Margaret would soon need a full-time nurse-housekeeper, the situation became critical when, at eighty-eight she had a serious fall on the cellar stairs. I had no idea of Margaret's financial position, but I was certain of two things: she was determined to remain in her own home for the remainder of her life and, although she had resisted all offers to sell her brother's paintings, she hoped that they would one day hang with the Collection at Kleinburg. I was deeply concerned that in her understandable determination to achieve the first objective (although she was stiff and lame, her mental alertness was unimpaired) Margaret might be forced to sell some of the paintings. Surely some way could be found to make both of her wishes possible?

Puzzling over this problem, it occurred to me that Margaret might be persuaded to sell some of her paintings if she knew that they would immediately become part of the McMichael Collection. Would Bob Laidlaw, I wondered, be willing to provide the necessary funds? Agreement on both sides would be absolutely necessary for the plan to work. Approaching two such close friends as Margaret and Bob, with a real possibility of disappointment if one or the other was not receptive, was a daunting task. The big question was who to see first.

I had some understandable hesitation about approaching Bob. Only a year earlier he had laid out nearly sixty thousand dollars on behalf of the Collection. A reluctance to repeat such a generous act would be understandable.

On the other hand, it would be the first time I had ever approached Margaret with a cash offer. In the past our discussions had never gone beyond the rhetorical question, "Would you consider selling?" Now, we would be talking about a real, not a hypothetical, sale and although I was convinced I was offering her the best of two worlds, I was anxious not to bring pressure to bear. Yet I was also conscious that a delay now might bring a forced sale by her later, at a time when the Collection might be in no position to buy.

Obviously, if I could get Margaret's approval, it would be absolutely essential to persuade our white knight, Bob Laidlaw, to again come to our aid. How? The answer came to me almost at once. I would offer him the finest Tom Thomson imaginable, Margaret's beloved *Wildflowers*, and three others of near equally superb quality, *Tamaracks, Snow in the Woods* and *Spring Break Up*.

To begin our acquisitions with Margaret's personal favourites would make persuasion doubly difficult, but I felt it was the key to success in this most delicate of negotiations.

I decided to go for broke.

Instead of the difficulties I had feared, Margaret seemed almost relieved, as if a great burden had been removed from her shoulders. The pictures would be in Kleinburg where she wanted them to be and she could continue to enjoy them from time to time. And, though she avoided mentioning a need for money, it was obvious she was fully aware of the high costs she would face in the coming years.

The other party to my negotiations was equally enthusiastic. When I described Margaret's panels as among the finest ever painted by Thomson and *Wildflowers* as the finest of its kind anywhere, Bob Laidlaw agreed without a sign of hesitation to purchase the four as soon as I could complete the necessary arrangements. As always, Bob lost no time putting his decision into effect. As I left his home he handed me a cheque and had only one question, "When can I come to Kleinburg and see them?"

Three years later, in July 1974, Margaret asked Signe and I to join her and her lawyer, Sarah Goldstick, at her Etobicoke home. Mrs. Goldstick notorized a gift agreement which Margaret had signed, giving her remaining seven Tom Thomson panels and a smaller earlier sketch to the McMichael Canadian Collection.

Five years later, before her death in 1979, she added a lovely panel by A. Y. Jackson — a true friend to Tom, to Margaret and to us.

5

From the start our major collecting emphasis was on works by members of the Group of Seven and their close associate Tom Thomson. But this was not to the total exclusion of other artists. We purchased a fine Kwakiutl Raven Hamatsa mask and a beautiful Eskimo carving many years before Native art came into vogue. I was also particularly interested in the paintings of Emily Carr and David Milne.

David Brown Milne was born in Paisley, Ontario where he grew up and taught school briefly. He moved to New York in 1912, where he spent several years painting in the city itself and in the Adirondack Mountains. In New York he met and married Patsy Mae Flaherty, who became the subject or model for many of his paintings of this period. He was also fortunate to meet and count as a friend an established New York illustrator, James Clarke. Clarke's summer home in the Adirondacks became one of Milne's favourite painting places and Clarke also offered Milne financial and other help.

In 1917 Milne came back to Canada briefly to join the Canadian army, and was commissioned as a war artist. After the war, he returned to New York and to his upstate painting haunts, and through the twenties continued to paint until he had achieved a very distinctive style. Brilliant colours, heavily applied, were favoured by the members of the Group of Seven, but Milne's colours were muted and applied in the extremely sparse manner often referred to as "dry brush". He was equally comfortable with oils and watercolours.

After his permanent return to Canada, Milne was very short of funds and made the rounds of Toronto art dealers in an attempt to sell some of his paintings. One of the most prominent dealers, Laing Galleries, agreed to accept two works on consignment. A few weeks later, Milne was delighted to learn that one of his works had been sold and that the purchaser was Vincent Massey. He promptly wrote to Mr. and Mrs. Massey stating that he needed help and that he was willing to sell his entire inventory of paintings for a lump sum.

At lunch during one of his visits with Signe and me at Tapawingo in 1966, Vincent Massey (by then the Right Honourable Vincent Massey, first Canadian-born Governor General of Canada) told us this story:

The Masseys had received David Milne's letter proposing to sell them almost all of his artistic output to that time for a set sum which, I believe, was three thousand dollars. The Masseys liked Milne's work and accepted his proposal. Some days later a shipment of several large packing cases arrived. An excited Vincent and Alice Massey began unpacking the shipment and soon realized the full extent of their acquisition — it ran into hundreds of works. Though Milne had made the offer and the Masseys were delighted to receive this full measure, this unexpectedly large number of paintings was much more than they anticipated. Indeed, they felt the arrangement they had agreed to was hardly fair to Milne. After sorting out the two hundred or so works which they liked best and intended to keep, they arranged a sale exhibition of the balance through their friends the Laings, with the understanding that most of the proceeds would go to Milne.

In the early 1930s Milne met Kathleen Pavey, who became his second wife and bore his only child, David. At about the same time he met Douglas Duncan, who would from that time on act as his agent.

After Milne's death in 1945, the disposition of his paintings, most of which Duncan held, became a matter of dispute between Patsy and Kathleen, which helps to explain why we were never able to purchase a Milne painting from Duncan. We were not, however, mistaken in our belief that Duncan wanted us to add Milnes to our collection. Many years later, in 1969, the Collection received a bequest from the estate of Douglas Duncan which included four choice Milnes as well as works by Lionel LeMoine FitzGerald.

Though by 1961 we had given up hope of acquiring Milne paintings through Douglas Duncan, another source unexpectedly opened to us. We had earlier confided to our friend, painter Yvonne McKague Housser, that we were trying to acquire Milne paintings, without success. She called to tell us that her nearby neighbour on the outskirts of Markham, Blodwen Davies, had several paintings by Milne which had been consigned to her for sale by Patsy Milne, the artist's first wife, who was at that time living in Little Current on Manitoulin Island. Blodwen, the author of the first published biography of Tom Thomson, had been considering a biography of David Milne for some time and during her research had come to know Patsy. Through Yvonne, I arranged to meet with Miss Davies at her bungalow, one concession road beyond the village of Markham.

Because of our deep interest in Tom Thomson, I had been anxious to meet Blodwen Davies and to discuss the Thomson book she had written in the mid-1930s. More particularly, I was interested in the detailed research into Thomson's life and death which she had carried out so many years earlier.

I'm not certain what I expected, but I was certainly not prepared for the style in the early Milne canvases (circa 1914) that Blodwen Davies laid out on her dining room table. These personal possessions of Patsy Milne were products of Milne's early New York period, entirely different from the more familiar works of the 1920s and 1930s. I saw brilliant colours, boldly painted and laid on with a heavy impasto; modern art conceived and painted well before it was generally accepted, even in New York. Milne had shown, in fact, several works in the landmark 1913 Armory Show, the first major introduction of modern art to the United States. There was, of course, no question of authenticity, but I found this bold early style both exciting and perplexing.

Years earlier, the canvases, most about eighteen by twenty inches, had been removed from their stretchers and rolled, so they were badly in need of cleaning, but the paint surface appeared to be in reasonably good condition. Even through the accumulated dirt of almost fifty years, the colours were strong and their application bold, not unlike work by the Fauves, who had at one time caused such a stir in Europe. Nevertheless, I was very impressed with what I was seeing. Few, if any, of Milne's works from this period had been publicly exhibited, and virtually none had been reproduced. There was no expert opinion to guide me, but I sensed that it might be now or never. As always, our budget had to be considered, but the price of two hundred dollars each seemed very reasonable. I decided to plunge.

Among the seven or eight pieces of limp canvas propped against sofa and chair backs, I was most impressed with three which were entirely different from each other in subject matter, colouration and technique. The one which struck me the most forcefully was a flat design of *Lilies*, dominated by white and raw brush strokes of vermillion, ultramarine and acid green. This dazzling composition was my first choice. I then chose a feathery impressionistic landscape of *Boston Corners*, in brilliant but less contrasting colours, and a winter scene from the Adirondacks. I left with the three roughly rolled canvases which were to become the foundation of our collection of David Milne's works.

By 1960, I was spending five days of every week in New York, returning to Kleinburg for weekends. During my weekends in Kleinburg, I continued my occasional visits with Blodwen Davies, during which we explored at some length our historical interest in Tom Thomson and David Milne. During one of these get-togethers, Blodwen mentioned James Clarke who, as I said, had been Milne's best friend from his earliest New York years. Blodwen had had considerable correspondence with Clarke, who was now living in retirement in Yonkers. The following Monday, I telephoned him and after a brief chat he invited me to join him for lunch at the Illustrators' Club in Manhattan. Two days later I met the lanky, white-haired, easygoing Clarke and enjoyed every minute of a two-hour lunch. It was to prove the beginning of a warm friendship which lasted over several years.

Clarke listened attentively as I told him about our collection and our plans for its future. I also told him of the three very early works which we had purchased from Patsy Milne through Blodwen Davies, and we discussed how different Milne's early work in New York was from that of the 1920s and 1930s.

"Dave and I became close friends shortly after his arrival in New York," Clarke reminisced. "He'd shown me some of his paintings and I was impressed more with his intense desire to be an artist than with those first works. His art meant more to him than worldly comforts. Thank heaven that he felt that way, because he sure didn't have many possessions or comforts."

Clarke, already a successful illustrator, had an eye for unusual talent and sensed that Milne was both gifted and determined. The two men occasionally went painting together and, although Clarke was making a financial success of his artistic career, he had a deep admiration for Milne's creativity even though it was financially unrewarding. Clarke was extremely modest, but I already knew of the many ways he had helped Milne — supplying materials, living accommodation and, at times, purchasing a painting or two.

In the weeks and months following our first meeting I often visited Jim Clarke and his second wife at their Yonkers home. (The first Mrs. Clarke, whom Milne had painted occasionally, had died some years earlier.)

Perhaps because these visits revived his interest, Clarke rummaged through his attic and turned up several Milne paintings which he had acquired during their long years of friendship — paintings of the country around Clarke's summer home in the Adirondacks, one of Milne's favourite painting places — of the house itself, and of the first Mrs. Clarke and Patsy Milne. Whatever the memories the paintings brought back, Clarke told me he felt that Milne's work was more likely to receive appreciation in Canada than in New York, where he was totally unknown except to a few personal friends. He would therefore be willing to sell.

Jim Clarke had continued to correspond with Patsy Milne on Manitoulin Island and, typically, he said it was his intention to send her any money he received from selling his Milnes to me. He and his wife then drove me the few blocks to the little Yonkers station, where I boarded the commuter train back to Manhattan with string-bound parcels of paintings under each arm. A few days later I had a short note from Jim and a copy of a poignant letter to Patsy in which he had enclosed a cheque for over two thousand dollars.

On a later visit Jim brought out three small paintings which he had done during one of his sketching trips with Milne in the Adirondacks. I was excited to see these, since they were among the few visual records of Milne's early painting years. I was struck by the similarity of the technique Clarke had used to record Milne hiking and painting in the Adirondacks and the technique Milne was using at that time. I felt these little paintings were a significant historical record and asked if I might purchase them.

"I haven't sold one of my great paintings for years," Jim chuckled. "I didn't really think I'd ever sell another one...mainly because I don't think anyone wants them. You can have these for ten dollars each, if you really want them."

"Sold!" I said as I promptly produced three ten dollar bills. "But I feel you're not asking enough. After all these are an important record. And besides they're fine little paintings."

"If you feel that way," he laughed, "you can treat them as Green

Stamps, a premium on your last purchase. After all, I don't rank myself with Dave Milne."

The paintings dated from 1921. Two of them, each about nine-and-a-half by thirteen inches, were crayon and ink on paper; the third was a watercolour. I asked Clarke if he could remember the circumstances or any special points of interest surrounding the sketches. One of the crayon drawings showed Milne painting in the doorway of his tar paper shack at Mt. Alander, New York, wearing the uniform of a private in the Canadian army, without insignia. Milne had undoubtedly found his old uniforms to be warm and rugged and, therefore, ideal clothing for hiking in the bush. The second drawing was of the interior of the painting shack, which was something like a Quonset hut made of thin sticks of wood and materials that probably had been salvaged from abandoned houses. Clarke made a little note:

> *Interior of Mt. Alander shack. Thoreau would have considered it too primitive. Snow shoes explained means of transit. Although he was expert on skis, bush here too thick for skis.*

Of the watercolour he wrote:

> *David Milne breaking trail for Clarke after an icy storm on a painting trip to Riga Lakes, Conn.-N.Y. Note the canvas and easel, one reason why D.M. did not paint large canvases.*

The two little crayon and ink drawings, in particular, are so much in the manner of Milne that they might have been mistaken for the work of the artist himself. Though I noted this similarity, I did not feel I could ask Clarke whether he had been influenced by Milne or had purposely drawn the sketches to mimic Milne's own style.

After we had acquired our first Milne painting, I was anxious to find, and possibly acquire, others. At that time, Douglas Duncan, who maintained his shop, the Picture Loan Society, in a third-floor loft above Coles bookstore at Yonge and Charles Streets, seemed to have a virtual monopoly on Milne's work. He had known Milne well and from the early 1930s had been the artist's confidant and agent. Duncan, unlike most dealers, rented out pictures with an arrangement that allowed the client to buy the work and apply the rental costs if the pictures were purchased.

Signe and I visited Duncan on several occasions and spent many hours with him looking at literally dozens of Milnes. When the question of price and availability for purchase arose, however, he was always extremely evasive. Perhaps he would sell this one or that one among our favourites. Again, perhaps he wouldn't sell it at that particular time. "I'll know better in a few weeks; I'll be in touch with you," became almost a stock statement.

On more than one evening, we invited him to Tapawingo for dinner and long chats that continued to a very late hour. He made suggestions as to the period, size and even subject matter of the Milnes that he thought we should have, and we usually ended up feeling that at last we would have the privilege of acquiring one or more of the Milnes he held. Within a few days we would get in touch with him again only to have our hopes dashed once more. It appeared to us then that he saw himself as far more than a seller of Milnes — he also felt a responsibility for placing the paintings with those who deserved to have them. In time we realized that whatever truth there was in our assessment, the real problem was that Milne's estate had not been settled.

By the spring of 1969, the Collection had so increased that even with selective hanging we knew we would soon be unable to display all of the important paintings. Furthermore, our continuing missionary work among possible donors of other equally significant pictures made us quietly confident that this rewarding growth would continue.

We remained committed to the idea of focussing the Collection on a special few great Canadian national painters and the distinctive arts of our Native peoples. From the first we had tried to be very selective — to acquire only the most significant works by our chosen artists. We were also determined to display the entire Collection on a full-time basis. All of these good intentions were in danger of being frustrated by our own hard work and good fortune. It was now clear that even with the 1968 wing, a shortage of space would soon be our number-one problem.

As our policies attracted more and more gifts and attendance increased, we looked ahead and decided it was imperative to have a substantial gallery room for each artist of the Group and for each of their outstanding contemporaries, Thomson, Carr and Milne. Smaller rooms could be devoted to five other selected artists who, while highly desirable, would require less space. We felt there should also be a large master gallery which would contain at least one major canvas from each of our featured painters.

According to our plan, the largest room of all would be designed as a combined tribute to the Northwest Indian people and the solitary artist who had painted their villages, their totems, their forests and mountains with such passion — Emily Carr.

Although our holdings of her paintings, as well as the Northwest Indian ceremonial carvings, were still very modest, we were convinced that a monumental room built of stone and massive, hewn Douglas fir logs with a high vaulted ceiling, not unlike the Indians' own great longhouses, would capture the imagination and, we hoped, inspire the generosity of potential donors.

Once again Tapawingo proved to be subject to the McMichael version of Parkinson's Law — galleries expand to encompass the treasures available to them. In June, ground was broken for a large, new, L-shaped wing extending along the hogback ridge and deep into the hilltop woods. The site provided intimate glimpses of secluded woodlands and sweeping panoramas of towering pines and maples, through which you could catch a glimpse of the river snaking through the broad valley far below. Vast windows made of a special light-filtering glass would protect the paintings, while permitting visitors to enjoy the spectacular views of a natural setting similar to those in some of the paintings.

We knew the great new "longhouse" would be impressive in size, design and materials, but we felt that so dramatic a gallery could be even further enhanced by an unmistakable focal point to underline its theme.

We needed a totem pole.

Totem poles belong exclusively to the Indian peoples of our Northwest Coast. They are not merely decorative, but an important part of the Northwest Indian culture. We knew that to acquire one of these historic symbols would be a tall order. From our reading and talks with experts and members of the Indian community we knew that most early poles, celebrated by potlatch or sanctified at the grave sites of prominent chiefs, had either succumbed to natural deterioration or had long since been removed to museums and storage areas where they could be preserved against the damp ravages of the coastal climate. Those which remained intact were considered sacrosanct by the communities in which they stood, stately symbols of a disappearing way of life.

The opening of the new wing was scheduled for the early summer of 1970. At first we were tempted to commission the carving of a totem, just the right height, by a contemporary West Coast Indian carver. During previous visits to the Coast we had discussed the possibility with Kwakiutl artist Douglas Cramner of Deep Cove, B.C. and had seen photographs of several fine poles he had carved for institutions in Canada, the United States and Europe. Behind his home we had seen a partially completed pole that he was working on for the Canadian Armed Forces base at Lahr, West Germany. We had also explored the idea with Kwakiutl carvers Tony and Kelvin Hunt of Victoria when we visited their well-equipped modern workshop. Our Haida friends, carvers Bill Reid and Bob Davidson, also offered helpful advice. Any one of these talented artists could, we knew, produce an authentic totem of great power and beauty. It was also the opinion of those most familiar with Northwest Indian culture that we could not expect to find more than decayed fragments, much less a complete pole, which would meet our height requirements.

Still we clung to a stubborn hope... somewhere in the vast Northwest wilderness a historic totem, twenty feet tall and in salvageable condition, was waiting for us.

In the meantime, the official opening was getting closer. The massive end wall of the more than three thousand square foot Northwest room cried out for a totem. My friend Dr. Ed Rodgers at the Royal Ontario Museum came to our rescue by agreeing to loan a massive grizzly bear house post, about ten feet tall, from their collection. It would serve our purpose nicely for a year or more until we could satisfy ourselves once and for all of the possibility — or impossibility — of acquiring our ideal pole.

Ed also arranged for the loan of several good masks which the museum had in storage. For the time being, they would join the raven mask I had acquired years earlier and several small pieces which had been added recently to the Collection. We had five works by Emily Carr, and with our habitual optimism we were convinced that one day thirty impressive canvases would take up all the space on the broad log walls of the room. Until that time, years hence, large Rocky Mountain canvases by Lawren Harris, A. Y. Jackson, F. H. Varley and J.E.H. MacDonald would be perfectly at home in this very special western gallery room.

Early in our planning I had thought about the scale of the room — larger than most ten-room houses, and envisioned a huge bench, forty feet long, down the centre. In my imagination, I pictured an enormous bench top made of one piece of wood which would offer dramatic evidence of the mammoth size of the Pacific forest trees. It would, I told myself grandly, be the largest one-piece wooden bench in the world.

Unfortunately, you don't find a piece of wood that size at your lumber dealer's, or even in the huge sawmills on the West Coast. They do produce large boards — but nothing like the colossal plank I had in mind. The largest one-plank board in the world threatened to remain a figment of my imagination. Then I learned of an association with headquarters in Vancouver which was dedicated to serving the technical, promotional and public relations interests of the lumber companies operating in British Columbia. Surely this organization might, with a little persuasion, see the promotional value of my idea and undertake, through its members, to find a prime tree trunk that could be transformed into a bench. Fortunately, their vision was equal to my fantasy. The British Columbia Council of Forest Industries did indeed survey its members and turn up a gigantic western red cedar trunk, rot-free and suitable for cutting, which provided a slab capable of comfortably seating two entire school classes back-to-back. It was, in fact, forty feet long and nearly four feet wide. In the years since its completion, millions have marvelled at our giant from the forest in the northernmost reaches of Vancouver Island, a tree so large that its weak heartwood and tapered top could be discarded and still leave a slab of one hundred and sixty square feet!

By now we were becoming quite knowledgeable about Northwest Indian craftsmanship, so we decided the bench should be finished with the smooth, yet textured, surface achieved by Indian carvers with a small adze, much like the hewn planes of their immense totems. I relayed this thought to the Council of Forest Industries along with the suggestion that they might contact carver Doug Cramner in the village of Deep Cove, not far from Vancouver. Cramner agreed to undertake the job.

The gigantic slab of red cedar and two equally long runners which would support it to form a bench were transported by coastal steamship to Vancouver, where arrangements had been made to rent a hockey arena which was unused during the summer months and could therefore serve as Doug's studio. In it, he would have ample space to hew the vast surface of the rough-sawn planks to form our mammoth bench and, in the process, create a small mountain of cedar chips.

On the day Cramner was to begin, he met with an official of the Forest Industries Council at the arena to review a letter and some drawings I had sent to Vancouver. Seeing that Cramner had apparently arrived without his working tools, the official asked if Doug intended to begin work that day.

"By all means," said Doug.

"But where are your tools?"

Reaching into the pocket of his jeans, Cramner brought out a miniature adze, known as a D-adze, whose cutting edge was no wider than a razor blade.

The official then watched with open-mouthed astonishment as Cramner seated himself on one end of the largest slab which had been mounted on heavy supporting trestles and, with his little D-adze, began scooping out woodpecker-sized chips.

Forty working days later, Doug Cramner had transformed the massive wooden plank into a piece of sculpture on whose pebbled surface countless derrières have found a comfortable resting place.

When the three huge components of the bench, swathed in protective bands of rough-cut wood, arrived at Kleinburg, we faced the same sort of dilemma as the legendary handyman who built a three-masted schooner in his basement, except that we were trying to get in, not out. However, after tape-measure calculations and the removal of some doors and trim, we rounded up ten strong young men from Kleinburg in addition to our own maintenance crew, and tackled the tricky task of moving the immense bench top through our front hall and around the corners of the five other galleries which led to the Northwest gallery. Placed on a dozen wooden dowel rollers, similar to the wringers of an old-style washing machine, the mammoth two-ton slab of wood was moved, inch by inch, as the rollers were re-inserted from rear to front at one-minute intervals, to its final resting place over an extra heavy supporting wall of concrete and brick.

Pictures of our fourteen robust young men straining with their ponderous burden were captured by a Canadian Press photographer. They appeared in newspapers across the country with the saga of the bench and its improbable travels from a northern Pacific forest to an Ontario art gallery which wanted to pay tribute to the magnificent forests from which it had come.

Even during the hectic final preparations for the official opening of the new wing by Premier John Robarts, Signe and I were planning our long anticipated journey to the West Coast and its remote Northwest Indian villages. We would be in search of our own particular Grail, a totem pole which would be a permanent focal point of the great new longhouse gallery, spacious enough for years to come, but still lacking in content.

In the years since my first memorable contact with Northwest Indian art, we had studied everything we could get our hands on, including two scholarly volumes on totem poles by Marius Barbeau. We also spent many hours listening to that old ethnologist's experiences among the Indian peoples and hearing him discuss the artistic precepts behind their designs and carving. But we were still neophytes in this complex discipline. We knew that on this first field trip we had much to learn.

Many areas of British Columbia are rich in Native culture — the Queen Charlotte Islands (Haida), the Skeena River area (Tsimshian), and northern Vancouver Island (Kwakiutl). Hundreds of villages in other areas are home to other well-known tribes and their impressive totems.

On this first trip we had no hope of visiting more than a few villages in one tribal region. Where to begin? Where were totem poles known to be standing? Where might we negotiate for the purchase of one? Since we could not possibly answer our own questions we did what we always do in a perplexing situation — spread the word of our problem and hope for help.

In Vancouver we learned that word of our arrival and our search had gone forth from our friends Michael and Sonja Koerner to Michael's father. Walter Koerner, one of British Columbia's most prominent lumber magnates, was also a highly respected private collector of Northwest Indian art. I was invited to join him for lunch at the University of British Columbia's Faculty Club, where we were joined by anthropologist Wilson Duff, a respected authority on the Northwest Indian peoples and their art.

Both men listened attentively to my enthusiastic description of our new Northwest gallery and seemed sympathetic to my desire to provide it with a totem. Each had travelled extensively through the Indian villages and knew many of the Native carvers and band leaders. They also knew that most of the older poles were in an advanced state of decay and that the odds against finding one in reasonably good condition, and which might be purchased, were formidable. They tried gently to dissuade me by explaining patiently that poles in the villages and their graveyards were considered almost sacred and that even to make enquiries about obtaining one might be considered offensive by the Native people. The best I could hope for might be partially decayed fragments, and even these had been well combed over by the countless anthropologists who had visited the sites.

The Indian people, I knew, believed that fallen totems, like fallen men, should return naturally to the earth from which they came.

We certainly did not question either the Indians' beliefs or their right to do as they wished with their great statuary. But we felt that surely there must be an old pole somewhere that had been abandoned by those for whom it had been carved. If we could discover such a forsaken image, perhaps all but forgotten by its owners, and if they could be located and were willing to sell, we would have the double satisfaction of providing a focal point for our Northwest longhouse gallery and, in the process, preserving one more historic totem as a lasting tribute to a vanishing custom. There were a lot of "ifs".

In some ways, we thought the final "if" might be the most difficult — if the pole was no more than twenty feet tall. We could not even consider cutting a taller pole to room height, although I did think that if we found a suitable pole which measured a few feet taller we might be able to add some type of dome or skylight to our roof to accommodate it.

Adding to our difficulties was the knowledge that the Collection's art fund was now zilch. We had recently called in our last remaining pledge, from Don Harvie of Calgary, to complete the purchase of some fine miniature argolite totems. We decided that if we found a totem which could be obtained within our personal means (another "if") we would be prepared to purchase it with our own funds. This was a rather foolhardy decision since we had not the slightest idea how much might be asked.

We had counted on getting expert and helpful advice during our few days in Vancouver. We had not counted on well-meant discouragement. Then, just at the moment that we began to concede that our search was futile, I found my hopes soaring after a fortunate meeting with Robin Kendall in the Vancouver office of the federal Department of Indian Affairs. Kendall had lived and worked among the Native peoples as an agent of the department. Fortunately for us, he had just read an article about the McMichael Collection and its new emphasis on Emily Carr and the Northwest Indian culture which had been written by Kay Kritzweiser, the Toronto *Globe and Mail*'s respected art critic.

As I outlined our hopes for the new gallery I realized with mounting excitement that he was both willing and able to give me the guidance I so desperately needed. To begin, he told me that of several regions he knew well, we might have the best chance of success among the Kwakiutl people who lived at the northernmost tip of Vancouver Island. Unfortunately, there were no roads fit for automobiles through the densely forested centre of the island. There was, however, a daily flight to the town of Port Hardy, a centre of logging and salmon fishing operations, largely populated by the Kwakiutls, who had abandoned their tiny settlements in favour of a consolidated school system and the services the town could provide. He also told me that in recent years many totems in abandoned or nearly abandoned hamlets have been stolen and empty houses ransacked, mostly, it was believed, by unscrupulous white traders. Understandably, the Indian community and the local R.C.M.P. were angry about this plundering, which had created mistrust and dissension between the Native peoples and the minority whites. Kendall emphasized that we would have to overcome that latent distrust of whites by being patient and very straightforward with the Native people we met.

"Let's face it," he said, "these people have been exploited right from the beginning of this century when we nearly wiped out their culture and civilization with that stupid *Potlatch Act*.*

"Don't expect the Indians to fall all over themselves welcoming you and your proposals. They've been burned too often ... and they don't forget easily. You should be frank about the purpose of your visit but don't ... I repeat, *don't*, press too hard. Most of the older people have time on their hands. Don't try to rush them. Let them get to know you ... to know you're not trying to steal them blind. The elders will be the ones to help you ... if anyone will.

"If you're lucky enough to make a deal for a totem, there are things you must remember. First, and I can't tell you how important this is, you must be sure you're dealing with the rightful owner.

"Second, let him set the price ... and try not to bargain. Accept his price or definitely refuse the deal. Don't get into an argument you can't win.

"Third, and most important, get a clearly written bill of sale which includes confirmation of the price. You may have to write this out yourself, but be absolutely sure the seller understands it and signs the bill, acknowledging that he has received payment in full.

"Finally, if possible, get a B.C.R. — a Band Council Resolution. Again, you will probably have to draft it and write it out in duplicate. It should state that the band council recognizes the seller as the rightful owner and something to the effect that they approve of the pole's removal and that it will be kept in your museum. The B.C.R. should be signed by a majority of the council and, if possible, by all members, unless some are away."

In one short meeting, Robin Kendall had given me not only directions to follow but, for the first time, real hope. It was obvious

*The potlach is a formal celebration of the passing of rights, privileges and names from one generation to the next, through the transfer of associated artifacts, crests, songs, powers and other ancestrally derived properties. The federal government maintained a ban on potlaches from 1884 to 1951, which was extremely damaging to Northwest Coast Native art and culture.

to me why he had the confidence of the Native peoples.

Then, almost as an afterthought, Robin scribbled a name on his scratch pad. "Look up Henry Bell in the Port Hardy area. He's a former chief ... a nice guy." He handed me a slip of paper.

Two days later, near the docks in Port Hardy, we registered at the town's main hostelry, better known for its beer parlour than its sleeping accommodations. Our small, linoleum-floored room, dominated by the "girlie" calendar on its wall, provided a quick introduction to the frontier community. However, the next morning we were cheerfully moved to a much larger room, carpeted, newly decorated, and with a view of the magnificent coastline and mountains ... The Bridal Suite.

Henry Bell's soft, slightly guttural voice answered my telephone call. I told him that Robin Kendall had suggested I call him, and we were immediately invited to join the Bells for morning coffee. Their well-kept, little white frame bungalow was just a short walk from the hotel, one of several of the same size and design. We caused a momentary stir in a group of Indian children who were playing outside, but they soon returned to their hoola hoops.

Although they were in their mid-seventies, and their faces were leathered by a lifetime in the outdoors, Henry Bell and wife were so alert and full of vigour that they seemed much younger.

While two little faces looked at us curiously through the window — grandchildren who lived next door — I told the Bells as briefly as I could about the background of our now public museum in Kleinburg and about our new Northwest gallery room, which we had tried to design in the manner of an Indian longhouse. Then, remembering Robin Kendall's advice, I told them frankly of our hope of obtaining a twenty foot totem pole. Although we were enthralled by the art and artifacts of the Northwest Indians, I went on, we could not consider ourselves experts but students, anxious to increase our knowledge by visiting the sites of earlier villages to see and learn from the remains of tribal houses and totems, or perhaps, fragments of the once splendid poles. We hoped to meet people whose families had lived in these abandoned settlements and we wanted to learn all we could about the area, its people, its history and its art.

Bell seemed interested. I was pleased that he did not appear to be offended that we wanted to buy a historic totem. Quite the opposite. When I talked about visiting long-abandoned villages, his eyes lit up and I realized he was hoping to see again the village of his childhood.

"Most of our old villages are on the islands," he said thoughtfully. "The waters around them are shallow. That's part of the reason... maybe the main reason that we left them and came to the mainland. In the days when I was a boy, we fished from big canoes made by burning and digging to hollow out big trees. When the new power boats came along, we knew the dugout's end was near. At first, some of the elders resisted change, but most could see that the new trawlers would take over. They could get a bigger catch of salmon with a lot less work. The younger men would not work in the old canoes when they saw how much better the new boats were doing. But the new boats needed deeper water. Some of the water around the islands is so shallow you couldn't run powerboats anywhere near them, so the old places where our fathers and grandfathers lived just disappeared. Sometimes whole villages were moved by floating the houses on log rafts to the deeper mainland harbours.

"Education had something to do with it too. The government agents said the schools should be built in places like Port Hardy, not on the islands. The old way of life is gone... we still have some ceremonies and dances at Alert Bay and Fort Rupert, but it's not the same as our old ways on the islands."

"Do you and your children ever go back to the island villages?" I asked.

"No, very rarely," he replied. "The best way to get out there nowadays is in a small float airplane, but that's expensive, so we just don't get back."

For a few minutes he seemed lost in memories and I sat quietly waiting until he was ready to continue.

"If we can arrange to hire a plane to take us out to the old villages, would you come along as our guide?"

As I expected, he was happy at the prospect of a visit to the islands, especially Village Island, where he was born, and immediately suggested that we could get a plane at the docks which would carry the three of us and a pilot.

Next morning, sitting with Henry Bell on the docks, we waited patiently while our pilot tinkered with the motor of a trim little seaplane. Minutes later we clambered aboard in jeans, loafers and light windbreakers over which we had slung the small backpacks holding cameras, picnic lunches and toilet paper, which Signe (practical as always) had thoughtfully packed.

Following takeoff, we flew at low altitude over small fishing trawlers whose nets formed vast circles larger than a football field. Further out we spotted four giant fish, repeatedly breaking the surface in a graceful water ballet.

"Surely those can't be salmon?" I asked, trying to sound knowledgeable.

Bell hid a grin. "Killer whales," he said laconically.

I was saved from further revelations of my ignorance by the view. For the first time we were seeing the country that we had only known on canvas or by printed word. Finally, Bell, who was sitting up front with the pilot, pointed to a small, heavily forested island. Dropping lower, they both scanned the water for submerged shoals as the plane made a tight circle. Then straightening out, we skimmed along a shoreline of giant firs and cedars to an opening in the forest and a sandy beach. The pontoons dug into the water, slowing us to a crawl. The plane turned into a small cove and toward a derelict wharf as easily as a car into a driveway.

From the shore an overgrown path led through a long tunnel of towering trees to a clearing and several dilapidated buildings. In front of the buildings — we could scarcely believe our eyes — were totem poles!

Unfortunately, our spirits were fated to fall as fast as they had risen. When we moved closer we found that, like the decaying houses of the ghost village, the brightly painted shafts were broken and scarred beyond repair. Some were standing askew, broken as though they had been struck by lightning with their tops lying rotted in the dense undergrowth while once outstretched wings and protruding beaks were either broken off or missing.

It was tempting to delude myself that in the hands of an expert restorer one, at least, might be salvageable. Large areas of rotted wood could be removed and the remainder stabilized. Missing figures or parts could be copied and inserted by an expert carver like Doug Cramner. Paint could be re-touched or the entire pole re-painted using the same colours and type of paint. Of course, if restoration with a high degree of fidelity to the original was to be undertaken, good early photographs of the pole *in situ* would be indispensable.

My delusion lasted only moments. Even if photographs existed I knew the wounds were mortal. Careful reconstruction would appear impressive, a tribute to the fine art of the conservator. Nevertheless, with perhaps fifty percent or more of the pole the result of restoration, could it be classified as an original historic pole? As well, the cost of such difficult and demanding conservation work would considerably exceed the cost of an entirely new pole of exactly the right height.

The return to Village Island and the ruins of his once-thriving village was a poignant experience for Henry Bell. Signe and I were also sad. The derelict poles brought home to us, as nothing else had, how hopeless our quest was probably going to be. We were, we realized, at least a decade or two too late. A silent threesome, we ambled back along a barely disturbed trail to the quiet cove where our pilot was engrossed in a paperback.

Our next touchdown at Tourner Island revealed only stumps of much older totems — bleached, sightless figures staring out between enormous firs and cedars from whose upper limbs the black ravens of legend seemed to follow our brief procession. They were fascinating but useless to us.

At Gilford Island, the story was much the same. Yet it was impossible not to be affected by the ghostly remains of these once-flourishing settlements. Even in decay, the lordly totems, with their boldly carved figures staring enigmatically from the forests, have a power which no museum totem can ever duplicate. The staring eyes seem frozen in time. But the mosses which thrive in their crevices and the wildflowers which form richly coloured topknots in their splintered scalps remind us they are not timeless. They, like their carvers, will return to the earth.

As we flew back to Port Hardy, Henry Bell suggested that on the following day we might enjoy visiting the still-inhabited village of Fort Rupert. He could not come with us — a previous engagement. At the local service station we were able to rent a car which had seen better years but was serviceable and unobtrusive for short jaunts.

The next morning we found Fort Rupert on the shores of Queen Charlotte Strait. The tiny hamlet consisted of a few dozen small houses, much older than those in Port Hardy, and a modest white clapboard church with an adjoining burial ground, not unlike the one in the well-known Emily Carr painting, *Indian Church*.

The village sees little outside traffic and even fewer strangers, so it was quite natural for the middle-aged couple in front of whose home we had stopped to ask us if we were lost. When we explained that we were not lost at all but just travellers who were interested in the village and Northwest Indian culture we were immediately welcomed into their home. Suddenly I remembered a passage from Margaret Craven's *I Heard the Owl Call My Name*. It said something like:

The Indian knows his village and feels for his village as no white man for his country, his town or even for his own bit of land. His village is not the strip of land four miles long and three miles wide that is his as long as the sun rises and the moon sets. The myths are the village and the winds and the rains. The river is the village, and the black and white killer whales that herd the fish to the end of the inlet the better to gobble them. The village is the salmon who comes up the river to spawn, the seal who follows the salmon and bites off his head ... The village is ... the silver-tipped grizzly who ambles into the village, and the little white speck that is the mountain goat ...

Reminded again of the special feeling the Indian people have for their villages, I realized how privileged we were. The warmth with which we were accepted at face value into Indian homes would remain in our hearts and memories.

We told our hosts about our previous day's visit to the abandoned island settlements and of the reason for our search for the distinctive carvings of the area. They listened with interest to my enthusiastic description of our Northwest gallery and our hopes of a display of ceremonial sculpture.

Nevertheless, they remained somewhat reserved and cautious. We felt they wanted to be helpful. We also knew we were being judged.

Leaving aside our primary goal we told them how excited we had been by our first sight of killer whales and the ravens, which were so important in their legends, totems and masks. They smiled indulgently, too polite to laugh at our childlike enthusiasm for sights that they took so much for granted. Yet we could see they were also pleased. Proudly they informed us that this village had been the home of Mungo Martin and several other carvers whose works were already in museums. Unlike some of their people, they seemed honoured by this recognition. The conversation was becoming focussed and Signe and I encouraged them to continue.

"There's an old family, the Johnsons, who live pretty much to themselves down by the cove," the man — who had not introduced himself by name — said. "He's in his late eighties and still has some of his masks from the early days. I doubt if he'll ever dance again ... getting too old ... and I don't think his son Paul is much interested in the masks. In fact he makes his own. Not as good as some his father has, but he likes them anyway."

We felt the collector's familiar surge of excitement and, having caught the scent, with almost unseemly haste we asked to be directed to Tom Johnson's old cottage.

After looking us over carefully, the old chief invited us into his rundown old cottage. Against roughly nailed plywood walls we found a few dilapidated pieces of furniture. Mrs. Johnson sat beside a window that had been crudely patched with plastic tape.

Still we were not social workers, but seekers, and I launched into an explanation of our visit. Caught up in my own enthusiasm I did not notice for several minutes that I was being met with blank stares — they did not understand English. I did not understand Kwakwala. Old chief Johnson silenced me with an index finger to his lips while his wife padded out the door. She returned in a few minutes with her son Paul and an attractive young woman to act as interpreter.

With our expressions of interest in their masks finally translated we waited while the Johnson family had a little powwow. Then, to our complete delight, the ceremonial masks for the Dance of the Animals were carried from a small storage room into the parlour. As each emerged, a few words passed between father and son and the interpreter then informed us of the price expected for each.

Two represented birds: the larger a kingfisher, the smaller, obviously designed to fit a child's face, a wren. Two others were humanoid faces, one topped by a killer whale, the other by a salmon. The largest and most dramatic was a green frog's head with red lips and bulging copper eyes. The old chief revealed that some had been made by his old friend Mungo Martin, others by various carvers, including his son Paul. He was unable or, it appeared, unwilling to identify each by its carver.

Noticing that the masks appeared to be freshly painted, we asked about their age. Chief Johnson explained through the interpreter that all had been repainted in the 1950s for a dance held in the village following the repeal of the hated *Potlatch Act*. The use of high-gloss commercial paint over earlier Native paints was disappointing and would also make it much more difficult to date them and identify the carvers.

We knew that in the past, the Johnsons had refused to sell some of their masks, which even to our untrained eyes varied widely in quality. Now, the interpreter told us they would sell the group as a package because they were unwilling "to break up a set". If we wanted the ones which appealed to us, we would have to buy their less desirable companions.

It occurred to us that those who referred to the Native peoples as "primitive" and "naive" had not dealt with the Johnsons!

I was no expert on either quality or prices, but I could not erase a mental picture of the bare areas in our newest gallery which cried out for carvings like these. Applying the total price to the five or six which I judged were the better pieces I found we would be paying about five hundred dollars for each. It was always possible I might come to see this purchase as a lucky coup. At worst, I reasoned, we would acquire display material of respectable quality which at some time might be sold or traded to upgrade the Collection's quality. (My beginner's judgement did, as a matter of fact, prove to be quite accurate. Four of the masks were judged to be good, although not great. The rest could not be considered to be of museum quality.)

We were not surprised when the Johnsons asked for immediate payment in cash of over twenty-five hundred dollars.

Earlier we had been advised that cash would be expected for any purchases we might be able to make. Many of the Indians did not have bank accounts or did not understand or trust cheques. Accordingly, we had visited the manager of the one bank branch in Port Hardy, asking that he telephone our bank manager in Toronto to establish a personal line of credit for us. We had little idea of how much we might need, we told him, but we would need it in cash.

The bank manager pointed out that we might have a problem. Because of its remoteness, Port Hardy airlifted all of its currency from Vancouver. Security and transport were costly and shipments of cash arrived only on a prearranged schedule. At times, the branch was so short of legal tender that cashing a cheque for a few thousand dollars could temporarily exhaust its supply. Nevertheless, the manager said he would do his best for us.

Now I quickly tried to think of a way to make both the Johnsons and the bank manager happy. Turning to the interpreter, I assured her that we would place the cash in the Johnsons' hands but that I knew there were very few secrets in a tiny community, and was worried about so large an amount of cash being kept by an elderly couple in this secluded cottage. I proposed that she and they accompany us in our car to the bank in Port Hardy. We would cash a cheque so that they could actually see and feel the money in their own hands. Then, keeping a small portion for immediate needs, they could deposit the balance for safekeeping.

After a brief conference in Kwakwala, there were smiles all around. Our aging rented car groaned slightly as it rolled towards Port Hardy carrying two pleased collectors, three happily chatting Indians and a trunk full of masks.

The following day, we made another trip to Fort Rupert. The

Bells had told us that a young girl who was very dear to them was being buried that day in Fort Rupert. Since they had no other way of getting there, we offered to drive them to the funeral.

At the white clapboard church nestled in a grove of giant firs, the Bells and most of the townspeople slowly climbed the entrance stairs while we, outsiders, squatted on a grassy patch of the bordering burial ground.

When all the mourners had been seated inside, four men bearing the blanket-wrapped body of the little girl crossed the lawn and with measured steps climbed to the arched doorway. As they entered, we could hear muted chanting within. In a monotonous lament the chorus poured out, as one voice, its sorrow at the loss of one so young, so loved. Then the hymn soared to a high-pitched wailing, a tribute to the higher station where the departed child's soul now rested. Perched on a limb, the omnipresent black raven looked down, cawing softly as if calling her name.

During our return to Port Hardy following the burial, the Bells barely spoke. Then, in a soft but firm voice, Henry said, "Please arrange the airplane for tomorrow morning. I think we should go to Blunden Harbour. The village is abandoned but there's a pole there I know about. Might be just what you're lookin' for. I spoke to the guy who by rights owns it. Says he will sell it. Wants fifteen hundred dollars ... cash."

The mere mention of Blunden Harbour was enough to conjure up visions of the legendary place, immortalized by Emily Carr in the early 1930s in one of her best-known paintings. We now know that Carr had never seen the remote island, but had painted its totems and wharves from a photograph given to her by the famous anthropologist, Dr. C. F. Newcombe, who had visited Blunden at the turn of the century.

We knew that Henry Bell had understood our disappointment with the ravaged totems on the other islands we had visited. Surely, if he was so insistent, this one would, at the very least, be intact and close to the height we sought. Maybe this would be it!

Early next morning, a telephone call came from the pilot. "I'm ready, and the plane is ready," he said, "but Blunden Harbour isn't. It's fogged in, as usual, but the fog should burn off in a few hours. I'll call you as soon as there's word from some of the other pilots who fly over that way."

Small islands lying off the Pacific coast gather themselves in shrouds of dense fog which cling long after visibility has been restored over the open waters. That morning, with the sun sparkling on blue waters, the jagged silhouettes of mountains stood out clearly far across Queen Charlotte Strait. It was difficult to imagine a tiny island nearby shrouded in "pea soup".

I was pacing back and forth impatiently when Henry Bell strolled onto the dock.

"Henry," I blurted with exasperation, "it seems there's still a heavy fog out at Blunden, even though it's so clear here."

Henry laughed at my agitation. Placing a gentle hand on my shoulder, he said calmly, "Stop fretting. It's been out there a long time and it'll still be there when the fog's gone.

"There isn't much you can tell me about fog," he continued, "but I'll tell you, when it clears, we better get out there fast. It can close in again without any notice. The pilot knows that too. He won't want to stay out there any longer than he has to. There's a lot of rocks and shoals around Blunden. And if there's two things pilots don't like, it's fog and shoals. For that matter, neither do I."

Eventually the word came and we took off. Bell again acted as navigator while the little plane made several circles around the isolated island which is shaped like a curled-up shrimp, its head and tail nearly meeting at a narrow channel, the only entrance to the island's snug harbour.

Setting down, the pilot feathered his propeller so that we were barely moving along the surface of the glassy water. Suddenly Bell opened his door, climbed down to a pontoon and, paddle in hand, directed our zigzag course through the barely submerged rocks now clearly visible just inches beneath the water.

Years earlier, every house, shed and wharf had been laboriously floated by the villagers to deeper coves on the mainland. Now a ghostly silence, broken only by the screams of seagulls, hung over the island. The only clue to its earlier inhabitants was a sharply inclined white wooden shaft near the shoreline we were slowly, cautiously approaching.

Two hundred feet off the sandy, rock-strewn shoreline the plane drifted to a halt. Straining our eyes, we could just make out carved figures whose once black and red paint had faded to soft pink and grey. A startling overall white had developed a hint of silver patina. The pole leaned for support on a thick clump of cedars at the water's edge, obscuring its lower carving.

"You'll hafta swim for it if you want a closer look," Henry Bell called up from the pontoon.

The pilot agreed, "Sorry, but he's right. I don't dare go any closer. You could easily wade in ... only to about your knees. Be careful not to cut your feet on the rocks ..."

Henry and Signe and I wasted no time in removing our shoes

and socks and rolling up our jeans while the pilot reached for the paddle, the only way to prevent the fragile floats from bumping against the treacherous rocks.

And there it was!

Since the pole was leaning at a forty-five degree angle, face down in a dense pillow of cedar boughs, its two bottom figures, Waco, the sea monster, and Tsonaqua, the wild woman of the woods, could not easily be seen. Crawling under the canopy of green boughs, I reached up to feel the carved surfaces. They felt as firm and undamaged as the middle figure of a raven which was exposed to sight and touch. The angle of its lean — face forward — had been a fortunate accident, providing considerable shelter from the elements, while the hollowed-out posterior had acted as a trough carrying away the rain and snow, shielding the painted carved figures from the deteriorating effects of the clear sunlight.

It would have been dangerous to attempt to clamber over the concave back for accurate measuring, but I felt quite certain it was no more than twenty-one feet long.

Suddenly, as I peered up through the cedar jungle into the departing mists, I caught the glimmer of a band of prismatic colour. We had found the treasure at the rainbow's end.

Almost an hour had passed since we stepped ashore. Now our pilot was whistling loudly and waving his arms. Those mists I had seen departing in the sunshine were actually a new fog bank rolling in.

After the haunting solitude of Blunden Harbour, little Port Hardy seemed a lively metropolis. Refreshed by a shower and a salmon sandwich at our hotel, we set out again for the Bells' where we found Henry and his wife, and a middle-aged man named Joe Seaweed, the son of the carver Willie Seaweed, who had lived at Blunden Harbour and had created the totem pole we had seen.

From Joe we learned that the totem, which had been commissioned and erected as a grave marker by another of the village's families some years earlier, had never been paid for. Willie Seaweed had died in 1967 so, as his sole heir, Joe Seaweed was considered the totem's rightful owner. However, since two sons of the family for whom the pole was raised now lived in Port Hardy, Joe had recognized that they possibly held some interest in it and had agreed to share the proceeds from its sale with them. Since the Blunden area was totally abandoned and the grave marker was facing inevitable destruction by the elements, no one would resent our proposed purchase and removal of the pole.

When we heard about this somewhat complex state of affairs,

we were thankful for the advice we had received in Vancouver and anxious to acquire not only a proper bill of sale but also an official Band Council Resolution. Here again, Henry Bell's knowledge and experience as a former band councillor proved very helpful.

We drafted the resolution and then Signe wrote it out in duplicate in her neat hand. Henry accompanied us to the homes of the five band councillors, all of whom lived in, or near, town. As in most small, tightly knit communities, they all knew Joe and had known his father, as well as something of the totem's history. Each signed the B.C.R. and we heaved a big sigh of relief as I handed the duplicate copy to the chief councillor.

Henry had also suggested, even though we had a signed bill of sale, that he should witness the exchange of cash between ourselves and Joe Seaweed and in turn between Joe and the two brothers with whom he would share it. For Joe's sake as much as our own, Henry felt there should be no possibility of misunderstanding or claims arising later.

After repeated rounds of smiles and handshakes, we returned home with Henry, where the ever-thoughtful Mrs. Bell had brewed a fresh pot of coffee.

It had been a full Friday!

It was apparent that the Bells shared our satisfaction and pleasure as we reflected on the events of the past eight hours. Now it only remained for us to arrange for the pole to be moved, with care, from its isolated home in Blunden to a warehouse in Port Hardy for crating in preparation for the long journey back to Kleinburg.

We also hoped to visit Alert Bay, perhaps the best-known Indian village on Vancouver Island, if not on the entire West Coast. When we mentioned this, Henry broke into a broad grin, "Hope you'll take me along. I have a nephew there."

The next morning, our pilot and his seaplane set us down, after a thirty-minute flight, at the fishing boat docks of Alert Bay.

The main drag, near the waterfront, winds past old homes, some fronted by totems, and small stores. It is mainly a walking street, where young and old from the surrounding region meet for leisurely discussions of their work, their families and local news and gossip. With fishing boats in and housework done, Saturday afternoon becomes a festive social rite of shopping and chatting.

Henry was almost immediately drawn into groups of old friends who were conversing animatedly in Kwakwala although he always courteously introduced us in English. Arranging to meet later at his nephew's home, we left him to his cronies and made our way to the village's edge to view some of the fine Kwakiutl grave posts, carved thunderbirds, ravens and other traditional images in the burial ground.

James Seiweid, son of Henry's sister, operated a small flotilla of salmon fishing vessels, a mainstay of the local economy. He was also a leader in the town's social and political life and his leadership and judgement had done much to improve his people's lot and to preserve their pride in their ancient traditions.

In his comfortable living room we chatted about Northwest culture and history, while his wife and teenaged children were busy in the kitchen preparing dinner. He told us he was much involved in measures to conserve the remaining symbols, particularly the graveyard figures, which were in desperate need of maintenance.

The conversation naturally led to the totem at Blunden Harbour. He knew the pole was deteriorating and the desirability of saving it, even though that meant its removal. He felt, however, that this attitude would not be shared by all members of the community.

"There are those who would see it destroyed, rather than removed," he said thoughtfully. "Bitter differences of opinion almost always surface when something like this is being done. Though we know your intentions are good, others feel that in removing it you are taking away a part of our heritage. It will be preserved and not ruined by the weather, yes. But it will be a great distance from its home. Few, if any, of our people will ever see it again. You must understand that to many of them its removal seems unnatural and therefore wrong."

I was stunned.

Legally, the totem was ours and had, until now, seemed within easy reach. We had followed the rules and complied with all the requirements as we knew them. We had achieved agreements we believed were final and binding. Suddenly, it looked as if our prize might be snatched from us. We owned the totem, but getting physical possession of it might be quite another matter.

"My best advice to you," James Seiweid said earnestly, "is that you should arrange to have the pole removed immediately ... tonight if possible. Word of its sale will get around very quickly. I am honestly afraid for it. There are those, especially now with the weekend drinking beginning, who might set out to destroy it."

Silently, Henry Bell nodded his agreement, but there was no time to plan further before dinner was served.

Dinner with the Seiweid family was an occasion Signe and I are not likely to forget. Eight of us, seated around a large harvest table, bowed our heads as one of the youngsters gave the blessing in Kwakwala, followed by another who said grace in English, no doubt for our benefit. Two young people then brought to the centre of the table an enormous bowl, decorated with Kwakiutl symbols and overflowing with immense quantities of cooked fresh salmon and fowl. It was followed by an equally large platter of fresh vegetables presented with almost ceremonial formality. The perfect meal ended with a traditional favourite, wild soapberries from the forest, whipped to a delicious froth.

I was determined not to allow Jimmy Seiweid's warning to spoil my enjoyment of this feast, but my thoughts kept returning to a totem on a desolate island.

After dinner when we were getting ready to leave, Signe gave the Seiweids a copy of the Collection book as a modest thank you and without a pause, Jimmy Seiweid presented us with a copy of a widely distributed book he had written on the life and legends of his people. Its appropriate title: *Guests Never Leave Hungry*.

During our return flight to Port Hardy I could see that Henry was deep in thought and I felt sure that he was searching for an answer to the concerns his nephew had raised.

As we walked from the docks he said, "Let me check with my son-in-law, Jimmy Walkus. He and his fishing crew are home for the weekend but might be willing to go out to Blunden, if they don't have guests and he can get his crew to go. They're about the only ones who don't spend Saturday night drinking. Phone me, or come over to the house in about a half an hour."

We waited anxiously at the hotel until it was time, once again, to head for the Bells'. There was no definite answer yet, Henry told us, but Walkus was at least willing to talk it over with me, even though Saturday was his one night ashore in the fishing season.

In the few steps to Walkus's house next door, I tried to muster some powers of persuasion, knowing that he was our only hope. But breaking in on the family during the one evening they could spend together, I felt about as welcome as mosquitoes at a nudist convention.

Whatever her feelings, Mrs. Walkus welcomed us and had the children shake hands before she led them away to their bedrooms. "My wife's not too happy, but she agrees I should go," Jimmy said, getting to the heart of things. "I'm not sure how my crew and their wives will feel."

Reaching for his Tide and Chart book, the size of a big city telephone directory, he ran his finger down the columns, then looked at his watch.

"High tide at Blunden comes at 2:07 in the morning. It's about four hours trip out there. We could just make it if we leave about ten o'clock. That's less than two hours from now and I'm not even sure my guys are home.

"For the boat and crew it'll cost you six hundred bucks 'cause it's all overtime, you know. How does that sound to you ... if I can get them?"

"I'm sure whatever you say is fair," I replied, thanking the foresight that had caused us to cash a large cheque for just such an emergency.

"I'll start calling," said Jimmy. "Check with me in half an hour."

While I put in a long half hour back at Henry's, I was haunted by visions of our defenceless totem facing destruction on a dark, lonely beach. A babe in the woods saga was rapidly becoming a cliff-hanger.

"Can't you settle him down? He's gonna have a breakdown," Henry said to Signe, and then to me, "Seriously, they're a pretty good bunch of guys and they'll do anything for Jimmy if they can. So relax!"

Henry Bell had become not only the key to success but a good friend. Payment had never been mentioned, but we intended to thank him in a tangible, if modest, way. This seemed the perfect moment and he seemed slightly surprised but obviously pleased as I handed him five one hundred dollar bills.

"Maybe you better keep it 'til you've got the pole," he teased as he tucked the money securely away in a pocket.

Minutes later the telephone rang. It was Jimmy Walkus. Within the hour, he and his crew would set sail for Blunden Harbour.

Shortly after eight on Sunday morning, Henry was on the telephone urging us to hurry down to the docks. Passing before us, as if in review, was Jimmy's little trawler with four of her crew on deck. Across her fo'c's'le, projecting to either side like giant seagull wings, was the dappled white shaft of our totem pole! We were almost overcome with joy when suddenly we became uneasy. The little trawler was being closely escorted by a powerful, high-speed launch. At its mast flew the flag of The Royal Canadian Mounted Police.

Later we learned that Walkus and his crew had gone ashore at Blunden Harbour six hours earlier. In the beam of the little boat's powerful searchlight, they had dug the pole's base from the ground and eased it into the water, floating it face up to the deeper water where the trawler was moored.

Heading for home with the strange catch straddling his bow, Jimmy was stopped for questioning by the Mounties. He explained that he had been retained by Dr. McMichael to move the pole. (I had received my first doctorate, *honoris causa*, at York University a few months earlier and was using my new title rather proudly.) Jimmy assured the ever-wary police that we had purchased the totem and that we would be taking it to a public museum near Toronto. The police, however, wanted proof. And that was the reason for the official escort service as the little trawler eased up to the dock in Port Hardy. More than ever thankful for Robin Kendall's earlier advice, I produced our copies of the bill of sale and Band Council Resolution for inspection and immediately received approval by the R.C.M.P. When the officer on duty recited cases of stolen and illegally removed totems in earlier years, I sincerely, if a bit smugly, congratulated the force on its vigilance.

During the formalities with the police, Signe had recruited extra help from among the curious who gathered on the dock. Passing out five dollar bills, she soon had half a dozen strong young men offering their shoulders to assist the crew. In a slow march, like some ancient rite, ten young Indian men bore the old totem several hundred yards to an incongruous, though temporary, resting place — the warehouse of the Port Hardy Building Supply Company.

After lunch and farewells to the Bells and Seaweeds, Signe and I left for the local airport and our flight to Victoria. We wanted to see the fine poles on display at the British Columbia Provincial Museum and, we hoped, gather more information about their symbolic figures, particularly those which made up our totem.

Peter McNair, Curator of Ethnology at the Provincial Museum listened intently as I described our totem and its site at Blunden Harbour.

"That's a Willie Seaweed," he agreed. "In my opinion he was one of the best, if not the best, of the Kwakiutl carvers."

He opened a file drawer and pulled out a folder from which he took a photograph, asking, "Is this the pole you're talking about?"

The picture was of a totem standing perfectly erect in a little clearing near the water's edge. I had not seen it in this position and without the growth of cedars around it, but it was unmistakably our pole!

"My predecessor, Wilson Duff, photographed it some years ago. He attributes it to Willie, and the fact that you purchased it from Joe Seaweed seems to confirm that his father was indeed the carver.

"Congratulations! For a beginner in this field, you've done very well."

We thought so, too.

Back in Kleinburg, our artist-in-residence, A. Y. Jackson, listened intently to our tales of derring-do in the Pacific Northwest. Although he was now in his eighty-eighth year, Alex could recall clearly the details of a painting trip he had made half a lifetime earlier with fellow artist Edwin Holgate and the enthnologist Marius Barbeau. In the Skeena River area, the two painters had completed dozens of oil sketches of humble Tsimshian Indian villages with their majestic totems, while Barbeau, working for Ottawa's Museum of Man, had studied and collected art and artifacts from the region.

"Marius was offered two large totems by the Indians as a gift," Jackson stated. "Excitedly, he sent a telegram to Ottawa explaining that he had been able to arrange for their shipment via CNR at no cost to the museum. Next day, he was very upset when he received a wire from the museum which said, 'Please do not accept totems ... no storage space available!' "

Seeing his friend's disappointment, Jackson had suggested to Barbeau that he should get in touch with the Royal Ontario Museum.

"Almost immediately, a telegram went off to the director of the ROM in Toronto with the same free offer," Jackson remembered. "Same story ... back came another refusal ... 'no storage space'.

"Well, we didn't want to lose the poles, they were good ones. So Marius and I put our heads together. We composed another telegram suggesting the poles would look fine if they were erected on the front lawn of the museum. Another reply — 'We collect only things which can be preserved permanently ... Poles would be destroyed by weather ...' "

Smiling, Alex Jackson said, "We weren't ones to give up easy, so we sent still another message saying that the totems on the front lawn could be protected against weather by marvelous new paints like Duco so they would last a hundred years.

"But the museum had the last word," Jackson chuckled. "Back came the final telegram, 'We do not consider one hundred years to be permanent!' "

When the totem arrived in Kleinburg, our men secured the long, heavy crate with chains to the bucket of the front-end loader of our tractor. Slowly, they and the tractor "walked" the long wooden container to the Collection's large maintenance workshop. With barely concealed curiosity they uncrated the treasure we had rescued from a foggy, abandoned island lying off the northern Pacific Coast.

A large room in our workshop building was now sealed off while the still slightly damp totem spent three days and nights enveloped in a highly toxic gas, professionally applied to fumigate it and kill any vermin.

Kwakiutl carver Douglas Cramner had talked with me about the conservation and restoration work the pole would require. Now, arrangements were made for him to travel to Kleinburg where he devoted several days to removing punky wood from the pole's backside and taking the steps necessary for the totem's permanent preservation. The painted side would be lightly retouched to restore its red and black colours to their original intensity. The white background, a dominant feature, had originally received at least three coats of white lead paint, which had contributed to the pole's durability. It required no new impainting.

During his visit to Kleinburg, the jocular Doug Cramner, a gifted artist, became part of our household. He slept on a divan in the studio adjoining the bedroom where A. Y. Jackson and his nurse, Zita, slept. On Sunday morning, after days of hard work on the totem, he slept slightly later than usual.

Always an early riser, Alex noticed the bundled figure on the couch as he made his way into his studio room. Unknown to him, Zita was already in the kitchen preparing breakfast so, momentarily confused, he shook the sleeping figure and said urgently, "Zita, time to get up."

Startled, Cramner sat bolt upright, still too much asleep to understand what had happened. Artist and artist stared at each other in astonished surprise until, coming to full consciousness at the same time, they both collapsed in laughter.

After careful study, Doug decided that six feet of punky cedar, the totem's underground stump, would have to be removed. With that necessary surgery over we found it soared to within inches of the high peaked ceiling of our Northwest Indian gallery. The old totem's figures, scowling, gazed over the hewn-log and stone gallery toward the other carved faces sharing a new home.

In Canada's centennial year, the City of Toronto sponsored a sculpture festival, during which artists from across the country were commissioned to work under the eyes of the public in the city's largest natural reserve, High Park. Among those engaged was Pauta, who had flown down from Baffin Island, his first journey south of the Arctic Circle. He was supplied with a huge square block of Queenston limestone and over several weeks carved it into his favourite animal, a larger than life polar bear tenderly clutching her cub. It was the largest piece of Eskimo sculpture in the world!

After the Centennial festivities, the mammoth stone bear and her cub were relegated to a remote area of the park, apparently for the edification of a large population of teenaged couples who could be found studying it from their parked cars after dark. Inevitably, the noble beast became a target for graffiti and senseless vandalism. Lipstick and paint added sexual organs, and filthy epithets scarred its smooth stone flanks. Park officials arranged to have the obscenities sandblasted from the surface. The hooligans took this as a challenge to return. Park officials cleaned the bear again. Hooligans responded. After several years of this unequal contest, the park management gave up in disgust. The obscenities stayed. Friends who knew of my interest in Inuit carving told me this sad little tale and I made a trip to High Park for a firsthand look at the desecration.

My first reaction was rage. My second was a determination to do something about the problem. Back in Kleinburg I called the city's parks commissioner, not to discuss my outrage but to ask if he and his family could join Signe and me for lunch at Kleinburg to consider a matter we felt would be of mutual interest. I was happy to learn from Commissioner Forest that he and his family had often visited the Collection and would be delighted to join us the following Sunday afternoon.

After lunch I mentioned, I thought casually, the Pauta bear in High Park. Forest was away ahead of me. He had seen the crowds viewing our Inuit works almost with reverence and needed no urging to become convinced that the great bear and her cub would find a new and more appreciative home at our front entrance. The proposal was duly presented to the Toronto city council and one municipal wit later commented that it would long be remembered as the only motion to be passed unanimously that year.

Of course, most of the additions to our Inuit collection were on a much smaller scale. In the years following our purchase of that small parka-clad figure in soapstone, Signe and I continued to search out other fine Inuit carvings. Among those we came to love most was one of a beaming mother with two children carved by Kiawak of Cape Dorset in the more unusual green soapstone. A very strong larger piece of a mother breast-feeding her infant by Peter Anowtok of Povungnituk and a highly stylized muskox by Angrnasungaaq from Baker Lake also ranked high on our list of favourites.

As with all art, Inuit sculpture requires that the collector take time to develop a discriminating eye. At times we were tempted by items which at first glance appeared unique and innovative but which, in truth, owed their initial appeal to a contrived cuteness. We learned to resist these impulses and to confine our buying to works born of honest creativity and to separate that quality from the calculated and often cleverly conceived gimmickry which has, so unfortunately, crept into Arctic art.

With the completion of a large, new entrance complex at the gallery in 1973, two long connecting halls provided a perfect area for both the Eskimo carvings and the striking stonecut prints we had acquired from virtually every settlement in the eastern Arctic where artistic co-operatives are located.

To reproduce the cold, clear light in which the carvings had been conceived we designed and built special units for their display. The tops of the waist-high cabinets were made up largely of a strong and rigid milk glass under which we installed fluorescent tubes. Their cold light shining through the transluscent tops creates an effect very much like that of the most appropriate background for the dynamic sculptures — ice.

Our Inuit sculpture has inspired another innovation. The cool, polished surface of soapstone begs to be touched. The massive Eskimo carvings, in no danger of being moved or tipped, are, fortunately, touchable. We are able, therefore, to depart from the "Do not touch" policy in force in other areas of the gallery. We not only permit, but invite, our visitors to experience the sculpture as it would often be experienced in the long Arctic nights — by touch more than by sight.

As a by-product of this innovation we have enjoyed some of our most heart-warming experiences. Among the thousands of school classes visiting Kleinburg there have been special groups of blind children. Few experiences could be more rewarding than witnessing the joy in those little faces as their small hands delicately caress the carved features of a northern animal or human, seeing it as surely as we might with our eyes.

Looking back to my childhood I can recall clearly seeing illustrations of Northwest totem poles and masks in books and travel folders of western Canada. I also remember the day my class from Runnymede Road Public School toured the Royal Ontario Museum. I caught my first glimpse of the two giant totem poles in its open stairwell. Later I saw for the first time, in a more natural outdoor, setting (now long gone), the pole that stood in Exhibition Park near Lakeshore Drive. The carved images of birds, animals and mythological creatures celebrating both tribal legends and the natural environment of the Pacific Coast made a lasting impression. Even at so young an age I knew I was seeing something special.

My recollections of works by the more local and familiar Iroquois and Ojibwa were much more mundane and centred around birch bark canoes and animal-skin moccasins decorated in floral or geometric patterns in quill or beads. Attractive and useful artifacts, but not commemorative art.

Those simple boyhood impressions, untutored and naive, were essentially correct. Through centuries, the Indian peoples of the Pacific Coast have carved and painted their legendary figures in wood, stone and, more recently, precious metals. Among their Ojibwa and Iroquois cousins in eastern Canada, the recording of legends in any visual form was taboo.

Such prohibitions by the tribal elders might have remained in force to this day were it not for a single man — artist Norval Morrisseau of Beardmore in northwestern Ontario. In the late 1950s, when he began painting his people's legends on birch bark, plywood and kraft wrapping paper from a local mill, he was defying a long-forbidden stricture of the Anishnabc culture.

Still, Morrisseau, a self-professed shaman, knew that in earlier centuries, paintings and drawings on birch bark scrolls and natural rock faces had recorded tribal rites and that these recordings were the prerogative of the shaman as tribal artist.

What was new was Morrisseau's intention, not just to preserve his people's legends but to make them known to a much wider world through the dealers and collectors of Toronto.

At almost the same time, another Ojibwa artist, Carl Ray in remote Sandy Lake, was painting the old legends in a different manner. These two pioneers were followed by Francis Kagige and Noel Ducharme and other native painters working in communities stretching from the Manitoba border to Manitoulin Island. Most owed much to the influence of Morrisseau, now considered the father of contemporary Woodland Indian art.

Although Morrisseau's first exhibition in 1962 brought considerable acclaim and was a sellout, there were many in the cultural establishment who, through the sixties and seventies, continued to believe that the new movement in aboriginal art would be transitory in spite of the fact that dozens of talented Indians (and some not so talented) were taking up the brush.

For Signe and me the new art of the Anishnabec seemed a

modern revival in paint of the motifs and legends of an ancient culture which had existed far too long without graphic expressions. We felt the forms of the Northwest Indian peoples and the Inuit, evolved over centuries, had moved far beyond the indigenous cultures which inspired them to become universally accepted Canadian symbols, perhaps even more appropriate than our not so exclusive maple leaf. In the 1960s it appeared possible that in the work of the new Woodland Indian artists we were witnessing the birth, or at least rebirth, of another indigenous art form whose origins and growth were entirely located north of the 49th Parallel. During that first decade we were fascinated to see the works of other, mostly young, Ojibwa painters building on the pioneer efforts of Morrisseau and Ray in a widespread phenomenon which we felt was almost certainly the growth of a major and permanent force in their culture and ours.

It soon became apparent, however, that the endurance, growth and viability of Ojibwa art depended at least as much on the enthusiastic acceptance of collectors in the south as it did on the approval of the Native people from whose culture it had sprung. While it is true that, within a few years, humanoid and animal figures of legend made their appearance in Indian community centres and homes and eventually achieved "traditional" status, it is doubtful this would have occurred except for the success of Woodland Indian art in the sales galleries of metropolitan centres in southern Ontario. Without the money from sales to collectors, it is quite certain that the Ojibwa artists could not have carried on the work long enough to establish their visual impressions as accepted symbols among their own people.

In a happy exception to the usual result when Native peoples and the larger society meet, both have emerged richer from this involuntary co-operation. Our homes and galleries are enriched by the art and legends of an ancient and proud people and the Woodland tribes have rejoiced in the development of the long-submerged talents and creativity of their artists.

Even in the early 1970s, the art of the Anishnabec, or Woodland Indian art, as it is more commonly known, was appreciated by only a very select number of dealers in the larger Ontario cities and an even smaller but enthusiastic and devoted handful of collectors and scholars. In the broader art world of dealers, auction houses and public art galleries it was scarcely considered and among the public at large, all but unknown.

Signe and I had followed with interest the half dozen scattered exhibitions of Morrisseau and Ray during the 1960s, but it was not until the early 1970s that our interest moved from passive to very active. It became apparent that the trail broken by Morrisseau and two or three other pioneers working in isolation was being followed by a widening band of young Native artists and would-be artists which stretched across an enormous corridor extending north from the Great Lakes to James Bay. We believed it was an art movement which, catching fire and spreading through the lands of the Ojibwa and Cree peoples, might, with time, become part of a great tradition — a significant part of the heritage of their people.

When we first visited the homes of some of the young painters at Wikwemikong and West Bay on Manitoulin Island, we were impressed by their untutored but quite skilful handling of paint and their innate design sense. Even more striking were their unfettered, almost childlike imaginations and their collective ability to give free rein to their individual interpretations of things unseen, the spirits and creatures of the legends they had learned from the elders of the tribe.

By this time some had seen Morrisseau paintings or those of one of his followers and his influence was obvious in their work. Others had developed styles influenced, perhaps unconsciously, by other artists. At Wikwemikong Reserve I was impressed by the surrealistic elements that a nineteen-year-old painter, James Simon, had introduced into his legend painting. Yet when I asked him if Salvador Dali's work had influenced his style he replied, thoughtfully, "I don't think so. What reserve is he on?"

At West Bay we became acquainted with a young artist, Blake Debassige, then in his first year at Laurentian University. He enjoyed spending long hours with the elders of his band, listening carefully as they recited the old legends which he conscientiously recorded in longhand as a basis for his paintings. When Blake was fifteen, Carl Ray had visited his school and after listening to Ray speak about his work, Blake told me a new feeling for the Anishnabec art had so excited him that he found himself waiting for sunrise and the light to begin a new day's work. He was not aware of any restrictions against painting the ancient legends, at least on Manitoulin Island, and felt that he was carrying on a tradition which went back to the rock paintings, and which had been used for generations to decorate his ancestors' hunting gear, canoes, and other possessions.

Talking with him and his wife-to-be, Shirley Chee Choo, was a refreshing experience. The young couple were very involved in community affairs and the work of the Ojibwa Cultural Foundation, to which Blake had contributed several thoughtful posters, one of which was captioned, "When Legends Fall Silent Our Ways Are Lost". Blake was constantly thinking of new ways to solve artistic problems and develop themes closely related to his people and their heritage. Among the first of his paintings which had been retained were a small series of ochre and black figures of legendary birds and animals in silhouette. The first of these hung proudly in his father's band council office at West Bay. I was fortunate enough to acquire the second in the series, *Bird and Friend*, painted when the artist was only sixteen years old.

Later, Blake had mastered the technique of depicting graphically the process of metamorphosis, a theme he used to show the shaman transforming himself into a bird. In his continuing search for truth in nature and in art he became aware of the preponderance of animal forms over plant forms in Anishnabec art. Since his people had always excelled in the practice of herbal medicine he began to redress this imbalance of subject matter by incorporating the floral shapes, which long had been the motifs of traditional bead designs, into his work. I was most impressed when I saw one of the earliest of these themes at his home about five years after our first meeting and acquired the work, which he had titled *Dependency*, for the Collection which by that time included several of his paintings.

As often happens in a new world not yet widely explored we met, in addition to many of the artists, others who had an abiding interest in the still young Anishnabec art movement. George Yost, whose midtown Toronto home was literally an open house for visiting Native painters, became a good friend and trusted adviser. Through him Signe and I came to know many fine young painters from remote areas who might otherwise have escaped our attention and from his knowledge and deep interest in their symbolism and design we gained a greater appreciation of the art which we believed would, in time, become a significant part of Canada's heritage.

Two other enthusiasts for the emerging Anishnabec expression whose scholarly advice and encouragement of our collecting were invaluable were Elizabeth McLuhan of the Native Affairs Branch of the Ontario government, and Dr. Bernard Cinader of the University of Toronto, an immunologist whose avocation was the study and collecting of Woodland Indian art.

By late 1974 we had met Carl Ray, Noel Ducharme, Joshim Kakegamic and his brother Goyce, Saul Williams and Roy Thomas, all from the far northwestern areas of Ontario, as well as Martin Panamick and several of the other Manitoulin Island painters.

As one of the pioneers, Carl Ray was an artist whose works held special interest for us and on his infrequent visits to Toronto we sometimes arranged to meet him at Toronto Airport and bring him to Kleinburg. After purchasing several works from the armloads he brought with him from remote Sandy Lake, we would deliver him to the city where he usually sold the remainder.

Almost all Anishnabec painters work exclusively in acrylic paints and many of Ray's most appealing and dramatic works were confined to black and one other colour, most often brown or blue, on heavy, pure white watercolour paper. We were always drawn first to the depictions of legends which he painted with swift and sure outlines, almost always accentuating a spiral twist he gave the spinal column of man or beast to heighten motion and give a three-dimensional aspect to the painting which almost made it seem that the creatures depicted were alive. The X-ray effect, revealing inner organs and strengths, is reduced to a skeletal pattern of dotted, crosshatched and veined shapes which add, rather than detract, from the power and often furious movement of figures drawn with the perceptive eye of one who is thoroughly familiar with them in nature.

As word of our serious collecting spread through the Native grapevine we met other fine young painters, almost all of whom lived in near solitude, close to nature. Johnson Meekis, Francis Kagige, Jackson Beardy, Randy Trudeau and Sam Ashe had each approached the creatures of the wild and the old legends with distinctly different, yet somehow related, motifs. Their variations on the two broad themes are as infinite as the imagination and talents of their creative minds.

Almost weekly, it seemed, we saw new works, some less than skilled in execution but apparently original and often charmingly naive in concept. Other works had obviously drawn heavily on the manners and ideas of the pioneer painters, most notably those of the movement's acknowledged giant, Norval Morrisseau.

He might be listed as a resident of Beardmore, a village near Thunder Bay, but without notice Morrisseau's nomadic ways can change his address to Winnipeg or Toronto or any of a dozen northern communities. If the spirit moves him, he will head to a camp high in the Rocky Mountains. It was, therefore, not entirely surprising that I was unable to track him down until the first days of January 1975 when, curiously, our roles became reversed. I became the hunted and he the hunter. I was easily tracked to our gallery in Kleinburg. My secretary suddenly appeared tiny as she ushered a powerful, charismatic figure dressed in a beaded moose-hide coat into my office. I needed no introduction to guess that the craggily handsome face surrounded by a long, unruly mass of black hair with strands falling over dark, piercing eyes belonged to Norval Morrisseau.

Grinning broadly to conceal his shyness, Morrisseau seated himself and became busy with a large disposable plastic shopping bag from which he slowly withdrew a giant-sized calling card, a brilliantly painted and highly stylized self-portrait. It was a startling and unforgettable introduction if, indeed, any further introduction had been needed.

As I stared intently at the dazzling colours of a fully bedecked figure carrying a sacred staff, Morrisseau's initial shyness vanished. The painting's strong black outlines and the flashing colours of amethyst, ruby and topaz resembled nothing so much as the stained glass in a great cathedral. It was, the artist said, the way he saw himself, a brave young warrior resplendent in the robes and crowning headpiece of his forebears. Then beside the striking profile he placed another, even more complex, companion piece whose largest figure faced his. He told me he had called it *Artist's Wife and Daughter*.

I could not take my eyes from the two brilliant adult figures and the complementary figure of the child. Morrisseau was in command and he knew it. As he spoke of his people and their legends, often in the present tense, the words seemed to flow as naturally as if he were reciting a familiar poem or recalling a recent and memorable experience. The traditions and fables seemed as real and believable in his words as a landscaper's reference to trees and hills. It was apparent he felt his paintings were not the stuff of fanciful imagination but representations of what he had been appointed to reveal and preserve.

I was entranced by his stories, but I thought I sensed that Morrisseau was anxious to move to more mundane subjects such as sales and money. I fully expected the prices of his paintings to be considerably higher than those of other younger and less prominent Native artists with whom we had talked. As much as I wanted to add the two glowing works to the Collection, I hoped that he recognized our need to justify purchase prices, especially those in a relatively new field in which firm market values were not yet well established. Equally important, I hoped he would not set arbitrarily high prices with a view to impressing me but with the intention of reducing them if I proved resistant. I was not prepared to bargain.

Yet, while I was quite certain that his purpose was to sell the pictures, he had made no mention of selling. I took refuge in a delay tactic, hoping he would open the negotiations.

He had placed the pictures against the back of a sofa for viewing. As a matter of habit I picked up one for closer examination. To my surprise I noticed that although the figures and their lavish dress were painted with a measurable thickness of heavily applied paint, the deep yellow background was completely free of brush marks as if it had been spray painted ... or even printed. Without mentioning this I asked Norval if I might show the picture to one of my associates in a nearby office. He promptly agreed.

Jim Hubbard, who had been in the picture framing business for some years, quickly confirmed my suspicion that the painting had been made on inexpensive preprinted matte board intended for bordering pictures and that this particular grade had a very high acid content which, over the years, would cause it to discolour and eventually ... to self-destruct. Not a happy prospect for any art collector, least of all a public art gallery.

When I asked him about the support medium he was using, Morrisseau answered honestly, if naively, that he had been using the board because it came in a variety of colours and was inexpensive compared to the cost of canvas or heavy bonded watercolour paper. Also, the background colour was supplied which saved a lot of paint.

Patiently I explained about the matte board's high acid content and the inevitable discolouration and eventual ruin of his art which was certain to occur, not next month or next year, but at a time when his paintings would be recognized as truly historic. It was his, and our, solemn duty to do everything possible to see that this did not happen.

"But what can I do?" he asked. "Canvas and stretchers are so expensive and difficult to carry with me. And with large pictures like I paint, watercolour paper is hard to work with and impossible to prop up or hold on an easel."

I thought for a moment. "Have you ever used Masonite?"

"No, what is it?" The name was obviously totally unfamiliar to him.

"It's a building material, a wallboard sold in lumber yards. When properly primed, in your case with acrylic primer, it is an excellent, stable material to paint on and it will last."

"I need to get some ... where?"

With an unexpected turn of events I felt the ball was now in my court. I asked him if he hoped to sell the paintings to us and if so what price he expected. Obviously delighted that I had broached the subject, Morrisseau said that he hoped to get twelve hundred dollars for the self-portrait and fourteen hundred for the one of his wife and child because it had two figures and a lot more paint. Without hesitating he went on to say that since I was not too happy with the board he had used he would make a big reduction in the prices. It was a handsome offer, but not what I had in mind.

I asked where he was staying and how long he expected to be in the area. He had a motel room nearby and no definite schedule. I proposed that if he was willing to paint the two pictures again, within a few hours we could supply him with two pieces of Masonite cut to size and properly primed and that upon delivery of the paintings we would pay the full twenty-six hundred dollars he had suggested. We would also like to see the two that had been painted on matte board destroyed.

He not only agreed but seemed genuinely excited at the prospect of using a support material entirely new to him, one which might help to solve problems in the future. In our supply room we picked up a small sample of Masonite, then I took him to see two oil paintings on Masonite which were hanging in one of our gallery rooms. Studying the sample, he asked a natural question, "This material is smooth and shiny on one side, dull and quite textured on the other. Which side should I paint on?"

"Your choice," I replied. "The textured side gives a bit more drag to your brush, something like coarse canvas, while the smooth side is more like the board you have been using. Either one provides a good painting surface, so it's up to you."

Two days later Morrisseau returned to our gallery grinning happily and carrying two fine paintings of himself and his family on Masonite. One was painted on the smooth side, the other on the textured. It was the beginning of a warm and lasting, if occasionally bumpy, relationship and over the years many of Norval Morrisseau's finest works have found their way to Kleinburg.

Years earlier, when we were planning Tapawingo's first wing, Signe and I had allowed ourselves the luxury of an indoor swimming pool on its lower level. As a bonus we gained humidity, particularly during winter months, through controlled ducts which carried the pool room's excess moisture to the rooms where our paintings were hung. By 1975 our pool was the last remaining area in the gallery's two main floors which was still reserved for our personal use. Three large wings had been added to provide additional public amenities and individual galleries for the works of the artists around whom the Collection had been built. Annual attendance had reached the hundreds of thousands and all space and facilities were being fully used to accommodate the increasing number of paintings and people.

There was simply no area of sufficient size available for the permanent display of the Woodland Indian art we had come to admire so highly. It was impossible, under the circumstances, to avoid thinking about the pool. The swimming pool area would be ideal. As so many times in the past, it was time for Signe and me to have another heart-to-heart talk, and as always when personal luxury was weighed against the needs of the Collection, the outcome of that talk was never in doubt. So one evening that spring we took a sentimental dip in a pool filled with memories of happy times with so many of our friends. It would be our last. The following morning our maintenance crew, supervised by Raymond Peel, one of our excellent carpenters, pumped out thousands of gallons of water and began the work which would transform our pool into a gallery for Ojibwa, Cree and Iroquois art.

With our decision to create a permanent area for their art, our relationship with many of Ontario's Indian peoples became closer and at the same time much more widespread. Often one of the artists led us to another, a potential competitor for our favour, but whose work he admired. That summer I met one of our most interesting artists, a most remarkable young Ojibwa named Benjamin Chee Chee, who was living in Ottawa at the time. Like Carl Ray in Sandy Lake, Chee Chee's childhood in Temagami had been one of extreme deprivation and, also like Ray, he possessed an ineffable charm. Both men were gifted, creative, impulsive, fascinating, unpredictable and vulnerable. In his thirties each had achieved a magnificent style combining his own very individual expression with equally distinctive and gracefully flowing line and form. Both became my friends for a few short years before senseless, wasteful and violent death ended their lives. The body of work they left behind was all too small.

Chee Chee was born to the northern forests and lakes and his recollections and understanding of moose, bear, otter and Canada geese — for which he had a special affection — remained strong. Working mainly in black line against the pure white of watercolour paper with accents usually in a brown stipple, he did not use the X-ray technique so familiar in the work of Ray and the legend painters but took as his personal idiom the abstracted lines of form and motion inherent in his animal subjects. The line thus produced is so graceful and elegant that it effectively enhances the already beautiful forms of nature.

Another friend was Daphne Odjig, who was an accomplished painter before Anishnabec art, as we know it, was given widespread contemporary expression. At Wikwemikong reserve on Manitoulin Island, where she was born and spent her childhood years, her favourite pastime was sketching, often in company with her grandfather, the community stonemason. When she was in her teens she moved to Toronto with her sister and later, after her marriage, to Winnipeg and then to British Columbia. In the cities much of her free time was spent visiting art galleries, where she broadened her knowledge of modern art, particularly the work of Picasso and the Cubists. They became, and remained, strong influences on her own developing style.

In Winnipeg she met the painters Carl Ray, Jackson Beardy, Alex Janvier and Norval Morrisseau before she returned to Wikwemikong. Home again on Manitoulin Island as a mature painter, she was deeply impressed by the vigorous revival of Native customs and legends and the introspection and personal growth which she found taking place in the 1960s and 1970s among her people. To further it she wrote and illustrated a number of books for children which dealt mainly with the legendary creature Nanabush fondly remembered from her childhood.

When I first got in touch with Daphne Odjig in the 1970s it was arranged that several of her canvases would be sent to Kleinburg so we could make a selection. Unlike most artists, she painted in several entirely different styles, choosing the one she felt best suited the subject matter and design of each picture. The three large canvases which we purchased were each as different in treatment as they were in subject and title. *Tribute to the Great Chiefs of the Past* had a formal, organized design not unlike a stained-glass window. *Conflict Between Good and Evil* depicted the age-old parable with two grotesque figures and a serpent, all with a vague resemblance to humans in writhing, contorted motion. *The Embrace* is a cubist treatment of a tender and very intimate moment between man and woman. None of these would be considered typical of Woodland or any other Native art.

In the years since we first acquired her work, Signe and I have come to know Daphne, a remarkable woman, whom we believe we can include among those we call close friends. Her intelligence, sensitivity, easy wit and great warmth are only exceeded by the contribution she has already made to the culture of both her race and her nationality, although she prefers to think of them as one — Canadian.

As central features of the new Woodland Indian gallery which was richly panelled in red cedar, we designed two impressive display cases for the exquisite artistic creations of the Iroquois. One was built into a massive granite column replacing what had been a fireplace while the other, occupying the centre of the room, was made up of large panels carved in pine by Six Nations artist Elwood Green. It depicted the symbols and legendary creatures of Iroquois mythology.

In the case, Green's principal oeuvre, silver carving and steotite stone carvings by Joe Jacobs and Duffy Wilson were displayed side by side with traditional cornhusk statuary and finely designed and executed bead and quill patterns; a distinct counterpoint for the surrounding paintings which were mostly by Ojibwa artists.

We felt proud that our specially designed permanent showcase room for Woodland Indian art was the first in any public art gallery and we wanted to underline the importance we placed on it. Through my friend Esmond Butler, principal secretary at Rideau Hall, we invited the Governor General of Canada to open what we felt was an important new departure in the development of Canadian art.

To our delight, Their Excellencies the Right Honourable Jules Léger and Madame Léger accepted the invitation to honour the Woodland artists with their presence on November 16, 1975. To mark the occasion in an appropriate way, the McMichael Collection presented His Excellency with a beaded moosehide jacket.

I was told later that this jacket could be seen whenever the Governor General took one of his frequent winter strolls in the beautiful grounds of Rideau Hall.

6

During the spring and summer of 1970, celebrations to mark the Group of Seven's fiftieth anniversary with a recreation of their 1920 exhibition were being held in Toronto, Ottawa and Montreal. The opening at Ottawa's National Gallery of Canada was scheduled for June 19, and A. Y. Jackson, now in his eighty-eighth year, had agreed to be present. On the morning of June 18, Prime Minister Trudeau asked his secretary, Mary MacDonald, to find out if it would be possible to arrange a private meeting with Jackson away from the fanfare of the gala opening events.

At almost the same moment, Zita Wilson, Jackson's nurse-companion, was fastening the seat belt in the front passenger seat of the Collection's green Buick station wagon. We expected to take Alex on a leisurely drive from Kleinburg to Ottawa's Château Laurier hotel. Shoulder belts were new at the time and as Alex sensed some new kind of restraint he muttered, "This contraption makes me feel like I'm going to the moon." Nevertheless, he settled back to enjoy the three hundred mile journey.

By four o'clock in the afternoon we were still some distance from the National Gallery, so I pulled into a gas station near Carlton Place and telephoned the director, Jean Boggs, to ask her to send two catalogues directly to the hotel.

"I'm so glad you have called, Mr. McMichael," said the secretary I reached. "We've been trying to contact you most of the day. The Prime Minister's office is most anxious to reach you. Please call this number at once and ask for Mary MacDonald.

In novels those who are ordered to reach prime ministers do so without delay. I had to dig around for some more change. Finally I heard the cheerful voice of Mary MacDonald. She asked where we were and then continued, "The Prime Minister has been anxious to meet A. Y. Jackson. I believe he's travelling with you? Would it be possible for you to bring him to Mr. Trudeau's office in the centre block within the next hour or so?"

"I'll certainly try. What's the speed limit in Ottawa?"

"Never mind that, but drive carefully of course. In fact if you are stopped by the police ask them to give you an escort to the Prime Minister's office."

That certainly sounded like fun, but my delusions of grandeur were short-lived. I had to ask how to find the Prime Minister's office.

"Drive directly to the Peace Tower. Park your car at the main portico. Someone will take it and I will be there to meet you."

Returning to the car, I found Alex asleep, so I speeded up. I asked Signe and Zita to lean forward so I could give them the news without fear that he would hear and become overexcited.

There was consternation in the back seat. "We're not even dressed," said Zita. "How can we meet Mr. Trudeau in slacks and sport shirts? I always dreamed I would meet him, and look at me! Even Dr. Jackson is wearing his old clothes!"

"I'm sure the Prime Minister will understand that we dressed comfortably for the trip," I told them. "After all, this is an unscheduled command performance. Besides, he wants to meet Alex and we might not even be invited in." Somehow that didn't seem to cheer them.

As we entered the outskirts of the city on the Queensway, I suggested to Zita that she should gently wake Jackson and at least brush his thinning hair into place. "But don't tell him until we're there." Jackson began noticing familiar landmarks and as we turned off Wellington Street into the main driveway of the Parliament

Buildings, he looked towards me in disbelief.

"You're lost, Bob," he said laughing. "This isn't the Château Laurier."

"Right. This is where Prime Minister Trudeau works," I replied, "and he's waiting to meet you."

Without any visible sign of concern he simply responded, "Is that right? I'd be happy to meet him."

At the Peace Tower a Mountie gave us a brisk salute as Mary MacDonald came down the steps to greet us. After brief introductions and apologies for our informal dress, she said, "Never mind, you made good time getting here and that's the important thing. The Prime Minister can be very informal at times too."

As the four of us were ushered into his office, Pierre Trudeau came from behind his desk and walked toward us with his hand extended. It was a dramatic moment for all of us. Jackson met him with a warm handshake, as though they had been friends for years. Signe and I again apologized for our casual dress. With that, Trudeau, impeccable in a hand-tailored grey suit and white shirt immediately undid his silk tie, opened his shirt collar and slouched with his arm thrown over the back of a handy chair. "There ... does that make you feel more comfortable?" he asked with a broad grin.

At ease, he began enthusing about the opening of the Group's Anniversary Show, about which he appeared to be very well informed. Then he confided to us, "Not many people know it, but as a teenager, I spent several summers at Ahmek, Taylor Statten's boys' camp in Algonquin Park. The first year, I was a junior camper. I think they called us 'polywogs'. The second year, I was a 'minnow' and the third year I became a counsellor. If you know the camps, you'll know that for three years I was practically raised on Tom Thomson, who unfortunately drowned in our lake, Canoe Lake...and the Group of Seven, most of whom also painted there." Turning to me he said, "In spite of my admiration for their paintings, I had never met any of the artists. Jackson, here, is perhaps the best known of the Group, and when I heard he was coming to Ottawa for the special exhibition I hoped it might be possible for us to meet."

As our conversation continued, Jackson began to make occasional comments — in French!

"Does he speak French?" Trudeau asked eagerly.

"Not as a rule," I replied, "but with all the time he spent painting rural Quebec, I'm certain he picked up more than a working knowledge of the language."

For the remainder of the meeting, Trudeau and Jackson carried on a conversation, slightly halting on Jackson's part, in French. As we were departing, the Prime Minister turned to me with a grin and asked, "Were you able to follow what he was saying?"

Apologizing for my almost forgotten high school French, I admitted that I had not been able to follow the conversation.

With a proud gleam in his eyes Trudeau beamed, "Years ago, he actually saw and listened to Laurier! He says that I remind him of Laurier."

A. Y. Jackson was the only member of the original Group whose pictures had hung in the first Group of Seven show in Toronto to see the anniversary exhibition a half century later. Arthur Lismer and Frederick Varley had died a year earlier and Lawren Harris, living in Vancouver, was unable to travel. Two younger members, Alfred Casson and Edwin Holgate, who joined the Group a few years later, were present, and paintings by them also featured in the triumphant fiftieth anniversary celebration. It was a joyful reunion of Group families, many of whom were now our valued friends.

It was fitting that Mrs. Eric Brown, widow of a much earlier National Gallery director, open the exhibition with reminiscences of the Group's heyday. Her husband, Eric Brown, had been director of the National Gallery during the Group's earliest years. In 1914 he and National Gallery trustee Sir Edmund Walker encouraged the revolutionary movement of young artists in the most tangible way by insisting that the Gallery purchase major works by Thomson, Lismer, Harris, MacDonald and Jackson. Almost sixty years later, Mrs. Brown obviously took considerable pride in her late husband's perspicacity at a crucial time for the young artists. Few others had shown interest in the radical quest which by 1970 had firmly established them as the nation's "old masters".

We were also proud. Sixteen works in that memorable anniversary exhibition had their permanent home in the McMichael Canadian Collection.

It is interesting to note in the catalogue of the show that a painting stated to be Arthur Lismer's first Canadian work, was, for that historic reason, included in the exhibition. It is entitled *The Banks of the Don* and it had been assigned an approximate date of 1912. At the time, we had no reason to question its status. A few years later, however, The McMichael Canadian Collection received *An Ontario Landscape* from the artist's daughter, Marjorie Lismer Bridges. It is signed and dated 1911.

When William Davis became Premier of Ontario in 1971, Keith Reynolds, who had been John Robart's chief of staff, moved to the newly created Ministry of Natural Resources as deputy minister. One of the Ministry's continuing tasks was assigning names to unnamed lakes and rivers as well as resolving the problems which had arisen because many areas had been named without reference to any centrally planned and approved system. (For example, there were dozens of Gull Lakes and Deer Lakes.) In the early years of the province many places had been named for the settlers who lived near them, but after the establishment of the Geographic Names Board in 1971 it had been an unwritten law that living people would not be honoured on the maps of Ontario. It was, therefore, quite a departure when the Province decided to make an exception for a man who, in 1972, was nearing his ninetieth birthday and had become literally a legend in his own time. In 1970, a small lake in the wilderness region north of Lake Huron was officially designated A. Y. Jackson Lake in honour of the painter who had painted more of his country than anyone before (or since).

When we told him of the honour, Alex remarked almost casually that he might have painted "his" lake since he had so often hiked through the area. Unfortunately, his failing strength ruled out a visit, which would have included a mile-long portage.

Two years later, following Jackson's death in 1974, it was decided that two more lakes in the same general area of the La Cloche mountains should honour two other members of the Group. Franklin Carmichael had painted in the area for many years, working out of the cottage he had built on nearby Cranberry Lake and A. J. Casson had also painted extensively in the area.

As a result, Casson would become the first Canadian artist to paint a lake which bore his own name. This historic occasion came after a ceremonial hanging of the certificates proclaiming Carmichael and Casson Lakes, conducted by M.P.P. Donald Deacon at the McMichael Collection. Plans were then made for Casson to visit "his" remote lake about one hundred miles north of Manitoulin Island.

A small seaplane which regularly patrolled the area picked up the artist, Keith Reynolds and I at a Natural Resources fishery station at South Baymouth. Forty minutes later the pilot was pointing his index finger straight down. Noses pressed to the plane's small windows, we had our first look at a mile-long, finger-shaped body of water glimmering in the morning sun.

Encircled by low but treacherous quartzite mountains, Casson Lake must be approached by an aircraft with a steep descent to avoid overshooting, but our experienced bush pilot made it seem easy. He also took off with ease from the watery runway which comes to an abrupt end at a steep rock wall. He was to pick us up in late afternoon.

Casting a practised eye along the shoreline and over the rocky hills beyond, Casson headed for a vantage point on the sharply sloping hillside. Sensing his intense concentration at this unique moment in a long painting life, Keith and I left him to sketch and stole away to explore the craggy edges of the lake which had been carved out by glaciers in the Pre-Cambrian period. Now, millenia later, it was rimmed by the tenacious northern forest and a nearly impenetrable tangle of vegetation and colourful northern wildflowers.

Sometime later we returned to base camp and found Cass still totally absorbed in his sketching. A picnic lunch finally persuaded him to set down his sketch box and brushes and Keith and I had an opportunity to see what he had been up to. His pencil had traced the outlines of hills, forest, rocks and water on several wooden panels, but as was his habit, he was waiting for the sun and summer clouds to create shadows and contrasts before beginning to apply colour.

During nearly sixty years of roaming through backwoods country, Alfred Casson had seen and painted any number of lakes and forest-clad hills like those he sketched that August morning. He had, in fact, even painted the enormous quartzite cliffs and unusual natural features of this range of small mountains, often in the company of his painting comrade, Frank Carmichael.

But this was special.

He was not taking advantage of the artist's licence to change contours or move mountains for the sake of heightening drama or improving composition. Instead, his pencil had moved with precision to trace true images of the far shoreline with its rock outcroppings which formed miniature peninsulas, bays and islands. Scattered clumps of tall, symmetrical black spruce at water's edge were dark sentinels advancing before the light green of deciduous trees marching down from a blue-grey mountainous horizon. Casson was disciplining himself to paint a true likeness, a glowing, somewhat flattering portrait of his namesake.

After lunch, Cass returned to his painting perch, looked over the pencil outlines he had completed on panels, then moved his folding stool and sketch box to a quite different vantage point. At once he was again completely immersed in his work and a fresh view of "his" lake and its surrounding wilderness.

Keith and I had brought along our cameras to record what we saw as a unique event. As we circled around him, looking for the best angles, Casson was a completely unself-conscious subject, oblivious to our presence and our cameras. So engrossed had he become in his sketching that he scarcely heard or noticed the arrival of our plane a few hours later. By then there were four panels in his sketch box depicting the lonely little lake which bore his name.

Today, among over seventy works by A. J. Casson in the McMichael Canadian Collection, the visitor can enjoy one of the panels he sketched that day. While it holds its own among his other landscapes, I feel its historic interest outweighs its artistic merit.

Geographic memorials were not the only honours received by members of the Group during their own lifetimes.

When A. Y. Jackson came to live with us at Kleinburg in 1968, the grand old man of Canadian painting, then in his mid-eighties, had already received just about all the honours a grateful country could bestow. Although proud of these tributes, which had come mostly in his later years, the ever-modest Jackson seldom mentioned them and never paraded them.

Seven Canadian universities had conferred honorary doctorates upon him and many people who did not know him well addressed him deferentially as "Dr. Jackson". Jackson himself would joke that perhaps he should start signing his name followed by LL.D.(7).

Some years earlier he had received the medal of a Commander of St. Michael and St. George and with it the right to use the initials C.M.G. In the ranking of that particular order, there was one higher station, Knight Commander of St. Michael and St. George, K.C.M.G. When asked what C.M.G. stood for Jackson would reply with an impish grin, "Call Me God — and there's a higher rank, K.C.M.G. — Kindly Call Me God." Yet for all his joking, he was extremely proud of the honours he received, particularly the highest honour Canada can confer on a citizen, Companion of the Order of Canada.

Most of the living members of the Group of Seven had received similar honours, but in the earlier years the youngest member, A. J. Casson, seemed to have been overlooked. His turn would come. Just after his seventy-second birthday in 1970 the University of Western Ontario in London, at its June convocation, conferred on him the degree of Doctor of Law, *honoris causa*. Just one week later, I was honoured at the convocation of York University,

Toronto, with the degree Doctor of Letters, *honoris causa*. It was another parallel in our lives.

Other honours, perhaps really honouring the Group, also came my way. In 1974, I was inducted into the Order of Canada by Governor General Jules Léger at Government House in Ottawa. In another parallel, Casson became an Officer of the Order of Canada a few years later. Signe and I rejoiced in the following years as three more Canadian universities honoured Casson and he and Margaret occupied seats in the front row in the fall of 1983 when the University of Waterloo conferred Doctor of Law degrees on Signe and me in a unique double ceremony.

I have shared many experiences in my personal life as well as in business and in art with Alfred Casson. Whatever the future holds for us, we will finally share one more — a small cemetery surrounded by young pines and maples on a hilltop in Kleinburg.

I met Prime Minister Pierre Trudeau again in November of 1975, at a small dinner held in conjunction with the opening of an exhibition of Northwest Indian art at Ottawa's Museum of Man.

We reminisced about his visit with A. Y. Jackson, who had since died, and knowing of his special interest in Tom Thomson and the other artists, I suggested that he and his family might enjoy a weekend at Kleinburg.

"I'd like that," said the Prime Minister. "Would you be kind enough to drop me a note reminding me of your offer? It may well fit into our schedule during the coming months."

Back at my office in Kleinburg the next morning I dictated a brief letter, giving Mr. and Mrs. Trudeau an open invitation to spend a weekend with us.

The following February, Signe and I spent ten days in the Bermuda sun. During our absence my secretary received a call from the Prime Minister's office asking whether it would be convenient for the Trudeaus to visit us the following weekend. The executive assistant would not hear of disturbing our vacation and suggested that he would call again.

Upon our return, I promptly dictated a letter to the Trudeaus telling them how sorry we were to have been away and expressing our hopes that we would receive another call. Towards the end of March the call came, suggesting the first weekend in April. They were scheduled to be in Toronto on the Friday evening for a dinner address which the Prime Minister was giving. We had a date.

On Wednesday, two security experts from the R.C.M.P. came

to take a walk through the galleries and to enquire about staff members who would have direct access to the building during the Trudeaus' visit. Who would prepare the food? Where would the Prime Minister and his wife and their son Sacha sleep? We were told in confidence that the Ontario Provincial Police and the York Regional Force would be patrolling the grounds surrounding the gallery and that shifts of plain-clothes security men, charged with the Prime Minister's safety, would be constantly on guard at the foot of the stairs leading to our private quarters. Others would be patrolling the building in co-operation with our own security people. We had asked one of our favourite guides, a young mother named Joy Treadwell, to be available as a baby-sitter and to assist Mrs. Trudeau in any possible way. Two of our young gallery restaurant waitresses were assigned to serve at meals. The R.C.M.P. were especially interested in meeting these three young women.

As dinner hour on Friday approached, Signe and I nervously re-checked the bedrooms as well as the living and dining rooms. As usual Stella and her staff had done an excellent job.

Suddenly our private telephone rang, causing us both to jump. "Who's nervous?" Signe asked and we both laughed. It was Margaret Trudeau, calling from the Toronto home of publisher Jack McClelland. She would be arriving with Sacha for dinner in about one hour. Her husband, who was speaking at a Liberal Association dinner, would not arrive until a little later in the evening.

Shortly after the arrival of our other guests, Keith and Maudie Reynolds, the intercom reported that an unmarked R.C.M.P. automobile, carrying Mrs. Trudeau and her son, was now approaching our front door.

During the day, Margaret and Sacha had attended the annual Easter Seal Daffodil parade in Toronto. To their delight and the anguish of the police, they had managed to slip away from their security guards to mingle with the crowds. It had been a big day for Sacha. Already in his mother's arms, he was a very tired little boy ready for bed.

At dinner, Margaret Trudeau talked about her sons. She hated the necessity of constant security and talked rather wistfully of their wilderness trips with the children. Her husband was an excellent canoeist. "That way," she said, "we get a little more privacy, because the Mounties have to follow behind in a separate canoe."

Towards the end of dinner Prime Minister Pierre Trudeau bounded into the room, accompanied by three men, each wearing a communicating radio like a hearing aid behind his ear.

Margaret sighed, "See what I mean?"

The Trudeaus told us they were looking forward to the time when they could build and enjoy their own country home, perhaps in the Laurentians. Both admired our cathedral ceilings and the twenty-two inch pine boards with which the room had been panelled.

Saturday morning, the hum of electric razors and splashing showers in the Trudeaus' rooms and our own blended with the chirping of a white-throated sparrow high in the trees which encircled Tapawingo's top floor. In a second sitting room between the two sets of bedrooms, the Prime Minister had caught his little son by the heels and was vigorously swinging him up above his head and between the exposed rafters of the open triangular ceiling to an accompaniment of delighted shouts of "Closer... closer!"

After a few moments, Sacha was walking hand in hand with his father toward the dining room, where our two guide-waitresses were standing very formally at attention, somewhat nervously waiting to serve breakfast. To their surprise the Prime Minister and Sacha walked by them with a nod and sauntered directly into the kitchen where Signe was supervising bacon and eggs. Completely at home, the Prime Minister opened a cupboard. "What would you like Sach?... Corn flakes... shredded wheat... bran flakes... maybe corn pops? Any tension which might have existed immediately dissolved as the five of us sat down to a family-style breakfast.

After breakfast I led the Trudeaus to a stairway which went directly into the galleries below, while Signe remained upstairs to oversee housekeeping chores and the preparation of fresh lobster and salads for lunch.

The first room we entered was the special gallery for Clarence Gagnon's fifty-four *Maria Chapdelaine* illustrations. I thought how proud Colonel McLaughlin would have been.

The Prime Minister was so enchanted with the display that I began to despair of ever getting through the twenty-five other gallery rooms before the public visitors were admitted at noon.

Finally we moved on and I noticed that Margaret, a serious semi-professional photographer, was busy with her 35 mm camera. Pierre Trudeau, keeping up a steady flow of intelligent questions about the artists and their pictures, appeared fascinated by the artists' interpretations of the Canadian landscape, perhaps because he had so many vivid recollections of visits to the same areas.

Before noon, Margaret and Sacha rejoined Signe in the apartment, but Pierre continued to be completely absorbed in the Collection. He mentioned that, like many others, he had always felt that there was a considerable similarity in the work of members of the Group. Now, after seeing the full scope of each artist, he recognized the distinctive and dramatic differences which made each painter unique.

Unfortunately, a lot of people think that if they've seen a few Group paintings, they've seen them all. The bent pine in the foreground and cobalt blue lakes are seen to be trademarks. To paraphrase Arthur Lismer, "the Group had hitched their wagon to the wild and the untamed". The images they created from primeval raw materials have become imprinted in our national consciousness.

Of course, members of the Group often painted similar subjects. But the display of each painter's work in continuous rooms at Kleinburg gives visitors a singular opportunity to compare distinctly different personal approaches to thematically similar subjects. Yet, underlying most of their work is an unabashed nationalism, a determination to celebrate Canadian themes in a distinctively Canadian manner.

By early afternoon, word of the Trudeaus' private visit had reached the media. Reporters and cameramen lined our front entrance walkway. As Sacha, in conductor's hat, burst out of the front door holding his father's hand, an alert photographer from the *Globe and Mail* captured the moment, which appeared on the paper's front page over the gleeful caption, "Me, too".

The Prime Minister took the end of his privacy good-naturedly and chatted amiably with surprised and delighted visitors, including a short-haired twelve-year-old, wearing jeans and a loose windbreaker, to whom he said in parting, "Good luck, son..."

The impish reply, "I'm a girl, Mr. Trudeau..." produced a smile and the now-famous shrug.

By 1975, eight years after the great Tom Thomson switch, from which we had emerged bruised and battered, we had amassed nearly seventy works by the legendary painter. These ranged from very early, stilted drawings and watercolours to more than fifty glowing oil panels from his brief but triumphant Algonquin period.

It was an impressive accumulation, but it lacked balance. We still had only three Thomson canvases — the medium-size *Afternoon, Algonquin* which Signe and I had purchased almost twenty years earlier and two important but much smaller ones, *Autumn, Algonquin Park*, a gift of Clare Wood, and *Silver Birches*, from the R. S. McLaughlin gift.

We knew that Thomson had probably produced perhaps fifteen large canvases. Of these, a few were painted before 1914 and the rest when the artist was at his peak of achievement — during the three years before his death in 1917. Most of these major canvases were in public art galleries and we could think of none of the remaining works in private hands which seemed likely to come on the market. After intensive research we had produced a list of private owners that included collectors in Toronto and Montreal and extended from California to England. We had met most of them and all seemed firm in their determination not to sell. Nevertheless, we continued to search and to hope.

During our first overseas jaunt in 1968 our search led us to a tiny village near Oxford and Dr. Frederick MacCallum, who taught there. We knew he owned a fine medium-size canvas, *Hardwoods*, from Thomson's later period.

Dr. MacCallum's father, Dr. J. M. MacCallum, a Toronto ophthalmologist, was Tom Thomson's "patron", his best customer. The elder MacCallum had owned an island and a large summer home at Go Home Bay, an inlet of Georgian Bay, and had taken an interest in Thomson and his friends from their earliest painting days. He was one of the few who were willing to purchase the artists' work and had invited them to make use of his island home during their painting trips. Many of Thomson's paintings from 1912 to 1914 are of Georgian Bay subjects.

In 1912, Jackson was living and painting in the area in a tiny shack which was neither winterized nor waterproof. One day in the late fall, while he was sketching near the shore, he noticed a motorboat approaching. Since most of the summer residents had long-since fled, he was surprised when the boat pulled up and Dr. MacCallum stepped out. MacCallum said later that he was appalled at Jackson's primitive living conditions, which provided little protection from the severe autumn storms. After the usual pleasantries, MacCallum looked over some of the sketches and then suggested tactfully that Jackson move into his well-equipped, heated, and above all, dry island home. It was the beginning of a close relationship which lasted until MacCallum's death thirty years later.

After his return to Toronto, MacCallum met Tom Thomson and spent many hours poring over his small oil panels. Thomson's work at this time was tight and laboured, giving little hint of the brilliant colour and bold technique of his later work. Yet, MacCallum realized, there was a feel for the northern wilderness that was by no means ordinary. "Dark they were, muddy in colour, tight, and not wanting in technical defects, but they made me feel that the North had gripped Thomson, as it had gripped me ever since I first sailed through its silent places as a boy of eleven."

After their first meeting, MacCallum saw little of Thomson until the spring of 1913. Thomson, who was earning a living as a commercial artist at Grip Limited, had been encouraged by his art director, Albert Robson, and artist friends J.E.H. MacDonald and Frederick Varley to enter in an exhibition what became a highly significant canvas, *Northern Lake*. It was the turning point in his career. Though reluctant, he was persuaded to submit it to the jury for the 1913 annual exhibition of the Ontario Society of Artists. To his surprise, it was accepted by the selection committee headed by Sir Edmund Walker, won the first prize money put up by the Government of Ontario and was purchased for two hundred and fifty dollars. It was Thomson's first significant sale.

For years the painting languished in a back hall of Ottawa Teachers' College until Ontario Premier Leslie Frost moved it to his office at Queen's Park. It occupied a place of honour over the mantle in the premier's office until 1972 when Premier William Davis was persuaded to turn it over to the Art Gallery of Ontario.

In the autumn of 1913, Dr. MacCallum proposed to guarantee Thomson's expenses through the purchase of paintings if Tom, by then working at Rous and Mann, would abandon his job and devote himself to painting full time. The arrangement ushered in Thomson's greatest period of creativity and gave MacCallum the largest collection of Thomson paintings.

At his death in 1943, MacCallum had willed most of his collection to the National Gallery of Canada. A few works went to his children. By the time of our visit only one canvas and one panel, both owned by Fred MacCallum, remained in the family. Understandably, he had not the slightest intention of parting with either.

Other owners of Thomson's larger works had made their unwillingness to sell equally clear. Our hope of ever adding a major Thomson canvas to the Collection had become very dim.

Then it happened!

A telephone call came from financier Allan Manford. For unstated reasons, he had decided to sell the cornerstone of his collection, Tom Thomson's *Woodland Waterfall*. He felt we might be interested and invited us to come and see it the following evening.

Sitting before the large Thomson canvas in Manford's living room, I finally plucked up courage. "Have you an idea of the price you would want?" I asked tentatively, well aware of Manford's reputation as a hard and astute bargainer.

"Yes, I know exactly. Three hundred thousand dollars."

I suddenly needed the drink in my hand.

The picture was irreplaceable. The price was unattainable. How on earth could I raise that kind of money?

I muttered something about that being by far the highest price ever asked for a Canadian work of art.

He was fully aware of that. He was also aware that this might well be the last large, late-period Tom Thomson which would ever be sold. No Canadian painting sold in recent years could compare with it. The opportunity was unique. We could take it or leave it. Other galleries or collectors would undoubtedly be interested.

I swallowed the last of my drink and left, torn between desire and despair.

In his book *The Group of Seven*, Peter Mellen writes:

> *Thomson's deep understanding of nature can be seen in works like* Woodland Waterfall *of 1916-17. The impression is one of having entered into a secluded world which had been seen before only by wild animals as they drink in the pool below the falls. It is a landscape where the presence of man is never felt, yet nature is neither threatening nor awe-inspiring. With a few deft changes to the scene before him, Thomson is able to impose order on an intrinsically disorganized setting, while maintaining its complete naturalness.*
>
> Waterfall *is a preview of the Group's work in the years to come. The bold painting of the foreground rocks and the thick rich colours appear at about the same time in MacDonald's work and were probably due to an interchange between the two artists. The dabs of pure red which form an arc across the lower part of the painting reappear a few years later in Jackson's* First Snow Algoma, *and the stylized treatment of the* Waterfall *can be found in Harris'* Waterfall Algoma *in 1918. The strong decorative quality, combined with a feeling for mood, became the trademark of the Group's work.*

During the eight years since our last encounter with major Thomson canvases, in which *Woodland Waterfall* had also figured, the Collection had undergone both phenomenal growth and administrative change. It now enjoyed the status of a provincial Crown corporation; a new name, the McMichael Canadian Collection; and a nine-member board of trustees.

We had been extremely fortunate in the choice of our first chairman. At the request of Premier William Davis we had made recommendations, but Bill Davis himself had his eye on J. Allyn

Taylor, who had recently stepped down from the presidency of Canada Trust. Canada Trust's last annual report under Taylor had taken nature conservation as its theme. It was illustrated with beautifully reproduced paintings by Thomson and the Group from the McMichael Collection. As a thank-you gesture, Canada Trust, with our advice and help, had purchased a Tom Thomson oil-on-panel from Mrs. Jocelyn Mitchell for ten thousand dollars and presented it to the Collection. Although the premier had known Allyn Taylor for some time, it was that annual report which suggested to Bill Davis that Allyn Taylor was the ideal choice for first chairman of the board of the McMichael Canadian Collection.

I received a call from Bill Davis's office asking if I knew Mr. Taylor and if I would concur with his appointment to the board, quite possibly as chairman. I told them we would be honoured to have either Mr. Taylor or Reg Dowsett as chairman and that I hoped that whichever was chosen, the other would agree to be vice-chairman.

Davis felt that the appointment of the Collection's first chairman was sufficiently important to require his personal attention and, after several attempts, finally located Taylor and asked him whether he would prefer to be chairman or vice-chairman.

Without hesitation Allyn Taylor answered, "I'll be whatever you want me to be, Mr. Premier."

The response was typical of the clear thinking we came to expect in the ten years that J. Allyn Taylor served as the first chairman of the board of trustees.

Allyn Taylor was, therefore, the first person I advised of the opportunity to purchase *Woodland Waterfall*. Then I telephoned Jack Wildridge of Roberts Gallery in Toronto. Jack had been on our advisory committee for years and was one of our nominees for trustee on the board of the new corporation. I asked him to join me for another look at the Thomson painting and a discussion with its owner.

We arrived at Manford's home a few minutes early and parked at a discreet distance from the house for a brief discussion before our meeting. There was no question of authenticity and we believed the picture to be in good condition. Knowing Manford as we did, we felt there would be little room for bargaining. It was some consolation that in purchasing the painting on behalf of Her Majesty in Right of Ontario, the usual five percent sales tax which, in this case, would have amounted to fifteen thousand dollars, would not have to be paid. We thought I could ask Manford if he would reduce the price by this amount.

Seated before the large Thomson canvas, Jack opened negotiations by asking the lowest price Manford would accept for the painting. Manford responded firmly with the three hundred thousand dollar figure. On cue, I suggested that we were very serious about purchasing it, but we felt that he should reduce the price by fifteen thousand dollars since the picture would attract no sales tax.

We arrived at an agreed price of two hundred and eighty-five thousand dollars.

I told Manford that if we decided to undertake a fund-raising campaign we would need to hang the painting at Kleinburg, on loan — on approval. To my surprise he readily agreed, adding that he did not wish to receive any payment or complete the sale for a year. He was prepared to give us a firm price and option to purchase effective one year from date.

Manford was aware, as we were, that Parliament had Bill C33 before it.

When it became law it would exempt the seller of a major Canadian work of art to an approved institution from capital gains tax. By waiting a year Manford could expect to avoid a very substantial tax. From our standpoint, such an arrangement was ideal. Holding both a written option and the painting would allow us to display it while we mounted an intensive fund-raising campaign.

Our fruitless attempts to acquire a major Thomson canvas in 1967 were much in our thoughts, but nine years had made a big difference. The Collection had experienced phenomenal growth in its holdings, its buildings and, even more importantly, in public awareness and support. The board and the government supported my proposal to buy *Woodland Waterfall* with what we hoped would be a cascade of money from major corporations and foundations.

As the first step in our campaign we decided to produce a limited edition print on canvas of the painting, about half the size of the original. It would be on a stretcher just like the original and would be treated with a special gel process which could be skilfully applied to duplicate the texture and impasto of an original oil. This would not only allow us to display a small version of the painting to prospective donors but also to offer one of these excellent copies to each major donor, framed and with a brass plaque indicating that the company or person to whom it was given had made an important contribution toward the purchase of the painting.

A few days after the opening of our campaign we received the first contribution of five thousand dollars — the contribution unit we had established — from Xerox Corporation. My list of appointments with senior management began to grow and with it our list of contributions and pledges. A contribution of five thousand dollars from the Royal Bank of Canada was soon followed by a similar amount from the Toronto Dominion Bank after a meeting with its chairman, Alan Lambert.

Twenty years earlier I had sold Lambert, then assistant general manager of the bank, our Vacation Paks as part of the bank's employee relations programme. Now I met with him and my old friend Ben Boyle in the chairman's suite of the Toronto Dominion Tower. Our relationship with Toronto Dominion and with Ben went back a long way to when Ben was the bank's agency representative in New York. At the height of our expansion in the United States, my American corporation had needed some short-term credit, but since we were newcomers without an American track record, Manufacturers-Hanover, our New York bankers, refused a loan. Toronto Dominion came to the rescue without hesitation. A few months later we were maintaining substantial credit balances and loaning money on term deposits to Manufacturers-Hanover, who had become considerably more cordial. Ben eventually rose to the Canadian bank's presidency.

My fund-raising efforts received a sympathetic hearing and I could not resist telling them, "You both played important roles when we built the foundations [of the Collection]. Now it is appropriate that you have a part in the topping-off."

Unfortunately, all my fund-raising was not that successful. Even with the advantage of the excellent reputation which the Collection now enjoyed, the task of convincing individuals and corporations that they should participate in the acquisition of a painting was far from easy. At any given time, thousands of individuals and organizations are seeking donations. The successful campaigns are usually backed up by teams of researchers, direct mail and public relations agencies, professional fund-raising consultants and committees, not to mention small armies of canvassers. All are aimed at the same targets — business, foundations and the wealthy. This relatively small group, compelled by custom and, often inclination, to support the traditional causes, necessarily applies very stringent standards to the hundreds of requests that come in every day.

I was naturally apprehensive, but I hoped that the painting itself would have such wide appeal that we would succeed. While I was willing, and eager, to do everything I could to raise money I felt it was a real drawback that my own name and the name of the McMichael Canadian Collection were the same. While there was undoubtedly value in a personal call from the founder, I worried that donors might think of this as my own personal charity. I tried to dispel any misunderstanding with a simple statement that I was the founder of the Collection which was owned by the Province of Ontario for the education and enjoyment of all Canadians. We now, I told prospects, have the opportunity of bringing a major painting by Tom Thomson, a national treasure, into the Collection for the benefit of this and future generations. We need your help!

A campaign to raise two hundred and eighty-five thousand dollars hardly warranted a fund-raising infrastructure, but it was a formidable challenge for one person. The few members of the board who might have been able and willing to help, all seemed fully occupied with their own businesses and other pursuits. Though Signe and I were already working ten and twelve hour days we knew it was up to us.

Since we had no professionally prepared lists I turned to the only source of information I knew — Maclean-Hunter's national list of sales, advertising and public relations executives. Armed with this, a copy of *Who's Who in Canada* and the Toronto telephone book, I waded in, doing research and listing possibilities in the evening while devoting business hours to making appointments and visiting prospective donors.

By mid-May of 1976 we had contributions and pledges totalling more than sixty thousand dollars. This was gratifying, but after two months of intensive campaigning, the climb appeared to be getting steeper. Almost daily we received letters beginning, "We have great admiration for ... however, we regret ...".

I would have given almost anything for the help and encouragement of a good committee. Instead, Signe was forced to take on the roles of assessor, comforter, cheerleader and fellow strategist. Thanks to her, our long evening sessions among the paintings usually ended on an upbeat note.

One source of encouragement was the growing list of blue-chip donors who had contributed five thousand dollars. In addition to Xerox, the Royal Bank and the Toronto Dominion Bank, we had received cheques from Shell Oil, Philips Electronics, the Canadian Imperial Bank of Commerce, Alcan Aluminum, Canada Packers, International Nickel, Pepsi Cola and Olivetti (Canada) Limited. Smaller but significant amounts came from Union Carbide, Dominion Foundries and Steel, Manufacturers Life Insurance and more modest donations from private individuals who had heard of our quest and contributed without solicitation. These responses, almost all from people we didn't know, were heartwarming and served as a real prod. If these people cared so much, we told ourselves, then surely others would find our cause worthwhile.

Just when our progress seemed to be lagging, I received a telephone call from an Edward Kernaghan, who was an admirer of Tom Thomson and who asked to meet me at the gallery the following Sunday afternoon.

Sunday was, as usual, our busiest day, with an attendance seldom numbered below two thousand and often over three thousand. I met the Kernaghans, a handsome young couple in their early thirties, in the lobby and suggested coffee in the gallery restaurant, which was overflowing with Sunday brunchers.

Ted Kernaghan told us that he was deeply interested in the paintings of the Group and that he had a modest collection, including one panel by Tom Thomson. He shared our opinion that Thomson was the greatest. Then, just as coffee was being served, he came to the reason for their visit.

"My wife and I feel you are doing a great job dedicating this Collection and gallery to the full recognition of these artists and particularly Tom Thomson. We know how hard you're working to acquire the *Waterfall* painting ... we would like to donate five thousand dollars towards its purchase!"

To their great amusement I choked and spilled my coffee. It was just the new direction we needed. If Ted Kernaghan could care that much, there must be more people out there who would respond.

I realized that up until my meeting with the Kernaghans I had forgotten one of the basic rules of salesmanship — believe fully in what you are selling and make your prospects see that you are not seeking a sale but offering an opportunity. I had been little more than a glorified beggar. That day I put my tin cup away forever and became a bearer of glad tidings. I did not hesitate to call on friends or friends of friends. To contribute to the acquisition of a Canadian master work was a privilege and I knew I could make prospective donors anxious to be part of the effort.

It was time to shift gears and broaden our campaign to take in everyone to whom we might have an entrée and who would be in a position to make a substantial contribution. Our list would include friends and friends of friends, people we had met at the gallery and those with no more than a passing interest in art and the Collection, who could, nevertheless, afford to help.

Over the years we had been introduced to hundreds of corporate and social leaders, but it had never occurred to us that we could ask them for help. Now, we realized we should give them an opportunity to share our excitement over the acquisition of *Waterfall*. We began to develop a composite picture of potential benefactors.

At the head of the list we found a family that seemed to fit our "most likely" description almost perfectly. Over the years, on various occasions we had met Mr. and Mrs. Peter Dalglish and Mr. and Mrs. Leslie Rebanks, Mrs. Charles Bernett and Mrs. Robert Mitchell. The four women, Camilla, Wendy, Miriam and Barbara, were daughters of the great Canadian industrialist and financier Garfield Weston, and three of them had spent childhood years living near Kleinburg!

Born in a room over his father's modest bakery on Toronto's Soho Street, Garfield Weston had built a worldwide commercial empire which included, in addition to Weston Bakeries, such familiar names as Loblaws, Neilson, Eddy Pulp and Paper Company and a host of others. His operations extended from Canada and the United States to West Germany, South Africa and Australia. He also had vast holdings in Great Britain, where he now lived. His commercial headquarters was on the top floor of London's famous department store, Fortnum and Mason, which he also owned, and it was said that his companies packed over half of the salmon on Canada's West Coast and baked over half of all commercial bakery products in Great Britain.

During the years that his interests were confined to Canada, Weston built an impressive stone manor on one hundred acres near Kleinburg for his large family.

Though few knew it, Garfield Weston's public service and private charity rivalled his achievements in commerce. I knew, for example, that during the Battle of Britain in 1940 he had learned that sixteen Spitfires had been shot down in one terrible night. At once he called his friend, expatriate Canadian Lord Beaverbrook, Minister of Aircraft Production, with an offer to pay for the replacement of the airplanes. "Unfortunately," he told me later, "I couldn't replace the brave boys who had been the pilots."

Most of Weston's donations in Canada were channelled through the W. Garfield Weston Foundation, which gave most of its support to medical research.

Our closest acquaintance was with Wendy, the sixth of nine Weston children, who had married the architect, Leslie Rebanks. She was a senior member of the Weston Foundation Board, so it was natural to telephone her, explain our proposal briefly, and ask how we might go about presenting our case to her father.

Wendy has one of those rare voices which reflect both thoughtfulness and cheerfulness in a way which has always made me feel my call was welcome. I felt that way now when she said, "I read about the picture and your fund-raising programme in Arnold Edinborough's column in the *Financial Post* and I was considering how we might help." Then, "Father takes a very personal interest in the individual projects in which we participate. As you probably know most of our contributions are for medical research, but we do on occasion help in unusual and worthy causes which catch his interest."

How I hoped our request would "catch his interest"! Wendy would be a very strong influence and I hoped she was as favourably inclined towards the Collection as we had always believed. I asked if she knew of any way we could present our story to her father.

"There just may be, Bob," she replied with the slightest hesitation. "He usually comes to Canada for a week or so to attend annual meetings and discuss Foundation business ... and of course to see the family and his grandchildren. He'll be in Toronto two weeks from now. One of my little nieces is about to undergo serious surgery and he's especially interested in spending some time with her. Now, I can't promise, but it's just possible he might enjoy the thought of a sentimental journey back to Kleinburg. His time during that week is quite fully booked, but it's possible that on the Saturday Camilla and I might be able to take him and some of the grandchildren for a little drive in the country. I don't think he's been back to Kleinburg since we lived there."

God bless you, Wendy, I thought, what could be more perfect? "Perhaps you could join us for lunch at the gallery?"

Wendy thought that would be a fine idea except that the children were very young. Could they have a little party of their own that would be more fun than grown-up food and conversation?

They certainly could. I promised a children's party in our log cabin snack shack with one of our guides as den mother and Wendy promised to confirm in ten days when she'd had a chance to talk to her father.

This news was too good for intercom talk, so I raced upstairs to the apartment where Signe, as a trustee, was dutifully signing a stack of cheques.

It was a long ten days. Then Wendy called to tell us that she and Camilla would drive to Kleinburg the following Saturday. They would bring Mr. and Mrs. Weston and four grandchildren with them.

Saturday dawned a beautiful May day filled with sunshine and the softest of breezes. It seemed to us that even the abundant wild apple trees on the grounds understood the importance of the occasion — they were in full blossom.

Shortly after noon our guests arrived and Signe and I were introduced to Mr. and Mrs. Garfield Weston and the grandchildren. Guide Pattie Rennie was our choice for den mother and within a few minutes she was leading her young charges on an exploration of the gallery and grounds, which would include a picnic at the snack shack. The Westons were fascinated by the tumbling waters of our lobby waterfall which, however, made conversation impossible until, in a loud voice, Signe announced that lunch was ready in the restaurant downstairs.

Mr. Weston said cheerfully that his wife was in charge of his diet and, while she studied the menu carefully, he told us of their flight in the new supersonic Concorde. They had breakfasted in London and arrived in New York in time for breakfast the same day!

Garfield Weston also spoke of his philosophy of business and of some of his interesting philanthropies. He recalled a conversation with Stanley Marks of Marks and Spencer, the worldwide department store chain. Mr. Marks had approached him on behalf of a fund-raising campaign for the State of Israel and was apparently surprised with the prompt response in the form of a donation in the seven-figure range.

"Remember, Stanley," Weston had told him with a smile, "it's my Holy Land as well as yours."

He also talked freely of his wide-ranging interests throughout the world and some of his special interests in his native Canada.

"When we become involved in a situation," he said, "it usually means outright purchase by us, or at very least fifty-one percent. Anything else is of no interest."

It was the maxim he lived by. In early life, he told us, he had realized that if a man immerses himself in a venture to which he contributes the resources, energies and judgement necessary for success without absolute assurance of continuing control, he courts disaster, for he will find that all of his achievements can be doomed by the ambitions or machinations of someone else.

We soon learned that Mr. Weston applied much of his business policy to his philanthropy. He would have no part of a buckshot approach — small amounts to many causes — but preferred substantial support for programmes which he and his foundation members found especially interesting and deserving.

Wendy, mindful of their schedule, suggested it was time to tour the Collection, and we had to break off this fascinating discussion.

As we moved from room to room rich with aboriginal art and the brilliant works of the Group of Seven, Mr. Weston said, "My daughters tell me you are attempting to acquire an important painting."

This was our moment of truth. "Yes," I said, without hesitation, "It's by Tom Thomson, and possibly the last large canvas by him which will ever come on the market. The subject is a waterfall deep in the woods of Algonquin Park. We believe it was painted in 1916 at the height of his career."

"Your mention of Algonquin Park reminds me of a place I have always loved," he said. "I owned a thousand acres next to the park ... magnificent country. I gave it to the Salvation Army to be used as a children's camp."

My hopes soared.

As we approached the master gallery in which one major canvas of each Group member was displayed, we caught the first glimpse of *Woodland Waterfall*. "How much will the picture cost?" he asked.

I mumbled something about others who were willing to contribute five thousand dollars each but that we had a long way to go.

"That isn't what I asked," he said. "How much will the picture cost?"

I have always found it difficult to be casual in talking about very large sums of money and I knew that this was the highest price ever to be negotiated for a Canadian work of art. After a slight hesitation I said nervously, "This masterpiece will cost two hundred and eight-five thousand dollars."

"Hmmmm."

Wendy and Camilla had seated themselves on a pine deacon's bench, which we had placed facing the picture. Mr. Weston and I sat down beside them and for a long minute the painting had his total attention. Then he turned to his daughters and I sensed, more than saw, an almost imperceptible wink as he slowly turned to me and announced, "We will buy the picture for you."

"Do I understand you correctly, sir?" My voice was shaking.

A broad grin and a twinkle. "You understand perfectly," said Mr. Weston. "My foundation will provide the full amount to pay for this beautiful painting. We may wish to spread payment over two or three years, but we will give you a written pledge."

The generous Weston family must have often seen incredulous beneficiaries. They will never see one more rapturous than I was.

Shortly afterwards, the children were retrieved from a romp in the woods and the Westons continued their day's outing. Oblivious to the other visitors and guides Signe and I threw our arms around each other and danced a little jig on the lawn.

Our chairman, Allyn Taylor, was at his home in London, so I had to telephone the good news. At first I think he thought the telephone was playing tricks. Then, always practical, he asked if we had anything in writing. "No," I replied, "but Mr. Weston was very clear, and he is a man of his word. He promised to send me a letter confirming the gift, and I am absolutely sure he will."

Just five days later the letter was placed on my desk:

Dear Bob,
It is with great pleasure I enclose a cheque for $100,000 from my Charitable Foundation to enable the McMichael Canadian Collection to acquire Tom Thomson's 'Waterfall'. Having seen this magnificent painting in your fine collection I am delighted to be able to help you keep this great Canadian picture where all Canadians may come to see and enjoy it.
In 1977 and 1978 my Foundation will send you further gifts of $100,000 and $85,000 to complete its purchase.
The delightful afternoon my wife, daughters and I spent with you and Signe was a memorable occasion, the tour round your collection was a fascinating experience.
With every good wish for your continued success with which I am tremendously impressed,

W. Garfield Weston

One problem was solved but another, albeit a far easier one, had arisen. How should we deal with the generous donors who had already contributed to the purchase of *Woodland Waterfall*?

After months of worry, hard work, and concern over reaching our objective, we were faced with a new experience. We were over-subscribed. Those who had given had done so with the understanding that they were helping to acquire a national treasure. It would be difficult to think of a comparable Canadian painting in private hands that we could acquire, but return of the money and pledges would be heartbreaking and embarrassing for us and, possibly, offensive to the donors. Still, it seemed to me the only honourable course unless an equally attractive and important painting could be found that would be available for purchase. All of this would have to be achieved in a very short time since news of the Weston gift would soon become known.

Through the years we had come to know virtually every Thomson canvas and its owner. With great care not to rule out even the most remote possibility, we reviewed our records and memories.

There was Dr. MacCallum in England. Remembering our discussions with him we concluded he had no interest in selling. The

Power Corporation of Montreal, we knew, had a nice canvas but, like us, they would be more interested in buying another Thomson than in selling the one they had. Mr. McCaulley, a wealthy Winnipeg lawyer, was justifiably proud to own the only Thomson canvas in western Canada. Art dealer Blair Laing was not even willing to discuss selling the one he owned. For smaller canvases the story was the same.

Finally we came to a couple we had come to know because of their ownership of a magnificent Thomson canvas, Richard and Barbara Le Sueur, who lived in the Rosedale section of Toronto. We had first seen the picture some twenty years earlier when it was loaned for the "Collector's Choice" exhibition at the Canadian National Exhibition. Ownership was then attributed to Richard's parents. In the intervening years, though his mother was still alive, the painting had been turned over to Richard.

We had exchanged several dinner invitations with the Le Sueurs and they knew of our interest in the painting but had never shown the slightest inclination to part with it.

Still, we were desperate. It was worth a try.

Sunday morning, after a long night of thinking about the best approach I telephoned the Le Sueurs ... ten rings, no answer. An hour later I tried again. "They're probably at church," Signe said in an encouraging voice. One o'clock came — and two and three o'clock. Pacing the floor, I pictured them on vacation in some far-away place, out of reach of radio or phone.

Time was now critical. I felt very strongly that our donors must be informed of the Weston gift well before the news was released or, heaven forbid, leaked, to the media. The essential corollary to informing donors was to seek their agreement to the purchase of another all-important canvas ... now. I was filled with self-recrimination. Why had I not approached the Le Sueurs before? They were unselfish, public-spirited people. Why had I not given them the opportunity to share their Thomson before we reached this emergency? Perhaps I should go to Douglas Drive and check with their neighbours?

In the midst of my frantic deliberations, Signe answered a telephone call from Jean Dowsett who asked if we might be free for dinner that evening. My mind was on one track, so when the invitation was relayed, I told Signe to tell Jean we would be delighted — providing I could use their telephone. Besides, I knew that the Dowsett's home on St. Leonard's Avenue in Lawrence Park would be only a scant fifteen minutes from the Le Sueurs' house in Rosedale.

When we reached the Dowsetts' they quickly sensed that something exciting was in the wind and I wasted little time bringing them completely up-to-date. They were not only among our dearest friends, but Reg, of course, was vice-chairman of the Collection's board of trustees.

Back to the phone ... still no answer.

One of Jean's satisfying dinners.

Still no answer ... then, on the fifth ring I heard Dick's welcome, "Hello."

"Dick, it's Bob McMichael. I've been trying to reach you most of the day. I hate to bother you on a Sunday, but I would like to talk with you for fifteen minutes about something that is very important. I'm in the city, not far from you in fact, and I'd like to come over to your house."

"Sounds pretty urgent," said Dick. "We've been out to our place in the country and just this minute got home. Give us half an hour to unpack and tidy up. Let's see, it's about eight. Would eight-thirty be alright?"

It certainly would. At eight-thirty, still wearing country clothes, Dick Le Sueur greeted me warmly and offered me my favourite chair facing the Thomson canvas that I had always called *Summer Shore, Georgian Bay*.

"Don't you ever worry about it when you're away from home?" I asked, full of guile.

"Yes, we do," a slight wrinkle creased Dick's forehead. "With so many stories about art thefts, we become more concerned all the time ... insurance costs seem to be skyrocketing and from what we hear of auctions, so do the prices of Canadian paintings."

Nothing ventured, I thought. Plunging right in I thanked him for seeing me on such short notice then outlined our campaign to date and pointed out that we had raised sixty-one thousand dollars before Mr. Weston's offer. I could see that Dick Le Sueur's thoughts were already running ahead of my story. The reason for my visit would be no surprise.

"I think you know, Bob, that we are sympathetic to the wonderful thing you and Signe are doing in Kleinburg, but this comes very suddenly and we would need to give it considerable thought. How much would you expect to pay for our painting?"

We had given a lot of thought to the answer to this inevitable question. To our knowledge, no Thomson canvas had been sold in almost ten years and at that time prices had ranged between fifty and one hundred thousand dollars. *Summer Shore* was only about half the size of *Woodland Waterfall*, but it had a brilliant colour quality and the appeal of its lofty pines, bent by a century of prevailing winds, could not be denied. In fact, its attraction was so great that I had hardly dared to look at it during our discussion.

With a deep breath I told him we would be prepared to pay one hundred and fifty thousand dollars.

There was no change of expression on Dick's face. "I'd like to discuss this with Barbara ... and I feel I should talk with mother. When do you need to know?"

I felt like saying "yesterday", but in spite of the pressure I was determined not to sound desperate. "Just as soon as possible, Dick, and I would hope within two days."

"Leave it with me, Bob," he said very quietly. "I'll be back to you, one way or the other."

After the events of the weekend, it was difficult to maintain silence, but I confided the story only to my secretary, asking her to be alert for a call from Mr. Le Sueur and also from prospective or confirmed donors. Jeanne Pattison, our public relations manager, had also been fully informed and was discreetly preparing press releases and photographs dealing with the Weston gift. It had been agreed that the announcement would be made on Thursday, so Wendy Rebanks could review the release for the Weston family. I prayed there would be time to hear from Dick Le Sueur and then to discuss our new proposal with committed donors before the Weston news was released.

The call from Dick came on Tuesday.

While I held my breath he told me that he had talked it over with his family and was willing to sell the Thomson painting to us at the agreed price. Years of hope and months of worry and tension melted away and I experienced a few moments of glorious fulfillment. Not one but two great Tom Thomson canvases would join our other fine works by Canada's most extraordinary artist to become high points of the Collection.

The next thirty-six hours were bedlam. Bursting with confidence, I began the phone calls which I hoped would allow us to shift money pledged for the purchase of *Woodland Waterfall* to the purchase of *Summer Shore*. My first call was to a donor whom I felt was totally committed to our cause. I outlined briefly the momentous events of the past few days and related in glowing terms the importance of *Summer Shore, Georgian Bay* and how fortunate we felt to be able to capture the very last major Thomson canvas which would ever be available for purchase.

As I hoped, when my calls were completed the corporations and individuals had given us a unanimous vote of confidence by consenting to the use of their donations toward the purchase of *Summer Shore*.

Allyn Taylor set up a meeting with the Honourable Robert Welch. Bob Welch was the first minister of the newly created Ministry of Culture and Recreation which, in addition to overseeing the province's cultural facilities, was also responsible for the new provincial lottery, Wintario. Its profits had been earmarked for matching grants to cultural and recreational projects. One-shot undertakings such as replacing a roof on a town arena, with the town putting up half the money, were its primary focus. It occurred to me that the rules might include, or be stretched to include, a matching grant for the purchase of a great Canadian painting. Why not?

Smiling broadly, Allyn Taylor and I seated ourselves in Welch's Queen's Park office and Allyn opened our discussion by saying, "Mr. Minister, I believe we have here the Bobby Orr of salesmen. And he sure has scored!" With that he turned to me and said, "Bob, I want you to tell the minister what you've done."

"Well, Mr. Welch," I said, "it isn't really what I have done, but what Mr. Garfield Weston has done. I'm sure you are aware of our campaign to raise funds for the purchase of a great Tom Thomson painting. Well, a few days ago, Mr. Weston and some of his family visited us at the Collection in Kleinburg. He saw Thomson's *Woodland Waterfall* and was very impressed. He has agreed to buy the painting for our gallery."

Bob Welch is seldom at a loss for words, but that left him literally open-mouthed.

With a grin, Allyn said, "Now you see what I meant. Bob and Signe ... and their Collection impressed Mr. Weston so much that he is actually buying the painting ... paying the full cost ... for the Collection."

The full impact was sinking in. "This has to be one of the most important ... May I inform the Premier?"

"Certainly," I replied. This was the moment to strike the Wintario iron. "But first, I'd like to make one request." I explained about the substantial cash donations which we had received and our good fortune in finding another important Thomson.

"We have raised over sixty thousand, and can certainly bring that up to seventy-five, which is half the price of *Summer Shore, Georgian Bay* by the great Tom Thomson. We need a matching grant from Wintario!"

The minister paused and rolled his eyes back in thought. "Come on, Bob," I challenged him, "make our day complete." He did.

Jeanne Pattison had arranged her public relations work well. Newspapers and the Canadian Press wire service received releases and photographs hand-delivered within minutes of each other. Television crews filmed and taped at the gallery in ample time to catch the dinner-hour national news broadcasts almost simultaneously.

By early evening, most Canadians had learned of Garfield Weston's spectacular gift of a national treasure to the McMichael Canadian Collection and, by extension, the country.

The story's impact was doubled by the simultaneous acquisition of *Summer Shore, Georgian Bay*. Television, press and radio commentators, pointing out the rarity of Thomson canvases, excitedly announced that Canadians could now enjoy two which had rarely been on public exhibition. From the media's viewpoint, the biggest news was the fact that the purchase price of *Woodland Waterfall* had established a new record for the amount paid for a Canadian work of art and that the combined purchase totalled a whopping four hundred and thirty-five thousand dollars.

The record was duly noted and the story along with an illustration of the painting appeared in the next edition of the Guinness Book of Records.

Someone asked, "Robert, how can you top this?"

It was a good question.

In the autumn of 1974, a few months after Alex's death, Signe and I made our second visit to London. On our first visit, six years earlier, we had been wide-eyed tourists; this time we arrived with a mission, carrying an informal introduction from a distantly related namesake, Montrealer Colin McMichael of the Bell Telephone Company, to Clifford Gerrard, Cultural Attaché at the Canadian High Commission.

Colin had worked with Gerrard on an exhibition to honour Alexander Graham Bell which was mounted at the newly established exhibition gallery in Canada House and had been delighted when, in the course of other discussions, Gerrard had expressed a desire to present an exhibition of works by the Group of Seven. Thinking immediately of the McMichael Canadian Collection, Colin suggested that he arrange to bring us together.

Later, when he telephoned me from Montreal, Colin asked if we would be prepared to mount a Group exhibition in London, made up of works from the Collection. Without hesitation I replied that we'd love to, and the groundwork was laid for a meeting in London.

Following a few hours sleep after our arrival on a Sunday morning, Signe and I, now feeling like seasoned travellers, set out to see London again. We were approaching Trafalgar Square, our eyes straining for the first glimpse of Nelson's famous column, when we swerved to avoid a poster kiosk and saw its astonishing message: "A. Y. Jackson, A Memorial Exhibition".

We knew nothing about it, but the Imperial War Museum was featuring a special showing of the paintings Alex had produced when he was an official Canadian army artist during World War I. Suddenly he seemed very close, and we felt how proud he would have been that this work — hardly noticed when it was produced — was finally receiving its due at the "seat of Empire".

Our casual sightseeing was casual no longer. Pausing only for directions, we took the first double-decker to Kensington and the Imperial War Museum. Even the gigantic turret with three fifteen-inch naval guns which guards the museum's entrance could not delay us as we rushed headlong for the exhibition. Although we had seen some of Alex's war paintings before, their power and brilliance in this major exhibition surprised us. What a contrast to the often stark, but tranquil, northern landscapes we knew so well!

Monday, we got back to business and our meeting with Clifford Gerrard. To my delight, there was no beating about the bush. He made it clear that he was determined to have an exhibition of the Group of Seven at the new Canada House Gallery. He also wanted the exhibition to tour major cities in Scotland. Together we pored over the Collection's catalogue and then I made notes of available wall space, mentally mapping out the number of panels and canvases needed to mount a well-balanced exhibition.

Gerrard was a man who got things done. By the time we had confirmed our return flight to Toronto, he had embarked on the mountain of paperwork — detailed budget estimates, including costs of transportation for both paintings and people, insurance, catalogues and other details — which would have to be completed before he could submit a proposal to Ottawa. He promised to keep in touch.

Nevertheless, it was more than a year later, in the last days of 1975, that I received a telephone call from Ottawa. Freeman Tovell, Cultural Affairs officer of the Department of External Affairs, would be in Toronto the following week to discuss the proposed British tour with me and with officials of the Ontario

Ministry of Culture and Recreation to whom we reported. Since I had received approval from the Collection's board of trustees, I was now free to begin working on the actual selection of works.

Freeman Tovell, whose brothers Vincent and Walter also occupied high places in the realm of Canadian culture, was a genial, sophisticated diplomat of the arts, knowledgeable about Canadian painting and especially so about the Group. At Kleinburg, reviewing hundreds of works, large and small, by Thomson and the Group, we had several lively but amiable sparring matches before we finally made the first cut in our selection.

Then, quite casually, Freeman dropped a bombshell. External Affairs had decided the exhibition should tour not only Great Britain but also the Union of Soviet Socialist Republics, with whom Canada had recently signed a cultural exchange treaty. Ottawa wanted to have Signe and me or a staff assistant travel to each city to assist with the hanging and introduction of our national art.

I had been excited by the thought that we would be exhibiting the Group's paintings in the shadows of Big Ben and Edinborough Castle. Now we were to have a glimpse behind the Iron Curtain, perhaps even a showing at the fabled Hermitage in Leningrad. We were excited for ourselves but almost more excited by the opportunity to see how the people of other nations would react to our national art.

That spring of 1976 was an exciting chapter in the Collection's history. Not the least of the excitements was the acquisition of the large Tom Thomson canvas, *Woodland Waterfall* and his splendid *Summer Shore, Georgian Bay*. Still, there was little time to rest and savour these accomplishments. The pace of our lives increased and we began to grapple with the responsibilities we had agreed to undertake for the international tour.

It would be launched during August in Glasgow. When we agreed to the date it did not seem too pressing. But we were neophytes. We somehow did not come to grips with the fact that many of our deadlines would come weeks, and even months, before the actual departure.

For one thing, we had undertaken to write texts and provide photographs and colour transparencies for the catalogues, which would be designed and printed in Great Britain and the U.S.S.R. for sale during the exhibitions. At first this appeared to be just one more assignment which Jeanne Pattison and I could work in quite easily between her regular public relations duties and my own responsibilities. That assumption went by the board when we discovered the lead time which was required for our copy to be reviewed in Ottawa and the changes that would have to be made before it could be sent overseas by diplomatic pouch. Nor had we realized how long it would take for each country to design, print and bind catalogues in totally different formats and languages. They expected finished copy about the time we had expected to start work.

It had also been decided that we should design and write a smaller, bilingual brochure catalogue for distribution without charge at the exhibitions in Scotland and England. Four-colour posters, which would be imprinted with the names of the galleries and cities and exhibition dates were also designed at Kleinburg for advance shipping from Ottawa. The decision to leave space for imprinting was wiser than we knew. By the time the tour was over posters had been produced in German and Norwegian as well as in English and Russian.

We had also assumed responsibility for designing and constructing cases for the paintings, which would have to withstand travelling and handling by airplane, ship, train, truck, forklift and dolly during their journey halfway around the world. These unusual containers were produced in our own workshops with some guidance from the National Gallery of Canada. Provisions against rough handling, excessive moisture and heat, and a system that would ensure consistent methods of unpacking and repacking were also incorporated into our planning. Since our treasures would be shipped and reshipped by people speaking many different languages, their exteriors were festooned with symbols similar to international road signs which warned handlers against exposing them to rain and snow, excessive heat and dropping, and also told them in graphic terms which end was up.

The rugged boxes, painted a brilliant yellow and overprinted with large, black stencilled letters and symbols were to become familiar old friends we were to meet again and again in gallery preparation rooms from Dublin to Kiev. They became a special source of interest to the staff of every gallery we visited. Several preparators were so impressed with their floating picture trays, each with photographic identification of its painting, that they photographed them inside and out so they could be copied for their own shipments.

As the date for the first exhibition in Glasgow drew nearer, Signe and I reached a pitch of excitement that was increased by an invitation from Prime Minister Pierre Trudeau to join cabinet members and their spouses at a small dinner for Her Majesty Queen Elizabeth II and Prince Philip, who were going to be in Montreal to open the 1976 Olympic Games. Opposition leader John Diefenbaker, Mayor Jean Drapeau and Quebec Premier Robert Bourassa would also be dinner guests at the historic old Beaver Club. Princess Anne, a member of the British equestrian team, would be joined by her brothers, Prince Charles, Prince Andrew and Prince Edward. After dinner the Queen would speak to the worldwide audience for the Olympics on television.

The media later reported that the dinner was of historical significance since it was the first time the entire Royal Family had dined together outside of the British Isles. It was widely agreed that it was a very fitting prelude to the Olympic Games. Privately, Signe and I felt it was a fitting send-off for our first international exhibition tour.

The travel arrangements for an international art exhibition are both expensive and complicated. Insurance coverage reached the millions. As a first step, arrangements had been made for Air Canada to transport the six large crates of paintings across the Atlantic on one of its largest cargo planes which would land at Prestwick, Scotland. For this service Air Canada's name appeared on all catalogues and posters associated with the tour. A few hours after the departure of the stars, Signe and I and the Collection's public relations manager Jeanne Pattison boarded a 727 for an overnight flight to Glasgow.

We allowed ourselves a few hours of sleep to overcome jet lag and then went to work to set up shop in our suite at the ornate old Station Hotel. Our first priority was publicity. We knew from our meetings with Alex Brodie, Canada's trade counsellor in Scotland, and Griselda Bear from the High Commission in London, that posters had been distributed and arrangements made for the formal official opening. But that was about it. We did not delude ourselves that Glasgow would beat a path to our door. We needed to let Glasgow know there was a door to which a path should be beaten.

Civil servants tend to be conservative, even cautious, in their approach to publicity, which they prefer to call "media liaison". Though we were employees of a government agency, we had learned much from our years in private enterprise and we knew that enthusiasm is not generated by procedure manuals and media liaison.

Our methods required a lot more effort and imagination than routine press handouts, but they had produced results. Moreover, they had already proved themselves in the years when we were struggling to promote the growth of the Collection and stir public interest in our dream, and we had learned to mount our promotion campaigns at lower costs. We never doubted that we were right, but we never expected to win any bureaucratic popularity contests either.

Our campaign in Scotland was typical. Jeanne Pattison listed the Scottish TV channels and radio stations, studying their programming and looking particularly for talk shows or those dealing with art and coming events. I picked up copies of Glasgow's newspapers, scanning them to get a feel for the audiences they catered to, their writing and photo styles.

In large British cities, newspapers are less alike than their counterparts in multi-paper cities in Canada and the United States. The contrasts are perhaps not as great in Glasgow as in London, for example, where *The Times* is the epitome of conservative dignity, sometimes dull, but read as a "bible" by its upper and upper-middle class subscribers. The much larger *News of the World*, brassy, sexy and sensational, appeals to millions who delight in its tantalizing headlines, stories and photos. Seeking publicity but failing to tailor our efforts to these differences would have doomed us to disappointment.

On that August day, the Glasgow papers announced that the Prime Minister of Great Britain, James Callaghan and Mrs. Callaghan would visit the city the following week to attend a meeting of the Labour Party's Scottish wing before they departed for a tour of Canada. When I read this exciting news to Jeanne and Signe they knew exactly what was in my mind.

"You wouldn't dare," they gasped almost in unison.

"It's a natural," I told them with the shameless bravado of a Hollywood press agent. "The Prime Minister is coming to Glasgow just in time for our opening and just before his tour of Canada. It's perfect!"

"I suppose," said Jean sarcastically, "we just pick up the phone and say, 'Prime Minister, we have a really good art show here in Glasgow. We'd like you and your wife to come and see it.' "

"Perhaps not quite so bluntly," I agreed, "but I feel there is something almost preordained about all of this. I think it would be good politics for the Callaghans and I also think they would enjoy this sort of visual briefing before their trip, to say nothing of what it could do for our show."

I had convinced them. A few minutes later, I had even managed to convince myself.

On the telephone I had surprisingly little difficulty getting the Prime Minister's number from the operator. Bravely, I dialed 10

Downing Street.

"Residence of the Prime Minister."

"May I speak to the Prime Minister's executive assistant?"

"Which one, please?"

"Hmmm ... It's in connection with his visit to Glasgow."

A pleasant, unhurried male voice came on the line. I explained briefly, with all the persuasiveness I could muster, that the first British exhibition of Canada's most famous landscape painters would open in Glasgow the following week at the time of the Callaghans' visit. Since they were scheduled to begin a tour of Canada, it would be particularly fitting for them to view the exhibition, so they could familiarize themselves with the country and its best-known artists. We would be honoured if they could visit the showing at Kelvin Grove Art Gallery.

After a slight pause, he asked, "What is your name again, and whom do you represent?"

I told him, with all the assurance I could muster, that I was the director and founder of the public collection which bore my family name. I explained that I was travelling with the exhibition on behalf of the Department of External Affairs and the Canadian High Commission in London. I did not tell him that I knew full well that this direct approach went well beyond the bounds of protocol.

Sounding genuinely interested, the executive assistant asked where I could be reached by telephone and promised to get back to me later that day.

Signe undertook the boring task of waiting for the phone to ring while Jeanne and I, briefcases filled with press releases and photographs, made the rounds of Glasgow's public media. Hours later, foot-weary but happy with the initial responses, we returned to the hotel where Signe was still at her post. Moments later, as if on cue, the call came from London.

The pleasant male voice assured me that the Prime Minister had been pleased by our invitation but that his Glasgow schedule was completely filled. Mrs. Callaghan, however, had some free time and would like very much to visit the Canadian exhibition. We discussed the date and time, then I thanked and silently blessed him as I put down the phone.

Five days later, on a sunny afternoon following the formal opening the previous evening, Kelvin Grove's director and three triumphant Canadians met a black Rolls Royce limousine and greeted the Prime Minister's wife and her personal secretary. Relaxed and unassuming, Mrs. Callaghan seemed happy to mingle with the gallery's trustees, who were as excited as we were by her visit.

We could see that Mrs. Callaghan was enjoying her tour of our pictures, but we were a little surprised when she asked, "Are your trees in Canada as brilliantly coloured as they appear in these pictures?"

We had forgotten how much we take our autumn glory for granted. Our blazing colours are never seen in the British Isles.

I explained that in some regions of our country, such as British Columbia, the climate was similar to Britain's and the dramatic colour change did not occur. However, since she and her husband would visit areas of Quebec and Ontario near our capital, Ottawa, in September, they would almost certainly see the crimson maples, the golden birches and aspens, and the brilliant sumacs just as they appeared in the paintings.

Photos of the popular Mrs. Callaghan viewing some of the larger Group paintings appeared in the British press and additional glossy photographs were rushed by overnight air express to Canadian Press. When we got home a few days later, the first thing I saw on my desk was a photo clipping from the *Ottawa Journal* showing the British Prime Minister's wife enjoying Canadian art in Glasgow. It had come from Anne Garneau of External Affairs with a one-word memo, "Bravo!"

I met with Anne, the tour co-ordinator, and her boss, Freeman Tovell, in Ottawa the following week to review the first exhibition and discuss the others which would follow. There was also a meeting at Rideau Hall with Esmond Butler, principal secretary to the Governor General. (Earlier he had arranged for Governor General Jules Léger to dedicate our new Woodland Indian gallery at the Collection in Kleinburg.) Unexpectedly, but to my delight, Butler invited me to join a luncheon that day for Prime Minister James Callaghan and his wife.

It had been only ten days since our meeting in Scotland. As I approached the honoured guests in the receiving line, my name was announced by an attendant. Mrs. Callaghan immediately remembered me, greeted me warmly, and introduced me to her husband. "Jim, this is Mr. McMichael, who told me about the beautiful coloured leaves we have been seeing in Canada."

"Ah, yes. Good to meet you," Prime Minister Callaghan said. "We have been enjoying the book of your Collection which you were kind enough to give to my wife."

As our Kleinburg woods were producing their annual autumn tribute to the Group of Seven — a case of life imitating art — I left, this time alone, for our second overseas exhibition at the Talbot-Rice Gallery of the University of Edinburgh.

While Glasgow is much larger, and serves as the country's centre of industry and finance, Edinburgh, at the heart of Scotland's history and culture, is the site of the National Gallery, the National Library, the Royal Scottish Academy, Parliament House, the Law Courts and, of course, the ever-present Castle.

Edinburgh is also the home of Scotland's most famous retail stores, such as Jenner's, purveyors of tartans and traditional Scottish dress to the Queen. Two centuries earlier my ancestors had come from Ayrshire to the New World. I had no trouble convincing myself that so close a connection should be honoured — I would commission Jenner's to produce a pair of slacks in my family's Stuart tartan without delay. Purveyors to R. McMichael? It had a good solid sound.

After some discussion with the store's staff, expert on such matters, I was informed that my simple desire for a sartorial link to my ancestors was not going to be simple at all. After reference to sanctioned books which listed the McMichaels along with several other clans properly entitled to wear the Stuart tartan, a highly knowledgeable draper excitedly explained that I was one of a select group — fortunates, qualified to wear not one, but four, distinctive tartans: the Royal Stuart, the Dress Stuart, the Black Stuart and the Hunting Stuart. It would indeed be a shame, he stated authoritatively, if a person of my lineage and standing could not have suitable clothing in all four.

As he began unrolling bolts of the finest Scottish woollens, appropriate for suits, jackets and "trews", I feebly suggested that "trews", perhaps two pair, would suffice. I might not have spoken. Instead, he began draping a length of Dress Stuart wool over my shoulder while easing me gently toward a full-length mirror. I had to admit it looked and felt great. At that moment, as if by magic, an assistant arrived carrying a beautifully tailored Dress Stuart jacket in my exact size. Standing tall before the mirror I was transformed into a laird, ready for a stroll on the moors or for a ball at the castle.

Of course, said my mentor, it requires these matching trousers, and he held aloft the perfect bottle-green slacks.

"Of course," I agreed. Lairds do not quibble, although I was mentally counting my American Express cheques.

"Now, about the Black Stuart. It makes beautifully into trousers," he continued without pause, holding a piece of the darker tartan against my leg. "There will be many times when you'll want to wear these with a wool sweater."

"Of course." They would be perfect for a walk with the dogs or just lounging around.

After taking some measurements he brought out the Hunting Stuart for an alternate pair of slacks. In my state of weakened resistance I meekly accepted that these, too, were essential. We were now building up to the finale. Producing the Royal Stuart he exclaimed, "The Royal would be perfect to complete your wardrobe with — the kilt!"

The laird found himself abruptly transported to the streets of Kleinburg. I drew the line. I would settle for a tie.

A week later, after overseeing the hanging at Talbot-Rice, attending the opening and talking with *The Scotsman*, Edinburgh's leading daily, I boarded a train for Aberdeen and an advance visit to the Aberdeen Art Gallery and the city's daily newspaper.

A brief flight to London made it possible for me to catch up on proposals for extending the tour and the day-to-day planning for a climactic opening the following January in the great city itself.

Some months earlier I had talked about the Canadian Landscape Painters tour with my friend Ken Thomson (properly known in England as Lord Thomson, a title inherited from his late father Roy, along with control of the vast Thomson newspaper chain). I had asked him who I might see in the editorial offices of *The Times*, their proudest acquisition, in the hope that the Canadian exhibition might get some attention in the difficult to crack London media. Ken told me that he and the Toronto head office of Thomson bent over backwards not to influence editorial policy but that he would send a letter of introduction to one of the *Times* people. He stressed however, that any decisions on a story and its contents would be made, not by him, but by the editors of *The Times*. I had better, he warned me, wear my best salesman's suit on my next visit to London.

The Times is located on Grey's Inn Road in an older, industrial area of London which was mercilessly bombed by the Luftwaffe. It had been largely rebuilt, but although the local people say they no longer smell it, thirty-five years after the blitz I could still detect the musty odour of incineration.

At the reception desk I was referred to Harold Evans, an editor of *The Sunday Times*, the rotagravure supplement, a respected staple of British weekend reading. Flipping quickly through the copy of the Collection's master catalogue which I had given him,

Evans said he was impressed with the freshness of colour and the painters' freedom of technique, quite different from what he had expected from a backwoods country in the early part of the century. Looking more closely at full-page colour reproductions, he asked, "Has the colour in the book been heightened from that of the original paintings?"

"No," I assured him. "In some pictures it may even be slightly diminished. The colour of Canada, particularly in autumn, is brilliant. That's the story of Tom Thomson and the Group of Seven. Earlier painters in Canada, influenced by European traditions, muted their colours and were often overly concerned with detail. This little group took off the smoked glasses, and painted the country in rich, pure colour, often directly from the tube. They were determined to paint it as they saw it. Sixty years later, that's the way most Canadians see their country. Granted, sixty years is not a long time in British or European art history, but Canada is a relatively young country. These painters are now our old masters." And here endeth the sermon, I reminded myself.

"When does the London showing open?" Evans asked.

"Early January, next year. At present the pictures are in Edinburgh and then we'll move on to Aberdeen ..."

"Oh! They're already in Britain. Glad you mentioned that. I'd like to see them for myself and perhaps take one of our photographers along. As a matter of fact, we have some work to do on another story in Aberdeen ... the North Sea oil is starting to pour through there, you know, and it's a hot topic ... in Britain and elsewhere."

Visions of a colour feature story in Britain's foremost weekend paper appeared before my eyes and I assured him I would make arrangements with the Aberdeen Art Gallery which would allow him and his photographer a free hand to study and photograph the works in private.

The roof of my London cab was no higher than my spirits as I headed back to Canada House to tell Christian Hardy, Deputy High Commissioner, and Griselda Bear, Information Officer, of my coup. They greeted my news with some caution, but soon we were all caught up with the promise of national publicity highlighting the Canadian Landscape Painters exhibition at their new gallery in Trafalgar Square.

They had equally exciting news for me.

John Halstead, Canada's ambassador to West Germany, had been in touch with Ottawa and London, requesting the Group of Seven show for three German cities, before or after the planned exhibitions in three major locations in the U.S.S.R.. Enquiries had been received also from Canadian embassies in Ireland and Norway.

It had been decided to produce, in England, a special glossy catalogue with some colour for the much anticipated London exhibition. Working with Mrs. Bear and her staff, I helped to bring together and condense material about the painters which would help them to produce an impressive booklet in the short period of time now left. The Canadian Embassy in West Germany was planning to produce a catalogue in German for the Canadian Landscape Painters exhibitions and I was asked to forward a suggested text along with reproduction photographs in colour and black and white to them in Bonn, via the diplomatic pouch out of Ottawa.

With so much to be done I flew home to Kleinburg a few days later to be told by Signe that I had an appointment the following day with a Mr. McLaughlin, curator of the Phillips Collection, whose gallery in Washington, D.C. was among the most highly regarded in the United States.

Over coffee with James McLaughlin the next morning I learned that Washington intended to celebrate a "Canada Week" the following February during which Prime Minister Trudeau would address a Joint Session of Congress. Among the other events, the Phillips Collection wished to present a major exhibition of the Group of Seven from the McMichael Canadian Collection. Were we willing to join with them in planning and presenting the exhibition? Paintings by individual Group members had been shown in earlier American shows, but this would be the first Group of Seven exhibition in the United States. The time was right. The location was right. Best of all, the Americans were prepared to produce, with our help, an impressive thirty-six page catalogue with all reproductions in full colour.

Thinking of my upcoming trip to Aberdeen, the London opening in early January and shows in Germany, probably in March, not to mention my responsibilities as director of the Collection, I felt I was probably developing the first of a bumper crop of ulcers. I wondered, too, whether the Collection could remove enough first-rate Group paintings to mount two important international shows during the same two-month period without seriously denuding its own walls at Kleinburg.

Of course, we could not refuse. To have our Collection proudly showing the flag in the capital cities of two great western nations simultaneously was much too heady a prospect to miss. I just hoped our feast of international honours would not bring on a mammoth attack of indigestion.

The major Canadian newspapers were now carrying large feature articles about the Canadian Landscape Painters tour of Great Britain, Russia and Germany. In the near future they would report that, following its success in these countries, exhibitions in Norway and Ireland were to be added to the itinerary and that a parallel show of the same size would be mounted in Washington.

In Kleinburg during the few weeks between each opening I tackled the accumulation of mail and administrative chores which always piled up during my increasingly frequent overseas trips. Since my name was directly associated with the Collection and I had agreed at the outset, when the schedule was a good deal less demanding, to help with gallery hangings and to attend the openings personally, it was difficult to send a substitute. Though Signe could have carried the name, neither of us felt that she should be forced to tackle an international hanging and opening alone. I was enjoying the challenge of visiting and presenting Canadian art in historic cities, but many times I wished that the timetable could have been spread over a much longer period. As it was, I found I had to be away almost two weeks out of every month.

Aberdeen, Britain's most northerly major city, established as a commercial centre and principal port in the twelfth century during the reign of William the Lion, had now become the nation's oil capital. Like most of the city's ancient and enduring buildings, the Central Hotel was constructed of solid granite blocks. Here, where Middle Eastern sheiks mingled with Texans and British oilmen, I had arranged to meet Christian Hardy, up from the Canadian High Commission in London to officiate at the third Scottish opening.

He and I were invited to high tea the following day at the Town House, official residence of Aberdeen's Lord Provost. We walked the few blocks at a leisurely pace through a November sprinkling of snow, not wishing to arrive prematurely for a three o'clock invitation.

Lord Provost Lennox and his wife served tea before the warm hearth of the handsome House and time passed quickly as we talked about the exhibition. I was pleased to be able to point out that in this very area, Aberdeenshire, a Thomas "Tam" Thomson was born in 1806, that he had emigrated to Canada in the 1830s, and that his grandson and namesake, born in 1877, had become Canada's most famous artist.

Leaving the warm surroundings in an increasingly heavy snowfall, Hardy and I were perplexed to find ourselves in total darkness.

"I can't believe we were that long," I said with some embarrassment, thinking we had certainly overstayed our welcome. We checked our watches. Both showed four o'clock. We had forgotten we were at nearly the same latitude as Churchill, Manitoba. As the song says, "the days (on the 57th Parallel) grow short when you reach November!"

Planning our travel for the London exhibition in the last days of 1976, Signe and I decided that it might minimize the long trans-Atlantic flight if we made it on a night we would, in any case, be up later than usual ... New Year's Eve. As a result we toasted 1977 four times.

Our expectations of publicity had actually materialized. An impressive spread of five pages in full colour had appeared in the *Sunday Times Magazine* of December 12, 1976 under the bold headline "Northern Lights". The accompanying review by the emminent British art critic, Marina Vaizey, urged Britons to see the work of the artists whose paintings had been a huge success in England at the Wembley exhibition fifty years earlier.

The show opened January 11, 1977 at Canada House, with a glittering social event hosted by the High Commissioner, the Honourable Paul Martin. Thousands of Britons, including former Prime Minister Harold Wilson, viewed the paintings in the six weeks that followed.

In London, newspaper art critics were enthusiastic. Writers in *The Times* and the *Daily Telegraph* described the Group's work as an important and bold expression of a developing national identity.

Paddy Kitchen of *The Times* wrote,

> *Their shared stylistic influence was a kind of optimistic impressionism.*
>
> *The excited brush strokes and vivid paint do not dramatize nature in order to express man's dark passions; rather they are used as a means of describing a landscape which is already so dramatic, and so blatantly techni-coloured under the northern light, that only a joyously fervid response could possibly convey its impact.*

Kitchen went on to speculate what prospective emigrants to Canada would make of the showing.

> *Do the thick glazes of paint that represent the vitality of rushing water, the gleam-and-slide of sun on snow, the autumns*

that seem to be pink, green, ochre, red, orange, but never somnolent gold, still seem like a breath of fresh cultural air?

If so, then perhaps they are sensing an essence, and invigoration, that the Seven wished to convey.

Terrence Mullaly of the *Telegraph* said the Group:

played an extremely important role in the history of Canadian art. Its influence extended beyond art, and this largely accounts for its hold upon the Canadian imagination.

Above all, the Group served to focus attention upon the beauties of the Canadian landscape, played a key role in fostering a sense of Canadian identity and it is around an emergence of such a sense of national identity that the whole history of Canada needs to be seen.

Newspapers in every part of Canada blossomed with such headings as "British Critics Praise Canada's Group of Seven", and "Canadian Paintings Spark Interest". One widely syndicated column, "Across the Atlantic" by Michael Cope, was headlined, "Group of Seven Restore Faith in Canadian Art". Another was "U.K. Art Reviewers Laud Group of Seven Exhibit".

In Kleinburg, Jeanne Pattison and the staff had been working overtime in preparation for the Washington show, which was to open January 22, barely a week after our return from London. A handsome catalogue in full colour was in production and final plans were being made for moving forty-four irreplaceable paintings, including such monumental works as Jackson's *First Snow, Algoma*, to the American capital. It had been decided that the security van carrying the works (insured for about two million dollars) would be escorted by an automobile carrying two of our staff who would be equipped to meet any unforeseen problems. Stopping only for gas and coffee, the little convoy would make its way from Kleinburg to Washington and the van would not be left unattended for even a moment.

Our small group, including Jack and Jennie Wildridge, Dick and Mary Mastin (daughter of Group of Seven artist Frank Carmichael) and the last living Group member Alfred Casson and his wife Margaret, flew to Washington for this first comprehensive exhibition of the Group of Seven to be seen in the United States. There we were joined by Marjorie Lismer Bridges, Arthur Lismer's daughter, who lived in nearby Ashton, Maryland.

After years of international obscurity, the Group's paintings were now, in the space of a single six-month period, arriving as honoured guests with suitable fanfare in three of the world's great capitals — London, Moscow and Washington.

And fanfare there was.

The *Washington Post* featured a front page review of the exhibition by Paul Richard highlighted with maple leaves printed in red. Under the bold heading "Canadian Colours" it read in part:

> *It is a lovely exhibition of paintings virtually unknown here. One can almost feel the crispness of the air and the shifting of the seasons in these freely brushed and brightly coloured paeans to the beauties of the wilderness of Canada.*

This was followed a few days later by a glowing review in the *Washington Star* by art critic Benjamin Forgey, under the headline, "Canadian Art in the Mainstream".

Exhibitions were scheduled for March and April in Munich and Bonn, after which the paintings would be moved to the U.S.S.R. for several months, returning for a third German exhibition in Hamburg in late autumn. The co-ordinator of the tour, Anne Garneau of External Affairs, accompanied me to the ancient walled city of Munich, where the exhibition would be housed in the ornate Residenz Museum, the home of earlier Bavarian monarchs. Canadian ambassador to Germany John Halstead and cultural attaché Fernand Tonguay had arranged a series of events for a "Canada Week" in the picturesque old city. They had also produced a well-illustrated catalogue of the exhibition, *Kanadische Landschaftz-Maler*, the first publication in German to deal with the Group of Seven.

Hildegard Hamm-Brücher, West German Minister of Cultural Relations, opened the exhibition and described "the McMichael Canadian Collection, near Toronto, as a gallery which must be unique in the world". She had visited it during a tour of Canada in 1975 and said she wished she could bring to the exhibit (in Germany) "a sense of the harmony of nature and art that I found in Kleinburg".

Reporting the opening in Munich, the *Ottawa Journal*'s visual arts critic, Pearl Oxorn, headed her four-column review, "Canada Puts Best Foot Forward in Germany".

The Hamburg opening that fall gave us one of the most exciting moments of the entire tour. Months earlier, Jean Halstead, wife of the ambassador, had asked Frau Schmidt, wife of West German Chancellor Helmut Schmidt, to open the exhibition officially in

Hamburg, the Schmidts' home town. Mrs. Schmidt had happily agreed. As opening night approached, Germany was virtually under seige by the Bäder-Meinhof Gang, which had recently kidnapped Hanns-Martin Schleyer of the West German Employers' Association, and a friend of the Chancellor's. Airports, communications centres and most government buildings were being patrolled by tanks and army patrols with automatic weapons at the ready. Attempting to negotiate with the ruthless gang, the Chancellor had seldom left his office in Bonn during the past several weeks, tirelessly monitoring efforts to save the industrialist's life. However, concerned for his health, his aides had insisted that he go home to Hamburg for the weekend.

On opening evening, as limousines dropped their passengers at the gallery, the rumble of an approaching military convoy could be heard. Led and flanked on all sides by armoured gun carriers laden with troops carrying machine guns, a long, sleek bullet-proof Mercedes pulled up to the main entrance and Chancellor Helmut Schmidt and his popular and attractive wife Loki emerged. Photo flashes popped over audible gasps as the couple, now rarely seen in public, made their way to the exhibition.

Naomi Jackson Groves, working in Germany on a Barlach book at the time, had been invited to give an introductory talk on the Group of Seven and her uncle, A. Y. Jackson, after which Loki Schmidt, speaking in German and English, officially opened the show. German television and radio stations recorded the event for broadcasts and telecasts in Germany and, a day later, in Canada.

During an informal chat, Chancellor Schmidt told me that in many ways the paintings reminded him of *Worpswede*, a band of German artists who had painted in northern Germany near Bremen in the early part of the century, but the German paintings, he felt, were less vivid and more inclined towards the romantic.

Even though I was pleased that the Chancellor was so impressed by our colourful Canadian paintings, I found my attention riveted on his snuff box. Perhaps the old custom was experiencing a revival in the continental *beau monde*? Not at all — the Chancellor was simply trying to give up cigarettes.

A few weeks after our return to Kleinburg we were shocked by a news report from Germany. The body of Hanns-Martin Schleyer had been found, brutally murdered by the German terrorists.

Selling and buying art is not always a simple matter of exchanging a cheque for an appealing work.

Even when the seller is a highly respected art dealer or auction house, errors of judgement and improper attribution can, and do, occur more frequently than many professionals care to admit. In private sales or those involving smaller salesrooms with less knowledgeable principals the possibility of misattribution, flawed judgement or outright fraud tends to increase, but size is no guarantee of integrity. I have often found a thoroughness and integrity in one-man shops sometimes lacking in larger organizations. In any case, where substantial amounts of money are involved, and in the fine arts they usually are, collecting is not a hobby to be taken up lightly by those who think they possess sufficient knowledge. The wise collector must always be certain of the integrity and reputation of the seller and, if the slightest doubt exists, he must be prepared to seek the advice of a knowledgeable, independent third party before making a purchase.

Misattributions may be made either knowingly and, therefore, fraudulently, or unknowingly by a seller who mistakenly believes that what he is offering is "right". In either case the buyer is the loser, even though the misattribution may not be discovered until after his death.

Most wrongly attributed pictures are sold as the work of well-known (often dead) artists and the prices asked or bid at auction are usually in line with going prices for the artists' work. Others are sold at suspiciously low prices which are usually a dead giveaway of doubtful authenticity. Certainly they are a signal calling for extreme caution. Yet in the pursuit of much sought-after works of art, collectors are often all too human. They believe what they want to believe.

When there is even the slightest doubt about a work of art, most reputable sellers will try to get second and third opinions but, short of absolute proof to the contrary, there is a quite natural reluctance to give up the opportunity to sell a work which they are personally convinced is "right". Similarly, when a picture seems convincing, many potential buyers, anxious to have it for their own, find it easy to satisfy themselves that the piece is what it appears, and is claimed, to be.

In the late 1950s and early 1960s scores of oil panels held out to be the work of Tom Thomson and other artists of the Group of Seven were sold by the Toronto auction house, Ward-Price Limited. Unfortunately, they were not genuine, and before the dishonest picture dealers, Leslie Lewis and Neil Sharkey, who had supplied the phony works, were exposed, prosecuted by the Ontario Provincial Police and convicted, a lot of otherwise highly intelligent people who could not resist a bargain were duped. The shady dealers were given time in jail to meditate on their ill-gotten profits but the hapless collectors, some of whom had made several purchases, were stuck with their "bargains".

A more subtle and fascinating case of misattribution occurred in May 1977 when the highly respected auction house, Sotheby Parke Bernet (Canada) Limited, and equally respected McCready Galleries were fooled by eighteen tempera paintings said to be by Clarence Gagnon, R.C.A. and related to the scenes from *Maria Chapdelaine*, which had come to the McMichael Canadian Collection from R. S. McLaughlin, who had bought them from the artist's estate.

The information in the auction catalogue in which six of the pictures were reproduced was so specific that eighteen identification numbers were listed indicating the paintings in the McMichael Collection to which each of the temperas was said to be related. It was assumed that the eighteen temperas, much larger than our paintings but depicting almost identical human figures and horses as well as similar rural terrain and buildings, were preparatory studies for some of the famous Gagnon illustrations which had been painted for the great Mornay edition of the classic novel. So highly regarded are these illustrations that paintings made in preparation for the final works which appeared in the book would command very high prices.

Gagnon completed the fifty-four illustrations for *Maria Chapdelaine* in Paris between 1928 and 1932. The eighteen tempera paintings, each twenty-five inches by nineteen inches were said, improbably but not impossibly, to have turned up at a Paris flea market and were being offered for sale through Sotheby Parke Bernet by a consignee who was not named in the sale catalogue. Shortly after the announcement of the sale I received a copy of the catalogue and I also learned that my friend, art dealer Phil McCready, would be bidding for the pictures on behalf of a client who was most anxious to have them.

Something about the pictures in the catalogue made me decide I should examine the actual temperas, which were on display at the auctioneer's showroom in advance of the sale. In spite of the great similarities of subject matter and painting style I was convinced that these eighteen large illustrations had not been painted by Clarence Gagnon. This assessment was based, not only on my own reactions, but on my conviction that neither the artist nor his widow Lucille would have allowed such similar studies of paintings he treasured so highly to leave his studio. I had been very impressed with Madame Gagnon's insistence when she sold our pictures to R. S. McLaughlin that the series must never be broken up, all fifty-four must be kept together always. Her devotion to these very special paintings and McLaughlin's strict observance of her conditions when he gave the works to the Collection satisfied me that the Gagnons never would have permitted very similar works to be sold by another person.

I felt I had to relay my misgivings to both Sotheby Parke Bernet and Phil McCready. Both said politely that they could understand my disappointment at learning that other Gagnon *Maria Chapdelaine* illustrations existed, but both pointed out that it would have been virtually impossible for the artist to create the complex final series without first having produced schematic or trial drawings and paintings.

Their reasoning seemed logical and I was quite certain they believed what they were saying, but I felt just as certain of my belief. As a last resort, knowing that Sotheby Parke Bernet had not the slightest intention of withdrawing the pictures, I suggested that a cautionary announcement be made at the auction to the effect that, based on my reservations, Sotheby's had some concern regarding the genuineness of authorship.

Yet I was quite sure they would not accept my recommendation. Their function was to sell pictures, not to cast doubt upon them.

On the evening of the auction I went downstairs to our gallery to examine our fifty-four Gagnon illustrations through a large magnifying glass. I wanted to make very precise comparisons between the illustrations in the Sotheby Parke Bernet sale catalogue and the final pictures in the Collection that they were said to presage.

To begin, I studied a horse and sled being driven at full tilt over a frozen river and compared it to one of the temperas showing what was obviously the same horse, sled and driver. The positions and actions of horse and driver as well as the most minute details of sled and harness were nearly photographically identical. Why would an accomplished artist, I asked myself, even experimenting with possible variations in a picture, copy a horse, driver and sled which he had already achieved with great feeling? If he was attempting to improve the feeling of action (which in this picture seemed perfect) wouldn't he change the driver's stance or the positions of the horse's straining legs or perhaps its head thrusting into the wind? Yet in the two pictures the angle of the driver's head and the action of the horse appeared identical right down to highlights and shadows.

Then I realized that in my close study of the foreground figures I had not noticed that the background in the tempera painting was entirely different from that in our Gagnon. Yet it was familiar. Suddenly I knew why. The church steeple, houses and a line of slow-moving horses and sleds — which lacked any relationship to the action in the foreground — had been copied from an entirely different picture in the Gagnon series.

I felt certain that moving a focal point of intense action from a simple setting to a distracting background was a transfer the sensitive Gagnon would never have contemplated, much less painted. With mounting excitement I compared the other illustrations in the catalogue. It was the same story — subjects and backgrounds copied with photographic accuracy but misfits when compared with our authentic Gagnons. I knew that something was very wrong!

Nevertheless, I still had no way of explaining how the eighteen pictures came to be painted or of proving they had not been painted by Clarence Gagnon.

While I was discovering these strange anomalies in the temperas, the Sotheby Parke Bernet auction held at Simpson's Arcadian Court was proceeding as scheduled, and as expected, Phillip McCready, acting for a determined client, was the successful bidder. Although the advance published estimates for the eighteen pictures ranged between fifteen and eighteen thousand dollars, the bidding was so spirited that when the hammer came down it was on McCready's whopping bid of fifty-eight thousand dollars. This high price would be enough to establish the paintings' authenticity for future buyers.

Since I had no doubt that the very existence of eighteen other *Maria Chapdelaine* paintings, accepted as the true work of Clarence Gagnon, would cast a shadow over the supposedly unique works in the McMichael Canadian Collection, I felt that any further suggestions or protests from me would be seen scornfully as nothing more than sour grapes. To pursue my convictions could only lead to bitter and futile exchanges with a respected auction house, a respected dealer who was also a friend, and a satisfied buyer. I had very little to gain and, without more proof, a lot of face to lose. There existed also the possibility that I was flirting with a lawsuit if I persisted. The odds were not attractive.

As I have done so many times when I have needed advice, not only on artistic matters but also on matters calling for good common sense, I decided to put my dilemma to my old friend, Alfred Casson. Sometimes it is difficult not to believe that fate does not intervene to force us to take the only step that will lead to the truth we are seeking.

When I reached Cass it almost seemed that he had been anticipating my call. He knew about the eighteen temperas which were coming up at auction and he was probably the only living person who knew the story behind them. Like me, he had been reluctant to get involved in a thankless controversy, so he had never revealed his "insider's knowledge" to anyone. Deep down, he had hoped that someone else would reject the temperas and prevent their sale. But the sale was now a *fait accompli* and he was appalled at the thought of an unwitting purchaser laying out well over sixty thousand dollars (including commissions) for eighteen pictures of very little value. Even more galling would be the knowledge that another set of fake paintings would become a part of the Canadian art scene — perhaps forever.

Alfred Casson did not merely welcome my call, it was very evident that he had been longing to resolve a perplexing dilemma without hurting his friends and mine at McCready Galleries and Sotheby Parke Bernet. My call provided the opportunity he needed.

Here is the story as Cass told it:

Years earlier he had attended an arts dinner in Montreal and quite by chance had been seated next to Clarence Gagnon's widow, Lucille. During the meal Madame Gagnon had told him of a Montreal painter who had asked her, as copyright holder, for permission to copy paintings of her late husband's illustrations for *Maria Chapdelaine* with the purpose of reproducing some of the pictures as Christmas cards. She was not happy about the proposal and refused to give her consent. Some time later she learned that the persistent painter, in spite of her refusal, had decided to make exact copies of the foreground pictures in the series. There would be no copyright infringement, he reasoned, since no one picture would be the same as any of Gagnon's illustrations.

Apparently some of these "mixed" illustrations were painted and shown to Madame Gagnon. She informed the tenacious copyist that she was still strongly opposed to what he was attempting and that if he persisted she would consider taking legal action. The Christmas cards were never produced and as far as Madame Gagnon knew that was the end of the matter.

Now, some years after Lucille Gagnon's death, it was apparent that the copied hybrid illustrations were being unscrupulously passed off as Gagnon originals.

Cass's astonishing story explained all the mysteries which had troubled me. After hearing these astonishing revelations I asked Cass if he would come to my gallery office the next morning. Then I phoned my good friend Phil McCready and urged him to join us for discussion of "a matter of the greatest importance".

When we demonstrated how the foregrounds and backgrounds had been interchanged and Casson repeated his conversation with Madame Gagnon, McCready immediately recognized that he and his client had been the victims of a scam, which, except for the fortunate accident of a casual conversation many years before, would have succeeded completely.

Weeks after the auction, after hearing Casson's and my own statements and after McCready had returned the pictures to them, Sotheby Parke Bernet maintained that the firm had no reason to believe that the works were not authentic and it was almost a year before they officially cancelled the sale to McCready.

Fortunately no one had been badly hurt. It was a classic example of what buyers and sellers didn't know but wanted to believe.

Like most Westerners, Signe and I were curious about life behind the Iron Curtain, so we did some intensive reading before our visits to three widely separated cities in the Union of Soviet Socialist Republics, each, in fact, in a different republic of the enormous nation whose land mass is larger than North America.

There were no good connecting flights between Toronto and Leningrad, so we decided to make our stopover and transfer in Denmark, Signe's birthplace. Air Canada had twice-weekly flights to Copenhagen from which there were twice-weekly non-stop flights to the U.S.S.R.'s most northerly major city. Our first exhibition in the U.S.S.R. was scheduled for June at Leningrad's fabled Hermitage Museum. It would be the first-ever show of Canadian art in what is believed to be the world's largest art museum.

For two days in Copenhagen we were voracious tourists, taking in the city's permanent year-round circus and the sights and sounds of the Tivoli Gardens and munching classic Danish foods on the narrow, colourful Walking Street. We felt very much at home, but all that changed during the Aeroflot flight from Copenhagen when we realized that none of the passengers or stewardesses had spoken anything but Russian. We prayed that an interpreter would be meeting us. Inside the customs-immigration room a young man, spotting without much difficulty our western clothes, approached us tentatively and said in halting English, "Mr. MacMikel?"

I enthusiastically nodded, offering my hand.

"I, Micha," he said, pointing at himself. "Please to follow," he continued, pointing to the shortest of several lines of arriving passengers.

Immediately in front of me as we approached the customs desk was a young Soviet man, obviously returning home. Opening his rather tacky, imitation leather suitcase, the customs officer began rummaging mercilessly until he came upon four obviously pornographic magazines. Lifting two of them between his fingers he looked the returning passenger straight in the eye with a silent question. There was an almost imperceptible nod of the head in front of me. Two of the banned magazines quickly disappeared into the customs officer's desk as the passenger re-packed and closed his luggage.

We had received our first lesson in "co-operative exchange", or the grey market. This incident was typical of a shady bargaining system which Soviet society and its government not only tolerate, but accept as normal, a bartering of goods and services among citizens. Without it, it would be difficult to imagine the Soviet social and economic systems being able to function. A worker, for example, in a glove factory will exchange hard to get quality gloves with a friend employed in making scarce automobile parts or with a box-office clerk at The Bolshoi. Recognized as Westerners, we were often asked to pay taxi fares with a package of our cigarettes rather than a much higher equivalent in rubles.

As we stepped towards the customs officer with our luggage, Micha quickly intervened, flashing a red identification card. We passed through, bags unopened. At the air terminal's curbside long lines of people were queuing patiently awaiting their turn to share a taxi. To our embarrassment we were led to the head of the line where Micha, again showing his magic red card, lifted our luggage into the first cab.

During our ride to the city, Micha explained haltingly that he spoke a little English and was not our interpreter but a representative of the Hermitage Museum. After giving me an envelope containing fifty rubles for spending money, he directed the driver to the old and ornate Astoria, the most prestigious hotel in the central area of Leningrad. Checking in and surrendering our passports, we were given identification cards and elaborate over-sized room keys like ceremonial keys to the city. Their moulded brass faces bore the city's original name, St. Petersburg. We were suddenly aware that we were holding relics from the days when the city was the czarist capital.

After a long flight we were ready for bed, but at eleven o'clock that June evening daylight still poured through our hotel windows. Once again I did a rapid calculation and decided that this great city of over three million people was at the same latitude as Whitehorse and Anchorage.

Leningrad, with its palaces, parks and museums is a special place — the most popular city for vacationers from all parts of the Soviet Union as well as visitors from other nations. Approaching the large open space surrounding the imposing buildings of the Hermitage, you pass block-long double lines of people patiently waiting their turn to enter the former Winter Palace of the Czars.

The Winter Palace was first built by Peter the Great and was later developed and improved by Catherine II. It is now, as the Hermitage Museum, the U.S.S.R.'s greatest cultural mecca as well as the historic site of the turning point in the Russian Revolution. After October 1917, czarist orders no longer issued from these enormous pavilions. Instead, they became immense storehouses of the nation's artistic and intellectual treasures — many of them confiscated or abandoned by their dead or fleeing owners.

Hordes of insatiable sightseers are a common sight at all the great museums of the world. What is striking about the Hermitage is the proportion of peasants and workers, often in colourful regional costumes, and kerchiefed old women, who seem to have come, perhaps less to see the museum's treasures than to visit the Winter Palace. The young take it for granted that the Winter Palace and the treasures of The Hermitage should be at their disposal for the sum of three rubles. But the older people still seem amazed to find themselves able to walk freely about the palace and the long-forbidden Throne Room.

The Hermitage has more than a thousand rooms, in which the arts of the ancient and modern worlds — ranging from thousands of tiny, exquisite gold ornaments of Scythian art of the sixth century B.C. to the paintings of Picasso and Matisse — are displayed. Works of DaVinci, Michaelangelo and Reubens hang side by side with Raphaels and Rembrandts and, in fact, with great artists of almost every period.

In addition to the works of western masters, sections are devoted to the arts of India, China, Ancient Egypt, Mesopotamia, Pre-Columbian America, and Greece and Rome. There is also a department of pre-historic art. Paintings represent only a part of the riches of the Hermitage. People also come to admire the extensive collections of tapestry, weapons, ivories, pottery and furniture.

The total collection of the Hermitage contains over a million works and during the summer months, between fifteen and twenty thousand people from all parts of the Soviet Union and the world visit the museum daily. The large gallery room set aside for the exhibition of Canadian Landscape Painters was located near the main entrance. Visitors to the Hermitage tend to follow a suggested route so as to see the greatest amount in a given time. It was easy, therefore, for us to calculate that in the one-month period during which our show would be on exhibit it would be seen by half a million people.

The morning after our arrival I received a telephone call from a clear voice speaking English with so little accent it could have been someone from Toronto or Vancouver. It was our assigned interpreter, Natasha, who would be our almost inseparable companion during the next two weeks.

She suggested we meet downstairs for breakfast. Coffee usually starts my day, so I was disconcerted to find that restaurants in the U.S.S.R. have little refrigeration equipment and do not serve cream or milk or even dry creamers. It was black or nothing. For me that meant nothing. At dinner I noticed, however, that ice cream was a favourite dessert. The next morning, after eggs and toast, I asked Natasha to order ice cream and to explain to a startled waitress that it was an old Canadian custom. Signe and I then gleefully stirred the vanilla ice cream into our morning coffee.

Our conversations with Natasha seemed as natural as talks with a Canadian college student. She was in her early twenties, doing post-graduate work for her master's degree in fine arts, a thesis on English theatre, for which her excellent grasp of the language must have been a great asset.

In that, she was quite different from most of the Soviets we met on our travels. Very few, whatever their status, spoke even one English word. The director of the Hermitage Museum, a Ph.D. with whom we enjoyed frequent discussions, could communicate with us only through Natasha, to whom we clung for guidance and enlightenment.

Unlike most Soviets, Natasha was permitted to read many publications from the West which were stored in a central library. Though she had never left her native U.S.S.R. she could read, speak and think in English, although she told us she didn't believe all she read. She had, however, come to accept certain facts through her reading and marvelled at the simple, everyday rights and freedoms we take for granted. Although she believed most of what she read, nothing in her experience enabled her to imagine what life with Western freedoms and rights would be like. She was also a little skeptical of Western abundance — a world of privately owned homes and automobiles (even for workers); a world of nylons, blue jeans and abundant food of all kinds; a world where you could read and listen and speak as you pleased; a world where governments which did not govern according to the wishes of the people could be removed — not the other way around. She accepted as truth our right to travel domestically and internationally or to relocate our homes if we so desired, but it was extremely difficult for her to visualize a life so free from governmental decree. In the Soviet Union, one cannot spend even one night in a hotel without a special and difficult to obtain permit.

During our conversations, Natasha asked us about employment, our households, appliances and furnishings and the many facilities available to the average Canadian. Our talks about everyday living in Canada and the easy availability of "luxuries", while seeming to amaze her, also confirmed what she had read and tried to picture in her mind.

She was not averse to discussing our totally different political and social systems or the East-West arms race. But such subjects, we noticed, were not discussed in our hotel suite. They were reserved for leisurely strolls in the broad avenues and parks.

A year earlier, Natasha told us, she had been assigned as interpreter to Jacqueline Kennedy and Thomas Hoving during their visit to Leningrad. After several days filled with visits to the magnificent fountains of Peterhoff and the palaces and museums, the time came for farewells. The former First Lady thanked Natasha and asked if there was something from the United States she particularly wished to have for herself.

Natasha mentioned two books on Western theatre which she dreamed of possessing and wrote down their titles and authors. Several weeks later, she received a formal letter from the Soviet Union's Ministry of Culture advising that a package addressed to her had been intercepted. The books had been placed in the central library with a note commending Comrade Natasha's generous "donation".

An eighty-page catalogue for the three U.S.S.R. exhibitions of Canadian Landscape Painters was designed and produced in the U.S.S.R. All forty-four paintings were reproduced in full-page size, eleven in colour. The text, printed entirely in Russian, was read and translated for us by our always willing and helpful young friend.

Natasha had mingled with the crowds of visitors viewing the Canadian exhibition on opening day, so she was able to pick up comments and reactions from first-time viewers. The Soviet people, with their closeness to the land, felt and understood these colourful landscapes showing a rocky, forested wilderness. The subjects were so similar to those in much of their own country that they felt the pictures could have been of the U.S.S.R.

On our last day in Leningrad, Signe began packing our bags. Not knowing in advance about laundry facilities in the U.S.S.R., she had brought a pair of new, plastic-wrapped pantyhose for every day away, plus a few extra. Now three pairs remained unopened. Knowing this luxury was unheard of in the U.S.S.R., she offered them as her gift to Natasha, who had read of, but never seen, sheer pantyhose.

"I couldn't, Mrs. McMichael. You'd never be able to replace them," Natasha looked longingly at the three packages. Assured that Signe could replace them with no difficulty, tears came to her eyes as she clutched the three packages.

"I'll save them for my wedding day."

Between overseas visits I managed to keep up with regular Collection business and the ever-present paperwork. I was also anxious to continue discussions with potential donors of major gifts to the Collection. Sizeable donations almost always involve delicate negotiations and timing is crucial.

Three situations required my attention and sent me on a trip to Montreal between the long trips to the Soviet Union.

The first concerned J. W. Morrice. I had been in contact by letter and telephone with David Morrice, nephew of the great painter, and his sister Eleanore, but I had never met them. I knew, however, that they had one of the finest private collections of their late uncle's works.

James Wilson Morrice was born in Montreal in 1865 and is regarded by many respected art historians as Canada's premier landscape painter. After graduation from the University of Toronto, he abandoned the law, for which he had been educated, to devote his life to painting. He spent his artistically formative years in France at the time when the Impressionists and Post-Impressionists were adding a vital chapter to art history.

Although much of Morrice's life was spent abroad in France,

North Africa and the Caribbean (he died in Tunis in 1924) some of his best-known paintings were made during return visits to his native Quebec — snowbound villages of the lower St. Lawrence and the older sections of Montreal and Quebec City.

His tiny, exquisite panels (like the larger ones of the Group of Seven a generation later) were, in themselves, finished compositions and, like members of the Group, he translated some into larger canvases.

Morrice was one of the few artists, Signe and I felt, whose work should be included in the Collection, in addition to those artists specifically named in the Gift Agreement of 1965. Although we already had nineteen of his scarce pictures I was anxious for more.

David Morrice and his sister Eleanore met me in their townhouse apartment in a garden court adjacent to the Montreal Museum of Fine Arts. I had assumed, correctly, that a major share of their collection would end up in that museum, but I wanted them to be fully aware of another public gallery on the Humber River, which Morrice had painted during his student years at Osgoode Hall law school, one that placed him in the company of a select few of his near-contemporaries and would honour him with a permanent gallery room.

As I had expected, the walls of their apartment were hung with Morrice's richly coloured, sensitive little panels, many no larger than five by six inches, the largest only about twice that size.

But value is not measured by size. Morrice's sensual handling of pigment and his love of healthy, lusty colour are a delight to the eye. In spite of its miniature size, each little study condensed on wood is a finished composition executed with a free hand. Most include little figures, their shapes indicated by certain mannerisms of his brush, quick twirls that stand as symbols for a skirt, a bonnet and a face or the head and mane of a horse in rich and oily pigments. I had only an hour with the Morrices but they could have been in no doubt about my regard for their uncle's work.

About three years later, I received a letter from Royal Trust in Montreal. David Morrice had died and his sister was terminally ill. Three choice works by J. W. Morrice were a special bequest made by them to the McMichael Canadian Collection and would be shipped to us upon receipt of our instructions.

My second mission was to meet with Mrs. Arthur Gill.

For several years I was in close touch with Arthur Gill, prominent in Montreal's world of finance, who had been for many years a serious collector of Canadian art, especially those artists who had painted in Quebec. Two great favourites whom he had known personally were Albert Robinson and Edwin Holgate, who, after 1965, had become more prominent in the Collection. Both painters had close associations with the Group — Robinson as a guest exhibitor at their exhibitions and Holgate as a later Group member.

Gill, a periodic visitor to Kleinburg during his frequent business trips to Toronto, had introduced himself on an early visit. Through the years we had become friends and I occasionally visited him in Montreal. He had encouraged us to expand our holdings of his two favourite artists and at his urging, Signe and I had purchased a large portrait, *The Cellist*, directly from Holgate. Then, after seeing Gill's Robinsons, our interest in the artist whom Alex Jackson had referred to as an *ex officio* member of the Group, increased and led us to include works by Robinson in the Collection.

On September 1, 1972, Arthur Gill wrote to me, saying that he wished to make a gift to the McMichael Collection of a fine Robinson canvas, *Haytime, Knowlton*, and asking if we would be prepared to accept the painting. I was so delighted with this Monday morning surprise that I picked up the telephone at once to thank him and tell him how much we looked forward to adding *Haytime*, a glowing Quebec farm landscape, to our three Robinson panels and single canvas, *St. Joseph*, a landscape in the R. S. McLaughlin gift.

Oddly, I got a hesitant response from Gill's secretary. "Mr. Gill is not in ... may I ask who is calling?" Then, hearing my name there was a longer pause followed by a trembling "Mr. McMichael, I'm so glad you've called ... I presume you have Mr. Gill's letter ... I hardly know how to tell you ... Mr. Gill is dead."

As I listened in shocked silence, she told me that mine was the last letter he had dictated and that she had had to remind him to sign it before he left for a Friday board meeting. It was at that meeting that he had asked to be excused to lie down. Half an hour later they found him dead. Her voice trembled as she said, "Mrs. Gill knows about his letter and I'm sure she would like to hear from you."

When I reached her, Mrs. Gill told me in a calm voice that she and her husband had discussed the gift and were in complete agreement. It had been his last wish and she was determined to honour it. The letter had covered the intention and now she wanted the painting to be in our hands as soon as safe delivery could be arranged.

I suggested that Jack Fenwick, my niece's husband, might pick it up, since I knew he and Penny would be driving to Kleinburg in the very near future. She had met Jack, a close friend who had accompanied me on visits to the Gill home, and felt this would be a very good arrangement.

Some time after Arthur Gill's death, I received a letter from Mrs. Gill asking if I could meet with her when I was next in Montreal. Over afternoon tea we reminisced about her husband's love of Canadian paintings. Then, without preamble, she pointed to his two favourites, Robinson's *Afternoon, St. Simeon* and Holgate's *Fishermen's Houses* and asked me to take them to Kleinburg, a gift from her and their son, Bruce, in memory of Arthur.

My third meeting during that brief trip to Montreal was with my old friend, Dr. Max Stern, Montreal's foremost art dealer.

I first met Max and his wife Iris in 1956 at their Dominion Gallery on Sherbrooke Street, directly across from the Montreal Museum of Fine Arts. I was on one of my regular business trips, and after visiting Arthur Lismer at the Museum's Children's Art Centre, I stopped in at the Dominion. I knew that Stern was the gallery owner who had acquired most of the works sold by Emily Carr before her death in 1945, a coup that had the Canadian art world buzzing.

In 1956 both our collection and our financial resources were very modest and in any case our priorities were Tom Thomson and the Group. We were, however, very aware of Emily Carr and I was anxious to see a wider variety of her work and to get some idea of prices.

Max or Iris Stern, equally knowledgeable, usually met and talked with visitors to their gallery, especially those who appeared to be serious customers. Since I was not yet in that category, I felt fortunate to have a discussion with them that lasted for almost an hour. Most of the Emily Carrs I was shown were works on paper — oils, watercolours and drawings offered at prices between one and three thousand dollars. They were elaborately and ornately framed, a hallmark of Max Stern's, carried over from the European traditions of his youth. He believed that an elaborate gilded frame improved any artist, any style, any subject. However, even in those early days, I felt that the twentieth-century paintings in which we were most interested demanded very simple, light-coloured frames.

While I admired several of the Emily Carrs being offered, I felt sure that the Sterns knew I had set my heart on a master work, even though I could not possibly afford it. Toward the end of my visit, Iris Stern invited me to the apartment above the gallery and I found myself viewing monumental Emily Carr canvases which would have made the most sophisticated collector giddy: powerful tree forms and mountains and shorelines painted with a magical inspiration forced me to catch my breath. Naively I asked if they were for sale. Iris replied with a question, "Would I sell my children?"

The memory of those paintings never dimmed. During the next five years, I visited the Dominion Gallery whenever I was in Montreal, renewing my acquaintance with the Sterns and always hoping I might again be invited upstairs. Then my Canadian business trips came to an abrupt end as I began seven years of commuting to the United States.

By 1967, Canada's Centennial, the McMichael Canadian Collection was into its second year of operation as a public gallery and my work in the United States was finished. Signe and I decided to combine a trip to Montreal and Expo '67 with a renewal of our acquaintance with the Sterns. In the intervening years we had acquired two magnificent Emily Carr canvases. Their superb quality had made us determined to add other major Carr paintings to the Collection, but this ambition was becoming harder and harder to achieve. Increased interest in Canadian art and wider recognition of Carr's genius had dramatically reduced the number of even her lesser works that were for sale. The major paintings we sought were tightly held by public galleries and a handful of private collectors, who were unwilling to part with them at any price.

Knowing that a major Carr was now probably beyond our reach, the Sterns, with an unspoken "we told you so" commiserated over our not having purchased Emily Carrs on their recommendation years earlier. We, in turn, reminded them that we had had little money. While our financial situation had improved, rarity and escalated prices seemed to have put a major Carr even further beyond our grasp. Our distress was even greater when Iris once again led us upstairs where their private Emily Carrs seemed even more breathtaking than I remembered.

Seven years later, on a summer day in 1974, my office intercom announced that Dr. and Mrs. Stern were in our gallery and had asked for me. Signe and I dropped everything with a prayer that the owners of the finest private collection of Carrs would be favourably impressed by their first visit to Kleinburg.

We were not surprised to find the Sterns had arrived unannounced and had already made a tour of the Collection. They wanted to make up their own minds about its quality and presentation, its strengths and weaknesses and perhaps even more important, they wanted to see and hear other visitors' responses to the Collection, now widely publicized and discussed in every part of Canada.

We persuaded them to return to the western Canada gallery room which now contained the Blunden Harbour totem pole, several Northwest Indian masks, a few western Canada subjects by Group members and five fine paintings by Emily Carr. We told them of our desire to have this, our largest gallery room, devoted entirely to Emily Carr paintings and the carvings of the Northwest Coast Indians which the painter had always admired.

Our Emily Carrs, all on canvas, included *Reforestation*, which Signe and I had purchased, *Shoreline*, which had been given to us by Norah dePencier in 1963 before our Agreement with the Ontario government, and *Old Tree at Dark*, from the R. S. McLaughlin gift. These three were the same size. Two smaller but equally fine works were *Swaying*, a gift of Yvonne Housser, and *New Growth*, which we had purchased more recently with the Collection's special art fund.

We held our breaths, hoping against hope that the majestic room of hewn Douglas fir logs and the five top quality paintings by their favourite artist would lead the Sterns to share our vision of a future Emily Carr memorial.

They did! For the first time in their lives, they told us, they would part with a major Emily Carr. A gift from their personal collection ... to the McMichael Canadian Collection.

Later that year Max Stern called to ask if I could visit him in Montreal to discuss the gift they had promised. In his office he handed me a large brown envelope crammed with photographs of paintings in their private collection. Most of them I remembered well from my earlier visits, but I was surprised to learn that for some time all had been on loan to the Edmonton Art Gallery and the Glenbow Institute in Calgary. Both galleries were quite new and were happy to have the works of western Canada's most famous artist for display and to secure them in their vaults when they were not on view. The arrangement was thus mutually helpful.

The Stern's concern for the security of their treasures had increased when, some months earlier, while investigating a series of crimes linked to robbery, extortion and murder, the Montreal police turned up a carefully detailed floor plan of a three-floor building with frontage, fire escapes and other features indicated in scale. It could have been any of thousands of buildings in the city, but the search was narrowed because it included detailed indications of a professionally installed burglar and fire alarm system.

The layout matched exactly that of Dominion Gallery and the apartment above it.

In Max's office, it soon became obvious that a serious discussion, let alone selection of a single painting, would be next to impossible during business hours. If he was not issuing instructions through a door kept ajar, he was on the telephone, often two telephones at the same time. Billing, packing and record keeping could be efficiently handled by his staff. Calls from potential buyers or sellers, locally or in New York, London or Trois-Rivières were the personal challenges on which he thrived, a human dynamo whirring and sparking with the energy which had made Dominion Montreal's leading gallery.

In a rare pause, Max made a reservation for a quiet dinner that evening at the Ritz where I was staying and I hastily retreated there, a block down the street, clutching under my arm a fat envelope of photographs with notes of sizes, dates and titles.

Once in my room I spread the eight by ten inch prints across the bed and on the floor, all but overwhelmed by the extent of the Stern's holdings. How could I ever narrow my choice to a single painting?

For a few minutes my eyes darted hungrily from picture to picture — the surging *Straits of Juan de Fuca*, soaring trees in rain forest cathedrals, native villages and striking totems, magnificent mountains and swirling skies. Then gradually I slowed down for the longer study of each than had been possible during my brief visits to the apartment years earlier.

Like most artists, Carr had experienced frustration when her brush could not capture all of her passionate and intense feelings. But during those fleeting hours and days when her mind, her eye and her hand had worked in perfect harmony, the images that emerged on her canvas had seized "the thing she had striven for ... the nameless something that carries beyond, what your finger cannot point to". Carr had yearned for honest appreciation, for others to see, to understand, to recognize the expressions of her all-consuming passion. Ira Dilworth, Lawren Harris, Marius Barbeau, Campbell McInnes, Norah dePencier and a small handful of others encouraged her, but national recognition came only after her death, in 1945.

While Max Stern was not the first dealer to recognize the strength, the dynamic movement, and the joyousness in Carr's paintings, he was the one who became convinced, not only of their rare qualities, but of their saleability.

Stern's European training and academic background were the

foundation of his magnificent self-confidence and his uncanny ability to judge an artist. That judgement had served him and his customers well. He had exhibited unknown painters whose names were later to become household words. Dominion was the first Canadian gallery from which now grateful clients had purchased the sculpture of such international giants as Marini, Manzu, Maillol and Henry Moore.

When he met with Emily Carr at her home in Victoria, he found himself so moved by her work that the line between dealer and collector became permanently blurred. He arranged to purchase every painting she was willing to sell, and in 1944 presented the single major exhibition to be mounted during Carr's lifetime.

He faced the dilemma which confronts most art dealers at one time or another. To sell, which his business required, or to keep, as his emotions demanded. The luxury of personal collection is a dangerous temptation most dealers try to resist.

Max and Iris Stern could not.

From almost five hundred paintings acquired in their trust purchase, the Sterns selected forty-three which would become the core of their private collection of Canadian art.

Sequestered with the photographs, only hunger pangs reminded me that through hours of studying, comparing and sorting, I had not paused for lunch. Yet with all my viewing and reviewing, I was no closer to selecting a single picture. Taking into account quality and general appeal, size, medium and date or period, the choice had been narrowed, but it was beginning to look as though I would have to close my eyes, take a couple of turns, and point.

Then inspiration struck.

As the foremost private collectors of Emily Carrs, I felt the Sterns should be represented by more than a single painting in the great Emily Carr-Northwest Indian room they had seen. There should not be a single Stern gift. There should be a Stern wall of Emily Carr paintings!

This was the kind of bold thinking which had led to Stern's own success. Max had spent his life convincing clients they should upgrade quality and increase quantity far beyond their own original intent. While giving could hardly be considered the same as selling or owning, I set about convincing myself that they would recognize the honour of having their names, in perpetuity, on bronze plaques directly associated with Emily Carr.

The Stern Memorial wall was easy to visualize.

It would be one of six large bays in the enormous gallery room, which divided by massive stone columns about twenty-five feet apart and each capable of displaying perhaps five canvases. Reaching for a scratch pad, I began jotting down picture widths. Most of them were twenty-seven inches. Allowing for good spacing and frame widths, I needed five major Emily Carrs.

Imagine, I told them in my imagination, five large swirling and soaring Carrs in the vibrant colours of her unique palette proudly proclaiming her position in Canadian art — all made possible by the generosity of Dr. and Mrs. Max Stern. Visions of the Stern wall and the room danced before me.

Immortality was calling. I felt sure the Sterns would answer. Or almost sure. Would they merely think me greedy? Would I appear ungrateful for the gift they had already offered?

My doubts were set aside by a firm conviction that the bigger undertaking would actually give them much more personal satisfaction. If I was wrong and the suggestion gave offence then I must be prepared to backpaddle, leaving the choice of one of my five favourites to them.

During dinner I learned much more about the Sterns, his fine art studies at Cologne, Vienna, Berlin and Bonn Universities, their marriage and escape from Germany a step ahead of Hitler's SS, their first years in Canada.

Max's first venture was a partnership in Montreal's Continental Galleries, but he soon found such an arrangement too confining. In 1950 he seized the opportunity to purchase the superb location on Sherbrooke Street and Dominion Gallery was born. Seeking out lesser-known artists of promise and acquiring the works of well-known international masters such as August Rodin, whom he believed to be very underpriced, Max soon established a loyal clientele. His worldliness and astute judgement soon attracted hosts of would-be collectors who became willing students and often disciples. Teaching them to really see and guiding their tastes had given him great satisfaction and his gallery a very satisfactory balance sheet.

After dinner, as a waiter served coffee, Max asked if I had selected a favourite painting from the photographs.

I took the plunge. "Yes, Max, in fact I've selected five."

Giving him no time to interrupt I assured him that although one would be a welcome addition to the Collection, a group of five, a magnificent Stern wall, would more honestly represent the contribution he and Mrs. Stern had made to the understanding and acceptance of Emily Carr as one of the nation's artistic giants.

Stunned silence. I held my breath. Max's eyes bore into mine and I forced myself not to blink.

He turned to Iris. "What do you think, dear?"

Iris's eyes were misty, "It's what we've always wanted, Max."

It was decided. Max turned to me and smiled. "The boss has spoken. Have you decided which pictures you want?"

The five photos were handy in my attaché case. On top was a magnificent example of Carr's classic elongated composition.

Max looked at it in silence then said apologetically, "I don't think we can part with that one right now."

Iris would have none of it. The painting would be included. But I remembered what she had said years earlier about selling her "children" and knew the bittersweet pleasure they were feeling. I wondered if they could have borne to part with their beloved paintings if they had not already been stored in distant galleries.

Before the evening was over, they were talking enthusiastically about the Stern wall and how the pictures would appear in that handsome log and stone room in Kleinburg. There would be no final parting. They could visit with their "children" whenever they wished.

That gift doubled the McMichael Canadian Collection's holdings of Emily Carrs. Almost more important, it increased the Sterns' desire to be even more involved in creating a permanent tribute to their favourite artist at Kleinburg. In the years that followed, nine more of Emily Carr's paintings, from her earliest to her later periods, would join the initial gift. With each contribution the Sterns' enthusiasm for the Collection seemed to increase. Eventually they also gave us four important canvases by A. Y. Jackson and one by J.E.H. MacDonald.

Several years later, in November 1980, Signe and I had dinner at the Ritz, this time with Max alone. Iris had died the year before. While he was signing the forms transferring six splendid canvases to the Collection he reminisced about Iris and chuckled again over her advice.

"Don't hold onto the pictures too long," she had told him. "Remember, you can't take them with you. And if you could they would only burn."

Our second exhibition in the Soviet Union was at the Museum of Western and Eastern Art in Kiev, capital of the Ukranian Soviet Socialist Republic.

Staff member Jim Hubbard and I flew to London where we made a tight connection for Moscow on a British Airways flight. We were met at Moscow's airport by an attractive young interpreter, Janya, who would accompany us by train to Kiev the following evening. Registering at the Rossia, reputed to be the world's largest hotel, we were quite ready for bed after two very long flights, but tired as we were that evening, we could not resist a short walk in the vast open space beside the hotel — Red Square.

The next morning I met with Guy Choquette, counsellor at the Canadian embassy, a converted mansion at 23 Starokonyushenny Perleulok, not far from Red Square and the Kremlin — a vast, walled complex of buildings, towers and spires.

It was arranged that Choquette would fly to Kiev on the evening before our opening. Since I would have a twin bed suite at the hotel, he would bunk in with me so we would not have to go through the tedious process of obtaining an extra permit for hotel accommodation.

Jim Hubbard and I had made the tight London-Moscow connection, but our luggage had not. It also failed to catch up with us during our day in Moscow. We boarded the train for Kiev that evening with only the clothes we wore and our briefcases. Fortunately, Jim had packed an electric razor in his.

Each evening in Kiev, we bathed ourselves and our only socks, underwear and shirts using the little red slab of carbolic soap that came with the room. In the sticky July weather we soon became conscious of a need for a western refinement we knew it would be hard to find in Kiev — deodorant. Was it only in our imaginations that people were standing a little further from us each day?

After several days of work at the museum, the evening of Choquette's scheduled arrival came and went with no Choquette. By opening day, we were seriously concerned, particularly when a telephone call to the Canadian embassy in Moscow shed no light on Guy's whereabouts.

Then, to our astonishment and relief, about noon, only two hours before the official opening, a slightly bedraggled Choquette arrived at our hotel. Before we could say a word he held up his hand, "Please ... don't ask! You wouldn't believe."

Later he told us his tale of horrors.

He had boarded his plane to Kiev the evening before and decided to nap because he knew from experience it was a boring flight. When the plane landed he gathered his belongings, walked into the terminal and asked for a taxi to the Kiev Hotel. Told there was no such hotel, he took another look at the depot and experienced a sinking feeling when he realized he had somehow come down in Odessa on the Black Sea.

Had the flight made its scheduled stop in Kiev? No. For reasons known only to the pilot, it hadn't. He was the only passenger for Kiev. Perhaps in the U.S.S.R. it was not considered necessary to accommodate one individual? In any case the by-passing of Kiev had not been announced.

"When is the next flight to Kiev?"

"Tomorrow morning."

"Book it, and take me to a hotel for tonight."

"May I see your hotel occupancy permit?"

End of conversation. Choquette spent a long night on a concrete bench in Odessa Airport's waiting room. We thought it better to omit our own adventures without luggage. We had a feeling he wouldn't be particularly sympathetic.

Oh yes, our luggage did arrive — that night.

The third showing of the Group's paintings and the climax of our Soviet tour took place at Moscow's famous Pushkin Museum.

Jeanne Pattison and I were met at Moscow Airport by a mature woman named Toya who had been assigned to us as interpreter. Moscow had two other commercial airports but "for security reasons" they are out of bounds to all but Soviet citizens.

Toya had a good command of English, but unlike Natasha or Janya, she lacked personal warmth. Her manner was crisp, at times even strident. When she told us proudly of her many experiences travelling abroad with cultural and athletic groups who were participating in international events we decided she was undoubtedly a member of the notorious KGB. We certainly had nothing to hide but we were, nevertheless, cautious in our conversations with her, avoiding any discussion of politics or other possibly touchy subjects.

Although we had several days work with the Pushkin's curators hanging the show, we found time for sightseeing and a visit to the Canadian embassy, where, to our delight, we found reproductions of Group paintings from the McMichael Collection hanging permanently.

In the Soviet Union, minor western luxuries like Coca-Cola and kleenex were, of course, unavailable. We were amused to see that the embassy staff and guests had a little supermarket away from home — basement shelves full of the little luxuries and comforts we take for granted.

Ambassador and Mrs. Robert Ford invited Jeanne and I for lunch in their private embassy quarters, a few hours before the ambassador was to join Vladimir Popov, Deputy Minister of Culture of the U.S.S.R., for the official opening of the Canadian Landscape Painters exhibition at the Pushkin Museum of Fine Arts.

Over coffee, Mrs. Ford told us an amusing story. Several years before, Soviet Foreign Minister Andrei Gromyko and his wife were making an official visit to Ottawa and the Fords, who speak fluent Russian, were accompanying them. While their husbands attended meetings, Mrs. Ford accompanied Mrs. Gromyko to the National Gallery of Canada, hoping to see the landscapes by the Group of Seven that Mrs. Ford had been praising to her visitors. Instead, they were greeted by gallery director Jean Boggs, guided firmly to the current exhibition which consisted entirely of coloured fluorescent tubes, some glowing on the walls, others on the floor. Mrs. Gromyko quietly declined the offer of a catalogue and indicated politely but firmly that she had come to see landscape paintings.

As the two women were leaving, Mrs. Gromyko, apparently having second thoughts, asked if she might have the catalogue of the light show after all. Jean Boggs was delighted to produce one. A twinkle in her eye, Mrs. Gromyko remarked, "My grandchildren will be amused."

The main galleries of the Pushkin Museum are reached from the lobby by a grand marble staircase. Robert Ford was crippled by a childhood illness, so I hurried down to assist him. I was met by four men carrying a sedan chair in which Ford sat like a stately prince borne by his retainers. Passing me on the stairs, he said grandly, "Bob, it's the only way to travel."

Following the three, month-long exhibitions in the U.S.S.R., the Canadian Landscape Painters exhibition was scheduled to move to Oslo's *Kunstforeningen*. A modest but informative Norwegian catalogue had been produced.

While we were in Oslo, Signe and I grasped the opportunity to visit Norway's National Gallery where arrangements were made for us to see some of the paintings which had been shown in the Exhibition of Contemporary Scandinavian Art at Buffalo's Albright Gallery in 1912. That historic exhibition had been seen by Lawren Harris and J.E.H. MacDonald, reinforcing their belief that northern nations such as the Scandinavian countries and Canada could achieve their own vital and distinctive indigenous art.

We spent most of one day in the *Munch-museet*, a renowned public gallery devoted entirely to Norway's most famous artist, Edvard Munch.

The it was off to Eire.

After almost two years in thirteen cities and six countries, the Group of Seven European tour concluded with two exhibitions in Ireland. The first was at the National Gallery of Ireland in Dublin and, following that, there was another in the art gallery of the impressive old stone castle at Kilkenny.

It had been the most extensive international cultural tour ever undertaken by Canada. To our ambassadors and cultural attachés, who measure reactions to Canada in the nations to which they are posted and attempt thus to evaluate Canada's diplomatic efforts, the Group of Seven exhibitions were high points.

Nations have long recognized that when major international cultural exchanges are undertaken, their appeal must be to the greatest number rather than to a narrow artistic elite. Older countries with much longer art histories than Canada's know that exhibitions of their best-known treasures will attract the widest audiences: The Netherlands has toured its Rembrandts and Van Goghs; Italy, the archeological riches of Pompeii; and Egypt, the treasures of King Tut. All have been cultural blockbusters.

Our relatively short history as a nation has not yet produced such universally recognized classics. Nevertheless, the paintings of the Group, although they are not widely known internationally, had impressed viewers as inspired interpretations of our landscape as seen through highly perceptive Canadian eyes. The dramatic, brilliantly rendered paintings proved to be vivid confirmations of the way millions of people, who had never seen our country, had imagined the terrain and spirit of Canada.

Less than a year after the Group of Seven tour terminated, the Collection was invited to present another exhibition in Hamburg, West Germany, and in addition, to participate with a number of major works in a second exhibition in the same city. This time the shows would focus on the arts of our Native peoples.

At the vast *Hamburgisches Museum fur Volkerkunde*, the larger exhibition, entitled *Donnervogel und Ruhwal* (Thunderbird and Killer Whale) and organized by Dr. Wolfgang Haberland, displayed an impressive assemblage of fine Northwest Indian works. Many of our finest pieces were on display, including exquisite carvings by the great Charles Edenshaw, among hundreds of other works representing virtually every facet of the rich West Coast Indian culture.

At the smaller Interversa Gallery, prominently located in the heart of Hamburg's business district, *Kinder des Nanabush* (Children of Nanabush) was one of the first large showings of contemporary Woodland Indian art to be presented in Europe. It featured paintings by many of the talented Anishnabec artists and was made up entirely of works from the McMichael Collection.

In Germany there are hundreds of clubs, similar to the service clubs and fraternal organizations we know in Canada, whose themes are woven around the romantic traditions of the North American Indians. They hold parades and powwows regularly, with participants decked out in feathers and paints, many riding horses and carrying tomahawks. Teepees are often set up for the festive occasions and the imitation rituals are taken quite seriously. Well over a century ago, German anthropologists were among the first to make serious studies of, and to collect the artifacts of our Indian peoples. Consequently, German interest in the customs of the North American Indian is unusually intense and we were proud to display two important segments of Indian arts in one of Germany's largest cities.

In that same year we were planning ahead for an extensive American tour of works by the Group of Seven and Tom Thomson. It was launched in December, 1982, in co-operation with several Midwestern art associations. Over a two-year period it visited thirteen American cities in nine states.

Curiously, previous to 1976, there had been few major exhibitions of Canadian art in other parts of the world. We were delighted to play a part in breaking new ground for the display of important sectors of our visual culture, which, unfortunately, are all but unknown beyond our nation's borders.

7

After nearly three years of touring and exhibitions in some of the world's most famous galleries, our road show finally came home to Kleinburg. We had acquired some magnificent new works by Morrice, Carr, Thomson, Jackson, MacDonald, Holgate and Robinson, and enlarged our collection of Native art. In the gallery rooms, we fancied that the timeless Indian and Inuit masks maintained a ceaseless vigil for the ever-increasing numbers of enthusiastic visitors who found their way to our woodland shrine.

Fifteen years had passed since we had signed away our log home and its treasures and signed on as the curators of an entirely new kind of public art gallery. We looked back on a quarter of a century of memories of people and paintings since the day when we first had decided to bring together nature, art and people at Kleinburg. We were looking forward, as well, to the new challenges of the 1980s, as we toasted the silver anniversary of the building of Tapawingo. Yet we could never dwell on the past for long. Our thoughts were always moving forward, planning how to best refine and add to the Collection. We felt that continuing improvement and fine-tuning would provide even more meaning for the seemingly endless thousands who were now happily making Tapawingo their own place of joy.

In twenty-five years our log cabin had grown from a private home to a large complex housing over one thousand important works of art plus approximately fifteen hundred works of a lesser or archival value. Annual attendance was now close to three hundred thousand, and the throngs of visitors were steadily increasing. We felt the Collection had made a real contribution to a heightened sense of national pride as more and more Canadians came to share our love affair with the artists who had depicted the wilderness in such a distinctively Canadian way. We had watched prices paid for their works at Toronto galleries and auction houses rise to astronomical heights.

The Collection restaurant, which had originally served a modest trade, now dealt with overflowing lineups during almost every hour of operation. The gift shop, opened in 1967 in a small room where visitors could buy catalogues and postcards, had been greatly enlarged and now did a thriving trade in reproductions of Collection paintings, Canadian art books and a wide selection of handicrafts. The pine-panelled shop became one of our major attractions and, to our delight, produced consistently handsome profits, even though most of its stock was moderately priced. The shop's great success was based on our constant search for attractive Canadian items, many of which were not available elsewhere. The most popular item was our own handbook. It included a brief written history of the Collection and its featured artists, and was lavishly illustrated with hundreds of pictures, over half of them in colour.

The book's appeal owed even more to its magnificent design, a gift of talent from my dear friend, Alfred Casson. Through all six editions, Casson's skilful layouts, unerring type selection and impressive cover designs have been primarily responsible for the fact that the McMichael Canadian Collection catalogue has sold more copies than any other art publication ever produced in this country.

Its success was especially gratifying since the government had agreed that all shop profits should be added to the art acquisition fund.

In the years which followed our gift in 1965, Signe and I devoted ourselves to the enlargement and improvement of the Collection and its buildings. We were also determined to increase public awareness of the new gallery. Our first big step was to complete (with our own funds) a new gallery wing with living space above it. By the time the wing was officially opened, in July 1966, we had moved into our small quarters and acquired new works of art sufficient to fill the four additional gallery rooms. We were tempted to sit back and bask in the glow of accomplishment, but somehow our thoughts were always racing ahead to fresh ideas and developments.

As a result of our relentless courting of favourable publicity, public interest and attendance continued to increase. Still, we were forced to admit that although the Collection and its setting were very appealing, they were not extensive or impressive enough to command the national, and possibly even international, attention that we sought. Yet if many more people were attracted to the gallery we would be hard-pressed to accommodate them — although it would be unthinkable to turn anyone away. We were at the awkward stage that every growing enterprise reaches: too large to be ignored yet not important enough to be compelling. How could we convince the government that our rosy predictions of growth were more than pipe dreams?

By 1968, the gifts of important collections from R. S. McLaughlin, Walter Stewart and Charles Matthews, plus additional paintings from Bob Laidlaw and a surprising number of other private collectors had increased our holdings significantly. Along with those works which Signe and I had bought, they added up to nearly two hundred important additions to the original Collection. That increase was sufficiently impressive to satisfy John Robarts that the time had come for the Government of Ontario to approve funding for the construction of two large new wings. They were completed in 1968 and 1970.

Growth and ever-increasing public attendance went hand in hand. Like the proud parents of a promising youngster, we mingled with the crowds hoping for enthusiastic or at least constructive comments. We overheard plenty. True to our optimistic forecasts, Canadians were excited by the magnificent art. Equally important, visitors were enchanted by the rustic yet inspired atmosphere that we had worked so hard to maintain, even in the enlarged gallery. The combination of art and setting was so appealing that in a few short months the number of visitors increased five-fold. Apprehensively we scanned a parking lot which once had seemed embarrassingly large but was now barely adequate. Lines of people waited patiently each day for the appearance of our guide supervisor with her magic key to open the Collection for another day of public viewing.

The attractive young women who acted as gallery guides wore forest green jumpers and slacks, and became affectionately known as "green legs". Although the guides' primary responsibility was security, they doubled as friendly hostesses who delighted in answering questions about paintings and artists. Tired as they often were toward the end of a long day, the young women prided themselves on never appearing bored, and they invariably gave polite directions to exits and washrooms.

By 1972, the McMichael Canadian Collection showed the most impressive collection of the Group of Seven on display anywhere in the world. Attendance had zoomed well into the six-figure range, bolstered by over a thousand classes of schoolchildren each year.

At this time, Ontario acquired a new premier, the Honourable William Davis. I knew Bill Davis and his wife Kathleen informally. On one pleasant occasion they had joined us for dinner at Tapawingo. In the early spring of 1972, I met with him for the first time in his official capacity at Queen's Park. We were seeking his approval for the construction of a large new entry-complex wing, urgently required to accommodate our growing hosts of visitors.

Well aware that the premier was very proud of his large family, I tried to set a light tone for the conversation by asking, "Bill, when you built your home did you ever think of planning a cloakroom for hundreds of children's coats?"

"No. I wish I had."

The ice was broken and I pointed out that we hadn't planned that far ahead either, and as a result we had become a huge theatre without a lobby. I showed him our latest attendance figures which were particularly impressive when compared with those of other art galleries. Without hesitation he gave a favourable nod to our plans for expansion.

Weeks later, the premier came to open officially an exhibition of cartoons by the *Toronto Star's* Duncan McPherson. Noticing a pattern of red wooden pegs on our front lawn he surmised correctly that they were markers for the new entrance complex.

In his speech to the crowd that had gathered around Duncan McPherson and his cartoons, the premier said, "You may have noticed a set of red pegs on the front lawn and thought they were Bob McMichael's idea of modern art. Well, they're not. I'm pleased to be able to tell you that they represent the outline for construction of an impressive new entrance for this Collection which my government has approved."

In our original discussion of the new entrance complex Davis had told me how pleased he was with the new operational format for the Art Gallery of Ontario. He believed that it would work well because it maintained the ownership by the Gallery's members that was such a valuable incentive for patrons while giving the provincial government a large measure of control through its appointments to the Gallery's governing board. It struck me at the time that although the McMichael Collection had been deeded by us to the Ontario government, our situation was in many ways similar to that of the Art Gallery of Ontario. Both organizations combined individual initiative with government stewardship and each appeared to be thriving in a spirit of partnership.

The premier then asked me if I would agree to the assignment of the McMichael Collection, by an act of the Legislature, to a more autonomous foundation in which the Collection would become a full-fledged Crown corporation.

The idea had considerable appeal. Such a designation, it seemed to me, would give the Collection a status similar to other large and well-established public institutions. It would also provide a more direct means of carrying on the administrative and financial business which had sometimes made operation of the Collection cumbersome. In addition, I hoped that the change would resolve our rather anomalous position. When asked about our exact status, my usual answer was to explain that although we were owned by Ontario our precise standing was difficult to describe, except to say that we were the result or product of a solemn Agreement. We were at times uncharitably referred to as a "nonentity".

Later, after months of preparation, Bill 216, *An Act To Establish the McMichael Canadian Collection,* came before the Legislature of Ontario. It had its second and third readings on November 23, 1972. I was a proud and attentive spectator in the public gallery. After all, how often can a person look on while an act bearing his name is debated?

Part of my pride came from the glowing tribute paid to Signe and me by the responsible minister, the Honourable Jack McNie, and several other members. Basking in that glow, I was surprised to hear J. A. Renwick of the New Democratic Party rise to express his concern that there was no specific reference to the 1965 Agreement in the new Act. He put his misgivings this way:

Mr. Speaker, we support the principle of the bill. I do, however, have two or three questions in connection with it, which I trust perhaps the minister would consider.

We share with all the members of the House the expression of gratitude to the McMichaels for the donation of this art treasure to the Province of Ontario, and the value which it lends to the enhancement of the cultural life of the Province.

I am, however, concerned in two respects about the way in which the foundation has been set up. And I want either some very clear assurance from the minister about it, or a protective provision or provisions inserted in the bill by way of amendment to allay the area of ambiguity that is involved in the bill.

That Agreement is an extensive agreement covering a large number of topics, and I don't intend to elaborate on them …

Secondly, there is at the end of the Agreement, the 1965 Agreement, a specific provision — and I am going to quote it in extenso *in order to make the point that I want to make. It is paragraph 30, the last paragraph of the Agreement entered into in 1965 and it states that:*

"Notwithstanding any of the foregoing provisions of the Agreement, in the event that the Province of Ontario establishes a foundation for any of the general purposes of preserving, maintaining or developing lands, buildings and collections of art for the public benefit, the Crown may assign the whole of the lands and premises and collection vested in it or subsequently acquired by it, pursuant to this Agreement, including all its rights, powers and privileges and subject to all its obligations in connection therewith to the said foundation, provided that the Crown agrees not to make such assignment until the foundation covenants to be bound by the provisions of the Agreement to the same extent as is the Crown herein."

I was struck on reading the bill that there is no reference whatsoever to that Agreement in the Act which is before us.

I think that it is most important, and not as a matter of legalities at all, I think it's essential that there be reference in the bill to the obligation of the foundation to carry out the obligations imposed on the Crown by that Agreement and that the bill itself contain as a schedule the Agreement of 1965 establishing the Collection so that the public statutes of Ontario will for all time contain the 1965 Agreement within the bounds of those statutes.

The minister, Jack McNie, replied, "Mr. Chairman, as I said earlier, I'm satisfied that the intent of the bill is to accomplish just that."

In light of the many verbal assurances we had been given we accepted the minister's response in the presence of the Legislature (duly recorded in Hansard) as an absolute commitment to the terms and intent of the 1965 Agreement. We were certain that the conditions covering the acquisition of art for the Collection would be honoured by every government of Ontario for all time. Reinforcing our conviction was a section in the new Act which stated: "The Board shall ensure that the art works and objects acquired from time to time as part of the Collection are not inconsistent with the general character of the Collection at the time of such acquisition."

I wondered why Mr. Renwick could not see, as we believed, how ironclad our Agreement remained. Many times since I have wished that I had appreciated the well-founded apprehension of that outstanding legislator!

The Act was officially proclaimed in the spring of 1973 and nine trustees including Signe and me were appointed to the new board. We knew them all and had given the premier's office our personal approval of each appointment as well as endorsing the selection of J. Allyn Taylor as chairman. The other six trustees were Warren Jones of the Metropolitan Toronto and Region Conservation Authority, Jack Wildridge of Roberts Gallery, David Bernstein, a former advisory committee member from the Office of the Attorney General, Geraldine Wilson, a supervisor from North York Board of Education and Hamilton Laratt Smith, a retired Peterborough lawyer. The former chairman of our advisory committee, Reg Dowsett, was appointed vice-chairman. I considered the board an excellent, well-rounded group.

Unfortunately, during the next seven years inevitable changes occurred. Reg Dowsett died. Dave Bernstein received a major promotion in the government service and was forced by his heavy new responsibilities to retire from the board. Geraldine Wilson and Warren Jones stepped down after two terms.

When openings on the board occurred, Allyn Taylor and I made joint recommendations to the minister, but its original chemistry had changed. Our endorsements went largely unheeded and new and unknown faces appeared in the boardroom. "The honeymoon is over," said Allyn.

As it grew, the gallery complex had been planned as a series of connecting gallery rooms through which visitors could pass on a suggested route. A sort of continuous loop, it would take them through all the rooms and return them to the entry lobby. An ever-increasing number of special events, symposia, concerts, and educational and cultural gatherings made it seem desirable that we build a modest auditorium slightly apart from the continuous flow of gallery traffic. The idea had added value because this space could also accommodate special incoming exhibitions — now on the increase — without disturbing the permanent Collection. It could be added with almost perfect symmetry to the end of the entry complex at relatively modest cost, without disrupting the regular daily functioning of the gallery. Underneath such an addition there would be ample space for an increasingly necessary conservation laboratory and receiving and shipping facilities.

Before embarking on yet another expansion it seemed appropriate to pause and reflect, to take stock of our strengths and weaknesses, our past successes and a seemingly limitless future.

In spite of our rapid growth, the staff had remained small, especially at the senior level. Since the beginning Signe and I had sought out virtually all new acquisitions; we also personally oversaw the necessary fund raising. Changes in the display of the art, and questions of traffic flow, security and public relations came in for our scrutiny. At the same time I continued to carry out the complex and difficult task of managing an organization which had grown from a small, very personal endeavour to the largest industry in our community.

Of course, we were not without help. I was able to delegate much of the responsibility and authority for individual departments to competent people like Frank Billings in finance, Jeanne Pattison in public relations, Margaret Barr in education, Dennis Jones in maintenance and purchasing, and Lee Guscott in the gift shop. Still, like many founders, I was reluctant to assign authority for senior management responsibilities or policy decisions to others. My schedule left little time for making contact with or getting to know good prospects for managerial responsibilities. Furthermore, our modest salaries (the result of government demands for restraint) did not attract the outstanding people that we wanted to the gallery. The price of our perpetual forward motion had been the sacrifice of management strength in depth.

When I realized the need for a senior executive assistant, it was natural for me to go looking for someone out of my own mould — a young entrepreneur with a proven record in business. I hoped to find someone who shared my passion for Canada's distinctive national art and understood the concept that had guided the growth of the gallery and Collection from the start.

In 1975, I met a young man who seemed to meet those requirements. In his early thirties, with an outgoing personality, intelligence, and youthful maturity, John Ingram had a talent for business that had made him a rising star at Xerox Corporation. His intense interest in Canadian art and particularly the Group of Seven had led him to membership in Toronto's Arts and Letters Club.

At mid-year our budget was too inflexible to permit us to offer

John a salary proportionate to his experience. Nevertheless, he very much wanted to join us at the Collection and my promise of a substantial salary increase, effective with our new budget, tipped the scales. He came to Kleinburg as the first of a projected team of qualified executives who could begin to shoulder much of the administrative load.

Only a few weeks later, we received a directive from the ministry freezing the amount by which salaries could be increased. At first I thought I could keep my promise to John by foregoing any increase in my own deliberately modest salary, but the directive was quite explicit and I soon realized it would not permit even the most adroit juggling.

Yet salary was only one consideration. I was aware that John missed the excitement of corporate life in the big city and sensed too that he was chafing under my gradual and possibly overcautious shifting of major responsibilities. I was disappointed, but not totally surprised, when John returned to the welcoming arms of Xerox a few months later in the spring of 1976.

For the next two years much of my time was absorbed by our international showings, the acquisition of several of our most important works and the necessarily intensive fund raising. Our continuing growth added to the Collection's administrative burdens, but it seemed difficult to find just the right people to add to our team. Finally, advice from management consultants, approved by our board of trustees, made it clear that a realignment of management responsibilities was not only necessary but overdue. I set out once more to find competent and congenial assistance.

With hindsight it is easy to see that we should have advertised widely and used the services of a good headhunter in our attempt to find the ideal person to manage the administrative side of the Collection. At least we should have realized the soundness of the criteria we had established earlier: imagination and initiative, a measure of experience and success in private enterprise and, most importantly, empathy with our aims for the Collection, its artists and its ambiance.

Unfortunately, in the two years since our first search our relationship with the government had changed. With the creation of the new Ministry of Culture and Recreation, complicated directives and intimidating forms arrived on my desk with increasing frequency. The machinations of a faceless bureaucracy became harder and harder to fathom. The mountains of paperwork grew ever larger. In the face of this bureaucratic muddle it seemed that creativity and empathy had become of secondary importance. We must have someone who could guide us through the government maze. I believed we needed our own civil servant.

My candidate was John Court. Although I had met him only once, I had been impressed with the apparent combination of what appeared to be a warm, obliging personality and a thorough schooling in and understanding of the mysterious and seemingly omnipotent bureaucracy.

Looking back, I suspect that the smiles I found so sympathetic actually masked amusement at my inability to understand that the ambition of some bureaucrats was not to seek meaningful results such as increased attendance, but to achieve only a disciplined enterprise that operated in conformity with predetermined rules. Personal success lay in obeying these rules — written and unwritten. How naive he must have found my unwillingness to accept that bureaucratic success was often demonstrated by increased budgets. I found it difficult to believe that the way to achieve an increased budget was to consistently arrive at a deficit by overspending allotted operating funds! Nor could I grasp the excitement that lay in the prodigious production of memos to cover every decision (and to protect one's backside). Paper made its way in an endless procession from desk to desk to wastebasket.

Had I taken a closer look I would have realized that there are two kinds of civil servants: the larger group is made up of honest, dedicated people who do a fine job in spite of a stifling system. The other, smaller flock are birds of slick plumage, often found in the outer recesses of ministerial offices. Their song is heard loudly in their native habitat (which they leave only to hop to a higher limb) but their voices are curiously muted in other surroundings. Their feeding habits are usually carnivorous.

Unfortunately, my knowledge of this tight little kingdom was scant. It was one of these latter birds that I had chosen to present to our board of trustees as a prospect to head the administrative side of the McMichael Canadian Collection. I must accept full responsibility for choosing him, but it turned out to be my most serious error in judgement.

I should have recognized that his talons were showing when as a condition of employment he sought immediate appointment as a trustee on our board. This request was refused, but I allowed him to take over my office, which contained all my business and personal files and I moved to a more remote location. On the basis of procedures standard in government agencies, he was seconded from the ministry for a one-year period during which he would be known as administrative director of the Collection. He would be accorded a firm and free hand in all decisions save those concerning the Collection's acquisitions of art, its ambiance and certain other areas which had always been my special preserve.

In the first months, all seemed orderly and quiet. Relieved of many of our most burdensome responsibilities, Signe and I blissfully took a brief but overdue vacation. On our return, just in advance of a board meeting, we were greeted by our new administrative director with a handful of submissions from consultants and a lengthy and detailed document which set out the terms of reference for a feasibility study, ostensibly required to obtain approval in principle for the building of the proposed addition to the gallery's working facilities. Our bright young man, who still enjoyed our full confidence, urged us to vote for the consulting firm of his choice. He earnestly suggested that we use our best efforts to persuade our chairman, Allyn Taylor, to give this firm his support. How happy he must have been when, without a murmur, we did as he asked.

After several weeks of poking into every nook and cranny of our operations, the consultants presented the board with a two-volume study. It arrived at almost the same time as Warren Jones, a friend and one of our trustees, appeared in my office with a handful of photocopies of letters, memos and bills, most highlighted in yellow. The documents had been presented to him, he told us, by our administrative director, who had interpreted certain statements in my correspondence as showing conflicts of interest. Jones had asked the new young appointee to organize the documents and state his conclusions. The material was now set out in a series of typewritten columns alleging a number of indiscretions drawn from my own freely available correspondence files. Shocked out of my complacency, I realized at last that our new employee was too ambitious to be satisfied with his own position — he wanted mine as well. Later, the chairman stated publicly that the documents showed nothing immoral or illegal but that my choice of words in some letters was indiscreet. He did not add, as he might have, that I had taken a long time to realize the necessity of protecting my derrière.

The feasibility study hit me and the board like a bombshell. Proposals for the much-needed modest new wing were absent. Instead, the report declared that the Collection buildings and even its lands provided inadequate public safety features and were particularly open to the danger of fire. They estimated that their recommended alterations would run into millions of dollars.

Central to the report was another recommendation: that I should resign as director and be replaced by a professional. I should be given a new, largely honorary, permanent title — Founder-Director Emeritus.

When we had all had time to read and digest this disturbing document, Allyn Taylor summed up his thoughts: "We sure walked into that one." On the basis of comments from certain other trustees he urged me to give up the directorship in favour of a much less demanding position and, of course, retention of Signe's and my continuing seats on the board. It was arranged that the administrative director, who was obviously hoping to replace me, would instead be terminated at the end of his one-year tenure and returned to his job at the ministry.

In 1980, after a long heart-to-heart talk with Allyn Taylor, I resigned as director to assume the new position of Founder-Director Emeritus. I assumed that when the change was actually made — almost a year later — I would be relieved of all day-to-day operational responsibilities.

I also assumed that the 1965 Agreement, and in particular the acquisition policy established by it, would remain inviolate. I was certain that physical changes to the gallery would be made as a result of the feasibility study report. Since I, as well as many fire-safety experts, felt it was overstated to the point of creating panic in the minds of trustees, I hoped that I would be able to exert enough influence to ensure that only necessary changes would be made and that the rustic atmosphere of Tapawingo would be preserved.

From the moment when we lovingly placed those first Lawren Harris and Tom Thomson panels on Tapawingo's massive walls we had been obsessed with the desire to bring together a much larger collection of art with an unabashedly nationalistic flavour. Around the paintings of Thomson and his Group friends, along with works by other selected artists, we would gather a meaningful array of fine arts by our Native peoples. In our log and stone lodge the combination of these symbols of the land and its cultures would be a stirring salute to nationhood. Any thoughts of a broader, less targeted museum of art never entered into our scheme to diffuse our singular purpose.

Years before, when Signe and I gave our lands, home and collection to the province it was with enthusiasm and a determination to honour the words and spirit of our pact with the province in the same way we felt sure that Ontario would forever honour its commitment to us. We believed we had an immutable agreement.

Even now, after the disturbing events of the past few years, we still believe so.

For us, the most crucial point was the government's guarantee that we should retain sufficient control over the acquisition policy and the ambiance of the gallery and surrounding property to ensure that they would retain their original character and continue to be an appealing presentation of a distinct theme. It was this key condition, more than any other, that persuaded us to donate our home and its treasures for the benefit of all.

To ensure that these conditions would be honoured in perpetuity, the government had created a five-member advisory committee. Signe and I were to have two permanent memberships on it, the government would appoint two members, and the fifth, a chairman, would be appointed by us jointly with the two government members. The appointments of the government members and chairman would last for two years. Signe and I would be members for life. Indeed, in the event of the death or incapacity of either McMichael it was set out that the other McMichael could appoint a substitute.

Among its main functions the committee was empowered to designate the artists whose works could be included in the Collection. The Agreement stated clearly and firmly that no work of art would be included unless it was first approved by the advisory committee.

In a further section the Agreement stated:

The Crown agrees that upon the death of the survivor of Robert and Signe McMichael, additions to the Collection shall be confined to works of art by the artists specifically named in section 13 above (i.e., Group of Seven members, Emily Carr and David Milne) or designated by the Advisory Committee pursuant to the said section 13.

To be sure that these terms and conditions would apply in perpetuity, the Agreement concluded with a section which stated that, notwithstanding any of the provisions of the Agreement, the Crown might assign the lands, buildings and Collection to an agency which might be established by the government. The agency would also receive all items subsequently acquired by the Collection including all its rights, powers and privileges. It would be subject to all the Collection's obligations in connection therewith — provided (and this was crucial) that the Crown agreed not to make such an assignment until the new agency had covenanted to be bound by the provisions of the Agreement to the same extent as the Crown.

In short, Signe and I, with the agreement of a chairman approved by us, or with the agreement of one government appointee, were empowered to accept or reject all works of art for the McMichael Collection. On our deaths the Collection would be confined, in perpetuity, to works by the artists the Committee had selected and any new agency to which the Collection might be assigned must be bound by all the provisions of the Agreement.

All of these conditions were contained in the document signed by us and by Premier John P. Robarts on behalf of Her Majesty the Queen in Right of Ontario, A.D. 1965.

After my decision to retire became known, Signe and I began receiving countless warm letters of thanks and even more honours than we had received during the years when we were actively creating the Collection. We were each made Fellows of the Ontario College of Art shortly before I became Director Emeritus. During the period of transition, Premier Davis and his cabinet gave us a huge testimonial dinner at Toronto's Royal York Hotel. We were overwhelmed to find ourselves escorted to the places of honour by the premier through aisles formed by hundreds of prominent well-wishers. The Ontario Society of Artists made us honorary members and presented us with their highest award in the form of a specially designed bronze sculpture engraved with our names. Not to be outdone, the Village of Kleinburg, at its famous annual Binder Twine Festival, presented us with a beautiful hand-lettered and framed certificate of appreciation. Two years later, Dr. Douglas Wright, president of the University of Waterloo, conferred on each of us the degree Doctor of Laws (*honoris causa*) on the recommendation of the University's senate.

It was difficult to give up active direction of the gallery but I felt an enormous sense of satisfaction in what had been accomplished. During the years between our signing of the Agreement in 1965 and my retirement as director in 1981 we had seen the Collection grow in numbers of visitors until it ranked among the top three galleries in all of Canada, with an annual attendance of well over one quarter of a million.

Yet in spite of the overwhelming success of our theme and the policies we had followed, it was not many months after my decision to step down before the designate for the position of director, and some trustees, were making unnerving proposals in the areas related to the Collection's art and ambiance. Signe and I, still conscious of our continuing responsibilities as trustees and members of the Art Acquisition Committee, felt that the overtures violated the terms and spirit of the 1965 Agreement. We could not acquiesce in these motions and so, for the first time, we found ourselves casting dissenting votes.

Of course, our two votes carried no influence with other trustees who apparently believed that our solemn Agreement was superseded by what was stated or, perhaps more important, not stated, in the Act.

At my final meeting as director of the Collection in June 1981 I brought before the board of trustees two superlative oil panels by Tom Thomson. The first was a study for the well-known canvas *Petawawa Gorges* in the National Gallery of Canada. The other was a superb sketch known as *Burnt Land*. Both were offered by Alan M. Cameron of Sudbury at a price generally considered modest for works of such importance. I persuaded my good friend, Major Fred Tilston, V.C., retired president of Sterling Drug of Canada Limited, to donate forty thousand dollars for the purchase of *Petawawa Gorges*. Our special art fund had the resources to buy *Burnt Land* at the same price. I felt that to acquire two such fine Tom Thomsons would be a very fitting climax to my term as chief executive.

I was stunned when trustee Cicely Bell (who would later become chairman of the Collection's board) asked in a mildly derisive voice, "Do we need any more Tom Thomsons?"

Fortunately, the other trustees were not swayed by her negative opinion and moved to approve my submission for the important purchase. Yet in that instant I realized that she and perhaps some of the other appointees were determined to change the direction of the Collection. The course which we and the government had set in our founding charter was to be set aside in favour of a much looser, less dedicated concept.

After two or three board meetings which resulted in divided votes, the trustees decided to attempt to resolve the impasse by passing a resolution that "The Board requests the Minister of Culture and Recreation to amend the *McMichael Canadian Collection Act, 1972*, to confirm that the powers of the Board and the Director are governed only by that Act and are not limited by the Agreement between Robert and Signe McMichael and Her Majesty the Queen, dated November 18th, 1965, and to the extent of any conflict or inconsistency between said Agreement and said Act the said Act shall, in all cases, prevail."

This resolution was more than humiliating — it was devastating — a sickening end to all our hopes and a mockery of the terms of our gift in 1965. It was also a monument to our naiveté and ignorance of the niceties of legislative language and procedure. Too late, we saw how wise J. A. Renwick had been.

We had no desire to drag such a betrayal into the limelight of public debate. However, when the board engaged the prominent Toronto lawyer Edwin Goodman to prepare a draft of the motion to be forwarded to the minister with a request for legislative action, we felt we had no option but to retain counsel ourselves. We abhorred the publicity which we knew would follow, but on the advice of our distinguished counsel, John J. Robinette, we approached Stuart Smith, leader of the Liberal opposition and three of the most respected members of his caucus, Sean Conway, Albert Roy and Hugh Edighoffer, to discuss with them the developments which we felt were now threatening the Collection as we had known it.

Following that discussion the Liberal opposition set the expert researchers in their office to work. They easily tracked down a draft numbered 4-W and headed "An Act to Amend the McMichael Canadian Collection Act". It stated:

The said Act is amended by adding thereto the following section:

18(a) (1) Effective the 2nd day of April, 1973, the agreement entered into on the 18th day of November, 1965 between Her Majesty the Queen in right of Ontario and Robert and Signe McMichael with respect to the McMichael Conservation Area and the McMichael Conservation Collection of Art is void and has no effect.

No mincing of words there!

We were so appalled by this bold indication of the government's intention that we failed to understand the implications of another subsection which read:

(3) Notwithstanding clause 8 (b), the Corporation may expend, administer or dispose of any money or property received under the agreement referred to in subsection (1), except for those objects provided for in subsection (2), in any way it considers proper.

The draft concluded with the usual words: "This Act comes into force on the day it receives Royal Assent." The short title of this Act is the *McMichael Canadian Collection Amendment Act, 1981*.

With this draft at hand, Stuart Smith made an eloquent address to the Legislature, castigating the minister and the government.

The fat was in the fire! For several days our phone never stopped ringing as reporters clamoured for interviews and information about the government's proposal to abrogate the 1965 Agreement. Filled with a kind of bitterness I had never before experienced, I felt tempted to take the phone off the hook and retire with Signe to suffer in private. But I knew we could not allow ourselves that luxury if our lifelong dream was to be saved. I accepted every request for an interview that I could possibly fit in. I wanted the public to know and understand what was being done in its name. By declaring void the 1965 Agreement, the government was, in effect, announcing that a partnership was no longer valid because sixteen years after its formation, one party was going to disavow the permanent written understanding. It was as if the destruction of a birth certificate would prove that a loving conception had never occurred.

In the following days, newspapers, radios and television sets screamed out the story to readers, listeners and viewers across the entire country. Letters, phone calls and telegrams poured into the offices of Ontario legislators — the largest number into the office of Premier William Davis. Hundreds of people also took the trouble to send copies of their letters to us, gestures of kindness that we truly appreciated in our state of low morale. Virtually all of the letters berated the government for going back on its word. Among our many angry supporters was a prominent Windsor business leader, a stalwart supporter of the government who wrote to his friend Premier Davis threatening to resign his membership in the Ontario Conservative Party.

During Question Period in the Legislature on November 17th, 1981, Stuart Smith directed a question to Reuben Baetz, the Minister of Culture and Recreation.

> *May I ask the minister further: when he decides to set the record straight, will he explain his assurance to this House that there is no desire to renege in any way on the agreement signed with the McMichaels by Premier Robarts? How can the minister say there is no desire to renege on the agreement when the draft bill says this agreement shall be rendered retroactively null, void and of no effect? How can one renege any more than that on any agreement?*
>
> *Will the minister explain what is the meaning of the clause in the draft bill if not to get rid of the agreement?*

The Minister responded:

> *This is neither the time nor the place to talk about a draft bill. The time to debate the bill is when I introduce it in the House. Why try to inflame a situation right now? Playing politics: that is all the members opposite are doing.*
>
> *In fairness to Mr. and Mrs. McMichael, I think the Leader of the Opposition had better hold off any further innuendoes and accusations until I introduce the legislation.*

Why was the government apparently so determined to use its

formidable power to pass legislation eliminating the terms and conditions under which our gift had been made? In the debate which followed Stuart Smith's speech, the minister stated that the government was acting because the McMichaels were, in effect, seeking veto power over new additions to the Collection and control of the aesthetic aspects of the entire operation.

Dr. Stuart Smith responded that it was not *individual* control but *joint* control with the government as set out in the 1965 Agreement that we were seeking. "It was not a veto," he pointed out, "but two and two and one, exactly as set out in the covenant Premier Robarts had signed."

In fact, Signe and I had already verbally agreed to some practical modification of our rights. When the Collection became a Crown corporation we agreed to a committee format which reduced our powers in the area of acquisitions. With the change in status the board of trustees had reduced the advisory committee (on acquisitions) to three: Signe, myself, and the board's vice-chairman. There was another important difference: each decision of this smaller committee was now subject to approval by the board. Majority decisions of the original advisory committee had been final.

We agreed to this change because we were satisfied that the new arrangement was an appropriate and balanced substitute in the spirit of the 1965 Agreement. We believed our interests to be fully safeguarded. The new arrangement worked well. The Collection continued to grow and refine its holdings, without dissension.

Now, in 1981, we found our acquiescence to the changes in the acquisitions committee had left us very vulnerable. A majority of the board had decided to grant the new director's demands for control over acquisitions and aesthetic changes through the formation of a new and larger committee. Although we had reason to believe the government had little stomach for the task, apparently it was willing to make a unilateral cancellation of the 1965 Agreement.

When the *McMichael Canadian Collection Amendment Act* was finally introduced for first reading, no one was more surprised than Signe and me. While it contained a change of words describing the nature of the Collection with which we were not entirely pleased, there was a far more significant difference from the draft bill.

The section which would have cancelled out the 1965 Agreement along with subsection (3) which might have had almost equally serious consequences for us and the Collection had been completely removed!

We felt, with reason, that the diligent work of the opposition and the pressure of public opinion had achieved an astounding victory. Later we learned that both the Attorney General and Premier Davis had publicly acknowledged the continuing force of the 1965 Agreement.

In his answer to a letter from one of his constituents, Attorney General Roy McMurtry underlined the government's position when he wrote: "The new bill (1981) does not alter the Board's commitment to uphold the terms and conditions of all gifts to the Collection. In particular the original 1965 Agreement with the McMichaels is being fully honoured."

At about the same time Premier Bill Davis wrote:

However, I am concerned about the misinformation held by a number of people regarding the bill introduced in the Legislature by the Minister of Culture and Recreation and the government's intent concerning the original agreement of 1965 ... contrary to the recent allegations, the government does not intend to break its agreement with the McMichaels or to destroy the character of the collection or the gallery building.

Clearly, the Government of Ontario fully understood the importance of the 1965 Agreement and the commitment to be bound by its terms and conditions.

But James Renwick, the NDP member who had so wisely and forcefully demanded an amendment to the original Act nine years before, was still determined that acceptance of the terms of the founding Agreement of 1965 should not be in the form of a verbal assurance of intent by a minister or even the premier. It had to be part of the Act.

He introduced what is known in parliamentary parlance as a Notice of Reasoned Amendment which was tabled on November 30, 1981. In essence it asked that second reading of the bill be deferred and that it be referred back to the minister with instructions to incorporate provisions which would ensure compliance by Her Majesty the Queen in Right of the Province of Ontario with the letter and spirit of the 1965 Agreement between the Crown and Robert and Signe McMichael.

In the formal language of the Legislature he asked, as he had almost ten years earlier, that the government write into the Act the assurances it was providing orally in the Legislature and in letters to interested correspondents. The combined opposition (Liberals and New Democrats) supported this Notice of Reasoned Amendment, and took the unusual step of voting against both the first and second readings of the bill in a stand-up head-count vote of the entire Legislature. They were, of course, defeated by a strong majority government which rallied fifty-six votes to their forty-five and some days later the bill went to debate on second reading.

Through day after day of impassioned speeches by the Liberal leader of the opposition, his colleagues and leading members of the NDP, the government continued to insist that the terms and the spirit of the Agreement would be honoured but that they would not be incorporated into the Act. Since its decision not to cancel the solemn promises in the founding Agreement the government had decided to at least pay it lip service but it was still determined not to enshrine its assurances in legislation.

Following the debate, Bill 175 was sent to committee for further study. A few weeks later, Signe and I, now suffering from severe nervous fatigue, took the advice of our counsel J. J. Robinette and signed a document prepared by the law firm of Goodman and Goodman which had been retained to represent the board of trustees. It reiterated in more pointed words what the Act already stated, that "the Board of Trustees is solely, fully and completely responsible for the management of the Corporation". It also contained an assurance of our support for Bill 175, now stripped of its most offensive section.

A few weeks later the *McMichael Canadian Collection Amendment Act* became law.

We had been through a painful and traumatic experience and were happy that the time of controversy seemed to be over. We wished only to return with some peace of mind to our primary concern, the continuing development of the Collection.

During the major renovations (climate control, a sprinkler system for fire protection, the replacement of stairs with ramps and other changes) which the board decided to undertake, the gallery was closed for about eighteen months and the staff and I were moved to temporary office quarters. All of the paintings were, of course, removed. Some were placed on display at the nearby Kortright Centre for Conservation and others went to the downtown Toronto College Park complex. If we ever had entertained any doubts about our insistence that the gallery retain its rustic character, this move would have resolved them. The paintings remained remarkable, but they lacked the impact they had in Kleinburg. They seemed to miss their home among the pines almost as much as we did.

In a year of living on the twenty-seventh floor of a luxurious highrise, we recognized two separate but undeniable truths. Our lives had become inseparable from the tall trees of our beloved hills and valleys but paradoxically, we had never lived apart from our work. When we purchased a lovely, weathered homestead nestled in fourteen acres of thickly wooded hills near the hamlet of Belfountain, twenty miles west of Kleinburg, we found the distance from work we had always needed and the nearness to nature we had always loved.

Throughout the long months of renovation the staff and board continued to function, but change was occurring in more than the gallery building. Warren Jones, Jack Wildridge and Hamilton Larratt Smith retired from the board. Along with Signe and me, only Chairman J. Allyn Taylor, who had obligingly agreed to another extension of his term of office until the reopening of the Collection, remained from the original trustees.

As part of the Collection's facelift, a new director was appointed. He hired, in turn, a curator and other staff. It soon became apparent that this predominantly new staff, supported by new trustees, was determined to institute major changes in the composition and presentation of the Collection.

When the renovated gallery finally opened, previous visitors could see that drastic changes had occurred. A new and younger crew, fresh from academe, had excitedly put their theories into practice. The display of art is, of course, somewhat subjective, yet Signe and I would have been the last to suggest that fresh eyes could not achieve improvements.

We could not and would not concede, however, that the changes that had taken place improved the Collection. The new staff had initiated a complete reversal of our most basic principle — that the Collection should always be displayed in a manner that emphasized the greatness and individuality of each principal artist, and that it be confined to the artists approved for inclusion by the advisory committee.

Looking back, we now see that what the Goodman agreement had said was far less important than what it did not say. It made no reference at all to the 1965 Agreement. It did not state that the board must at all times administer the Collection in accordance with the law!

The importance of compliance with the law became apparent when we realized how the new curator and director, with the concurrence of the acquisition committee, were changing both the ambiance and the nature and purpose of the Collection. We began to search for some way of curbing the new policies before irreparable damage was done. A close friend who was very knowledgeable about matters of law and legal terminology pointed out the significance of a subsection of the Act. It was part of the original Act of 1972 and remained unchanged in the Amendment Act of 1982. It was, therefore, the law.

The subsection states in no uncertain terms that the Collection Corporation is bound by the provisions of the 1965 Agreement, just as Premier Robarts, acting in behalf of Her Majesty the Queen in Right of Ontario, had promised in 1965. Specifically, clause (b) of section 8 of the *McMichael Canadian Collection Act* states:

The Corporation may expend, administer or dispose of any such money or property in furtherance of its objects, subject to the terms, if any, upon which such money or property was given, granted, bequeathed, leased or otherwise acquired by the Corporation.

It required no special expertise to see that in retaining this subsection the government had agreed that the corporation may administer any property in furtherance of its objectives, but always subject to the terms, if any, upon which the property had been given or otherwise acquired by the Corporation. Since the conditions set out in the 1965 Agreement applied to our gifts of lands, buildings and works of art, the board was required by law to administer the Collection under the terms and conditions established in 1965.

When the precise meaning of the subsection was confirmed by the respected legal and legislative authorities that we consulted, we wrote a lengthy letter to the minister of the day, pointing out that in many ways the Collection was *not* being administered subject to the terms, conditions and spirit of our 1965 Agreement. It was, therefore, operating in contravention of the law. Several weeks later we received a letter, signed by the minister, which we thought deserved an award for its bureaucratic evasiveness. It made no reference to clause 8(b), or even to the 1965 Agreement, but simply stated in general terms the minister's belief that the law was being obeyed.

The long controversy had brought us a great deal of pain and Signe and I just could not face another period of anguish. In spite of the favourable opinions we had received about the significance of 8(b) we knew that taking the matter to court would reopen wounds that were just beginning to heal. We had neither the resources nor the will to enter into prolonged litigation with the board and the province.

Our lovingly assembled art, the rustic yet noble structures we built and even the forests that we planted are in the hands of an appointed staff over which we hold no influence. An unsympathetic chairman presides over a board which is committed to altering the fundamental character of the Collection. The most devastating changes have affected the display of our beloved art.

The Collection's warm ambiance no longer exists, the themes which inspired us have been replaced.

Also among the changes of recent years has been the eradication of Signe's role in choosing art for the Collection. My solitary voice is seldom heard among five appointees who hang on the words of a curator determined to change rather than to preserve a precious vision.

With the passage of time we have nurtured a fading hope that our beloved paintings would someday be at home again in the welcoming rooms and natural settings we created for them. We yearn for a return of the splendor and warmth of spirit that had characterized our unique woodland dwelling.

Recently, a ray of sunshine has pierced the dark clouds. After more than forty years, a new party is in power in Ontario...a party that, in opposition, gallantly attempted to persuade the former government to honour our solemn agreement. We believe that the far-seeing members who once fought our battles in the legislature will now move to accomplish in power what they were unable to do in opposition.

I often think back to earlier years, when Signe and I both worked long days at our photography studio and in our advertising business. At night in our small adjoining apartment, we dreamed and planned our future.

When we discovered a wooded hilltop and valley, we found a place to settle, a snug, log home much like those of earlier settlers. Our pioneering spirit was awakened, and our adventure had only begun.

We fell under the spell of works by a few passionate artists who had captured not only the form and colour of the wilderness that we loved, but its very soul. To the beauty of the nature which surrounded us, we set out to add beauty created by man. The magnificent portrayals of the untamed land that adorned our walls reflected our world. As our collection grew, somehow we knew that Tapawingo would become a place of joy, not only for us, but for everyone. And though we will not always be here, we hope that our log house on the hilltop among the trees will remain forever filled with images of this blessed land in which we dwell.

Would we do it over again?

Certainly. And not very differently.

INDEX